How to Master CCNP TSHOOT

René Molenaar

Copyright © 2015 René Molenaar
All rights reserved.
ISBN: 1491272279
ISBN-13:   978-1491272275

All contents copyright C 2002-2015 by René Molenaar. All rights reserved. No part of this document or the related files may be reproduced or transmitted in any form, by any means (electronic, photocopying, recording, or otherwise) without the prior written permission of the publisher.

Limit of Liability and Disclaimer of Warranty: The publisher has used its best efforts in preparing this book, and the information provided herein is provided "as is." René Molenaar makes no representation or warranties with respect to the accuracy or completeness of the contents of this book and specifically disclaims any implied warranties of merchantability or fitness for any particular purpose and shall in no event be liable for any loss of profit or any other commercial damage, including but not limited to special, incidental, consequential, or other damages.

Trademarks: This book identifies product names and services known to be trademarks, registered trademarks, or service marks of their respective holders. They are used throughout this book in an editorial fashion only. In addition, terms suspected of being trademarks, registered trademarks, or service marks have been appropriately capitalized, although René Molenaar cannot attest to the accuracy of this information. Use of a term in this book should not be regarded as affecting the validity of any trademark, registered trademark, or service mark. René Molenaar is not associated with any product or vendor mentioned in this book.

Introduction

One of the things I do in life is work as a Cisco Instructor and after teaching CCNP for a few years I've learned which topics people find difficult to understand. This is the reason I created http://gns3vault.com where I offer free Cisco labs and videos to help people learn networking. The problem with networking is that you need to know what you are doing before you can configure anything. Even if you have all the commands you still need to understand *what* and *why* you are typing these commands. I created this book to give you a compact guide which will provide you the answer to *what* and *why* to help you master the CCNP exam.

CCNP is one of the well-known certifications you can get in the world of IT. Cisco is the largest supplier of networking equipment but also famous for its CCNA, CCNP and CCIE certifications. Whether you are new to networking or already in the field for some time, getting a certification is the best way to prove your knowledge on paper! Having said that, I also love routing & switching because it's one of those fields in IT that doesn't change much...some of the protocols you are about to learn are 10 or 20 years old and still alive and kicking!

I have tried to put all the important keywords in **bold**. If you see a **term or concept** in **bold** it's something you should remember / write down and make sure you understand it since its core knowledge for your CCNP!

One last thing before we get started. When I'm teaching I always advise students to create mindmaps instead of notes. Notes are just lists with random information while mindmaps show the relationship between the different items. If you are reading this book on your computer I highly suggest you download "Xmind" which you can get for free here:

http://www.xmind.net/

If you are new to mindmapping, check out "Appendix A – How to create mindmaps" at the end of this book where I show you how I do it.

Enjoy reading my book and good luck getting your CCNP certification!

René Molenaar

P.S. If you have any questions or comments about this book, please let me know:

E-mail: info@gns3vault.com
Website: gns3vault.com
Facebook: facebook.com/gns3vault
Twitter: twitter.com/gns3vault
Youtube: youtube.com/gns3vault

Index

Introduction 4
1. Network Maintenance and Troubleshooting methods............................ 1
2. Tools for Troubleshooting 15
3. Troubleshooting Switching 43
4. Troubleshooting RIP 94
5. Troubleshooting EIGRP.. 113
6. Troubleshooting OSPF 149
7. Troubleshooting BGP 199
8. Troubleshooting Network Services 223
9. Troubleshooting Network Management Protocols............................ 245
10. Troubleshooting IPv6 255
11. Troubleshooting Full Labs 283
12. Final Thoughts 319
Appendix A – How to create mindmaps 320

1. Network Maintenance and Troubleshooting methods

In this first chapter we will first look at some maintenance methods for networks. There are different models that will help you to maintain your networks and make your life easier. In the second part of this chapter we will look at some theoretical models that will help you with troubleshooting.

If you want to jump right into the technical action and start troubleshooting you might want to skip this chapter for now and get back to it later. However, on your CCNP TSHOOT exam you might encounter a couple of questions regarding network maintenance models and troubleshooting techniques so I do recommend you to read this chapter sometime.

Having said that, let's start talking about network maintenance! Network maintenance basically means you have to do what it takes in order to keep a network up and running and it includes a number of tasks:

- Troubleshooting network problems.
- Hardware and software installation/configuration.
- Monitoring and improving network performance.
- Planning for future network growth.
- Creating network documentation and keeping it up-to-date.
- Ensuring compliance with company policies.
- Ensuring compliance with legal regulations.
- Securing the network against all kind of threats.

Of course this list could be different for each network you work on and perhaps you are only responsible for a number of these tasks. All these tasks can be performed in the following way:

1. **Structured tasks.**
2. **Interrupt-driven tasks.**

Structured means you have a pre-defined plan for network maintenance that will make sure that problems are solved before they occur. As a network engineer this will also make your life a whole lot easier. **Interrupt-driven** means you just wait for trouble to occur and then fix it as fast as you can. Interrupt-driven is more like the "fireman" approach...you wait for trouble to happen and then you try to fix the problem as fast as you can. A structured approach where you have a network maintenance strategy and plan reduces downtime and it's more cost effective.

Of course you can never completely get rid of interrupt-driven tasks because sometimes things "just go wrong" but with a good plan we can reduce the number of interrupt-driven tasks for sure.

You don't have to think of a complete network maintenance model yourself; there are a number of well-known network maintenance models that we use. It's best to use one of the models that is best suited for your organization and adjustments if needed.
Here are some of the well-known network maintenance models:

- **FCAPS**:
    - Fault management.
    - Configuration management.
    - Accounting management.
    - Performance management.
    - Security management.

The FCAPS network maintenance model was created by the ISO (International Organization of Standardization).

- **ITIL**: IT Infrastructure Library is a set of practices for IT services management that focuses on aligning IT services with the needs of business.
- **TMN**: Telecomunications Management Network is another maintenance model that was created by the ITU-T (Telecommunications Standartization Sector) and is a variation of the FCAPS model. TMN targets management of telecommunications networks.
- **Cisco Lifecycle Services:** Of course Cisco has it's own network maintenance model which defines the different phases in the life of a Cisco network:
    - Prepare
    - Plan
    - Design
    - Implement
    - Operate
    - Optimize

If you decide to study CCDA (Cisco Certified Design Associate) you will learn a lot about the Cisco lifecycle which is also known as PPDIOO (Prepare, Plan, Design, Implement, Operate and Optimize).

Choosing which network maintenance model you will use depends on your network and the business. You can also use them as a template to create your own network maintenance model.

To give you an idea what a network maintenance model is about and what it looks like, here's an example for FCAPS:

- Fault management: we will configure our network devices (routers, switches, firewalls, servers, etc.) to capture logging messages and send them to an external server. Whenever an interface goes down or the CPU goes above 80% we want to receive an e-mail so we can see what is going on.

- Configuration management: Any changes made to the network have to be logged. We will use a change management so relevant personnel will be notified of planned network changes. Changes to network devices have to be reported and acknowledged before they are implemented.
- Accounting management: We will charge (guest) users for usage of the wireless network so they'll pay for each 100MB of data or something. It's also commonly used to charge people for long distance VoIP calls.
- Performance management: Network performance will be monitored on all LAN and WAN links so we know when things go wrong. QoS (Quality of Service) will be configured on the appropiate interfaces.
- Security management: We will create a security policy and implement it by using firewalls, VPNs, intrusion prevention systems and use AAA (Authorization, Authentication and Accounting) servers to validate user credentials. Network breaches have to be logged and a appropiate response has to be made.

You can see FCAPS is not just a "theoretical" method but it truly describes "what", "how" and "when" we will do things.

Whatever network maintenance model you decide to use, there are always a number of routine maintenance tasks that should have listed procedures, here are a couple of examples:

- **Configuration changes**: Business are never static but they change all the time. Sometimes you need to make changes to the network to allow access for guest users, normal users might move from one office to another so you'll have to make changes to the network to facilitate this.
- **Replacement of hardware**: Older hardware has to be replaced with more modern equipment and it's also possible that production hardware fails so we'll have to replace it immediately.
- **Backups**: If we want to recover from network problems such as failing switches or routers then we need to make sure we have recent backups of configurations. Normally you will use scheduled backups so you will save the running-configuration each day, week, month or whatever you like.
- **Software updates**: We need to keep our network devices and operating systems up-to-date. Bugs are fixed but also to make sure we don't have devices that are running older software that has security vulnerabilities.
- **Monitoring**: We need to collect and understand traffic statistics and bandwidth utilization so we can spot (future) network problems but also so we can plan for future network growth.

Normally you will create a list with the tasks that have to be done for your network. These tasks can be assigned a certain priority. If a certain access layer switch fails then you will likely want to replace it as fast as you can but a failed distribution or core layer device will have a much higher priority since it impacts more users of the network. Other tasks like backups and software updates can be scheduled. You will probably want to install software updates outside of business operating hours and backups can be scheduled to perform each day after midnight or something. The advantage of scheduling certain tasks is that network engineers will less likely forget to do them.

Making changes to your network will sometimes impact productivity of users who rely on the network availability. Some changes will have a huge impact, changes to firewalls or access-list rules might impact more users then you'd wish for. For example you might want to install a new firewall and planned for a certain result. Accidentally you forgot about a certain application that uses random port numbers and you end up troubleshooting this issue. Meanwhile some users are not able to use this application (and shouting at you while you try to fix it...;).

Larger companies might have more than 1 IT department and each department is responsible for different network services. If you plan to replace a certain router tommorow at 2AM then you might want to warn the "Microsoft Windows" guys department because their servers will be unreachable. You can use change management for this. When you plan to make a certain change to the network then other departments will be informed and they can object if there is a conflict with their planning.

When you want to implement change management you might want to think about the following:

- Who will be responsible for authorizing changes to the network?
- Which tasks will be performed during scheduled maintenance windows?
- What procedures have to be followed before making a change? (for example: doing a "copy run start" before making changes to a switch).
- How will you measure the success or failure of network changes? (for example: if you plan to change a number of IP addresses you will plan the time required to make this change. If it takes 5 minutes to reconfigure the IP addresses and you end up troubleshooting 2 hours because something else is not working you might want to "rollback" to the previous configuration. How much time do you allow for troubleshooting? 5 minutes? 10 minutes? 1 hour?
- How, when and who will add the network change to the network documentation?
- How will you create a rollback plan so you can restore a configuration to the previous configuration in case of unexpected problems?
- What circumstances will allow change management policies to be overruled?

Another task we have to do is to create and update our network documentation. Whenever a new network is designed and created it should be documented.

The more challenging part is to keep it up-to-date in the future. There are a number of items that you should find in any network documentation:

- Physical topology diagram: This should show all the network devices and how they are physically connected to each other.
- Logical topology diagram: This should show how everything is connected to each other. Protocols that are used, VLAN information etc.
- Interconnections: It's useful to have a diagram that shows which interfaces of one network device are connected to the interface of another network device.
- Inventory: You should have an inventory of all network equipment, vendor lists, product numbers, software versions, software license information and each network device should have an organization tag assess number.
- IP Addresses: You should have a diagram that covers all the IP addresses in use on the network and on which interfaces they are configured.
- Configuration management: Before changing a configuration we should save the current running-configuration so it's easy to restore to a previous (working) version. It's even better to keep an archive of older configurations for future use.
- Design documents: Documents that were created during the original design of the network should be kept so you can always check why certain design decisions were made.

It's also a good idea to work with step-by-step guidelines for troubleshooting or using templates for certain configurations that all network engineers agree on to use, here are some examples to give you an idea:

```
interface FastEthernet0/1
 description AccessPoint
 switchport access vlan 2
 switchport mode access
 spanning-tree portfast
```

Here's an example for access interfaces connected to wireless access points. Portfast has to be enabled for spanning-tree, the access points have to be in VLAN 2 and the switchport has to be changed to "access" manually.

```
interface FastEthernet0/2
 description VOIP
 interface FastEthernet0/2
 description ClientComputer
 switchport access vlan 6
 switchport mode access
 switchport port-security
 switchport port-security violation shutdown
 switchport port-security maximum 1
 spanning-tree portfast
 spanning-tree bpduguard enable
```

Here's a template for interfaces that connect to client computers. The interface has to be configured for "access" mode manually. Port security has to be enabled so only 1 MAC address is allowed (the computer). The interface has to go into forwarding mode immediately so we configure spanning-tree portfast and if we receive a BPDU the interface should go into err-disabled. Working with pre-defined templates like there will reduce the number of errors because everyone agrees on the same configuration. If you give each network engineer instructions to "protect the interface" you'll probably end up with 10 different configurations...

```
interface GigabitEthernet0/1
 description TRUNK
 switchport trunk encapsulation dot1q
 switchport mode trunk
 switchport trunk nonegotiate
```

Here's one more example for trunk links. If you tell 2 network engineers to "configure a trunk" you might end up with one interface configured for 802.1Q encapsulation and the other one for ISL encapsulation. If one network engineer disabled DTP and the other one configure the interface as "dynamic desirable" then it will also fail. If you instruct them to configure a trunk according to a template then we'll have the same configuration on both sides.

Enough about network maintenance, in the second part of this chapter we'll take a look at the theory of troubleshooting.

There are different reasons why things go wrong on our networks, humans make errors in their configurations, hardware can fail, software updates may include bugs and changing traffic patterns might cause congestion on our networks. To troubleshoot these errors there are different approaches and some are more effective than others.

Troubleshooting consists of 3 steps:

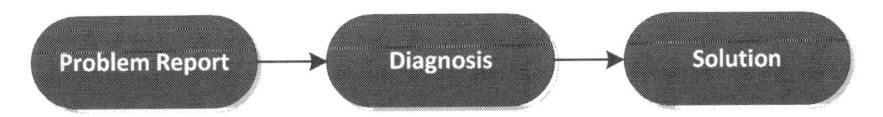

Problem Report → Diagnosis → Solution

It all starts when someone or something **reports a problem**. Often this will be a user that calls the helpdesk because something is not working as expected but it's also possible that you find issues because of network monitoring (you do monitor your network right? ☺). The next step is to **diagnose** the problem and it's important to find the root of the problem. Once you have found out the problem you will implement a (temporary) solution.

Diagnosing the problem is one of the most important steps to do because we need to find the root cause of the problem, here's what we do to diagnose the problem:

- **Collect information**: Most of the time a problem report doesn't give us enough information. Users are very good at reporting "network is down" or "my computer doesn't work" but this doesn't tell us anything. We need to collect information by asking our users detailed questions or we use network tools to gather information.
- **Analyze information**: Once we have gathered all information we will analyze it so see what is wrong. We can compare our information to previously collected information or other devices with similar configurations.
- **Eliminate possible causes**: We need to think about the possible causes and eliminate the potential causes for the problem. This requires thorough knowledge of the network and all the protocols that are involved.
- **Hypothesize**: After eliminating possible causes you will end up with a couple of possible causes that could be the problem. We will select the most likely cause for the problem.
- **Verify hypothesis**: We will test our hypothesis to see if we are right or wrong. If we are right we have a victory…if we are wrong we test our other possible causes.

If you don't use a structured approach for troubleshooting you might just "follow your gut feeling" and get confused because you forget what you already tried or not. It's also easier if you work together with other network engineers because you can share the steps you already went through.

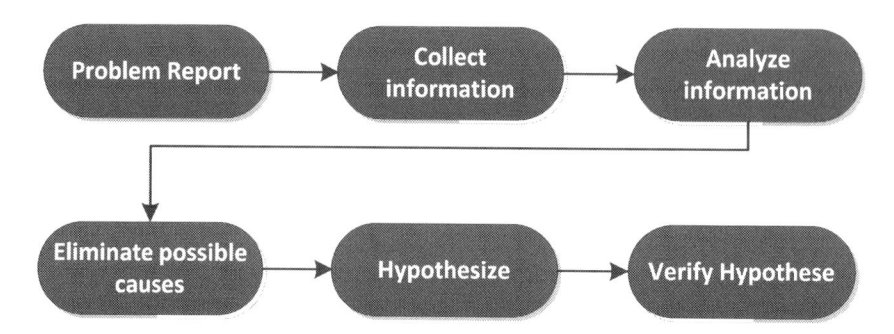

```
Problem Report → Collect information → Analyze information
                                              ↓
Eliminate possible causes → Hypothesize → Verify Hypothese
```

Here are the steps in a nice flowchart; we call this the **structured troubleshooting approach**. However if you have a lot of experience with the network you are working on and as you become better at troubleshooting this approach might be too time-consuming.

Instead of walking through all the different steps in the structured troubleshooting approach we can also jump from the "collect information" step directly to the "hypothesize" step and skip the "analyze information" and "eliminate possible causes" steps If you are inexperienced with troubleshooting it's best to use the structured troubleshooting approach. As you become better at troubleshooting you might want to skip some of the steps...we call this the **shoot from the hip** approach.

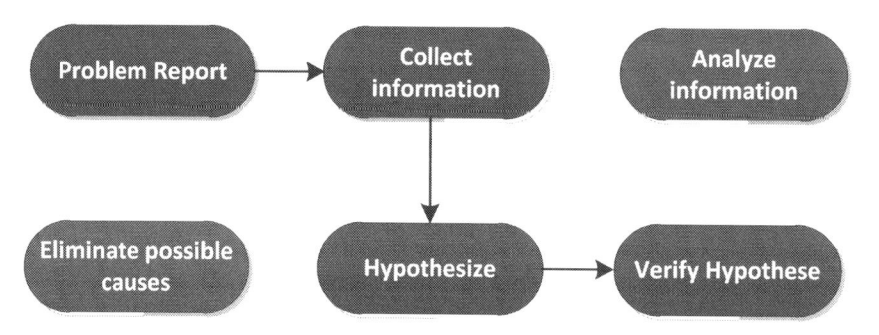

```
Problem Report → Collect information     Analyze information
                       ↓
Eliminate possible causes    Hypothesize → Verify Hypothese
```

Here's the shoot from the hip model. The steps that we skip are in blue. If your instincts are wrong you won't lose your life but you will lose valuable time.
If you are right however you'll save a lot of time (or become the new sheriff in town).

Eliminating possible causes is an important step in the troubleshooting process and there are a couple of approaches how you can do this, here they are:

- **Top-down.**
- **Bottom-up.**
- **Divide and conquer.**
- **Follow the traffic path.**
- **Spot the difference.**
- **Replace components.**

Let's walk through the different approaches one-by-one!

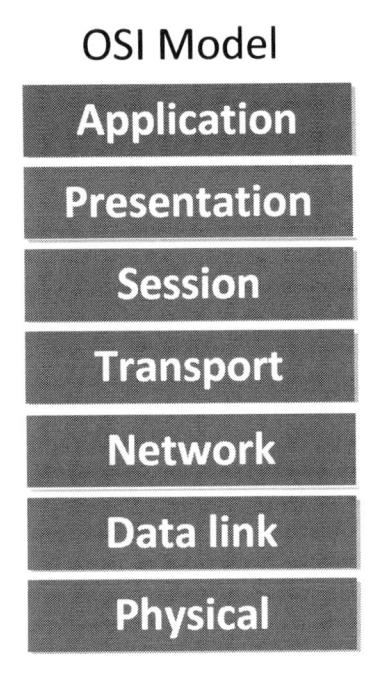

OSI Model

- Application
- Presentation
- Session
- Transport
- Network
- Data link
- Physical

Top-down means we start at the top of the OSI model (application layer) and work our way further down to the bottom. The idea is that we will check the application to see if it's working and assume that if a certain layer is working that all the layers below are also working. If you send a ping from one computer to another (ICMP) you can assume that layer 1,2 and 3 are operational. The downside of this approach is that you need access to the application that you are troubleshooting.

OSI Model

| Application |
| Presentation |
| Session |
| Transport |
| Network |
| Data link |
| Physical |

Bottom-up means we start at the bottom of the OSI model and we'll work our way up. We will start with the physical layer which means we check our cables and connectors, move up to the data link layer to see if Ethernet is working, Spanning-tree is working ok, port security is not causing issue, VLANs are configured properly and then move onto the network layer. Here we will check our IP addresses, access-lists, routing protocols and so on. This approach is very thorough but also time-consuming. If you are new to troubleshooting I would recommend to use this method because you will eliminate all the possible causes for problems.

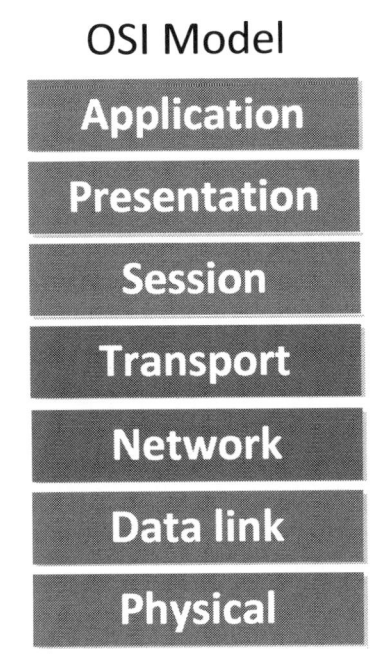

OSI Model

Application
Presentation
Session
Transport
Network
Data link
Physical

Divide and conquer means we start in the middle of the OSI-model. You can use this model if you are not sure if top-down or bottom-up are more effective. The idea is that you'll try to send a ping from one device to another. If the ping works you know that layer 1-3 are operational and you can work your way up in the OSI model.

If the ping fails you know something is not right and you'll work your way to the bottom of the OSI model.

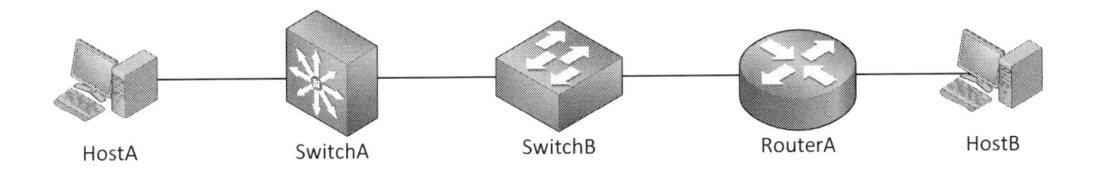

HostA — SwitchA — SwitchB — RouterA — HostB

The **follow the traffic path** is very useful. First we'll try to send a ping from HostA to HostB. If it fails we'll check all the devices in its path. First we'll verify if SwitchA is configured correctly, it it's looking good we'll move onto SwitchB, verify it and then move onto RouterA.

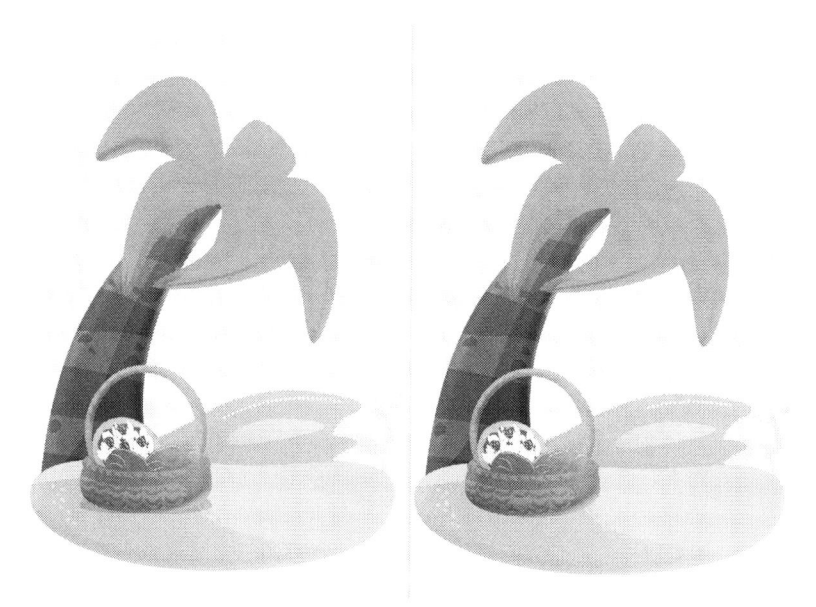

You've probably done one of these before. **Spotting the difference** in configurations or the output of show commands can be useful but it's very easy to miss something. If you have a number of branch routers with a similar configuration and only one is not working you can see if there's a difference in the configuration. Network engineers that don't have a lot of experience usually use this approach. You might be able to solve the problem but there's a risk that you don't really know what you are doing.

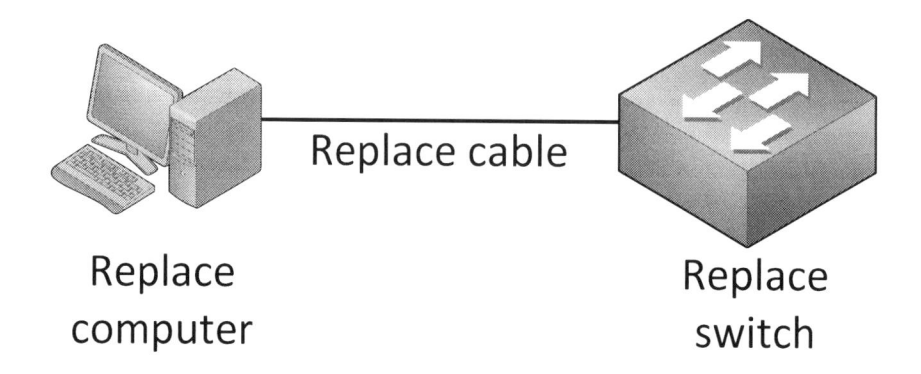

The last approach to solve our problem is to **replace components**. Let's say we have a scenario where a computer is unable to access the network. In the example above I could replace the computer to eliminate any chance of the computer being the problem. We could replace the cable and if we suspect the switch we can replace it with a new one and copy the old configuration to see if there are any hardware problems.

This is all the theory I wanted to share with you about network maintenance and troubleshooting.
We can talk all day long about different methods and such but the key to

12

becoming an expert with troubleshooting consists of two things:

- Truly **understand** all the different networking protocols like OSPF, EIGRP, BGP, spanning-tree and everything else you learned in CCNA and CCNP ROUTE/SWITCH. You can't fix something if you have no idea how it works.
- **Gain experience by doing labs** and **troubleshoot** broken networks!

You can read all the books about driving a car, how an engine works, what a clutch is or how to use your mirrors but at the end of the day…you have to **sit in a car** and **start driving** to learn how to drive a car. In the upcoming chapters of this book you will learn about all the different things that could go wrong with all the protocols and I will teach you how to troubleshoot them. I will also refer to some of the troubleshooting labs on GNS3Vault that I created for you to practice!

2. Tools for Troubleshooting

Before we start looking at the troubleshooting of the different protocols I want to give you an overview of all the different tools you can use for troubleshooting. Some of these might be familiar to you already but some are probably new to you. In this chapter we'll walk through all the different tools you can use and I'll give you some examples how to use them.

"If I had eight hours to chop down a tree, I'd spend six hours sharpening my ax"
~Abraham Lincoln

The first item we'll look at is NTP. Once you start working with logging information and debug output you need to make sure they show the correct date and time or your information will be useless. Cisco devices can be configured to use an external NTP server to synchronize their clocks. You can also configure most Cisco devices to become a NTP server.

```
Router(config)#ntp server pool.ntp.org
```

First I configure an external NTP server with the **ntp server** command. I've chosen to use one of the NTP servers from ntp.org.

```
Router#show ntp status
Clock is synchronized, stratum 3, reference is 217.121.137.227
nominal freq is 250.0000 Hz, actual freq is 250.0000 Hz,
precision is 2**18
reference time is D35E243C.A5B38A7C (13:03:56.647 UTC Wed May 16 2012)
clock offset is -10.1544 msec, root delay is 29.10 msec
root dispersion is 52.75 msec, peer dispersion is 2.40 msec
```

If everything is OK it should show you that the clock is now synchronized. We still have to configure the correct time zone.

```
Router(config)#clock timezone CET +1
```

I configured my time zone to be CET (European Time Zone). You can type in whatever name you want for the time zone, it doesn't matter. It's important that you configure the correct offset however.

In Europe we have a summer time which means we turn the clock one hour forward on the last Sunday in March from 02:00 to 03:00. On the last Sunday of October we turn the clock backwards from 03:00 to 02:00. This is something we'll have to configure on our Cisco device.

```
Router(config)#clock summer-time CETrecurring las sun mar 02:00 last sun oct 03:00
```

This takes care of the clock configuration. It's important that we enable the date, time and timezone in our debug and logging information. When you store logging or debug information it's important that they have the correct date and time on them.

```
Router(config)#service timestamps debug datetime msec localtime show-timezone year
Router(config)#service timestamps log datetime msec localtime show-timezone year
```

Use the **service timestamps** command to add the correct date and time to debug and logging information.

```
May 16 2012 15:16:23.214 CET: RIP: sending v2 flash update to 224.0.0.9 via FastEthernet0/0 (192.168.81.154)
May 16 2012 15:16:23.214 CET: RIP: build flash update entries
May 16 2012 15:16:23.214 CET:   1.1.1.0/24 via 0.0.0.0, metric 1, tag 0
May 16 2012 15:16:23.218 CET: RIP: sending v2 flash update to 224.0.0.9 via Loopback0 (1.1.1.1)
```

This is an example of a debug. You can see it adds the correct date, time and time zone. It's a good idea to configure one or two devices in your network to synchronize with an external NTP server. You can configure a Cisco device to become a NTP server for the rest of the devices in your network. If you want an example how to do this I can recommend you to try this lab:

http://gns3vault.com/Network-Management/ntp-network-time-protocol.html

Now our clocks are working correctly we can take a look at logging. Everything that happens on your router or switch can be logged. We have different levels of importance for logging information. By default you'll see the logging information on your console, like this one:

```
May 16 2012 15:24:53.080 CET: %LINK-5-CHANGED: Interface FastEthernet0/0, changed state to administratively down
May 16 2012 15:24:54.080 CET: %LINEPROTO-5-UPDOWN: Line protocol on Interface FastEthernet0/0, changed state to down
```

This is an example of an interface that's going down.

```
May 16 2012 15:25:19.893 CET: %SYS-5-CONFIG_I: Configured from console by console
```

You have probably seen this one before; you'll see it when you exit the global configuration mode. There are different severity levels for logging information. An interface that goes down is probably more important to know than a message that tells us we exited the global configuration.

Here are the severity levels:

0. Emergencies
1. Alerts
2. Critical
3. Errors
4. Warnings
5. Notifications
6. Informational
7. Debugging

By default you'll see all of these messages on the console. If you don't want to see everything you can change this behavior:

```
Router(config)#logging console errors
```

For example you can use configure the **logging console** command so it only shows you severity level 3 (errors) and lower. The message about the interface that was going down is a **notification** in case you were wondering.

```
Router#show logging history
Syslog History Table:1 maximum table entries,
 saving level warnings or higher
 29 messages ignored, 11 dropped, 0 recursion drops
 2 table entries flushed
 SNMP notifications not enabled
   entry number 3 : LINK-3-UPDOWN
     Interface FastEthernet0/0, changed state to up
     timestamp: 1688
```

We can use the **show logging history** command to see the logging history of this Cisco router. It doesn't store everything. You can see it says "saving level warnings or higher". This logging information is saved in the RAM of your device. Once you reboot it you will lose this logging history.

```
Router(config)#logging buffered 4096
```

You can change the size of the buffer if needed. As soon as the buffer is full old logging information will be discarded. In the example above we have 4096 bytes we can use for logging information.

It's not a good idea to store logging information locally on your device. One reboot and you'll lose valuable information. It's best to use an external server for this.

```
Router(config)#logging 192.168.1.100
```

Use the **logging** command to set the IP address for your logging server. All logging information will be sent towards this server with the exception of debugging (level 7) messages by default.

Normally you probably only want to see debug information on your console or telnet/SSH session but you can store it in on your logging server too if you want:

```
Router(config)#logging trap 7
```

You need to use the **logging trap** command to 7 so it will also store debug information on your logging server.

Besides syslog there is another method to store logging information to an external server. **SNMP (Simple Network Management Protocol)** can be used to collect statistics from network devices including Cisco routers and switches. SNMP consists of 2 items:

- **NMS (Network Management System)**
- **SNMP Agents**

The NMS is the external server where you want to store logging information. The SNMP agents run on the network devices that we want to monitor. The NMS can query a SNMP agent to collect information from the network device. SNMP has multiple versions, the most popular ones being:

- SNMP version 2c
- SNMP version 3

SNMP version 3 offers security through authentication and encryption which SNMP version 2c does not. SNMP version 2c however is still more common. Let me show you a simple example for SNMP version 2c:

```
Router(config)#snmp-server community TSHOOT ro
```

First we'll have to configure a **community string**. Think of this as a password that the SNMP agent and NMS have to agree upon. I called mine "TSHOOT". The **ro** stands for **read-only**. SNMP isn't just for retrieving information; we can also use it to instruct our routers and switches to perform an action.

```
Router(config)#snmp-server location Amsterdam GNS3Vault Lab
Router(config)#snmp-server contact info@gns3vault.com
```

These two steps are not required but it's useful to specify a **location** and **contact**. This way you'll at least know where the device is located whenever you receive information through SNMP.

```
Router(config)#snmp-server host 192.168.12.2 version 2c TSHOOT
```

The messages that the SNMP agent sends to the NMS are called **SNMP traps**. Of course we want to send these to an external server so I'll configure the IP address of the SNMP server. I also have to specify the version and the community string.

```
Router(config)#snmp-server enable traps
```

Last but not least I'll have to enable the SNMP traps. If I use the **snmp-server enable traps** command it will enable **all SNMP traps**.

```
Router#show run | include traps
snmp-server enable traps snmp authentication linkdown linkup coldstart warmstart
snmp-server enable traps vrrp
snmp-server enable traps ds1
snmp-server enable traps tty
snmp-server enable traps eigrp
snmp-server enable traps casa
snmp-server enable traps xgcp
snmp-server enable traps bulkstat collection transfer
snmp-server enable traps isdn call-information
snmp-server enable traps isdn layer2
```

This is only a portion of everything that you'll see in the running-configuration. This is a great way to test SNMP but on a production network it's better to take a look at the different traps and only enable the ones you feel are necessary. One of the SNMP traps in the example above is related to EIGRP. If anything happens with the EIGRP routing protocol a SNMP trap will be send towards the SNMP server.

If you never tried saving syslog information to an external server or played with SNMP I recommend trying "Solarwinds Kiwi Syslog server". You can download a 30 day trial and practice the commands above yourself:

http://www.kiwisyslog.com

Let's continue by looking at some methods how we can save our configs.

```
Router#copy running-config startup-config
Destination filename [startup-config]?
```

You are probably familiar with this command...if not, shame on you! ☺ This is the simplest method of copying your running configuration to the startup-config file which is stored in your nvram. It's a good method to store your configuration but you'll lose your configuration if your device has a hardware failure.

It's a good idea to have a backup server somewhere in your network; this could be something as simple as running a FTP or TFTP server on your own computer. Tftpd32 is a nice free windows utility for running a TFTP server. You don't even have to install it, it runs as an executable:

http://tftpd32.jounin.net/

We can use the copy command to copy our configuration and/or files on the flash to a wide range of devices, for example:

```
Router#copy running-config
ftp://username:password@192.168.1.1/myconfig.cfg
Address or name of remote host [192.168.1.1]?
Destination filename [myconfig.cfg]?
```

If you studied CCNA you are probably familiar with using the copy command like this. The command above will help you to copy your running-config to a FTP server. The downside of this method is that you have to type in the FTP username and password yourself.

```
Router(config)#ip ftp username myusername
Router(config)#ip ftp password mypassword
```

If you want you can save the FTP username and password in your configuration. By default it will be saved in cleartext. You can use the "service password-encryption" command to encrypt it using the Cisco type 7 proprietary encryption but don't forget that this can be easily decrypted!

```
Router#copy http://www.gns3vault.com/config.txt flash:/
configs/config.txt
```

You can also use HTTP to copy files from a webserver to your device.

FTP and HTTP are easy methods to copy configuration files and/or IOS images from and to your device but everything will be sent in **clear-text**. You can also use HTTPS or SCP to copy so traffic will be encrypted!

You've probably played with the copy command before but do you also know there's a method to archive configurations on your Cisco device? Let me show you how it works!

```
Router(config)#archive
Router(config-archive)#path ftp:/archive/$h-config
Router(config-archive)#write-memory
Router(config-archive)#time-period 60
```

First you need to use the **archive** command to get into the archive configuration. I configured my router to create an archive on the FTP server and the configuration files should be saved in the "archive" folder. The filenames will be appended with the hostname of the device because I used the **$h** parameter in front of the filename.

Every time someone copies the running configuration to the NVRAM the device will store a copy on the FTP server because of the **write-memory** command. The **time-period** command can be used to configure a schedule. Every 60 minutes the running-configuration will be "archived" to my FTP server. 60 minutes is very short and on a production network you probably want to configure this to 1440 minutes (24 hours) or maybe 10080 minutes (1 week).

```
Router#show archive
 The next archive file will be named ftp:/archive/Router-config-5
  Archive #  Name
     0         ftp:/archive/Router-config-1
     1         ftp:/archive/Router-config-2
     2         ftp:/archive/Router-config-3
     3         ftp:/archive/Router-config-4
```

You can use the **show archive** command to check how many backup configurations you have stored. In my example there are 4 backup configurations and the next one will be saved as "Router-config-5". It's important to have multiple backups of configuration files instead of just saving the "last" one. In case of trouble or misconfiguration you can always rollback to one of the earlier configurations that you archived.

Let's say someone changed the running-configuration on my device, made some errors and I want to roll back to a previous version. What would be the best way to do this? Of course I could do a reload and hope that they didn't overwrite the startup-config.
The downside is that a reload could take a couple of minutes and it will disrupt network services. Anything else we can do?

```
Router#copy startup-config running-config
```

If the startup-config is still good we could use the copy command. If you studied CCNA you might recall that copying something to the running-config will **not replace** it but the two configurations will **merge**. There is a command however that lets you replace the running-configuration **without rebooting** your device.

```
Router#configure replace ftp:/archive/Router-config-1 list
This will apply all necessary additions and deletions
to replace the current running configuration with the
contents of the specified configuration file, which is
assumed to be a complete configuration, not a partial
configuration. Enter Y if you are sure you want to proceed. ?
[no]: yes

!List of Commands:
```

```
no hostname Router
hostname MyRouter
end

Total number of passes: 1
Rollback Done

MyRouter#
```

We can use the **configure replace** command to do this. I will use one of my archived configurations on the FTP server to replace my running-configuration. The **list** parameter will show me all the commands that are different between the archived configuration and the running-configuration. In my example I'm using the first archived configuration file to copy it into the running-configuration. The only difference is the hostname of my router which has changed from "Router" to "MyRouter". This is a clean method of restoring the running-configuration without reloading your device.

Enough about configurations, there are more tricks that you should be familiar with in order to become a good troubleshooter. I want to show you some techniques for "show" commands that will be helpful.

```
Router#show ip route
Codes: C - connected, S - static, R - RIP, M - mobile, B - BGP
       D - EIGRP, EX - EIGRP external, O - OSPF, IA - OSPF inter area
       N1 - OSPF NSSA external type 1, N2 - OSPF NSSA external type 2
       E1 - OSPF external type 1, E2 - OSPF external type 2
       i - IS-IS, su - IS-IS summary, L1 - IS-IS level-1, L2 - IS-IS level-2
       ia - IS-IS inter area, * - candidate default, U - per-user static route
       o - ODR, P - periodic downloaded static route

Gateway of last resort is not set

C    192.168.12.0/24 is directly connected, FastEthernet0/0
     1.0.0.0/24 is subnetted, 1 subnets
C       1.1.1.0 is directly connected, Loopback0
     2.0.0.0/24 is subnetted, 1 subnets
D       2.2.2.0 [90/156160] via 192.168.12.2, 00:00:16, FastEthernet0/0
```

Let's start with **show ip route**. Let's imagine this router receives an IP packet destined for IP address 2.2.2.2 and I want to see if it knows where to send it. I can type "show ip route" and browse through the routing table myself. This will work but I'll have to scan the table myself.

```
Router#show ip route 2.2.2.2
Routing entry for 2.2.2.0/24
  Known via "eigrp 1", distance 90, metric 156160, type internal
  Redistributing via eigrp 1
  Last update from 192.168.12.2 on FastEthernet0/0, 00:02:12 ago
  Routing Descriptor Blocks:
  * 192.168.12.2, from 192.168.12.2, 00:02:12 ago, via FastEthernet0/0
      Route metric is 156160, traffic share count is 1
      Total delay is 5100 microseconds, minimum bandwidth is 100000 Kbit
      Reliability 255/255, minimum MTU 1500 bytes
      Loading 1/255, Hops 1
```

I can also type in **show ip route 2.2.2.2**. This will scan the routing table and it will show me the network that matches the IP address that I'm looking for. In the example above you can see that 2.2.2.0/24 matches the IP address that I was looking for. It also gives me more detailed information.

```
Router#show ip route 3.3.3.3
% Network not in table
```

If you are looking for an IP address that does not match any networks you'll get a nice message that the network is not in your routing table. However don't be too fast with drawing conclusions. If you have a default route in your routing table it won't show up as the network for this IP address, let me show you what I mean:

```
Router(config)#ip route 0.0.0.0 0.0.0.0 192.168.12.2
```

Let's create a default route; I don't care what it is I just want something in my routing table.

```
Router#show ip route

Gateway of last resort is 192.168.12.2 to network 0.0.0.0

C    192.168.12.0/24 is directly connected, FastEthernet0/0
     1.0.0.0/24 is subnetted, 1 subnets
C       1.1.1.0 is directly connected, Loopback0
     2.0.0.0/24 is subnetted, 1 subnets
D       2.2.2.0 [90/156160] via 192.168.12.2, 00:16:44, FastEthernet0/0
S*   0.0.0.0/0 [1/0] via 192.168.12.2
```

You can see I now have a default route in my routing table.

```
Router#show ip route 3.3.3.3
% Network not in table
```

If I do a lookup for IP address 3.3.3.3 it will tell me there is no network that matches this IP address. It matches the default route however, keep in mind to check the routing table yourself to see if there is a default route or not.

Our "show ip route" command offers us a nice way to check a certain entry in the routing table but not all show commands have similar options. There are some generic options that we can use for **all show** commands.

Show commands can be filtered by using the | character (it's called a pipe) and combining it with the **begin, section, include or exclude** parameters. Let's take a look at some examples!

```
Router#show run | begin router eigrp

router eigrp 1
 network 0.0.0.0
 no auto-summary
```

If I want to check my EIGRP configuration in the running-configuration I can type in "show run" and hammer the space or enter button to get to the EIGRP section of the configuration. *To make things easier* - I can also use the **begin** parameter. By using the "**show run | begin router eigrp**" command it will skip everything in the running configuration until the first line that matches "router eigrp".

```
Router#show run | section vty
line vty 0 4
 password vault
 login
```

We can also use the **section** keyword. In the example above I'm jumping straight to the "vty" section of the running configuration.

```
Router#show ip interface brief
Interface              IP-Address      OK? Method Status                Protocol
FastEthernet0/0        192.168.12.1    YES manual up      up
Loopback0              1.1.1.1         YES manual up      up
Loopback1              unassigned      YES unset  administratively down down
```

This is an example of the "show ip interface brief" command without any filters.

```
Router#show ip int brief | include administratively
Loopback1              unassigned      YES unset  administratively down down
```

If I want a quick overview of all the interfaces with a "shutdown" command on them I can use the **"show ip int brief | include administratively"** command. This will **only** show the lines that have the word "administratively" in them.

```
Router#show ip int brief | include admini
Loopback1              unassigned      YES unset
administratively down down
```

Of course you don't have to fully type what you are looking for; just typing "admini" will match "administratively" as well. This gives me a nice clean overview of what I'm looking for.

```
Router#show ip interface brief | exclude up
Interface              IP-Address      OK? Method Status
Protocol
Loopback1              unassigned      YES unset
administratively down down
```

I can also use the **exclude** keyword to filter all the lines that have "up" in them.

In the examples above I used the begin, section, include or exclude parameters and combined them with a word or sentence like "vty", "router eigrp" or "administratively". We can also use regular expressions. If you studied CCNP ROUTE you have seen regular expressions in combination with BGP.

```
Router#show ip int brief | include ^Loo
Loopback0              1.1.1.1         YES manual up
up
Loopback1              unassigned      YES unset
administratively down down
```

Here's an example of a regular expression. The ^ symbol means that the line has to start with whatever I type behind the ^ symbol. ^Loo means I want to see all lines that start with "Loo". In this case it will show me all the loopback interfaces.

```
Router#show processes | include ^CPU|ARP Input
CPU utilization for five seconds: 0%/0%; one minute: 0%; five
minutes: 0%
  16 Mwe 605F6A3C         12          78      153 4732/6000    0
ARP Input
  91 Mwe 6068862C          0           1        0 5616/6000    0
RARP Input
```

A good example of the power of regular expressions is by demonstrating it with the "show processes" command. The ^CPU means I want to see all lines that start with "CPU". The "ARP Input" will show me all lines that contain "ARP

25

Input". As a result I have a nice overview with just the ARP information.

```
Router#show processes | include ARP Input
   16 Mwe  605F6A3C        12       80       150 4732/6000   0
ARP Input
   91 Mwe  6068862C          0        1         0 5616/6000   0
RARP Input
```

If I don't add the ^CPU part then it will only show me the two lines containing "ARP Input" which isn't very useful...

Using the begin, include, exclude and section parameters makes my show commands far more useful. Right now I only see the output of the show command on my screen but it's also possible to redirect the output to a file.

```
Router#show tech-support | redirect
tftp://192.168.12.100/techsupport.txt
```

If you ever required support from Cisco they might have asked for the "show tech-support" command. This show command produces a lot of output and instead of copy/pasting whatever you see on your screen it might be easier to save the output in a file. Using the **redirect** parameter we can copy the output to a (TFTP) server and save it as a file called "techsupport.txt". The redirect parameter saves the output in a file and does **not show you the output on your screen**.

```
Router#show run | tee flash:myconfig.txt
Building configuration...

Current configuration : 714 bytes
!
version 12.4
service timestamps debug datetime msec
service timestamps log datetime msec
no service password-encryption
!
hostname Router
```

The **tee** parameter does the same thing as the redirect parameter but it **does show** the output of the show command on my screen. In the example above I'm also saving the output on the flash in a file called "myconfig.txt".

```
Router#dir flash:
Directory of flash:/

    1   -rw-         775                  <no date>  myconfig.txt
```

Use the **dir flash:** command to see the contents of the flash.

```
Router#more flash:myconfig.txt
Building configuration...

Current configuration : 714 bytes
!
version 12.4
service timestamps debug datetime msec
service timestamps log datetime msec
no service password-encryption
!
hostname Router
```

You can look at the contents of a file on your device with the **more** command. In the example above I'm looking at the contents of the myconfig.txt file.

```
Router#show tech-support | append flash:techsupport.txt
```

Redirect and tee will overwrite the old file if you use the same filename. We can also use **append** which is the same as redirect but it will add the output to the file instead of overwriting it. Not all file systems support append so it's possible that you get an error if you try this.

The last show commands I want to "show" you are the ones we use when we troubleshoot hardware-related issues.

```
route-views.optus.net.au>show processes cpu sorted 5min
CPU utilization for five seconds: 0%/0%; one minute: 2%; five
minutes: 3%
 PID Runtime(ms)      Invoked      uSecs    5Sec    1Min   5Min TTY
Process
 172    424120884     2295242      184788   0.00%   1.35%  1.58%   0
BGP Scanner
   4    382944880    20406399       18766   0.00%   0.89%  1.24%   0
Check heaps
 137         21640  2030982109           0  0.15%   0.12%  0.12%   0
HQF Shaper Backg
 138         18472  2030982311           0  0.15%   0.10%  0.08%   0
HQF Input Shaper
  88      17871980   267174489          66  0.00%   0.07%  0.07%   0
IP Input
 235      22159976   138390034         160  0.00%   0.06%  0.07%   0
BGP Router
  50      10475216     3398459        3082  0.00%   0.06%  0.05%   0
Net Background
```

I used one of the looking glass servers from http://www.bgp4.as/looking-glasses to telnet to and check the CPU load with the **show processes** command. Looking glass servers are BGP routers with a partial or full internet routing table. You don't have enable access but you can use some of the show commands to look at. In my example I used the **cpu sorted 5min** parameter to sort the processes based on a 5 minute interval. The load of the CPU is only

3% on a 5 minute interval. BGP scanner is the process that uses 1.58% of the CPU on a 5 minute interval.

Normally you shouldn't see a very high CPU load on a Cisco router or switch. Switches use a ASIC (Application Specific Integrated Circuit) which means that the forwarding of frames is done using hardware tables, not in software (CPU). Routers nowadays use CEF (Cisco Express Forwarding) which uses specialized tables so we don't have to use the CPU for each IP packet entering the router.

```
route-views.optus.net.au>show memory
              Head      Total(b)     Used(b)      Free(b)     Lowest(b)
Largest(b)
Processor   641DBCA0   417479404    365773404    51706000      180220
16777164
      I/O   E000000     33554432      3920924    29633508     26613200
29273820
Transient   7D000000    16777216        10208    16767008     16110700
16766732
```

We can also verify the memory. Especially if you run BGP and have the full Internet routing table you'll need quite some memory. You can use the **show memory** command to verify this. If your router runs out of memory you will see a %SYS-2-MALLOCFAIL message on your console indicating that a process was unable to get enough memory.

Another thing you might want to check if you think your router or switch has hardware errors are your interfaces.

```
Router#show interface gi0/1
GigabitEthernet0/1 is up, line protocol is up
  Last clearing of "show interface" counters never
  Input queue: 0/1000/0/114 (size/max/drops/flushes); Total
output drops: 4
  Queueing strategy: fifo
  Output queue: 0/40 (size/max)
  5 minute input rate 12000 bits/sec, 15 packets/sec
  5 minute output rate 15000 bits/sec, 17 packets/sec
     299904796 packets input, 1017879192 bytes, 0 no buffer
     Received 1433615 broadcasts (0 IP multicasts)
     0 runts, 0 giants, 0 throttles
     10 input errors, 6 CRC, 2 frame, 0 overrun, 12 ignored
     0 watchdog, 35502363 multicast, 0 pause input
     366840355 packets output, 3958512366 bytes, 0 underruns
     8 output errors, 2 collisions, 3 interface resets
     0 unknown protocol drops
     0 babbles, 0 late collision, 0 deferred
     1 lost carrier, 0 no carrier, 0 pause output
     0 output buffer failures, 0 output buffers swapped out
```

There are a number of things we can check with the **show interfaces** command. The **input queue drops** indicates that our device received more traffic than it could handle. It's possible that this happens during a traffic peak but it's also possible that the CPU was too busy to handle all the traffic. If you see a lot of drops you might want to investigate further what is going on.

Output queue drops means that you have congestion on the interface. When you receive traffic on a 100Mbit interface and forward it on a 10Mbit interface you'll see congestion which causes packet loss and high delay. Applications that use TCP can use retransmissions but Voice over IP is an application that is very sensitive to packet loss, high delay and a variation in delay which causes jitter. If you see a lot of output queue drops you'll have to start thinking about implementing QoS (Quality of Service).

If you see **input errors** you probably have hardware-related issues. In my example you see 6 CRC errors which indicates that we didn't receive the frames properly. This can be caused because of hardware errors, damaged cabling or duplex mismatches.

Output errors indicate that there was an error with the transmission of the frame. Nowadays we use full-duplex (FastEthernet, Gigabit) so we don't have collisions anymore and the CSMA/CD (Carrier Sense Multi Access / Collision Detection) is disabled.
On half-duplex networks we can have collisions so it's possible to have issues with the transmission of frames. If you do see output errors on a full-duplex network you probably have a duplex mismatch error.

When you are looking at the interface statistics you don't have to panic right away when you see input or output errors. These statistics are logged from the moment the router was booted so it's possible that those errors happened during weeks or months. In my example you can see that we have 299904796 packets that were received on the interface and only 10 input errors...this is no reason for concern. If I would see 100 packets and 20 of them had errors then I would have a reason to further investigate this. It's a good idea to use the **clear counters** command...let it run for a couple of hours or days and then check the statistics again to get a better picture.

These are all the show command parameters that I wanted to show you for now. If these are new to you I would highly recommend trying them yourself on your Cisco devices! Show commands are useful but they only produce "static" information. If we want to see what is going on real-time on our Cisco devices we'll have to use some debug commands.

> *Debugging is very powerful but will put a load on your CPU. Some debug commands produce more output than others. Typing in 'debug ip packet' without a filter will show the output of **ALL** IP packets on your screen...not a good idea!*

You have probably seen a debug before but did you know you can combine them with access-lists for more specific information? This will help you to reduce the load on the CPU and gives you more specific information. Let me

29

give you an example.

```
Router(config)#access-list 100 permit tcp 192.168.12.0 0.0.0.255 any
```

First I will create an access-list that matches on TCP traffic from source network 192.168.12.0 /24 to any destination.

```
Router#debug ip packet 100 detail
IP packet debugging is on (detailed) for access list 100
```

Next step is to enable debugging of IP packets showing details information. I will refer to access-list 100 that I created earlier and use the **detail** parameter to see more specific information.

```
Router#
*Mar  1 03:12:01.127: IP: tableid=0, s=192.168.12.1 (FastEthernet0/0), d=192.168.12.2 (FastEthernet0/0), routed via RIB
*Mar  1 03:12:01.127: IP: s=192.168.12.1 (FastEthernet0/0), d=192.168.12.2 (FastEthernet0/0), len 44, rcvd 3
*Mar  1 03:12:01.127:     TCP src=40054, dst=23, seq=402773320, ack=0, win=4128 SYN
*Mar  1 03:12:01.131: IP: tableid=0, s=192.168.12.2 (local), d=192.168.12.1 (FastEthernet0/0), routed via FIB
*Mar  1 03:12:01.135: IP: s=192.168.12.2 (local), d=192.168.12.1 (FastEthernet0/0), len 44, sending
*Mar  1 03:12:01.135:     TCP src=23, dst=40054, seq=2538821922, ack=402773321, win=4128 ACK SYN
*Mar  1 03:12:01.151: IP: tableid=0, s=192.168.12.1 (FastEthernet0/0), d=192.168.12.2 (FastEthernet0/0), routed via RIB
*Mar  1 03:12:01.151: IP: s=192.168.12.1 (FastEthernet0/0), d=192.168.12.2 (FastEthernet0/0), len 40, rcvd 3
*Mar  1 03:12:01.151:     TCP src=40054, dst=23, seq=402773321, ack=2538821923, win=4128 ACK
```

Here's an example of a debug that shows the TCP 3-way handshake. You can see the port number (23) that tells me that this is a session with a telnet server. If you have issues with dropping connections or sessions that won't establish you use a debug like this to see what is going on.

That's all I wanted to show you about debugging for the moment. Let's continue with some other useful tools.

How to Master CCNP TSHOOT

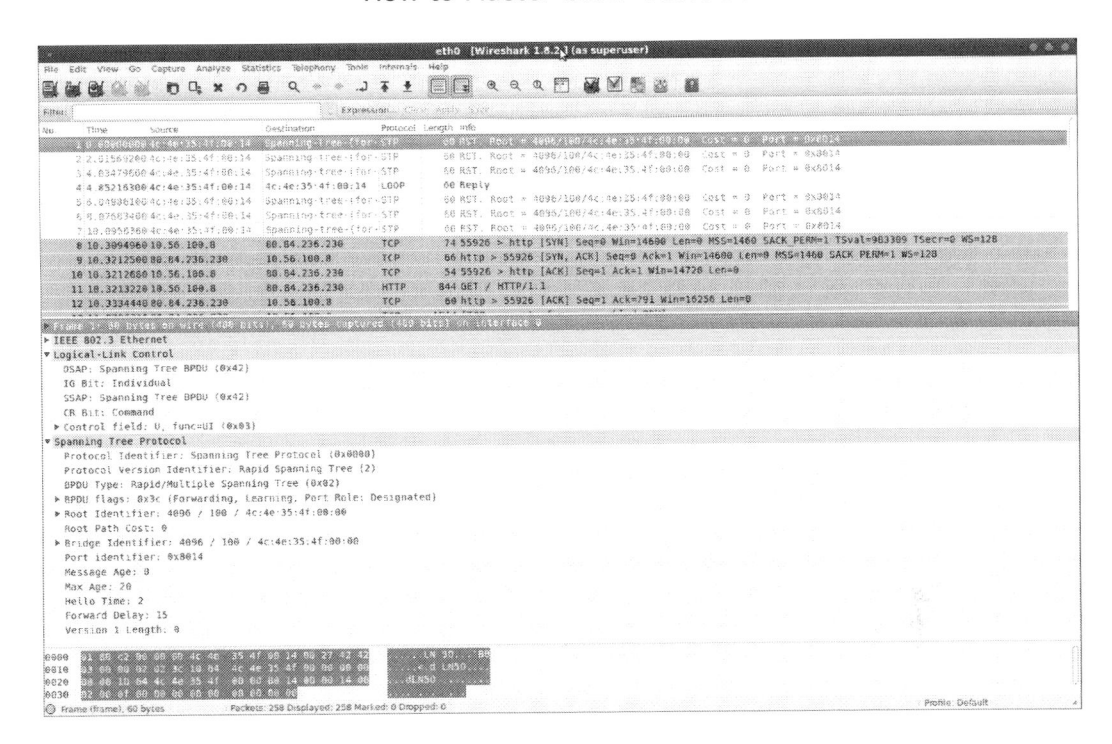

You have probably seen Wireshark before, it's the most popular protocol analyzer and it's open source. A protocol analyzer is a very powerful tool because you can see the actual traffic on your network. You can spot protocol errors or retransmissions and exactly see what is going on. In order to make this a useful tool there are two things you need to understand:

- Learn how to work with filters so you don't just see "everything" but maybe just the conversation between 2 hosts or perhaps you only want to see the "HTTP" traffic that is going on. You also need to understand how to work with the different graphical views.
- Understand all the different protocols and applications. If I'm having issues with TCP…I need to understand how TCP works…the 3-way handshake, the window size, retransmissions, etc. If you are troubleshooting HTTP related errors you need to understand how HTTP behaves. If you want to solve Voice over IP related issues you need to understand how protocols like SIP work and how VoIP packets are sent using RTP.

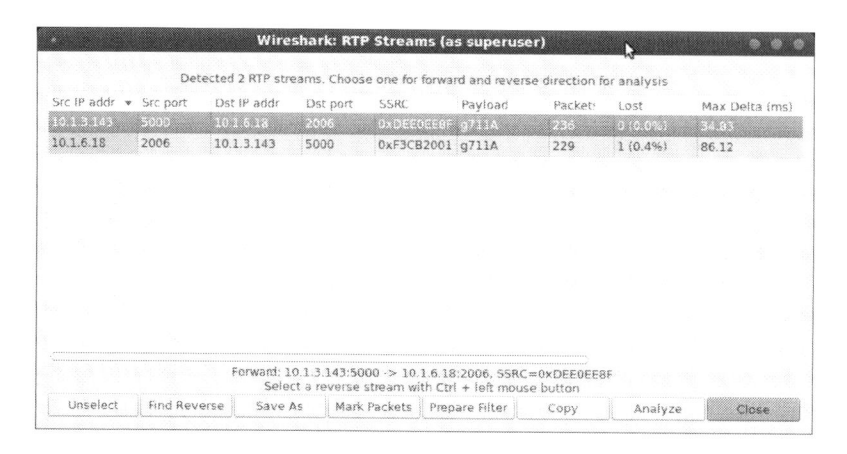

To give you an example of the power of Wireshark look at the example above. Voice over IP engineers can use a protocol analyzer like Wireshark to capture all the RTP packets on the network (RTP is used for sending voice samples on the network). Wireshark will filter out the RTP streams for me and it will even show me the delay between the different RTP packets, the packet loss in % and it's even possible to playback the voice conversation!

If you want some more examples of Wireshark I recommend you to take a look at the Wireshark website and especially the "Video and Presentations" part. There are some videos where they show you how network issues were solved using Wireshark:

http://www.wireshark.org/docs/

Learning how to work with Wireshark (or any other protocol analyzer) isn't something you learn in 5 minutes but it's well worth your time. If you want to become an expert at Wireshark I can highly recommend you to take a look at the Wireshark Network Analysis book written by Laura Chappell:

http://www.wiresharkbook.com/

If you want to capture traffic and analyze it with a protocol analyzer there are a number of things we have to think about.

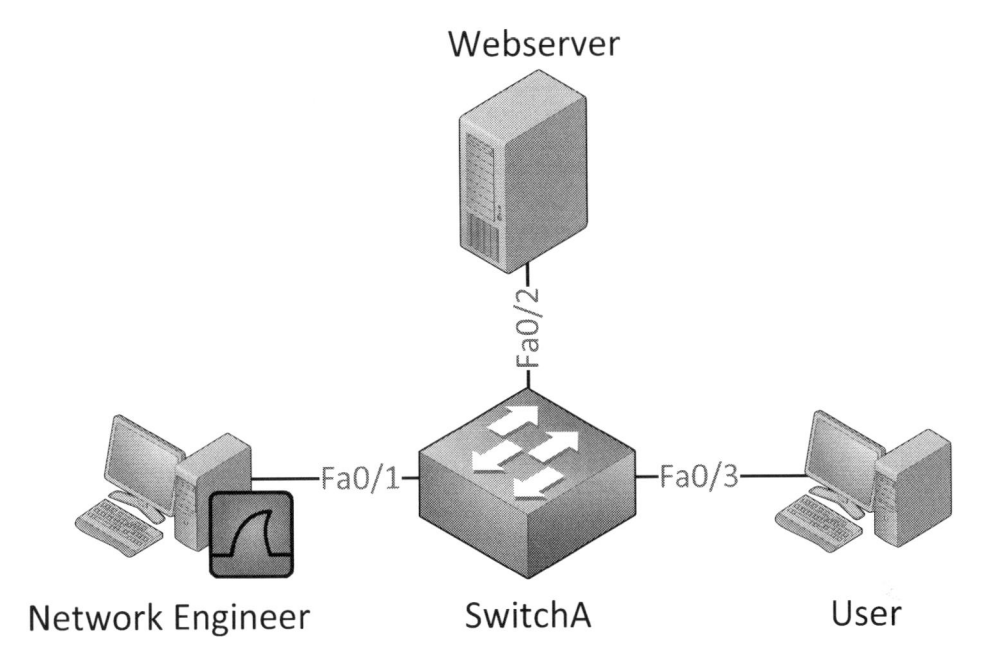

Webserver

[Diagram: Webserver connected to SwitchA via Fa0/2; Network Engineer connected to SwitchA via Fa0/1; User connected to SwitchA via Fa0/3.]

Take a look at the picture above. Our network engineer is running Wireshark on his computer and is connected to the fa0/1 interface of SwitchA. A user is connected to fa0/3 and there's a webserver connected to the fa0/2 interface. The user is browsing some webpage from the webserver and is having issues that our network engineer wants to investigate. As soon as we start Wireshark the only traffic that you will capture is **between your computer and the switch**. That's right you'll only see whatever is happening on the fa0/1 interface. If we want to see the traffic between our user and the webserver we'll have to configure **SPAN**.

SPAN (Switched Port Analyzer) will copy traffic from one interface or VLAN to an interface. Let's take a look how we can use SPAN to see traffic from the webserver:

```
SwitchA(config)#monitor session 1 source interface fa0/2
SwitchA(config)#monitor session 1 destination interface fa0/1
```

We use the **monitor session** command to configure SPAN. You can pick any session number you like...I used number 1. In my example I'm copying all traffic from the fa0/2 interface (the webserver) to the fa0/1 interface (our network engineer's computer).

If you start sniffing with Wireshark you'll see everything that happens on the fa0/2 interface.

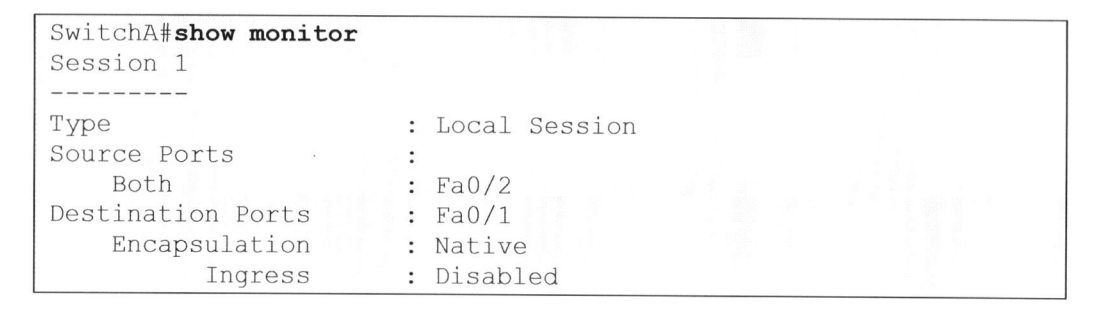

```
SwitchA#show monitor
Session 1
---------
Type                    : Local Session
Source Ports            :
    Both                : Fa0/2
Destination Ports       : Fa0/1
    Encapsulation       : Native
         Ingress        : Disabled
```

You can use the **show monitor** command to verify your configuration.

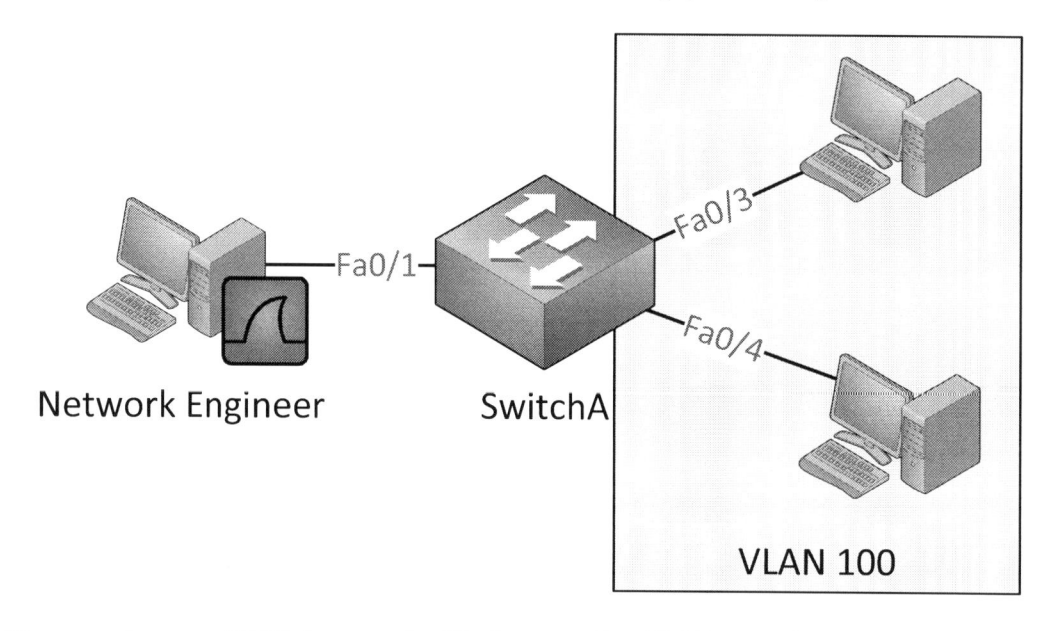

We can also use SPAN to copy traffic from entire VLAN to a destination interface. In the example above we have 2 computers in VLAN 100, let's copy their traffic to the fa0/1 interface so we can sniff it.

```
SwitchA(config)#monitor session 1 source vlan 100
SwitchA(config)#monitor session 1 destination interface fa0/1
```

Configure SPAN to use VLAN 100 as the source and copy it to the fa0/1 interface. All traffic from VLAN 100 will now be copied so we can sniff it!

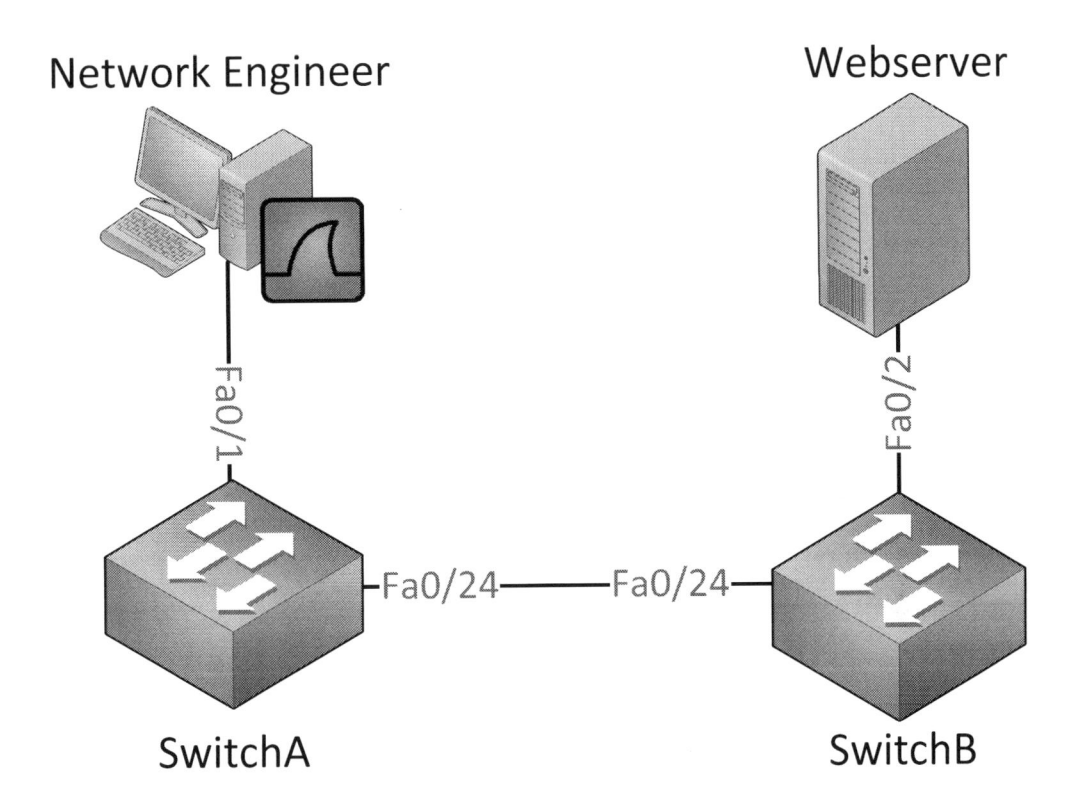

What if the webserver is connected to another switch? This time the webserver is connected to SwitchB while our network engineer is still connected to SwitchA. **RSPAN (Remote SPAN)** to the rescue! It's possible to sniff traffic from a remote switch, let me show you how:

```
SwitchB(config)#vlan 50
SwitchB(config-vlan)#name RSPAN
SwitchB(config-vlan)#remote-span
SwitchB(config-vlan)#exit
SwitchB(config)#monitor session 1 source interface fa0/2
SwitchB(config)#monitor session 1 destination remote vlan 50
```

Since we are sending the traffic from SwitchB to SwitchA we'll need something to carry our traffic. We have to use a VLAN for this and tell the switch that we'll use it for remote SPAN. In my example I'm using VLAN 50. Traffic from the fa0/2 interface on SwitchB should be copied to VLAN 50.

```
SwitchA(config)#vlan 50
SwitchA(config-vlan)#name RSPAN
SwitchA(config-vlan)#remote-span
SwitchA(config-vlan)#exit
SwitchA(config)#monitor session 1 destination interface fa0/1
SwitchA(config)#monitor session 1 source remote vlan 50
```

On SwitchA we'll configure RSPAN so everything from VLAN 50 will be copied to the fa0/1 interface. This will ensure that we can sniff traffic from the webserver. SPAN and RSPAN are very useful but depending on the switch platform you are using it might have some limitations, it's best to check the configuration guide of your switch to find out what options you can use.

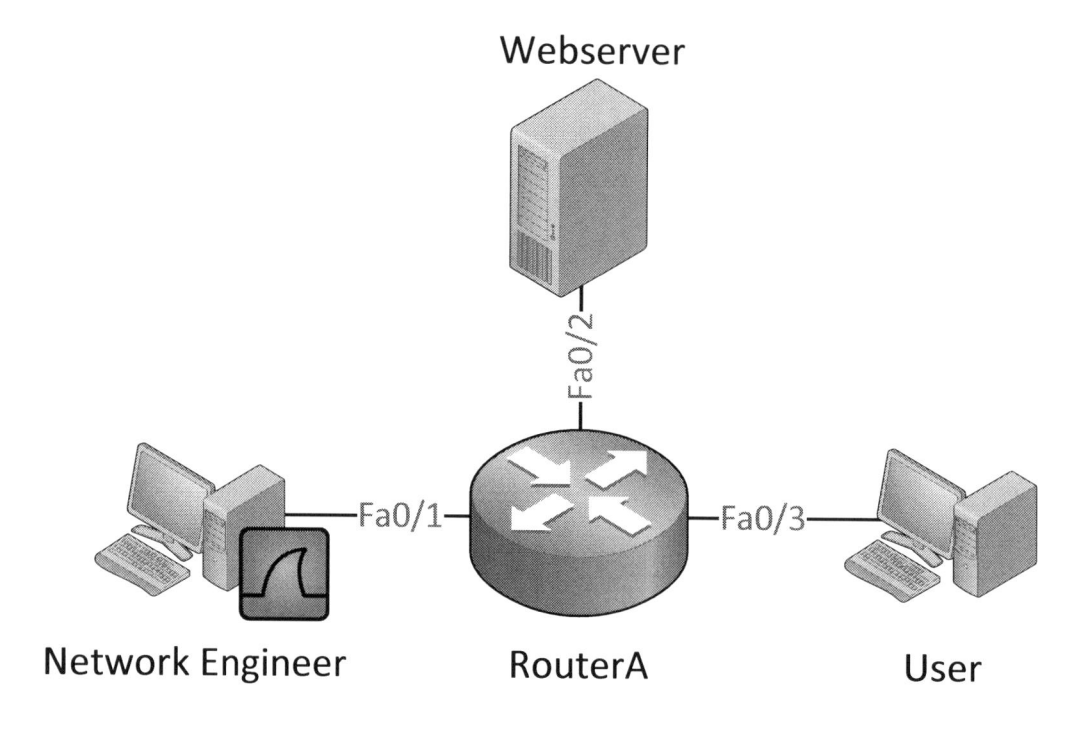

```
                        Webserver
                            |
                          Fa0/2
                            |
    ---Fa0/1---   RouterA   ---Fa0/3---
Network Engineer                         User
```

What if we have a router instead of a switch? SPAN doesn't exist for routers but we do have something called **RITE (Router IP Traffic Export).** RITE allows us to copy IP packets to a destination interface just like SPAN does. Let me show you an example:

```
RouterA(config)#ip traffic-export profile MYEXPORT
RouterA(conf-rite)#interface fastEthernet 0/1
RouterA(conf-rite)#mac-address 1111.1111.1111
```

This is RITE in its most simple form. We use the **ip traffic-export profile** command to create a new profile which I called "MYEXPORT". Next step is to specify the destination interface which will be fa0/1 in my case. We also have to configure the MAC address of the device that is running Wireshark.

```
RouterA(conf-rite)#bidirectional
```

By default only **inbound** IP packets will be copied to the destination interface. Use the **bidirectional** command to copy inbound AND outbound IP packets.

```
RouterA(conf-rite)#incoming access-list ?
  <1-199>      IP access list (standard or extended)
```

```
<1300-2699>   IP expanded access list (standard or extended)
WORD          Access-list name
```

Optionally you can apply an access-list. In my example I'm only interested in traffic from the webserver so I could use an access-list that will only match traffic on destination port 80 (HTTP) and port 443 (HTTPS).

```
RouterA(config)#interface fa0/2
RouterA(config-if)#ip traffic-export apply MYEXPORT
%RITE-5-ACTIVATE: Activated IP traffic export on interface
FastEthernet0/2
```

We still need to activate RITE on the interface. In my example I want to copy all IP packets from the webserver so I'll type **ip traffic-export apply MYEXPORT** on the fa0/2 interface that is connected to the webserver. You'll see a notification message that RITE has been activated. All IP packets from the webserver will now be copied to the fa0/1 interface!

That's all that I have for you about Wireshark, SPAN and RITE. Let's continue by looking at ping and telnet.

Let's start with the **ping** command. You are probably familiar with the ping command to see if you can reach certain IP addresses but this command is a classic example of *"there's more than meets the eye".*

```
Router#ping 192.168.12.2 repeat 1000
```

The first parameter **"repeat"** for ping is easy. By default 5 IP packets will be sent, in my example above I'm sending 1000. This can be useful if you have packet loss in your network, you can use the ping command as a quick tool to generate traffic.

```
Router#ping 192.168.12.2 size 1500
```

We can change the size of our IP packet with the **"size"** parameter. This is useful for 2 reasons:

- You can create larger packets to see what the maximum MTU (maximum transmission unit) is in the network.
- You can combine it with the repeat parameter to generate some load on your network.

```
Router#ping 192.168.12.2 size 1476 df-bit
Type escape sequence to abort.
Sending 5, 1476-byte ICMP Echos to 192.168.12.2, timeout is 2
seconds:
Packet sent with the DF bit set
!!!!!
Success rate is 100 percent (5/5), round-trip min/avg/max =
184/189/193 ms
```

If you want to check the maximum MTU you need to use the **df-bit (don't fragment)** parameter. In the example above I have set the size of the IP packet to 1476 bytes and you can see that the ping is working.

```
Router#ping 192.168.12.2 size 1477 df-bit
Type escape sequence to abort.
Sending 5, 1477-byte ICMP Echos to 10.1.221.1, timeout is 2
seconds:
Packet sent with the DF bit set
M.M.M
Success rate is 0 percent (0/5)
```

In this example I've set the size to 1477 bytes and you can see the pings are failing. This can sometimes occur when you are using a tunneling mechanism like GRE or IPSEC.
The tunnel will add overhead so it's possible that we exceed the maximum MTU of 1500 bytes. We can conclude that there is a host in the path to destination 192.168.12.2 that has a maximum MTU size of 1476 bytes.

In the previous example I have to specify the size myself which is kinda annoying, it's also possible to use a variety of IP packet sizes so we don't have to do the guesswork ourselves.

```
Router#ping
Protocol [ip]:
Target IP address: 192.168.12.2
Repeat count [5]: 1
Datagram size [100]:
Timeout in seconds [2]:
Extended commands [n]: y
Source address or interface:
Type of service [0]:
Set DF bit in IP header? [no]: yes
Validate reply data? [no]:
Data pattern [0xABCD]:
www.CareerCert.info
Loose, Strict, Record, Time stamp, Verbose[none]:
Sweep range of sizes [n]: y
Sweep min size [36]: 1300
Sweep max size [18024]: 1500
Sweep interval [1]:
Type escape sequence to abort.
```

```
Sending 101, [1300..1500]-byte ICMP Echos to 10.1.221.1, timeout
is 2 seconds:
Packet sent with the DF bit set
!!!!!!!!!!!!!!!!!!!!!!!!!!!!!!!!!!!!!!!!!!!!!!!!!!!!!!!!!!!!
!!!!!!
!!!!!!!M.M.M.M.M.M.M.M.M.M.M.
Success rate is 82 percent (83/101), round-trip min/avg/max =
4/4/16 ms
```

Use the ping command without any parameter and just hit enter. It will ask you for a variety of options. In this case I want to set a size of ranges. In the example above I set the lowest MTU size to 1300 and the highest MTU size to 1500. The first pings are OK and the ones with the larger MTU size fail. 83 IP packets were sent successfully and we started with a MTU size of 1300 bytes. This means there's a host that has a maximum MTU size of 1383 bytes.

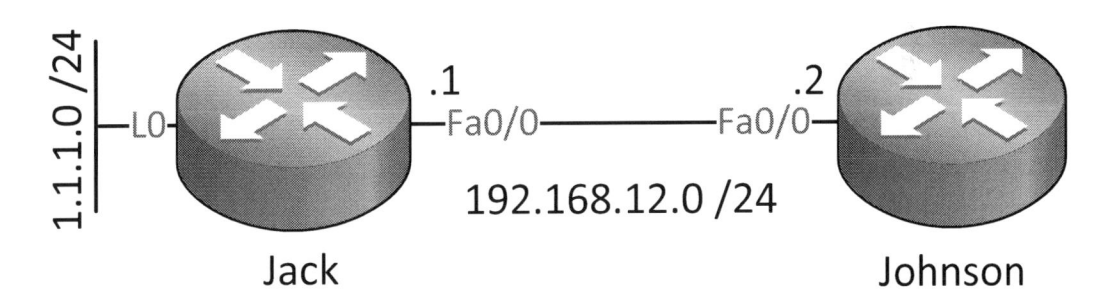

The ping command can also be used to check routing issues by using the **source** parameter. In the example above I have 2 routers, they are directly connected using their Fa0/0 interfaces and they have an IP address from the 192.168.12.0 /24 subnet. Router Jack also has a loopback0 interface with IP address 1.1.1.1 /24.

```
Jack#ping 192.168.12.2

Type escape sequence to abort.
Sending 5, 100-byte ICMP Echos to 192.168.12.2, timeout is 2
seconds:
!!!!!
Success rate is 100 percent (5/5), round-trip min/avg/max =
4/8/24 ms
```

If I use the ping command my router will use the IP address of the directly connected interface, this is what the IP packet will look like:

- Source: 192.168.12.1
- Destination: 192.168.12.2

Router Johnson will receive the IP packet, determine the packet is meant for him and will respond to the ping (ICMP echo-request) with an ICMP echo-reply.

The packet will look like this:

- Source: 192.168.12.2
- Destination: 192.168.12.1

Router Johnson will do a routing table lookup and determines that IP address 192.168.12.1 falls within network 192.168.12.0 /24 which is directly connected for him. The IP packet can be sent towards router Jack.

```
Jack#ping 192.168.12.2 source loopback 0

Type escape sequence to abort.
Sending 5, 100-byte ICMP Echos to 192.168.12.2, timeout is 2 seconds:
Packet sent with a source address of 1.1.1.1
.....
Success rate is 0 percent (0/5)
```

This time I'm sending another IP packet with an ICMP echo-request but we change the source IP address to 1.1.1.1 (loopback0) using the **source** parameter. The IP packet will look like this:

- Source: 1.1.1.1
- Destination: 192.168.12.2

The IP packet will make it to router Johnson; he will respond with an ICMP echo-reply and do another routing table lookup. This time we need to figure out where to send IP packets with destination address 1.1.1.1. Router Johnson doesn't have anything in its routing table that matches this IP address and will drop the packet. As a result my pings are failing. By using the ping command like this we can check if a router has certain entries in its routing table or not.

The next tool I want to talk about is telnet. Telnet uses TCP and port 23 but we can also use it to connect to other ports.

```
Router#telnet 192.168.12.2 80
Trying 192.168.12.1, 80 ... Open
123test blablabla
HTTP/1.1 400 Bad Request
Date: Fri, 01 Mar 2002 02:36:35 GMT
Server: cisco-IOS
Accept-Ranges: none

400 Bad Request

[Connection to 192.168.12.2 closed by foreign host]
```

I can telnet to other port numbers. If I see a message that says **open** like my example above I know that I can connect to this port number using TCP. Some applications might even respond to my input.

```
Router#telnet 192.168.12.1 22
Trying 192.168.12.1, 22 ... Open
SSH-1.99-Cisco-1.25


[Connection to 192.168.12.1 closed by foreign host]
```

Here's another example but this time I telnet to port 22 (SSH). You can see the SSH server shows me a banner.

```
Router#telnet 192.168.12.1 22 /source-interface loopback 0
```

Besides changing the port number to connect to we can also specify the source interface. This will change the source IP address. This can be useful if you want to test certain access-lists and see if your IP packets match your access-list statements where you filter on TCP traffic.

These are all the tools that I wanted to share with you and this is the end of the chapter. Hopefully you learned some new tricks that you can add to your troubleshooting toolkit.

Now it's finally time to dive into troubleshooting some protocols!

3. Troubleshooting Switching

If we want to work our way from the bottom of the OSI model to the top we'll have to start with the protocols that we use on the switches. Think about VLANs, trunking, etherchannels and spanning-tree. I'm going to walk you through the different protocols and I'll show you different scenarios where "something" is wrong. We'll tackle these problems by using a combination of show and debug commands. First stop...interface issues!

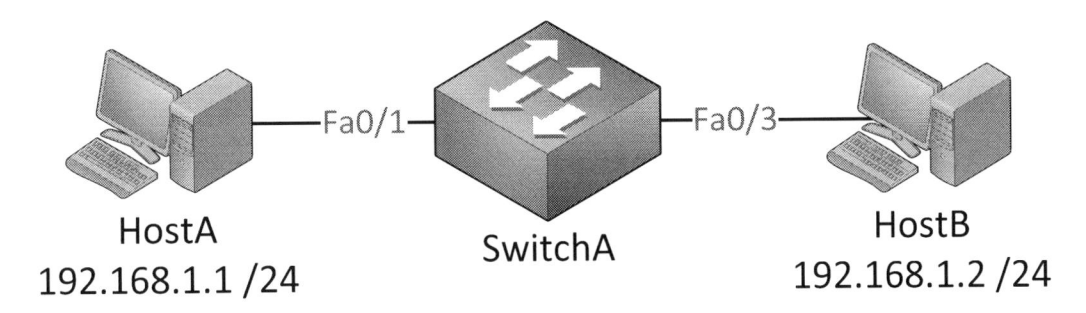

HostA —Fa0/1— SwitchA —Fa0/3— HostB
192.168.1.1 /24   192.168.1.2 /24

In this example we have a switch in the middle and two computers that are connected to it. Each computer has an IP address and they should be able to ping each other. We'll assume the computers are configured correctly and there are no issues there (after all this isn't a Windows / MAC / Linux course).

```
C:\Documents and Settings\HostA>ping 192.168.1.2

Pinging 192.168.1.2 with 32 bytes of data:

Request timed out.
Request timed out.
Request timed out.
Request timed out.

Ping statistics for 192.168.1.2:
    Packets: Sent = 4, Received = 0, Lost = 4 (100% loss),
```

Unfortunately our pings are not working. What's the first thing we should check? Our interfaces of course!

```
SwitchA#show interfaces fa0/1
FastEthernet0/1 is down, line protocol is down (notconnect)
  Hardware is Fast Ethernet, address is 0011.bb0b.3603 (bia 0011.bb0b.3603)
  MTU 1900 bytes, BW 100000 Kbit, DLY 100 usec,
     reliability 255/255, txload 1/255, rxload 1/255
  Encapsulation ARPA, loopback not set
  Keepalive set (10 sec)
  Half-duplex, Auto-speed, media type is 10/100BaseTX
  input flow-control is off, output flow-control is unsupported
```

```
  ARP type: ARPA, ARP Timeout 04:00:00
  Last input 00:26:47, output 00:19:17, output hang never
  Last clearing of "show interface" counters never
  Input queue: 0/75/0/0 (size/max/drops/flushes); Total output
drops: 0
  Queueing strategy: fifo
  Output queue: 0/40 (size/max)
  5 minute input rate 0 bits/sec, 0 packets/sec
  5 minute output rate 0 bits/sec, 0 packets/sec
     3457 packets input, 309301 bytes, 0 no buffer
     Received 2407 broadcasts (1702 multicasts)
     0 runts, 0 giants, 0 throttles
     0 input errors, 0 CRC, 0 frame, 0 overrun, 0 ignored
     0 watchdog, 1702 multicast, 0 pause input
     0 input packets with dribble condition detected
     42700 packets output, 8267872 bytes, 0 underruns
     0 output errors, 0 collisions, 1 interface resets
     0 babbles, 0 late collision, 0 deferred
     0 lost carrier, 0 no carrier, 0 PAUSE output
     0 output buffer failures, 0 output buffers swapped out
```

FastEthernet 0/1 is showing down. This could indicate a layer 1 problem like a broken cable, wrong cable (crossover instead of straight-through) or maybe a bad NIC. Note that this interface is running in **half duplex**. If you are lucky you might get a duplex message through CDP that tells you that there is a duplex mismatch. If you are unlucky it's possible that your interface goes down. Keep in mind that a Gigabit interface doesn't support half-duplex.

```
SwitchA(config)#interface fa0/1
SwitchA(config-if)#duplex auto
```

I'll change the interface to duplex auto so the switch can figure it out by itself.

```
SwitchA#
%LINK-3-UPDOWN: Interface FastEthernet0/1, changed state to up
%LINEPROTO-5-UPDOWN: Line protocol on Interface FastEthernet0/1,
changed state to up
```

That's looking better!

```
C:\Documents and Settings\HostA>ping 192.168.1.2

Pinging 192.168.1.2 with 32 bytes of data:

Request timed out.
Request timed out.
Request timed out.

Ping statistics for 192.168.1.2:
    Packets: Sent = 4, Received = 0, Lost = 4 (100% loss),
```

Maybe we are lucky...not this time, the ping isn't working.

```
SwitchA#show interfaces fa0/3
FastEthernet0/3 is down, line protocol is down (notconnect)
  Hardware is Fast Ethernet, address is 0011.bb0b.3605 (bia 0011.bb0b.3605)
  MTU 1900 bytes, BW 10000 Kbit, DLY 1000 usec,
     reliability 255/255, txload 1/255, rxload 1/255
  Encapsulation ARPA, loopback not set
  Keepalive set (10 sec)
  Auto-duplex, 10Mb/s, media type is 10/100BaseTX
  input flow-control is off, output flow-control is unsupported
  ARP type: ARPA, ARP Timeout 04:00:00
  Last input 00:38:09, output 00:01:42, output hang never
  Last clearing of "show interface" counters never
  Input queue: 0/75/0/0 (size/max/drops/flushes); Total output drops: 0
  Queueing strategy: fifo
  Output queue: 0/40 (size/max)
  5 minute input rate 0 bits/sec, 0 packets/sec
  5 minute output rate 0 bits/sec, 0 packets/sec
     1908 packets input, 181819 bytes, 0 no buffer
     Received 858 broadcasts (826 multicasts)
     0 runts, 0 giants, 0 throttles
     0 input errors, 0 CRC, 0 frame, 0 overrun, 0 ignored
     0 watchdog, 826 multicast, 0 pause input
     0 input packets with dribble condition detected
     46861 packets output, 9365341 bytes, 0 underruns
     0 output errors, 0 collisions, 1 interface resets
     0 babbles, 0 late collision, 0 deferred
     0 lost carrier, 0 no carrier, 0 PAUSE output
     0 output buffer failures, 0 output buffers swapped out
```

Interface fa0/3 that is connected to HostB is also down. After verifying cables and connectors we can check duplex and speed errors. Duplex is on auto so that shouldn't be a problem. Speed has been set to 10Mbit however while this interface is a FastEthernet (100Mbit) link.

```
SwitchA(config)#interface fa0/3
SwitchA(config-if)#speed auto
```

Let's change the speed to auto and see what happens.

```
SwitchA#
%LINK-3-UPDOWN: Interface FastEthernet0/3, changed state to up
%LINEPROTO-5-UPDOWN: Line protocol on Interface FastEthernet0/3, changed state to up
```

It seems the speed mismatch caused the interface to go down. Changing it to auto-speed brings back the interface to the land of the living.

```
SwitchA#show ip interface brief
Interface              IP-Address      OK? Method Status
Protocol
FastEthernet0/1        unassigned      YES unset  up
up
FastEthernet0/3        unassigned      YES unset  up
up
```

This is what we are looking for. The interfaces that I'm working with are both showing up/up. At least we now know that there are no cable, speed or duplex errors.

```
C:\Documents and Settings\HostA>ping 192.168.1.2

Pinging 192.168.1.2 with 32 bytes of data:

Reply from 192.168.1.2: bytes=32 time<1ms TTL=128
Reply from 192.168.1.2: bytes=32 time<1ms TTL=128
Reply from 192.168.1.2: bytes=32 time<1ms TTL=128
Reply from 192.168.1.2: bytes=32 time<1ms TTL=128

Ping statistics for 192.168.1.2:
    Packets: Sent = 4, Received = 4, Lost = 0 (0% loss),
Approximate round trip times in milli-seconds:
    Minimum = 0ms, Maximum = 0ms, Average = 0ms
```

Now our ping is working. **Lesson learned: Check your interfaces and see if they show as up/up.**

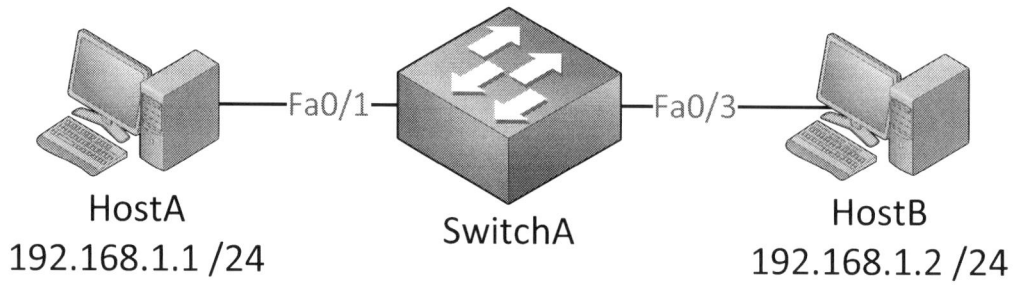

HostA —Fa0/1— SwitchA —Fa0/3— HostB
192.168.1.1 /24   192.168.1.2 /24

Same topology but there's a different problem here.

```
C:\Documents and Settings\HostA>ping 192.168.1.2

Pinging 192.168.1.2 with 32 bytes of data:

Request timed out.
Request timed out.

Ping statistics for 192.168.1.2:
    Packets: Sent = 4, Received = 0, Lost = 4 (100% loss),
```

HostA is unable to ping HostB. We'll start by checking the interfaces:

```
SwitchA#show ip interface brief
Interface            IP-Address      OK? Method Status    Protocol
FastEthernet0/1      unassigned      YES unset  down      down
FastEthernet0/3      unassigned      YES unset  up        up
```

FastEthernet 0/3 is looking fine but something is wrong with FastEthernet 0/1. Let's take a closer look at it:

```
SwitchA#show interfaces fa0/1
FastEthernet0/1 is down, line protocol is down (err-disabled)
```

Hmm it says **err-disabled**. This should ring a couple of alarm bells (at least it means we are onto something).

```
SwitchA#show interfaces status err-disabled

Port   Name           Status         Reason              Err-disabled Vlans
Fa0/1                 err-disabled   psecure-violation
```

Use the **show interfaces status err-disabled** command to see **why** the interface got into error-disabled mode. It's telling me port-security is the reason.

```
SwitchA#show port-security interface fa0/1
Port Security                : Disabled
Port Status                  : Secure-shutdown
Violation Mode               : Shutdown
Aging Time                   : 0 mins
Aging Type                   : Absolute
SecureStatic Address Aging   : Disabled
Maximum MAC Addresses        : 1
Total MAC Addresses          : 1
Configured MAC Addresses     : 1
Sticky MAC Addresses         : 0
Last Source Address:Vlan     : 000c.2928.5c6c:1
Security Violation Count     : 1
```

We can look at the port security configuration and we see that only 1 MAC address is allowed. The last MAC address seen on the interface is 000c.2928.5c6c.

```
SwitchA#show port-security interface fa0/1 address
         Secure Mac Address Table
-------------------------------------------------------------------
Vlan    Mac Address        Type                    Ports    Remaining Age
                                                            (mins)
----    -----------        ----                    -----    -----
   1    0019.569d.5742     SecureConfigured        Fa0/1      -
-------------------------------------------------------------------
Total Addresses: 1
```

Here we see that another MAC address has been configured for port security. This is the reason that the port went into err-disabled mode.

```
SwitchA(config)#interface fa0/1
SwitchA(config-if)#no switchport port-security
```

Let's get rid of port security to fix the problem.

```
SwitchA(config)#interface fa0/1
SwitchA(config-if)#shutdown
SwitchA(config-if)#no shutdown
```

This is something you should not forget. After getting rid of the port security configuration your interface is **still** in err-disabled mode. You need to do a shutdown and no shutdown to make it alive again!

```
SwitchA#
%LINK-3-UPDOWN: Interface FastEthernet0/1, changed state to up
%LINEPROTO-5-UPDOWN: Line protocol on Interface FastEthernet0/1, changed state to up
```

The console tells us that the interface is now up.

```
C:\Documents and Settings\HostA>ping 192.168.1.2

Pinging 192.168.1.2 with 32 bytes of data:

Reply from 192.168.1.2: bytes=32 time<1ms TTL=128
Reply from 192.168.1.2: bytes=32 time<1ms TTL=128

Ping statistics for 192.168.1.2:
    Packets: Sent = 4, Received = 4, Lost = 0 (0% loss),
Approximate round trip times in milli-seconds:
    Minimum = 0ms, Maximum = 0ms, Average = 0ms
```

We can now ping between the computers. Problem solved**! Lesson learned: Check if an interface is in err-disabled and if so: A) check why this happened and B) solve the problem.**

> *Not seeing err-disabled doesn't automatically mean there are **no** port-security issues. The default **violation mode** for port security is **shutdown** which will put the interface in **err-disabled** mode. The **restrict** mode will keep the interface up but shows a log message on the console. **Protect** mode also keeps the interface up but **doesn't** show any console messages. It's not a bad idea to take a **quick look** to see if port security is active or not...it's also a good idea to use **show mac address-table** to see if the switch learned the MAC addresses on the interfaces.*

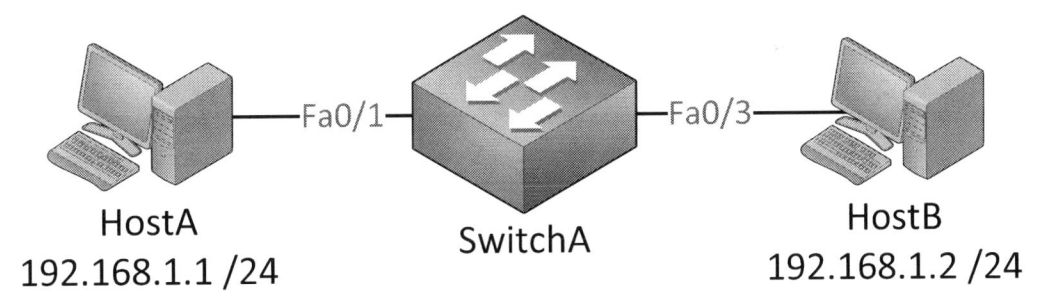

HostA —FaO/1— SwitchA —FaO/3— HostB

HostA
192.168.1.1 /24

HostB
192.168.1.2 /24

Let's continue with another problem. Same topology but something else is wrong.

```
C:\Documents and Settings\HostA>ping 192.168.1.2

Pinging 192.168.1.2 with 32 bytes of data:

Request timed out.
Request timed out.
Request timed out.
Request timed out.

Ping statistics for 192.168.1.2:
    Packets: Sent = 4, Received = 0, Lost = 4 (100% loss),
```

The two computers are unable to ping each other (what a surprise!).

```
SwitchA#show ip int brief
Interface              IP-Address      OK? Method Status     Protocol
FastEthernet0/1        unassigned      YES unset  up         up
FastEthernet0/3        unassigned      YES unset  up         up
```

The interfaces are looking good, no errors here.

```
SwitchA#show port-security
Secure Port   MaxSecureAddr   CurrentAddr   SecurityViolation   Security Action
              (Count)         (Count)       (Count)
---------------------------------------------------------------------------
---------------------------------------------------------------------------
Total Addresses in System (excluding one mac per port)     : 0
Max Addresses limit in System (excluding one mac per port) : 6144
```

Let's practice what I preach. Port security is disabled on this switch as you can see above. At this moment we at least know that there are no interface issues and port security isn't filtering any MAC addresses.

```
SwitchA#show vlan

VLAN Name                  Status    Ports
---- ---------------------- --------- -------------------------------
1    default                active    Fa0/1, Fa0/2, Fa0/4, Fa0/5
                                      Fa0/6, Fa0/7, Fa0/8, Fa0/9
                                      Fa0/10, Fa0/11, Fa0/12, Fa0/13
                                      Fa0/14, Fa0/15, Fa0/16, Fa0/17
                                      Fa0/18, Fa0/19, Fa0/20, Fa0/21
                                      Fa0/22, Fa0/23, Fa0/24, Gi0/1
                                      Gi0/2
2    VLAN0002               active    Fa0/3
```

At this moment it's a good idea to check the VLAN information. You can use the **show vlan** command to quickly verify to which VLAN the interfaces belong. As you can see our interfaces are not in the same VLAN.

```
SwitchA(config)#interface fa0/3
SwitchA(config-if)#switchport access vlan 1
```

We'll move interface fa0/3 back to VLAN 1.

```
C:\Documents and Settings\HostA>ping 192.168.1.2

Pinging 192.168.1.2 with 32 bytes of data:

Reply from 192.168.1.2: bytes=32 time<1ms TTL=128
Reply from 192.168.1.2: bytes=32 time<1ms TTL=128
Reply from 192.168.1.2: bytes=32 time<1ms TTL=128
Reply from 192.168.1.2: bytes=32 time<1ms TTL=128

Ping statistics for 192.168.1.2:
    Packets: Sent = 4, Received = 4, Lost = 0 (0% loss),
Approximate round trip times in milli-seconds:
    Minimum = 0ms, Maximum = 0ms, Average = 0ms
```

Both computers are now in the same VLAN. This solves our problem! **Lesson learned: Make sure the interface is in the correct VLAN.**

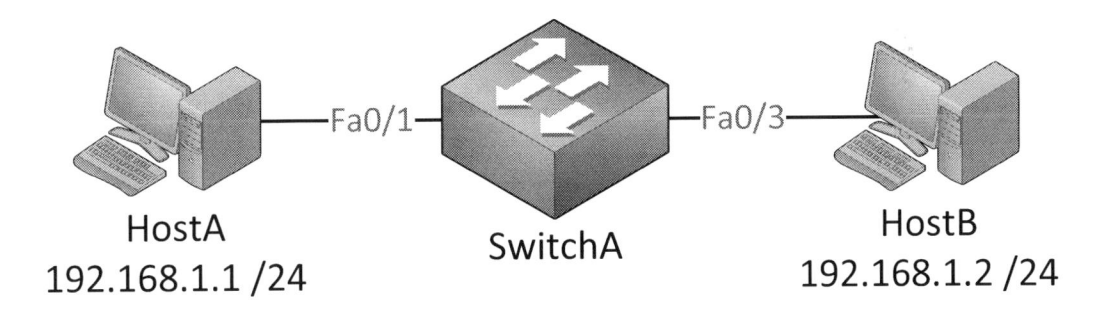

HostA —Fa0/1— SwitchA —Fa0/3— HostB
192.168.1.1 /24   192.168.1.2 /24

Time for another problem! Our two computers are unable to ping each other and I think by now you know what a failed ping looks like so I won't post it again.

```
SwitchA#show ip interface brief
Interface         IP-Address      OK? Method Status  Protocol
FastEthernet0/1   unassigned      YES unset  up      up
FastEthernet0/3   unassigned      YES unset  up      up
```

The interfaces don't show any errors.

```
SwitchA#show vlan

VLAN Name                            Status    Ports
---- -------------------------------- --------- ----------------
1    default                          active    Fa0/2, Fa0/4,
Fa0/5, Fa0/6
                                                Fa0/7, Fa0/8,
Fa0/9, Fa0/10
```

		Fa0/11, Fa0/12,
Fa0/13, Fa0/14		Fa0/15, Fa0/16,
Fa0/17, Fa0/18		Fa0/19, Fa0/20,
Fa0/21, Fa0/22		Fa0/23, Fa0/24,
Gi0/1, Gi0/2		
10 VLAN0010	active	Fa0/1

We'll take a look at the VLAN assignment. You can see that FastEthernet 0/1 is in VLAN 10 but I don't see FastEthernet 0/3 anywhere. Here are the possible causes:

- Something is wrong with the interface. We proved this wrong because it shows up/up so it seems to be active.
- The interface is not an access port but a **trunk**.

```
SwitchA#show interfaces fa0/3 switchport
Name: Fa0/3
Switchport: Enabled
Administrative Mode: trunk
Operational Mode: trunk
Administrative Trunking Encapsulation: dot1q
Operational Trunking Encapsulation: dot1q
Negotiation of Trunking: On
Access Mode VLAN: 10 (VLAN0010)
Trunking Native Mode VLAN: 1 (default)
```

A quick look at the switchport information shows us what we need to know. We can confirm that interface fa0/3 is in trunk mode and the native VLAN is 1. This means that whenever HostB sends traffic and doesn't use 802.1Q tagging that our traffic ends up in VLAN 1.

```
SwitchA(config)#interface fa0/3
SwitchA(config-if)#switchport mode access
SwitchA(config-if)#switchport access vlan 10
```

We'll turn fa0/3 into access mode and make sure it's in VLAN 10.

```
SwitchA#show vlan id 10

VLAN Name                             Status    Ports
---- -------------------------------- --------- -------------------
10   VLAN0010                         active    Fa0/1, Fa0/3
```

Both interfaces are now active in VLAN 10.

```
SwitchA#show interfaces fa0/3 switchport | include Operational
Mode
Operational Mode: static access
```

It's maybe better to check the switchport information.

```
C:\Documents and Settings\HostA>ping 192.168.1.2

Pinging 192.168.1.2 with 32 bytes of data:

Reply from 192.168.1.2: bytes=32 time<1ms TTL=128
Reply from 192.168.1.2: bytes=32 time<1ms TTL=128
Reply from 192.168.1.2: bytes=32 time<1ms TTL=128
Reply from 192.168.1.2: bytes=32 time<1ms TTL=128

Ping statistics for 192.168.1.2:
    Packets: Sent = 4, Received = 4, Lost = 0 (0% loss),
Approximate round trip times in milli-seconds:
    Minimum = 0ms, Maximum = 0ms, Average = 0ms
```

Now I can send a ping from HostA to HostB...problem solved! **Lesson learned: Make sure the interface is in the correct switchport mode (access or trunk mode).**

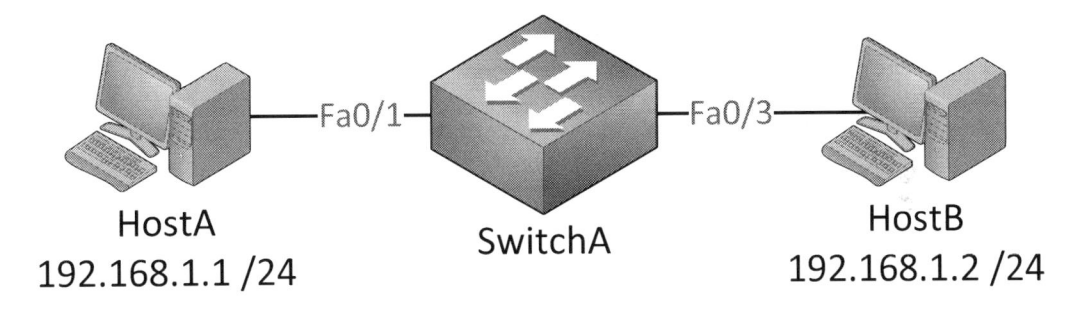

HostA —Fa0/1— SwitchA —Fa0/3— HostB

HostA
192.168.1.1 /24

SwitchA

HostB
192.168.1.2 /24

Same two computers, same switch. This scenario is a bit more interesting though. The computers are unable to ping each other so let's walk through our list of "possible" errors:

```
SwitchA#show ip interface brief
Interface         IP-Address      OK? Method Status
Protocol
FastEthernet0/1   unassigned      YES unset   up
up
FastEthernet0/3   unassigned      YES unset   up
up
```

The interfaces are looking good, up/up is what we like to see.

53

```
SwitchA#show vlan
VLAN Name                               Status    Ports
---- -------------------------------- --------- -------------------
1    default                           active    Fa0/2, Fa0/4,
Fa0/5, Fa0/6
                                                 Fa0/7, Fa0/8,
Fa0/9, Fa0/10
                                                 Fa0/11, Fa0/12,
Fa0/13, Fa0/14
                                                 Fa0/15, Fa0/16,
Fa0/17, Fa0/18
                                                 Fa0/19, Fa0/20,
Fa0/21, Fa0/22
                                                 Fa0/23, Fa0/24,
Gi0/1, Gi0/2
10   VLAN0010                          active    Fa0/1, Fa0/3
```

Both interfaces are in VLAN 10 so this looks ok to me.

```
SwitchA#show port-security
Secure Port   MaxSecureAddr   CurrentAddr   SecurityViolation   Security Action
              (Count)         (Count)       (Count)
---------------------------------------------------------------------------
---------------------------------------------------------------------------
Total Addresses in System (excluding one mac per port)     : 0
Max Addresses limit in System (excluding one mac per port) : 6144
```

Just to be sure...there's no port security. This is an interesting situation. The interfaces are up/up, we are in the same VLAN and there's no port security. Anything else that could block traffic?

```
SwitchA#show vlan filter
VLAN Map BLOCKSTUFF is filtering VLANs:
  10
```

You bet! This might not be something you think about immediately but we can use VACLs (VLAN access-list) to permit or deny traffic within the VLAN. If you are troubleshooting switches then this is something you'll have to look at if everything else seems fine. In this case there's a VACL attached to VLAN 10, let's inspect it.

```
SwitchA#show vlan access-map
Vlan access-map "BLOCKSTUFF"  10
  Match clauses:
    ip  address: 1
```

```
    Action:
      drop
Vlan access-map "BLOCKSTUFF"  20
  Match clauses:
  Action:
    forward
```

There are two sequence numbers...10 and 20. Sequence number 10 matches on access-list 1 and the action is to drop traffic. Let's take a look what this access-list 1 is about:

```
SwitchA#show access-lists
Standard IP access list 1
    10 permit 192.168.1.0, wildcard bits 0.0.0.255
```

Don't be confused because of the permit statement here. Using a permit statement in the access-list means that it will "match" on 192.168.1.0 /24. Our two computers are using IP addresses from this range. If it matches this access-list then the VLAN access-map will drop the traffic.

```
SwitchA(config)#vlan access-map BLOCKSTUFF 10
SwitchA(config-access-map)#action forward
```

Let's change the action to forward and see if it solves our problem.

```
C:\Documents and Settings\HostA>ping 192.168.1.2

Pinging 192.168.1.2 with 32 bytes of data:

Reply from 192.168.1.2: bytes=32 time<1ms TTL=128
Reply from 192.168.1.2: bytes=32 time<1ms TTL=128
Reply from 192.168.1.2: bytes=32 time<1ms TTL=128
Reply from 192.168.1.2: bytes=32 time<1ms TTL=128

Ping statistics for 192.168.1.2:
    Packets: Sent = 4, Received = 4, Lost = 0 (0% loss),
Approximate round trip times in milli-seconds:
    Minimum = 0ms, Maximum = 0ms, Average = 0ms
```

There we go, our ping is now working. **Lesson learned: If everything else seems to be ok, make sure there's no VACL!**

VLAN 10

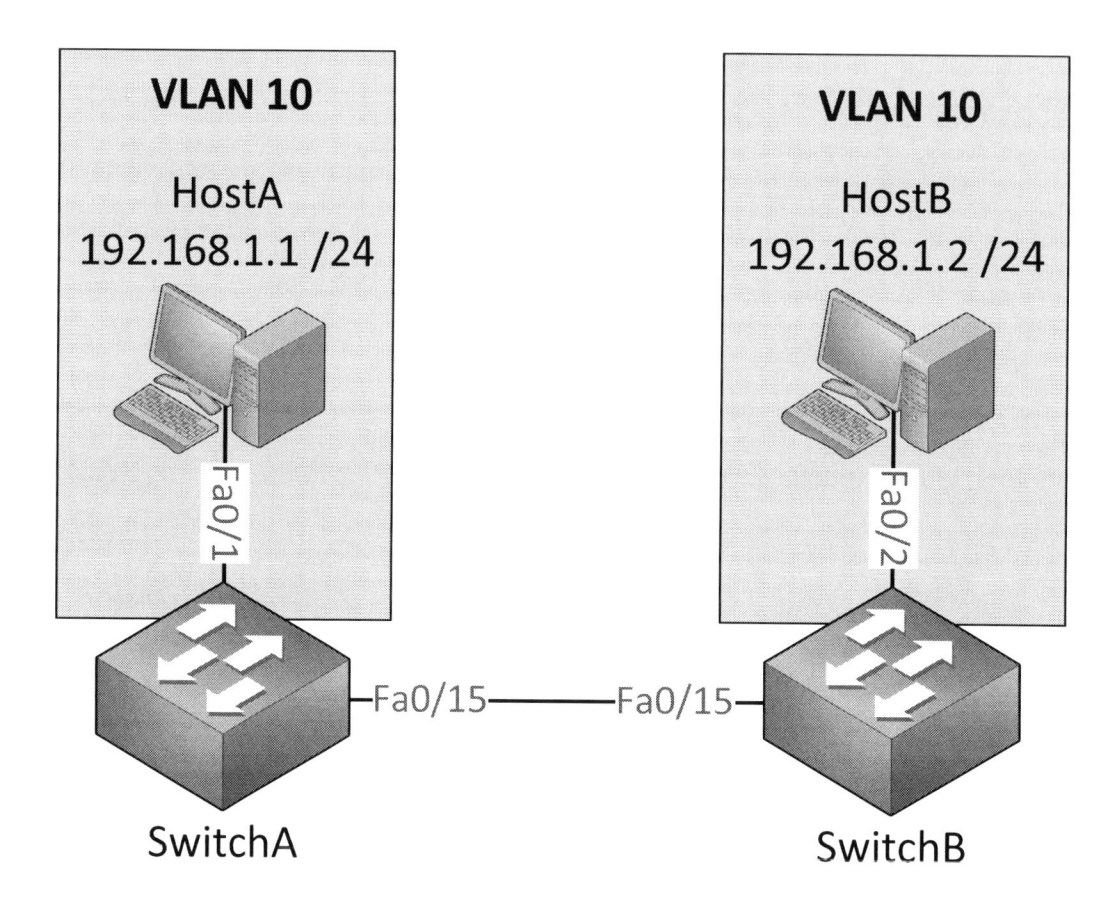

HostA
192.168.1.1 /24

VLAN 10

HostB
192.168.1.2 /24

SwitchA —Fa0/15————Fa0/15— SwitchB

Let's continue with another topology. By now you know we need to check the interfaces first and then the VLANS. In this example I have the same two computers but now we have two switches. The ping from HostA to HostB is failing so where do we start looking?

```
SwitchA#show interfaces fa0/1
FastEthernet0/1 is up, line protocol is up (connected)
```

```
SwitchA#show interfaces fa0/1 switchport
Name: Fa0/1
Switchport: Enabled
Administrative Mode: dynamic auto
Operational Mode: static access
Administrative Trunking Encapsulation: negotiate
Operational Trunking Encapsulation: native
Negotiation of Trunking: On
Access Mode VLAN: 10 (VLAN0010)
```

```
SwitchA#show port-security interface fa0/1
Port Security                : Disabled
```

First I'll verify the fa0/1 interface on Switch1. The interface is up and running, it's a switchport and assigned to VLAN 10. This is looking good so far. Port security is not enabled so we don't have to worry about it.

```
SwitchB#show interfaces fa0/2
FastEthernet0/2 is up, line protocol is up (connected)
```

```
SwitchB#show interfaces fa0/2 switchport
Name: Fa0/2
Switchport: Enabled
Administrative Mode: dynamic auto
Operational Mode: static access
Administrative Trunking Encapsulation: negotiate
Operational Trunking Encapsulation: native
Negotiation of Trunking: On
Access Mode VLAN: 10 (VLAN0010)
```

```
SwitchB#show port-security interface fa0/2
Port Security                : Disabled
```

I'll check the same things on Switch2. The interface is operational and it has been assigned to VLAN 10.

At this moment we know that the interfaces to the computers are looking good. At this moment you could do two things:

- Connect another computer to Switch1 and assign it to VLAN 10. See if you can communicate between computers in VLAN 10 when they are connected to the same switch. Do the same on Switch2.
- Check the interface between Switch1 and Switch2.

I'm going to focus on the interface between Switch1 and Switch2 because there's plenty that could go wrong there!

```
SwitchA#show interfaces fa0/15
FastEthernet0/15 is up, line protocol is up (connected)
```

```
SwitchB#show interfaces fa0/15
FastEthernet0/15 is up, line protocol is up (connected)
```

The interfaces are showing no issues, time to check the switchport information.

```
SwitchA#show interfaces fa0/15 switchport
Name: Fa0/15
Switchport: Enabled
Administrative Mode: trunk
Operational Mode: trunk
Administrative Trunking Encapsulation: isl
```

```
Operational Trunking Encapsulation: isl
Negotiation of Trunking: On
Access Mode VLAN: 1 (default)
Trunking Native Mode VLAN: 1 (default)
```

SwitchA is in trunk mode and using **ISL encapsulation**.

```
SwitchB#show interfaces fa0/15 switchport
Name: Fa0/15
Switchport: Enabled
Administrative Mode: trunk
Operational Mode: trunk
Administrative Trunking Encapsulation: dot1q
Operational Trunking Encapsulation: dot1q
Negotiation of Trunking: On
Access Mode VLAN: 1 (default)Trunking Native Mode VLAN: 1
(default)
```

SwitchB is also in trunk mode but using **802.1Q encapsulation**. Be aware that (depending on the switch model) the default administrative mode might be **dynamic auto**. Two interfaces that are both running in dynamic auto mode will become an **access port**. It's best to change the interface to trunk mode by yourself. In our case both interfaces are trunking so that's good but we have an encapsulation protocol mismatch.

```
SwitchA(config)#interface fa0/15
SwitchA(config-if)#switchport trunk encapsulation dot1q
```

We'll change the encapsulation type so both switches are using 802.1Q.

```
C:\Documents and Settings\HostA>ping 192.168.1.2

Pinging 192.168.1.2 with 32 bytes of data:

Reply from 192.168.1.2: bytes=32 time<1ms TTL=128
Reply from 192.168.1.2: bytes=32 time<1ms TTL=128
Reply from 192.168.1.2: bytes=32 time<1ms TTL=128
Reply from 192.168.1.2: bytes=32 time<1ms TTL=128

Ping statistics for 192.168.1.2:
    Packets: Sent = 4, Received = 4, Lost = 0 (0% loss),
Approximate round trip times in milli-seconds:
    Minimum = 0ms, Maximum = 0ms, Average = 0ms
```

Problem solved! Our ping is working. **Lesson learned: Make sure you use the same encapsulation protocol when configuring trunks.**

VLAN 10

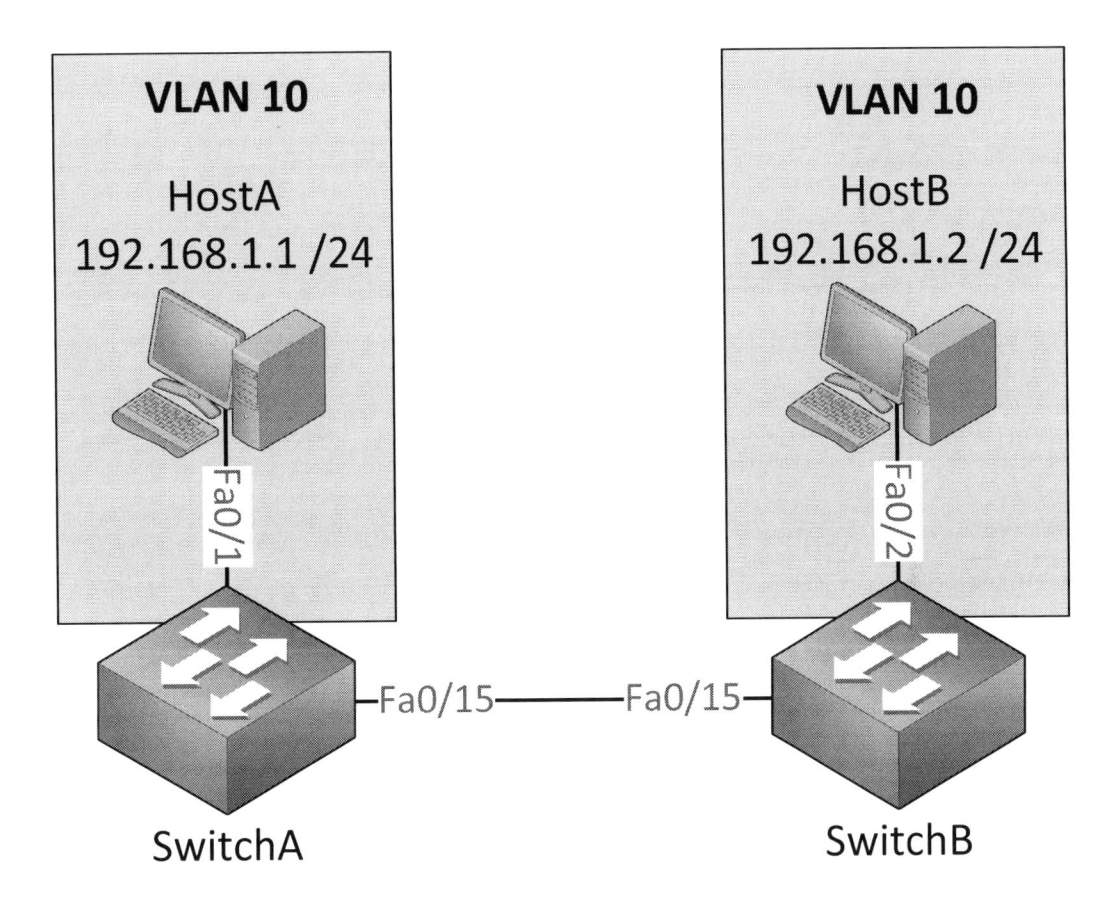

HostA
192.168.1.1 /24

VLAN 10

HostB
192.168.1.2 /24

SwitchA — Fa0/15 ——— Fa0/15 — SwitchB

Here's the same scenario again. I want to show you something else that is important to check when solving trunk issues. Assume we checked and verified that the following items are causing no issues:

- Interfaces (speed/duplex).
- Port-security.
- Switchport configuration (VLAN assignment, interface configured in access mode).

```
C:\Documents and Settings\HostA>ping 192.168.1.2

Pinging 192.168.1.2 with 32 bytes of data:

Request timed out.
Request timed out.
Request timed out.
Request timed out.

Ping statistics for 192.168.1.2:
    Packets: Sent = 4, Received = 0, Lost = 4 (100% loss),
```

Unfortunately the ping between the computers is still not working.

Let me show you the fa0/15 interfaces on the switches:

```
SwitchA#show interfaces fa0/15 switchport
Name: Fa0/15
Switchport: Enabled
Administrative Mode: trunk
Operational Mode: trunk
Administrative Trunking Encapsulation: dot1q
Operational Trunking Encapsulation: dot1q
```

```
SwitchB#show interfaces fa0/15 switchport
Name: Fa0/15
Switchport: Enabled
Administrative Mode: trunk
Operational Mode: trunk
Administrative Trunking Encapsulation: dot1q
Operational Trunking Encapsulation: dot1q
```

I'll verify that both interfaces are in trunk mode and that we are using the same encapsulation protocol (802.1Q). No problems here. Anything else that can go wrong with this trunk link? You bet!

```
SwitchA#show interfaces fa0/15 trunk

Port        Mode              Encapsulation    Status        Native
vlan
Fa0/15      on                802.1q           trunking      1

Port        Vlans allowed on trunk
Fa0/15      20
```

```
SwitchB#show interfaces fa0/15 trunk

Port        Mode              Encapsulation    Status        Native
vlan
Fa0/15      on                802.1q           trunking      1

Port        Vlans allowed on trunk
Fa0/15      20
```

The trunk might be operational but this doesn't mean that all VLANs are allowed over the trunk link. In the example above you can see that **only VLAN 20** is allowed.

```
SwitchA(config)#interface fa0/15
SwitchA(config-if)#switchport trunk allowed vlan all
```

```
SwitchB(config)#interface fa0/15
SwitchB(config-if)#switchport trunk allowed vlan all
```

Let's allow all VLANs to pass the trunk.

```
C:\Documents and Settings\HostA>ping 192.168.1.2

Pinging 192.168.1.2 with 32 bytes of data:

Reply from 192.168.1.2: bytes=32 time<1ms TTL=128
Reply from 192.168.1.2: bytes=32 time<1ms TTL=128
Reply from 192.168.1.2: bytes=32 time<1ms TTL=128
Reply from 192.168.1.2: bytes=32 time<1ms TTL=128

Ping statistics for 192.168.1.2:
    Packets: Sent = 4, Received = 4, Lost = 0 (0% loss),
Approximate round trip times in milli-seconds:
    Minimum = 0ms, Maximum = 0ms, Average = 0ms
```

VLAN 10 is now able to pass the trunk link between the two switches. As a result I can ping between the computers....another problem bites the dust!
Lesson learned: Always check if a trunk allows all VLANs or not.

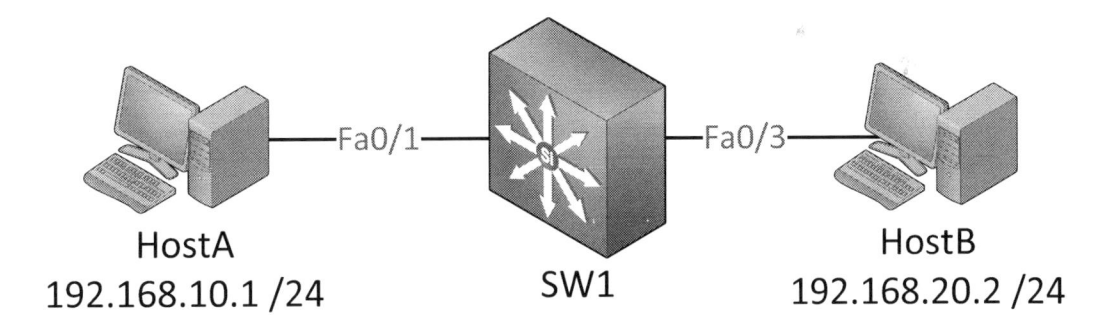

HostA —Fa0/1— SW1 —Fa0/3— HostB
192.168.10.1 /24   192.168.20.2 /24

Here's a new scenario for you. Two computers but you can see they have different IP addresses. The switch has another icon because it's a multilayer switch. Since the computers are in different subnets we have to worry about routing.

```
C:\Documents and Settings\HostA>ping 192.168.20.2

Pinging 192.168.1.2 with 32 bytes of data:

Request timed out.
Request timed out.
Request timed out.
```

```
Request timed out.

Ping statistics for 192.168.1.2:
    Packets: Sent = 4, Received = 0, Lost = 4 (100% loss),
```

A quick ping from HostA to HostB shows us that the two computers can't reach each other. Where should we start troubleshooting?

```
C:\Documents and Settings\HostA>ipconfig

Windows IP Configuration

Ethernet adapter Local Area Connection:

        Connection-specific DNS Suffix  . :
        IP Address. . . . . . . . . . . . : 192.168.10.1
        Subnet Mask . . . . . . . . . . . : 255.255.255.0
        Default Gateway . . . . . . . . . : 192.168.10.254
```

This isn't a book about windows but we do need to pay attention to our hosts. Since the computers need "to get out of their own subnet" we have to verify that the default gateway IP address is ok and reachable.

```
C:\Documents and Settings\VMWare>ping 192.168.10.254

Pinging 192.168.10.254 with 32 bytes of data:

Reply from 192.168.10.254: bytes=32 time=3ms TTL=255
Reply from 192.168.10.254: bytes=32 time=1ms TTL=255
Reply from 192.168.10.254: bytes=32 time=2ms TTL=255
Reply from 192.168.10.254: bytes=32 time=1ms TTL=255

Ping statistics for 192.168.10.254:
    Packets: Sent = 4, Received = 4, Lost = 0 (0% loss),
Approximate round trip times in milli-seconds:
    Minimum = 1ms, Maximum = 3ms, Average = 1ms
```

HostA is able to reach the default gateway so we at least know that hostA is working fine.

```
C:\Documents and Settings\HostB>ipconfig

Windows IP Configuration

Ethernet adapter Local Area Connection:

        Connection-specific DNS Suffix  . :
        IP Address. . . . . . . . . . . . : 192.168.20.2
        Subnet Mask . . . . . . . . . . . : 255.255.255.0
        Default Gateway . . . . . . . . . : 192.168.20.254
```

Here's the IP configuration of hostB. Let's see if we can reach the default gateway!

```
C:\Documents and Settings\HostB>ping 192.168.20.254

Pinging 192.168.20.254 with 32 bytes of data:

Reply from 192.168.20.254: bytes=32 time=4ms TTL=255
Reply from 192.168.20.254: bytes=32 time=2ms TTL=255
Reply from 192.168.20.254: bytes=32 time=2ms TTL=255
Reply from 192.168.20.254: bytes=32 time=1ms TTL=255

Ping statistics for 192.168.20.254:
    Packets: Sent = 4, Received = 4, Lost = 0 (0% loss),
Approximate round trip times in milli-seconds:
    Minimum = 1ms, Maximum = 4ms, Average = 2ms
```

That's also working. We know that the computers are not the issue because they know how to get out of their own subnet and the default gateway is reachable. Time to check out the switch (we are network guys after all...).

```
SwitchA#show interfaces fa0/1 switchport | include VLAN
Access Mode VLAN: 10 (VLAN0010)
SwitchA#show interfaces fa0/3 switchport | include VLAN
Access Mode VLAN: 20 (VLAN0020)
```

We can see that hostA is in VLAN 10 and hostB is in VLAN 20. I didn't check if the interfaces were up/up because I was already able to ping the default gateway IP addresses. This proves that fa0/1 and fa0/3 are working but I didn't know yet to what VLAN they belong.

```
SwitchA#show ip int brief | include Vlan
Vlan1                  unassigned      YES TFTP    up
down
Vlan10                 192.168.10.254  YES manual  up
up
Vlan20                 192.168.20.254  YES manual  up
up
```

Two SVI interfaces have been configured. These are the IP addresses that the computers use as default gateway. So why isn't our switch routing traffic?

```
SwitchA#show ip route
Default gateway is not set

Host               Gateway                    Last Use    Total Uses
Interface
ICMP redirect cache is empty
```

Having IP addresses on interfaces doesn't automatically mean that we are going to route traffic. In order to do so we require a routing table. This switch doesn't have one...

```
SwitchA(config)#ip routing
```

Let's enable routing on this switch.

```
SwitchA#show ip route connected
C    192.168.10.0/24 is directly connected, Vlan10
C    192.168.20.0/24 is directly connected, Vlan20
```

This is looking better. The switch now knows where to forward IP packets to.

```
C:\Documents and Settings\HostA>ping 192.168.20.2

Pinging 192.168.20.2 with 32 bytes of data:

Reply from 192.168.20.2: bytes=32 time<1ms TTL=127
Reply from 192.168.20.2: bytes=32 time<1ms TTL=127
Reply from 192.168.20.2: bytes=32 time<1ms TTL=127
Reply from 192.168.20.2: bytes=32 time<1ms TTL=127

Ping statistics for 192.168.20.2:
    Packets: Sent = 4, Received = 4, Lost = 0 (0% loss),
Approximate round trip times in milli-seconds:
    Minimum = 0ms, Maximum = 0ms, Average = 0ms
```

There we go...the two computers can now reach each other! Problem solved ☺
Lesson learned: If you use a multilayer switch for interVLAN routing make sure the SVI interfaces are configured correctly and that routing is enabled.

You have now seen the most common errors that can happen with our interfaces, VLANs, trunks and routing issues when using multilayer switches. In the next part of this chapter we'll take a look at spanning-tree. Spanning-tree is a pretty robust protocol but there are a number of things that could go wrong, maybe you expect a certain output but your switches are telling you something different. Also because of misconfiguration some funky things can happen...let's take a look at some scenarios:

SwitchA ROOT
Priority 24576

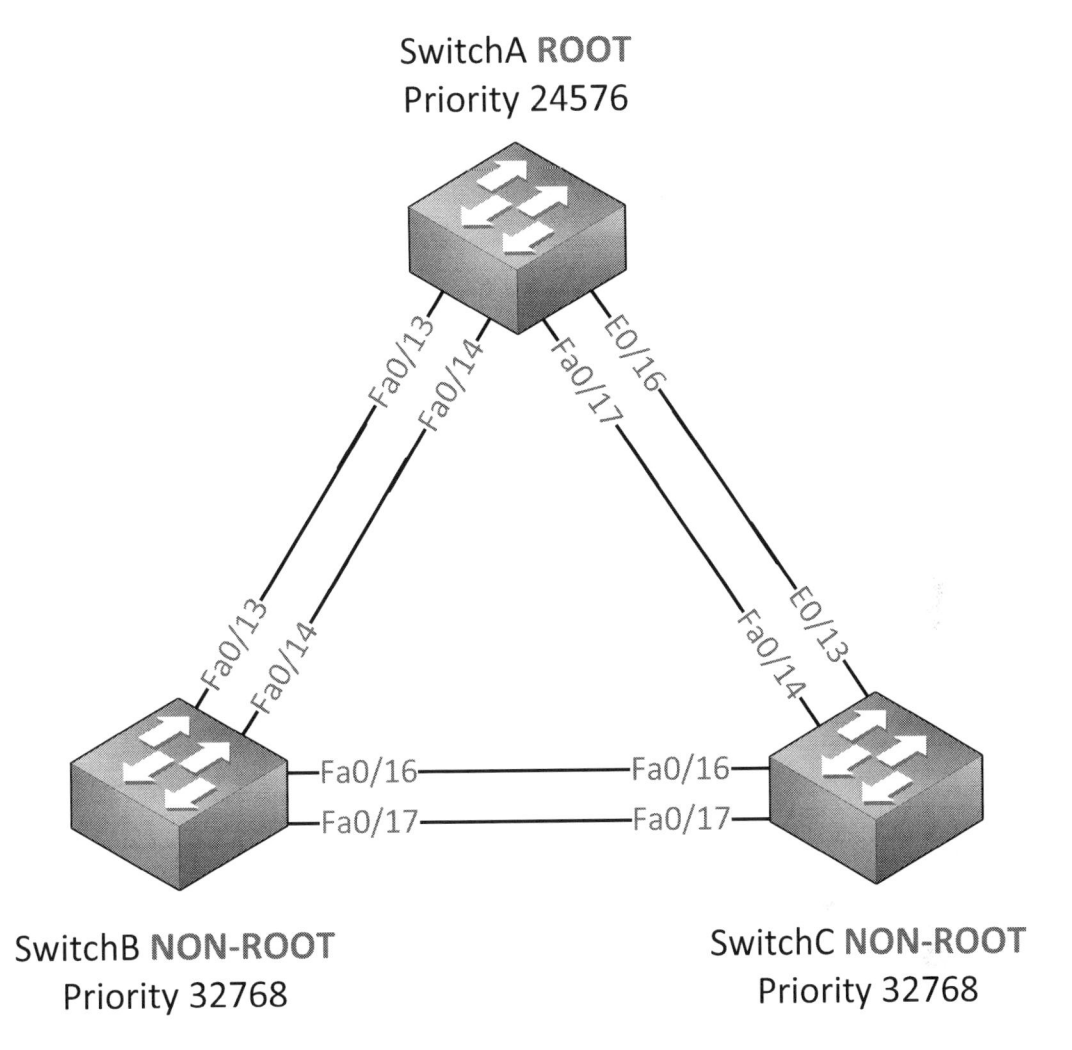

SwitchB NON-ROOT
Priority 32768

SwitchC NON-ROOT
Priority 32768

Here's a topology for you. Three switches and between the switches we have two links for redundancy. SwitchA has been elected as the root bridge for VLAN 1. When you are dealing with spanning-tree it's best to draw a small picture of the network and write down the interface roles for each switch (designated, non-designated/alternate or blocked). Note that one of the links between SwitchA and SwitchC is an Ethernet interface (10Mbit). All the other links are FastEthernet.

SwitchA ROOT
Priority 24576

SwitchB NON-ROOT
Priority 32768

SwitchC NON-ROOT
Priority 32768

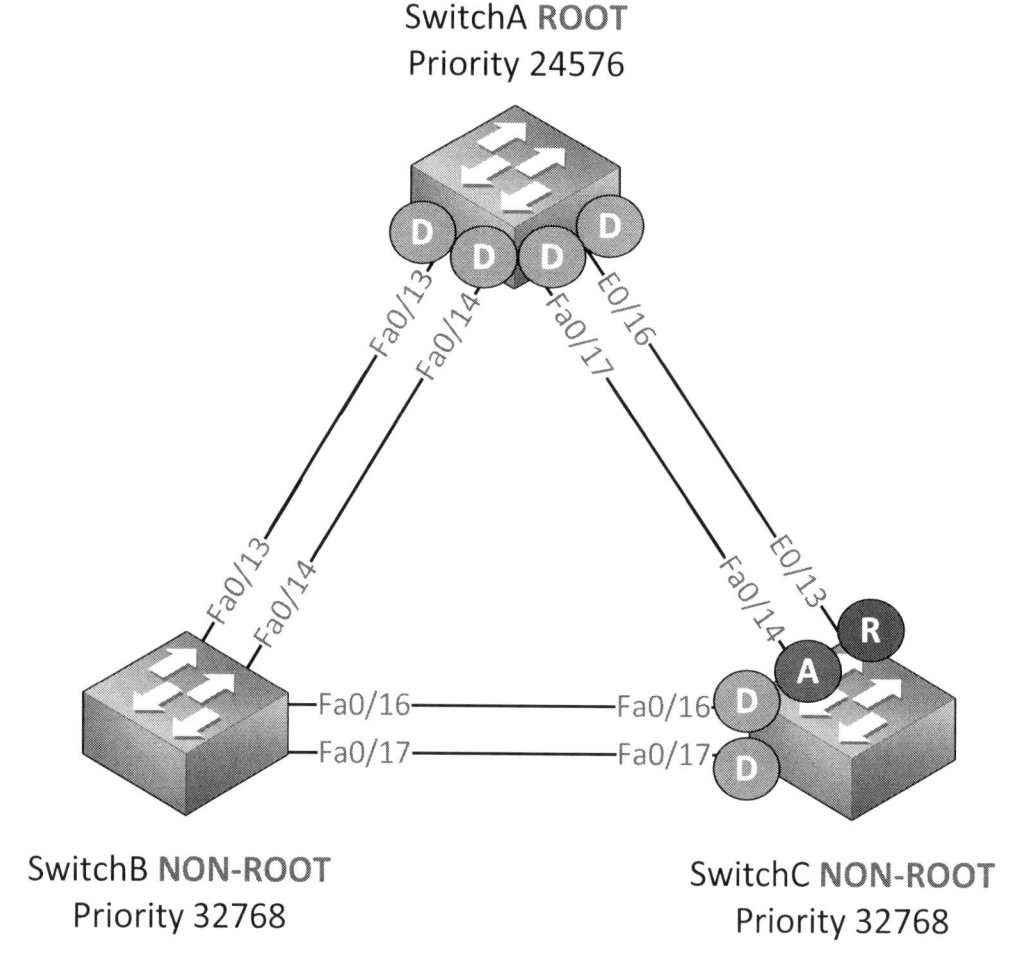

I used the show spanning-tree command to verify the interface roles for SwitchA and SwitchC. As you can see SwitchC has elected its Ethernet 0/13 interface as its root port and the FastEthernet 0/14 interface is elected as an alternate port. This is not a very good idea. It means we'll send all traffic down the 10Mbit link while the 100Mbit is not used at all. When a switch has to elect a root port it will select one like this:

1. Choose the interface that has the lowest cost to the root bridge.
2. If the cost is equal, select the lowest interface number.

Normally the cost of an Ethernet interface is higher than FastEthernet so it should select the FastEthernet interface. Why did SwitchC pick the Ethernet 0/13 interface?

```
SwitchC#show spanning-tree vlan 1

VLAN0001
  Spanning tree enabled protocol ieee
  Root ID    Priority    24577
```

```
                Address      0011.bb0b.3600
                Cost         19
                Port         13 (FastEthernet0/13)
                Hello Time   2 sec  Max Age 20 sec  Forward Delay
15 sec

  Bridge ID     Priority     32769  (priority 32768 sys-id-ext 1)
                Address      000f.34ca.1000
                Hello Time   2 sec  Max Age 20 sec  Forward Delay
15 sec
                Aging Time 15

Interface              Role Sts Cost      Prio.Nbr Type
-------------------    ---- --- --------- -------- --------------
----------------
E0/13                  Root FWD 19        128.13   P2p
Fa0/14                 Altn BLK 19        128.14   P2p
Fa0/16                 Desg FWD 19        128.16   P2p
Fa0/17                 Desg FWD 19        128.17   P2p
```

We can see that the Ethernet 0/13 and FastEthernet 0/14 interface have the same cost. SwitchC will then select the lowest interface number which is interface Ethernet 0/13.

```
SwitchC#show run interface fa0/13
Building configuration...

Current configuration : 102 bytes
!
Interface Ethernet0/13
 switchport mode dynamic desirable
 spanning-tree cost 19
```

We'll check the interface configuration and you can see that someone has changed the cost of the interface to 19 (the default for FastEthernet interfaces).

```
SwitchC(config)#interface Ethernet 0/13
SwitchC(config-if)#no spanning-tree cost 19
```

Let's get rid of the cost command.

```
SwitchC#show spanning-tree vlan 1

VLAN0001
  Spanning tree enabled protocol ieee
  Root ID     Priority    24577
              Address     0011.bb0b.3600
              Cost        19
              Port        14 (FastEthernet0/14)
```

```
                    Hello Time    2 sec   Max Age 20 sec   Forward Delay
15 sec

  Bridge ID  Priority     32769   (priority 32768 sys-id-ext 1)
             Address      000f.34ca.1000
             Hello Time    2 sec   Max Age 20 sec   Forward Delay
15 sec
             Aging Time 15

Interface            Role Sts Cost      Prio.Nbr Type
-------------------  ---- --- --------- -------- ----------------
-----------------
E0/13                Altn BLK 100       128.13   P2p
Fa0/14               Root FWD 19        128.14   P2p
Fa0/16               Desg FWD 19        128.16   P2p
Fa0/17               Desg FWD 19        128.17   P2p
```

After we removed the cost command you can see that the port state has changed. FastEthernet 0/14 is now the root port and the cost of the Ethernet 0/13 interface is 100 (which is the default for Ethernet interfaces). Problem solved! **Lesson learned: Make sure the interface you want to be the root port has the lowest cost path.**

SwitchA ROOT
Priority 24576

SwitchB NON-ROOT
Priority 32768

SwitchC NON-ROOT
Priority 32768

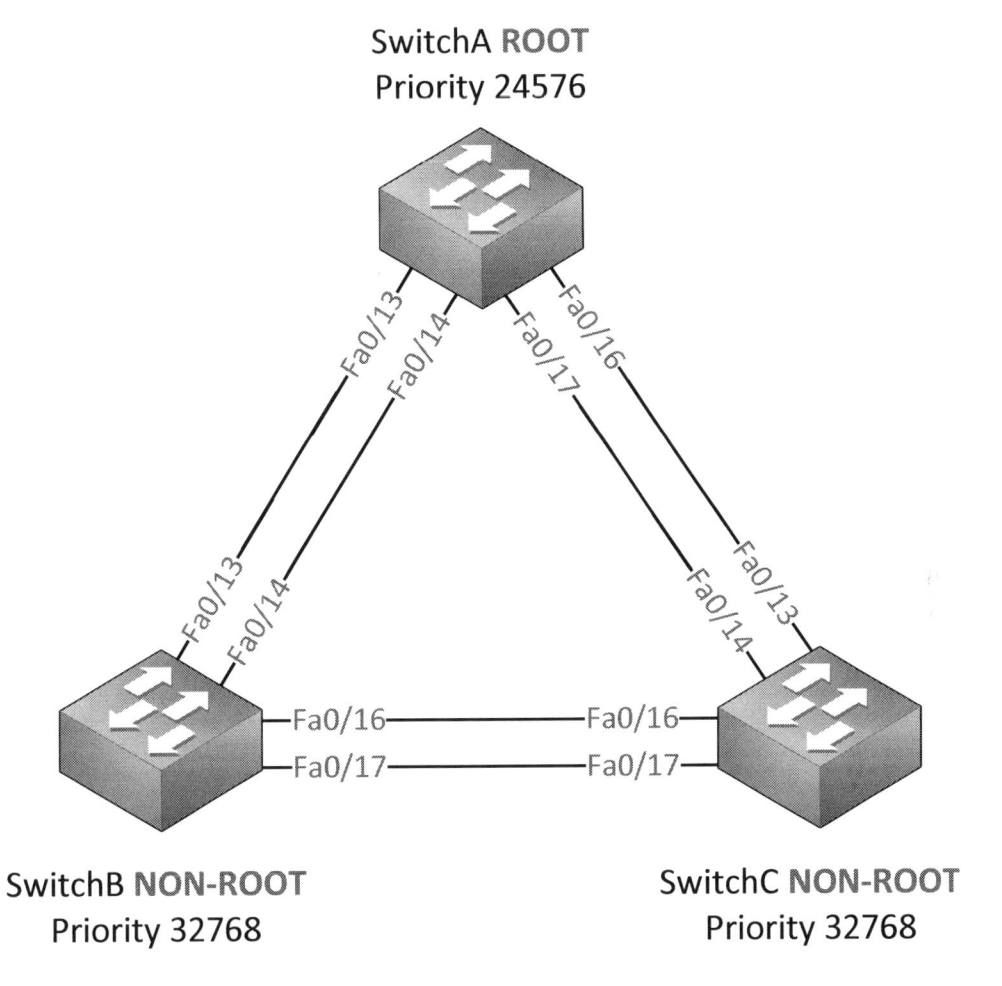

Here's a new scenario for you. All the interfaces are equal (FastEthernet). SwitchA is the root bridge for VLAN 10 and after checking the interface roles this is what we find:

SwitchA ROOT
Priority 24576

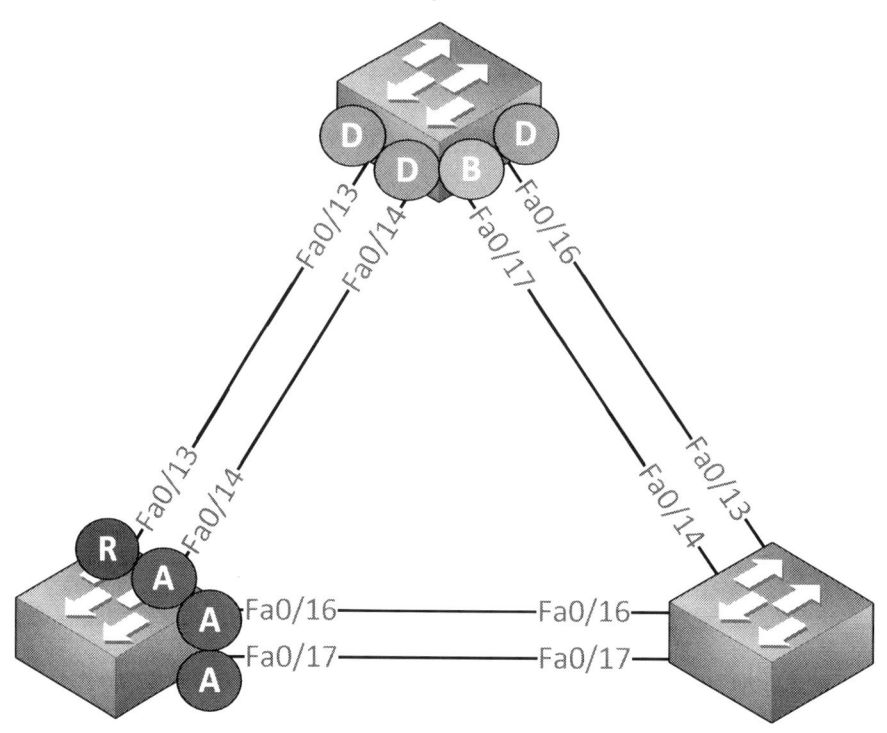

SwitchB NON-ROOT
Priority 32768

SwitchC NON-ROOT
Priority 32768

Hmm interesting...SwitchA is the root bridge and FastEthernet 0/17 has been elected as a **backup port**. Now that's something you see every day. SwitchB has elected a root port and all the other interfaces are alternate ports. I don't see anything on SwitchC.

```
SwitchA#show spanning-tree vlan 10

VLAN0010
  Spanning tree enabled protocol ieee
```

```
SwitchB#show spanning-tree vlan 10

VLAN0010
  Spanning tree enabled protocol ieee
```

```
SwitchC#show spanning-tree vlan 10

Spanning tree instance(s) for vlan 10 does not exist.
```

We can see that SwitchA and SwitchB are running spanning-tree for VLAN 10.

SwitchC however is not running spanning-tree for VLAN 10. What could be the issue?

```
SwitchC#show interfaces fa0/13 | include line protocol
FastEthernet0/13 is up, line protocol is up (connected)
```

```
SwitchC#show interfaces fa0/14 | include line protocol
FastEthernet0/14 is up, line protocol is up (connected)
```

```
SwitchC#show interfaces fa0/16 | include line protocol
FastEthernet0/16 is up, line protocol is up (connected)
```

```
SwitchC#show interfaces fa0/17 | include line protocol
FastEthernet0/16 is up, line protocol is up (connected)
```

Of course it's not a bad idea to check if the interfaces on SwitchC are working or not (but of course this is something that you already learned and did in the first part of this chapter ☺).

```
SwitchC#show interfaces trunk

Port        Mode            Encapsulation   Status          Native vlan
Fa0/13      desirable       n-isl           trunking        1
Fa0/14      desirable       n-isl           trunking        1
Fa0/16      desirable       n-isl           trunking        1
Fa0/17      desirable       n-isl           trunking        1

Port        Vlans allowed on trunk
Fa0/13      1-4094
Fa0/14      1-4094
Fa0/16      1-4094
Fa0/17      1-4094

Port        Vlans allowed and active in management domain
Fa0/13      1,10
Fa0/14      1,10
Fa0/16      1,10
Fa0/17      1,10
```

The interfaces are looking good. VLAN 10 is active on all interfaces of SwitchC. This means that spanning-tree should be active for VLAN 10.

```
SwitchC#show spanning-tree vlan 10

Spanning tree instance(s) for vlan 10 does not exist.
```

Let's take another look at this message. It says that spanning-tree for VLAN 10 does **not exist**. There are two reasons why could see this message:

71

- There are no interfaces active for VLAN 10.
- Spanning-tree has been disabled for VLAN 10.

We confirmed that VLAN 10 is active on all interfaces of SwitchC so maybe spanning-tree has been disabled globally?

```
SwitchC(config)#spanning-tree vlan 10
```

Let's give it a shot by typing in **spanning-tree vlan 10**.

```
SwitchC#show spanning-tree vlan 10

VLAN0010
  Spanning tree enabled protocol ieee
  Root ID    Priority    24586
             Address     0011.bb0b.3600
             Cost        19
             Port        13 (FastEthernet0/13)
             Hello Time   2 sec  Max Age 20 sec   Forward Delay 15 sec

  Bridge ID  Priority    32778  (priority 32768 sys-id-ext 10)
             Address     000f.34ca.1000
             Hello Time   2 sec  Max Age 20 sec   Forward Delay 15 sec
             Aging Time 300

Interface           Role Sts Cost      Prio.Nbr Type
------------------- ---- --- --------- -------- --------------------
Fa0/13              Root FWD 19        128.13   P2p
Fa0/14              Altn BLK 19        128.14   P2p
Fa0/16              Desg FWD 19        128.16   P2p
Fa0/17              Desg FWD 19        128.17   P2p
```

There we go...that's looking better! Spanning-tree is now enabled for VLAN 10 and is working...problem solved! This issue might sound a bit lame but I do see it every now and then in the real world. A scenario I encountered before is a customer that was told by their wireless vendor to disable spanning-tree for the interfaces that connect to the wireless access point. This is what the customer typed in on the switch:

```
SwitchC(config)#interface fa0/1
SwitchC(config-if)#no spanning-tree vlan 10
SwitchC(config)#
```

On the interface they typed **no spanning-tree vlan 10** but you can see you end up in the **global configuration mode**. There is no command to disable spanning-tree on the interface like this so the switch thinks you typed in the global command to disable spanning-tree. The switch accepts the command, disabled spanning-tree for VLAN 10 and kicks you back to global configuration mode...problem solved! Lesson learned: **Check if spanning-tree is enabled or disabled.**

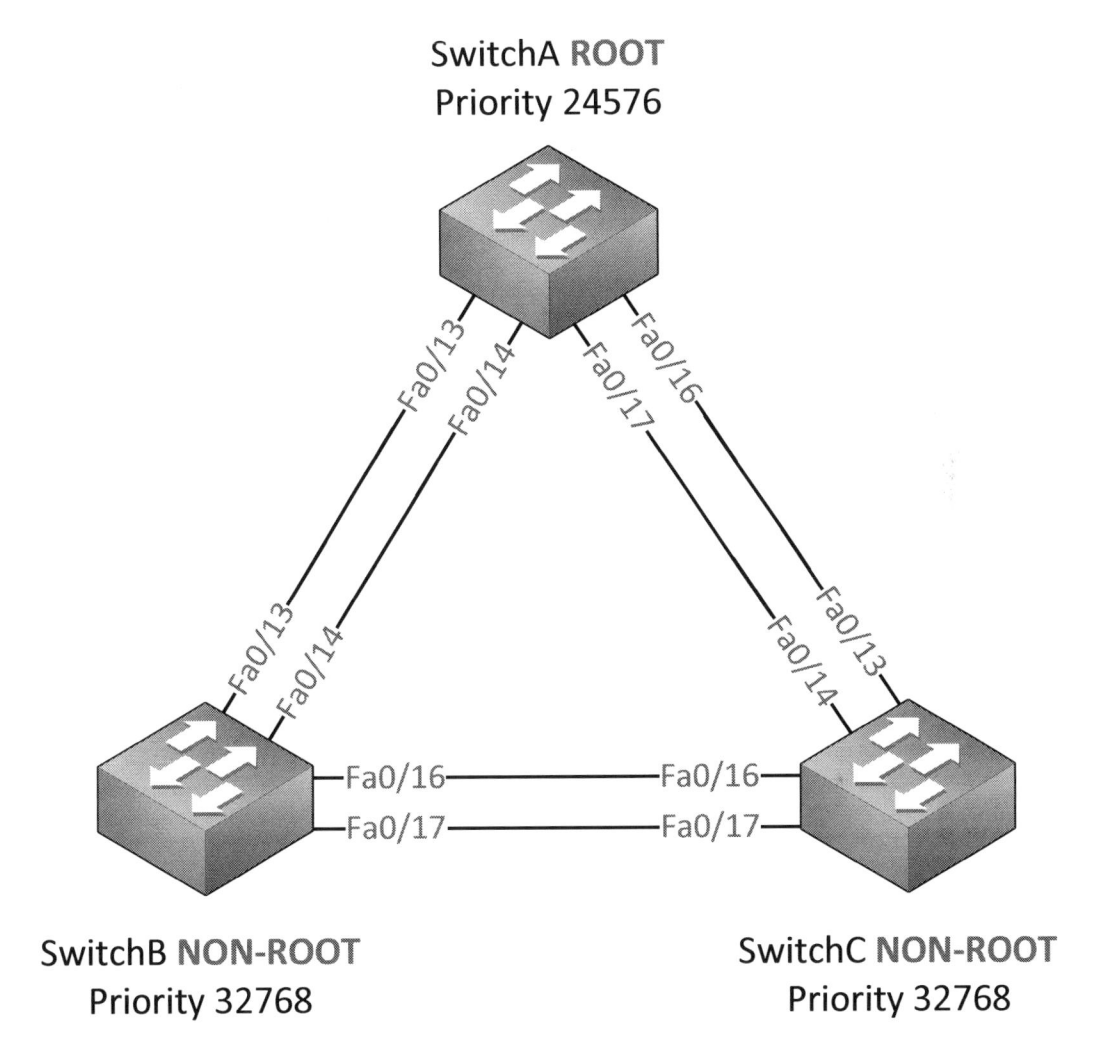

SwitchA ROOT
Priority 24576

SwitchB NON-ROOT　　　　　　　　**SwitchC NON-ROOT**
Priority 32768　　　　　　　　　　**Priority 32768**

Let's continue with another scenario! Same topology...our customer however is complaining about bad performance. We'll start by verifying the roles of the interfaces:

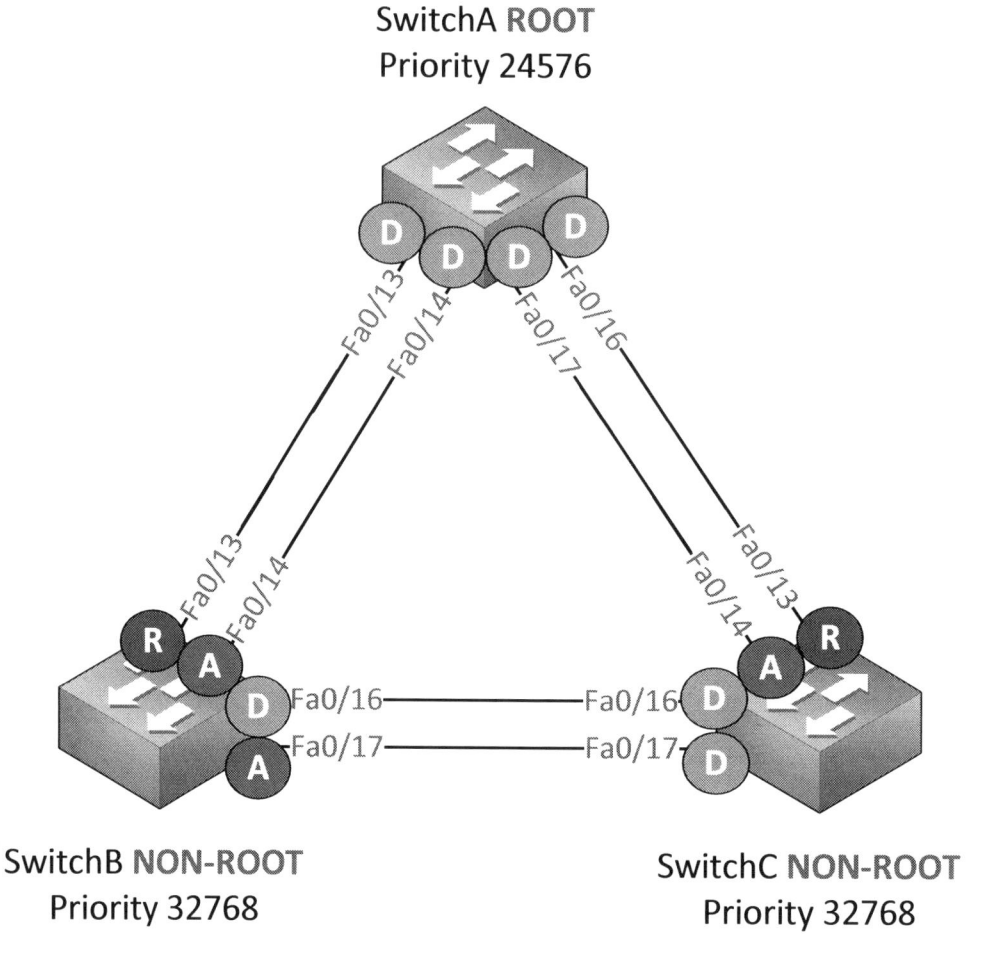

Take a look at the picture above. Do you see that Interface FastEthernet 0/16 on SwitchB and SwitchC are designated? On SwitchA all interfaces are designated. What do you think happens once one of our switches forwards a broadcast or has to flood a frame? Bingo! We'll have a loop...

Normally in this topology the FastEthernet 0/16 and 0/17 interfaces on SwitchC should both be alternate ports because SwitchC has the worst bridge ID. Since they are both designated we can assume that SwitchC is not receiving BPDUs on these interfaces.

So why did spanning-tree fail here? An important detail to remember here is that spanning-tree **requires BPDUs sent between the switches** in order to **create a loop-free topology**. BPDUs can be filtered because of MAC access-lists, VLAN access-maps or maybe something from the spanning-tree toolkit?

```
SwitchA#show vlan access-map
```

```
SwitchB#show vlan access-map
```

```
SwitchC#show vlan access-map
```

There are no VLAN access maps on any of the switches.

```
SwitchA#show access-lists
```

```
SwitchB#show access-lists
```

```
SwitchC#show access-lists
```

There are no access-lists...

```
SwitchA#show port-security
Secure Port  MaxSecureAddr  CurrentAddr  SecurityViolation  Security Action
             (Count)        (Count)      (Count)
---------------------------------------------------------------------------
---------------------------------------------------------------------------
Total Addresses in System (excluding one mac per port)     : 0
Max Addresses limit in System (excluding one mac per port) : 6144
```

```
SwitchB#show port-security
Secure Port  MaxSecureAddr  CurrentAddr  SecurityViolation  Security Action
             (Count)        (Count)      (Count)
---------------------------------------------------------------------------
---------------------------------------------------------------------------
Total Addresses in System (excluding one mac per port)     : 0
Max Addresses limit in System (excluding one mac per port) : 6144
```

```
SwitchC#show port-security
Secure Port  MaxSecureAddr  CurrentAddr  SecurityViolation  Security Action
             (Count)        (Count)      (Count)
---------------------------------------------------------------------------
---------------------------------------------------------------------------
Total Addresses in System (excluding one mac per port)     : 0
Max Addresses limit in System (excluding one mac per port) : 6144
```

There's no port security...what about spanning-tree related commands?

```
SwitchB#show spanning-tree interface fa0/16 detail | include
filter
    Bpdu filter is enabled
```

```
SwitchB#show spanning-tree interface fa0/17 detail | include
filter
    Bpdu filter is enabled
```

We found something! BPDU filter has been enabled on the FastEthernet 0/16 and 0/17 interfaces of SwitchB. Because of this SwitchC doesn't receive BPDUs from SwitchB.

```
SwitchB(config)#interface fa0/16
SwitchB(config-if)#no spanning-tree bpdufilter enable
SwitchB(config-if)#interface fa0/17
SwitchB(config-if)#no spanning-tree bpdufilter enable
```

Let's get rid of the BPDU filter.

```
SwitchC#show spanning-tree vlan 10 | begin Interface
Interface           Role Sts Cost      Prio.Nbr Type
------------------- ---- --- --------- -------- --------
Fa0/13              Root FWD 19        128.13   P2p
Fa0/14              Altn BLK 19        128.14   P2p
Fa0/16              Altn BLK 19        128.16   P2p
Fa0/17              Altn BLK 19        128.17   P2p
```

Now you can see that FastEthernet 0/16 and 0/17 are both alternate ports and blocking traffic. Our topology is now loop-free...problem solved! **Lesson learned: make sure BPDUs are not blocked or filtered between switches.**

SwitchA **ROOT**
Priority 24576

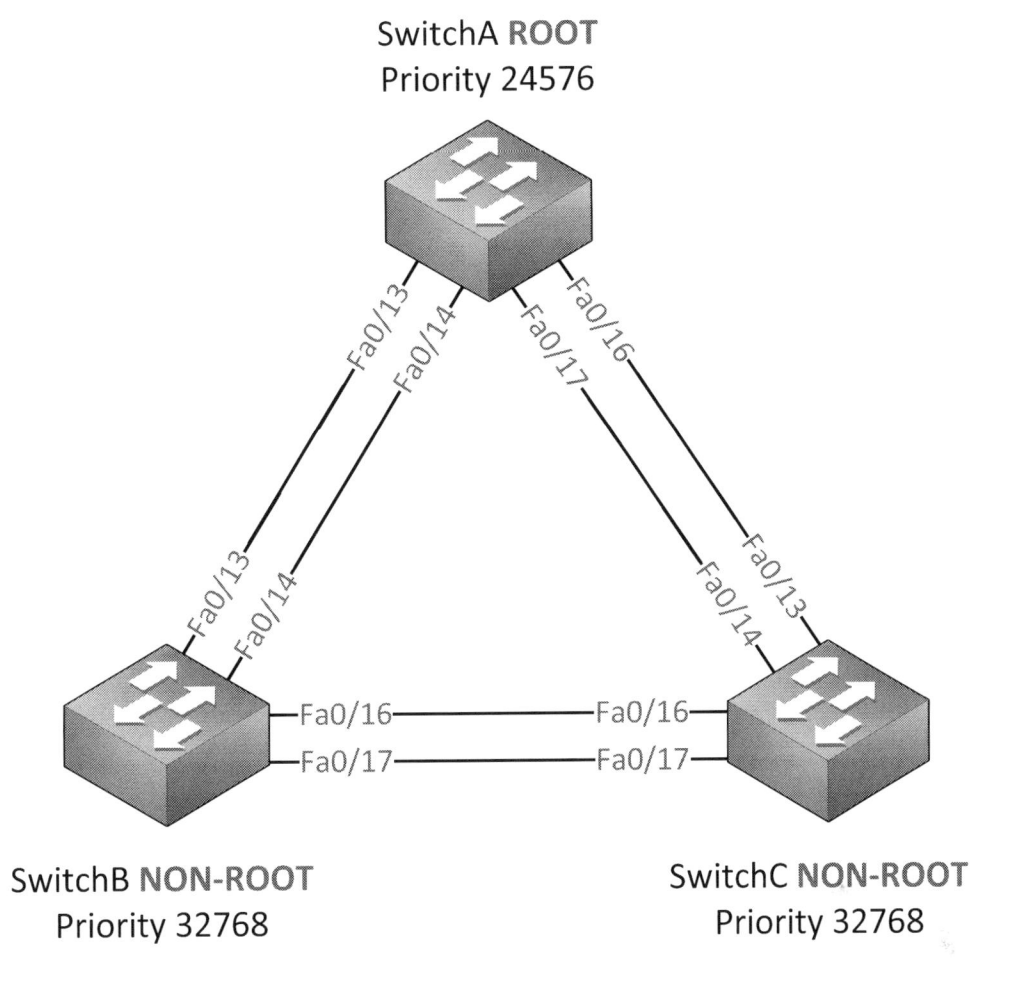

SwitchB **NON-ROOT**
Priority 32768

SwitchC **NON-ROOT**
Priority 32768

Here's a new topology for you. SwitchA has been elected as the root bridge for VLAN 10. All the interfaces are FastEthernet links.

SwitchA **ROOT**
Priority 24576

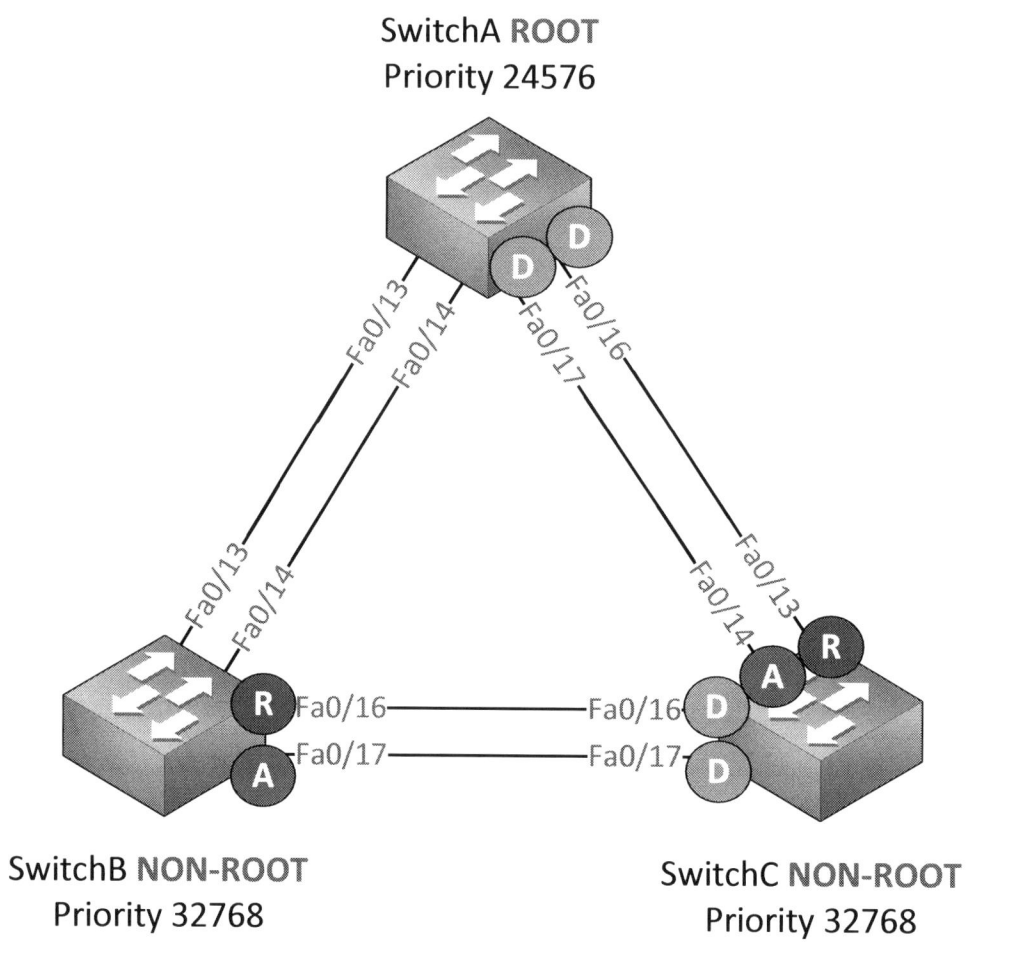

SwitchB **NON-ROOT**
Priority 32768

SwitchC **NON-ROOT**
Priority 32768

After using the **show spanning-tree vlan 10** command this is what we see. All interfaces are equal but for some reason SwitchB decided to select FastEthernet 0/16 as its root port. Don't you agree that FastEthernet 0/13 should be the root port? It has a lower cost to reach the root bridge than FastEthernet 0/16.

```
SwitchB#show spanning-tree interface fa0/13

Vlan                Role Sts Cost      Prio.Nbr Type
------------------- ---- --- --------- -------- --------------------
VLAN0001            Root FWD 19        128.15   P2p
```

```
SwitchB#show spanning-tree interface fa0/14

Vlan                Role Sts Cost      Prio.Nbr Type
------------------- ---- --- --------- -------- --------------------
VLAN0001            Altn BLK 19        128.16   P2p
```

We can use the **show spanning-tree interface** command to check the spanning-tree information per interface. As you can see there's only a spanning-tree for VLAN 1 active on interface FastEthernet 0/13 and 0/14.

There are a number of things we could check to see what is going on:

```
SwitchB#show spanning-tree vlan 10

VLAN0010
  Spanning tree enabled protocol ieee
  Root ID    Priority    24586
             Address     0011.bb0b.3600
             Cost        38
             Port        18 (FastEthernet0/16)
             Hello Time   2 sec  Max Age 20 sec  Forward Delay 15 sec

  Bridge ID  Priority    32778  (priority 32768 sys-id-ext 10)
             Address     0019.569d.5700
             Hello Time   2 sec  Max Age 20 sec  Forward Delay 15 sec
             Aging Time  300

Interface           Role Sts Cost      Prio.Nbr Type
------------------- ---- --- --------- -------- ----------------
Fa0/16              Root FWD 19        128.18   P2p
Fa0/17              Altn BLK 19        128.19   P2p
```

First it's always a good idea to check if spanning-tree is active for a certain VLAN. It's possible to disable spanning-tree by using the **no spanning-tree vlan X** command. In this scenario spanning-tree is active for VLAN 10 because we can see FastEthernet 0/16 and 0/17.

```
SwitchB#show interfaces fa0/13 switchport
Name: Fa0/13
Switchport: Enabled
Administrative Mode: dynamic auto
Operational Mode: static access
Administrative Trunking Encapsulation: negotiate
Operational Trunking Encapsulation: native
Negotiation of Trunking: On
Access Mode VLAN: 1 (default)
```

```
SwitchB#show interfaces fa0/14 switchport
Name: Fa0/14
Switchport: Enabled
Administrative Mode: dynamic auto
Operational Mode: static access
Administrative Trunking Encapsulation: negotiate
```

```
Operational Trunking Encapsulation: native
Negotiation of Trunking: On
Access Mode VLAN: 1 (default)
```

We know that spanning-tree is active globally for VLAN 10 but that doesn't mean it's active on all interfaces. I can use the **show interfaces switchport** command to check if VLAN 10 is running on interface FastEthernet 0/13 and 0/14. This reveals us some interesting information. You can see that these interfaces ended up in **access mode** and they are in VLAN 1.

```
SwitchB(config)#interface fa0/13
SwitchB(config-if)#switchport mode trunk
SwitchB(config-if)#interface fa0/14
SwitchB(config-if)#switchport mode trunk
```

Let's change the interfaces to trunks so VLAN 10 traffic can flow through these interfaces.

```
SwitchB#show spanning-tree vlan 10

VLAN0010
  Spanning tree enabled protocol ieee
  Root ID    Priority    24586
             Address     0011.bb0b.3600
             Cost        19
             Port        15 (FastEthernet0/13)
             Hello Time   2 sec  Max Age 20 sec  Forward Delay 15 sec

  Bridge ID  Priority    32778  (priority 32768 sys-id-ext 10)
             Address     0019.569d.5700
             Hello Time   2 sec  Max Age 20 sec  Forward Delay 15 sec
             Aging Time 300

Interface        Role Sts Cost      Prio.Nbr Type
---------------- ---- --- --------- -------- ----------------
Fa0/13           Root FWD 19        128.15   P2p
Fa0/14           Altn BLK 19        128.16   P2p
Fa0/16           Altn BLK 19        128.18   P2p
Fa0/17           Altn BLK 19        128.19   P2p
```

This is looking better. VLAN 10 traffic now runs on interface FastEthernet 0/13 and 0/14 and you can see that interface FastEthernet 0/13 is now elected as the root port. Problem solved! **Lesson learned: make sure the VLAN is active on the interface before looking at spanning-tree related issues.**

These are all the spanning-tree issues I wanted to show you. Before you start looking at spanning-tree commands you should verify that all your interfaces are operational and that the VLANs are passing your trunk links. Spanning-tree relies on BPDUs that are exchanged between the switches so make sure these are not filtered. If you are still facing issues you should check the spanning-tree configuration itself.

The last part of this chapter will be about troubleshooting Etherchannels. Most of the issues with etherchannels are because of **misconfiguration**.

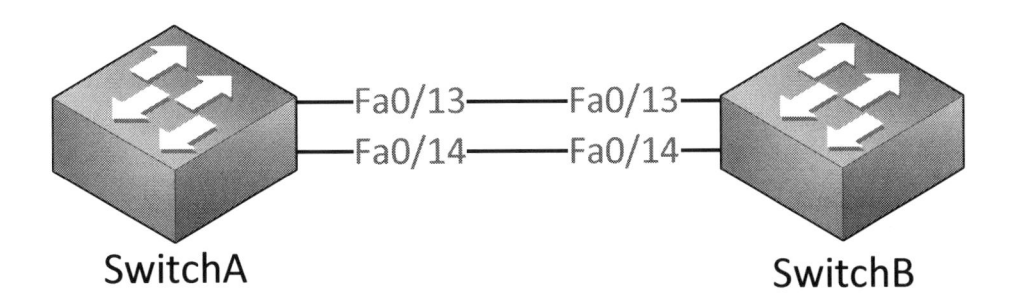

```
         Fa0/13——————Fa0/13
         Fa0/14——————Fa0/14
SwitchA                        SwitchB
```

In this scenario there are only two switches and two interfaces. The idea is to form an etherchannel by bundling the FastEthernet 0/13 and 0/14 interfaces but this is not working...

```
SwitchA#show interfaces fa0/13 | include line protocol
FastEthernet0/13 is up, line protocol is up (connected)
```

```
SwitchA#show interfaces fa0/14 | include line protocol
FastEthernet0/14 is up, line protocol is up (connected)
```

```
SwitchB#show interfaces fa0/13 | include line protocol
FastEthernet0/13 is up, line protocol is up (connected)
```

```
SwitchB#show interfaces fa0/14 | include line protocol
FastEthernet0/14 is up, line protocol is up (connected)
```

First I'll check if the interfaces are all up and running, this seems to be the case.

```
SwitchA#show ip int brief | include Port
Port-channel1          unassigned      YES unset  down                  down
```

```
SwitchB#show ip int brief | include Port
Port-channel1          unassigned      YES unset  down                  down
```

We can verify that a port-channel interface has been created but it is down.

```
SwitchA#show etherchannel summary | begin Group
```

```
Group     Port-channel   Protocol      Ports
------+-------------+-----------+-----------------------------
------------
1         Po1(SD)        LACP          Fa0/13(I)    Fa0/14(I)
```

```
SwitchB#show etherchannel summary | begin Group
Group     Port-channel   Protocol      Ports
------+-------------+-----------+-----------------------------
------------
1         Po1(SD)        PAgP          Fa0/13(I)    Fa0/14(I)
```

Here's a nice command to verify your etherchannel. Use the **show etherchannel summary** to see your port-channels. We can see that SwitchA has been configured for LACP and SwitchB for PAgP, this is never going to work.

```
SwitchA#show etherchannel 1 detail
Group state = L2
Ports: 2   Maxports = 16
Port-channels: 1 Max Port-channels = 16
Protocol:    LACP
Minimum Links: 0
         Ports in the group:
         -------------------
Port: Fa0/13
------------

Port state      = Up Sngl-port-Bndl Mstr Not-in-Bndl
Channel group = 1              Mode = Active          Gcchange = -
Port-channel  = null           GC   =  -              Pseudo port-channel
= Po1
Port index    = 0              Load = 0x00            Protocol =   LACP

Flags:  S - Device is sending Slow LACPDUs   F - Device is sending fast
LACPDUs.
        A - Device is in active mode.        P - Device is in passive
mode.

Local information:
                              LACP port     Admin        Oper       Port
Port
Port       Flags   State     Priority      Key          Key        Number
State
Fa0/13     SA      indep      32768         0x1          0x1        0xF
0x7D

Age of the port in the current state: 0d:00h:11m:59s

Port: Fa0/14
------------

Port state      = Up Sngl-port-Bndl Mstr Not-in-Bndl
Channel group = 1              Mode = Active          Gcchange = -
Port-channel  = null           GC   =  -              Pseudo port-channel
= Po1
```

```
Port index       = 0              Load = 0x00              Protocol =    LACP

Flags:   S - Device is sending Slow LACPDUs    F - Device is sending fast
LACPDUs.
         A - Device is in active mode.         P - Device is in passive
mode.

Local information:
                             LACP port    Admin      Oper       Port
Port
Port       Flags   State    Priority     Key        Key        Number
State
Fa0/14     SA      indep    32768        0x1        0x1        0x10
0x7D

Age of the port in the current state: 0d:00h:12m:38s

                 Port-channels in the group:
                 ---------------------------

Port-channel: Po1    (Primary Aggregator)

------------

Age of the Port-channel   = 0d:00h:12m:55s
Logical slot/port         = 2/1           Number of ports = 0
HotStandBy port = null
Port state                = Port-channel Ag-Not-Inuse
Protocol                  =    LACP
Port security             =  Disabled
```

The best command to use is **show etherchannel detail**. This gives you a lot of information but I'm particularly interested in seeing if LACP is configured for **passive** or **active** mode. Interfaces in active mode will "actively" try to form an etherchannel. Interfaces in passive mode will only respond to LACP requests.

```
SwitchB#show etherchannel 1 detail
Group state = L2
Ports: 2   Maxports = 8
Port-channels: 1 Max Port-channels = 1
Protocol:    PAgP
Minimum Links: 0
        Ports in the group:
        -------------------
Port: Fa0/13
------------

Port state       = Up Sngl-port-Bndl Mstr Not-in-Bndl
Channel group = 1          Mode = Desirable-Sl     Gcchange = 0
Port-channel  = null       GC   = 0x00010001       Pseudo port-channel
= Po1
Port index    = 0          Load = 0x00             Protocol =    PAgP

Flags:   S - Device is sending Slow hello.  C - Device is in Consistent
state.
```

```
                A - Device is in Auto mode.        P - Device learns on
physical port.
                d - PAgP is down.
Timers: H - Hello timer is running.         Q - Quit timer is running.
        S - Switching timer is running.     I - Interface timer is
running.

Local information:
                                    Hello    Partner  PAgP     Learning
Group
Port        Flags State   Timers  Interval Count   Priority  Method
Ifindex
Fa0/13      U4/S4   H      30s      0       128       Any    10013

Age of the port in the current state: 0d:00h:15m:25s

Port: Fa0/14
------------

Port state      = Up Sngl-port-Bndl Mstr Not-in-Bndl
Channel group = 1              Mode = Desirable-Sl    Gcchange = 0
Port-channel  = null           GC   = 0x00010001      Pseudo port-channel
= Po1
Port index    = 0              Load = 0x00            Protocol =    PAgP

Flags:  S - Device is sending Slow hello.  C - Device is in Consistent
state.
        A - Device is in Auto mode.        P - Device learns on
physical port.
        d - PAgP is down.
Timers: H - Hello timer is running.         Q - Quit timer is running.
        S - Switching timer is running.     I - Interface timer is
running.

Local information:
                                    Hello    Partner  PAgP     Learning
Group
Port        Flags State   Timers  Interval Count   Priority  Method
Ifindex
Fa0/14      U4/S4   H      30s      0       128       Any    10014

Age of the port in the current state: 0d:00h:15m:28s

                Port-channels in the group:
                ---------------------------

Port-channel: Po1
-----------------

Age of the Port-channel   = 0d:00h:15m:51s
Logical slot/port         = 2/1          Number of ports = 0
GC                        = 0x00000000   HotStandBy port = null
Port state                = Port-channel Ag-Not-Inuse
Protocol                  =    PAgP
Port security             = Disabled
```

Here's the output of show etherchannel detail of SwitchB. We can see that it has been configured for PAgP and the interfaces are configured for **desirable** mode. If they would have been configured for **auto** mode we would see the **A** flag.

```
SwitchB(config)#no interface po1
SwitchB(config)#interface fa0/13
SwitchB(config-if)#channel-group 1 mode passive
SwitchB(config-if)#exit
SwitchB(config)#interface fa0/14
SwitchB(config-if)#channel-group 1 mode passive
```

Let's get rid of the port-channel interface first, if we don't do this you'll see an error when you try to change the channel-group mode on the interfaces.

```
SwitchA# %LINK-3-UPDOWN: Interface Port-channel1, changed state to up
```

```
SwitchB# %LINK-3-UPDOWN: Interface Port-channel1, changed state to up
```

After changing the configuration we see the port-channel1 going up. Problem solved! **Lesson learned: Make sure you use the same EtherChannel mode on both sides.**

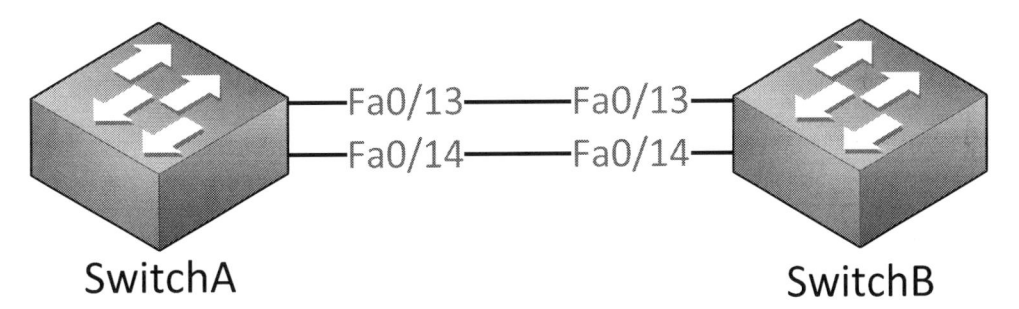

```
         —Fa0/13——Fa0/13—
         —Fa0/14——Fa0/14—
   SwitchA                    SwitchB
```

Time for another error! Same topology and an etherchannel that is not functioning:

```
SwitchA#show ip interface brief | include Port
Port-channel1          unassigned      YES unset  down     down
```

```
SwitchB#show ip interface brief | include Port
Port-channel1          unassigned      YES unset  down     down
```

We can verify that the port-channel interface exists but it's down on both sides.

85

```
SwitchA#show etherchannel 1 summary | begin Group
Group  Port-channel  Protocol      Ports
------+-------------+-------------+-----------------------------
1       Po1(SD)       PAgP          Fa0/13(D)   Fa0/14(D)
```

```
SwitchB#show etherchannel 1 summary | begin Group
Group  Port-channel  Protocol      Ports
------+-------------+-------------+-----------------------------
1       Po1(SD)       PAgP          Fa0/13(D)   Fa0/14(D)
```

We can also see that interface FastEthernet 0/13 and 0/14 have both been added to the port-channel interface.

```
SwitchA#show ip interface brief | begin FastEthernet0/13
FastEthernet0/13        unassigned       YES unset  up
up
FastEthernet0/14        unassigned       YES unset  up
up
```

```
SwitchB#show ip interface brief | begin FastEthernet0/13
FastEthernet0/13        unassigned       YES unset  up
up
FastEthernet0/14        unassigned       YES unset  up
up
```

The FastEthernet interfaces are looking good so we know this is not the issue. Let's dive deeper into the etherchannel configuration.

```
SwitchA#show etherchannel 1 port
        Ports in the group:
        -------------------
Port: Fa0/13
------------

Port state     = Up Sngl-port-Bndl Mstr Not-in-Bndl
Channel group  = 1           Mode = Automatic-Sl     Gcchange = 0
Port-channel   = null        GC   = 0x00010001       Pseudo port-
channel = Po1
Port index     = 0           Load = 0x00             Protocol =
PAgP

Flags:  S - Device is sending Slow hello.   C - Device is in
Consistent state.
        A - Device is in Auto mode.         P - Device learns on
physical port.
        d - PAgP is down.
Timers: H - Hello timer is running.         Q - Quit timer is
running.
```

```
                S - Switching timer is running.    I - Interface timer
is running.

Local information:
                                    Hello    Partner   PAgP
Learning   Group
Port         Flags State     Timers  Interval Count    Priority
Method     Ifindex
Fa0/13      A    U2/S4       1s      0        128      Any      10013

Age of the port in the current state: 0d:00h:11m:38s

Port: Fa0/14
------------

Port state      = Up Sngl-port-Bndl Mstr Not-in-Bndl
Channel group   = 1            Mode = Automatic-Sl    Gcchange = 0
Port-channel    = null         GC   = 0x00010001      Pseudo port-
channel = Po1
Port index      = 0            Load = 0x00            Protocol =
PAgP

Flags:  S - Device is sending Slow hello.  C - Device is in
Consistent state.
        A - Device is in Auto mode.        P - Device learns on
physical port.
        d - PAgP is down.
Timers: H - Hello timer is running.        Q - Quit timer is
running.
        S - Switching timer is running.    I - Interface timer
is running.

Local information:
                                    Hello    Partner   PAgP
Learning   Group
Port         Flags State     Timers  Interval Count    Priority
Method     Ifindex
Fa0/14      A    U2/S4       1s      0        128      Any      10014

Age of the port in the current state: 0d:00h:11m:41s
```

We can see that FastEthernet 0/13 and 0/14 on SwitchA are both configured for PAgP Auto mode (because of the "A" flag).

```
SwitchB#show etherchannel 1 port
        Ports in the group:
        -------------------
Port: Fa0/13
------------

Port state      = Up Sngl-port-Bndl Mstr Not-in-Bndl
Channel group   = 1            Mode = Automatic-Sl    Gcchange = 0
```

```
Port-channel   = null          GC   = 0x00010001      Pseudo port-
channel = Po1
Port index     = 0             Load = 0x00            Protocol =
PAgP

Flags:  S - Device is sending Slow hello.  C - Device is in
Consistent state.
        A - Device is in Auto mode.        P - Device learns on
physical port.
        d - PAgP is down.
Timers: H - Hello timer is running.        Q - Quit timer is
running.
        S - Switching timer is running.    I - Interface timer
is running.

Local information:
                                Hello    Partner   PAgP
Learning  Group
Port        Flags State   Timers  Interval Count   Priority
Method    Ifindex
Fa0/13      A    U2/S4    1s      0        128     Any        10013

Age of the port in the current state: 0d:00h:13m:13s

Port: Fa0/14
------------

Port state     = Up Sngl-port-Bndl Mstr Not-in-Bndl
Channel group  = 1             Mode = Automatic-Sl    Gcchange = 0
Port-channel   = null          GC   = 0x00010001      Pseudo port-
channel = Po1
Port index     = 0             Load = 0x00            Protocol =
PAgP

Flags:  S - Device is sending Slow hello.  C - Device is in
Consistent state.
        A - Device is in Auto mode.        P - Device learns on
physical port.
        d - PAgP is down.
Timers: H - Hello timer is running.        Q - Quit timer is
running.
        S - Switching timer is running.    I - Interface timer
is running.

Local information:
                                Hello    Partner   PAgP
Learning  Group
Port        Flags State   Timers  Interval Count   Priority
Method    Ifindex
Fa0/14      A    U2/S4    1s      0        128     Any        10014

Age of the port in the current state: 0d:00h:13m:13s
```

FastEthernet 0/13 and 0/14 on SwitchB are also configured for PAgP auto. This is never going to work because both switches are now waiting passively for PAgP messages.

```
SwitchB(config)#interface fa0/13
SwitchB(config-if)#channel-group 1 mode desirable
SwitchB(config-if)#interface fa0/14
SwitchB(config-if)#channel-group 1 mode desirable
```

Let's change one of the switches so it will actively send PAgP messages.

```
SwitchA# %LINEPROTO-5-UPDOWN: Line protocol on Interface Port-channel1, changed state to up
```

```
SwitchB# %LINEPROTO-5-UPDOWN: Line protocol on Interface Port-channel1, changed state to up
```

The etherchannel is now working...problem solved! **Lesson learned: When using PAgP make sure at least one of the switches is using desirable mode or in case of LACP make sure one switch is in active mode.**

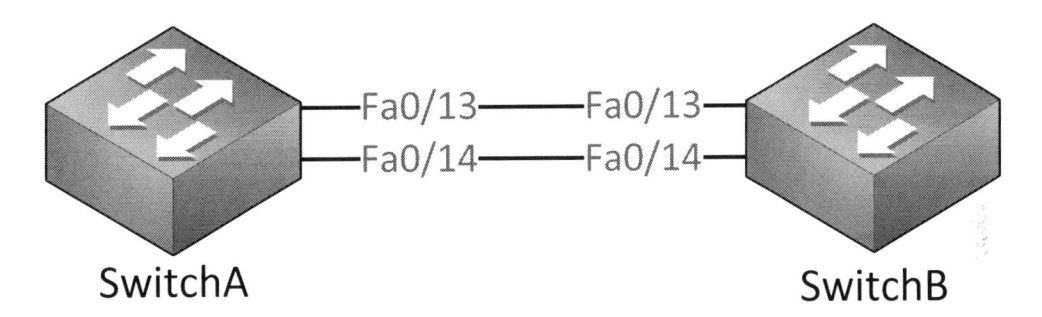

SwitchA   SwitchB

One last scenario for you: An etherchannel is configured between SwitchA and SwitchB but the customer is complaining that the link is slow...what could possibly be wrong?

```
SwitchA#show ip int brief | include Port
Port-channel1          unassigned      YES unset  up
up
```

```
SwitchB#show ip int brief | include Port
Port-channel1          unassigned      YES unset  up
up
```

A quick check tells us that the port-channel interface is operational.

```
SwitchA#show etherchannel 1 detail
Group state = L2
Ports: 2    Maxports = 8
```

```
Port-channels: 1 Max Port-channels = 1
Protocol:    PAgP
Minimum Links: 0
      Ports in the group:
      -------------------
Port: Fa0/13
------------

Port state     = Up Cnt-bndl Suspend Not-in-Bndl
Channel group = 1            Mode = Automatic-Sl   Gcchange = 0
Port-channel  = null         GC   = 0x00000000     Pseudo port-channel
= Po1
Port index    = 0            Load = 0x00           Protocol =    PAgP

Flags:  S - Device is sending Slow hello.  C - Device is in Consistent
state.
        A - Device is in Auto mode.        P - Device learns on
physical port.
        d - PAgP is down.
Timers: H - Hello timer is running.        Q - Quit timer is running.
        S - Switching timer is running.    I - Interface timer is
running.

Local information:
                                  Hello    Partner  PAgP      Learning
Group
Port       Flags State    Timers  Interval Count    Priority  Method
Ifindex
Fa0/13     dA    U1/S1    1s      0        128      Any       0

Age of the port in the current state: 0d:01h:10m:37s

Probable reason: speed of Fa0/13 is 100M, Fa0/14 is 10M
Port: Fa0/14
------------

Port state     = Up Mstr In-Bndl
Channel group = 1            Mode = Automatic-Sl   Gcchange = 0
Port-channel  = Po1          GC   = 0x00010001     Pseudo port-channel
= Po1
Port index    = 0            Load = 0x00           Protocol =    PAgP

Flags:  S - Device is sending Slow hello.  C - Device is in Consistent
state.
        A - Device is in Auto mode.        P - Device learns on
physical port.
        d - PAgP is down.
Timers: H - Hello timer is running.        Q - Quit timer is running.
        S - Switching timer is running.    I - Interface timer is
running.

Local information:
                                  Hello    Partner  PAgP      Learning
Group
Port       Flags State    Timers  Interval Count    Priority  Method
Ifindex
Fa0/14     SAC   U6/S7    HQ  30s 1        128      Any       5001
```

```
Partner's information:

          Partner              Partner              Partner              Partner
Group
Port      Name                 Device ID            Port                 Age    Flags
Cap.
Fa0/14    SwitchB              0019.569d.5700       Fa0/14               15s SC  10001

Age of the port in the current state: 0d:00h:04m:29s

        Port-channels in the group:
        ---------------------------

Port-channel: Po1
------------

Age of the Port-channel  = 0d:01h:30m:23s
Logical slot/port        = 2/1              Number of ports = 1
GC                       = 0x00010001       HotStandBy port = null
Port state               = Port-channel Ag-Inuse
Protocol                 =    PAgP
Port security            = Disabled

Ports in the Port-channel:

Index   Load    Port     EC state          No of bits
------+------+------+------------------+-----------
  0      00    Fa0/14   Automatic-Sl        0

Time since last port bundled:     0d:00h:04m:31s    Fa0/14
Time since last port Un-bundled:  0d:00h:08m:12s    Fa0/14
```

The show etherchannel detail command produces a lot of output but it does tell us what's going on. You can see that interface FastEthernet 0/13 and 0/14 both have been configured for this port-channel but the switch was unable to bundle them because FastEthernet 0/14 is configured for 10Mbit. You can see this in the **probable reason** that I highlighted.

```
SwitchB#show etherchannel 1 detail | include reason
Probable reason: speed of Fa0/13 is 100M, Fa0/14 is 10M
```

This is a good reason to use one of the operators for show command. I'm only interested in seeing the probably reason that the "show etherchannel detail" command produces.

```
SwitchA(config)#interface fa0/14
SwitchA(config-if)#speed auto
```

```
SwitchB(config)#interface fa0/14
SwitchB(config-if)#speed auto
```

Let's change the speed to auto. We need to make sure that FastEthernet 0/13 and 0/14 both have the same configuration. It's not a bad idea to do a show run to check if they have the same commands applied to them.

```
SwitchA# %LINEPROTO-5-UPDOWN: Line protocol on Interface Port-
channel1, changed state to down
%LINK-3-UPDOWN: Interface Port-channel1, changed state to down
%LINK-3-UPDOWN: Interface Port-channel1, changed state to up
%LINEPROTO-5-UPDOWN: Line protocol on Interface Port-channel1,
changed state to up
```

```
SwitchB# %LINEPROTO-5-UPDOWN: Line protocol on Interface Port-
channel1, changed state to down
%LINK-3-UPDOWN: Interface Port-channel1, changed state to down
%LINK-3-UPDOWN: Interface Port-channel1, changed state to up
%LINEPROTO-5-UPDOWN: Line protocol on Interface Port-channel1,
changed state to up
```

You will probably see a couple of messages about your interfaces bouncing down and up.

```
SwitchA#show etherchannel 1 summary | begin Group
Group  Port-channel  Protocol    Ports
------+-------------+-----------+-----------------------------
---------------
1      Po1(SU)       PAgP        Fa0/13(P)   Fa0/14(P)
```

```
SwitchB#show etherchannel 1 summary | begin Group
Group  Port-channel  Protocol    Ports
------+-------------+-----------+-----------------------------
---------------
1      Po1(SU)       PAgP        Fa0/13(P)   Fa0/14(P)
```

Now we see that both interfaces have been added to the port-channel...problem solved! **Lesson learned: Make sure all interfaces that will be added to the port-channel have the exact same configuration!**

This is it...the end of the troubleshooting switching chapter. I showed you the most common errors for interfaces, vlans, trunks, spanning-tree and etherchannel. In the next chapter we'll move our way further up the OSI model and look at routing protocols.

4. Troubleshooting RIP

In this chapter we'll take a look RIP, an old distance vector routing protocol that uses hop count as its metric. Unlike OSPF or EIGRP, RIP doesn't establish a neighbor adjacency. Most of the RIP troubleshooting issues are about missing routing information.

Here are a number of things that could go wrong with RIP:

- **Wrong network command(s):** the network command is used to tell RIP what networks to advertise but also where to send RIP routing updates to. Wrong (or missing) network commands will cause issues.
- **Interface shut**: A network on an interface that is in shutdown will not be advertised.
- **Passive interface:** An interface that has been configured as passive will not send any RIP updates.
- **Version mismatch:** RIP has two versions, both routers should use the same version.
- **Max hop count:** When the hop count is 16, the network is considered unreachable.
- **Route Filtering:** Filters might prevent RIP updates from beint sent or received.
- **Authentication:** Both RIP routers should have the same authentication parameters.
- **Split horizon:** Networks that are learned on an interface are not advertised out of the same interface.
- **Auto-summarization:** Causes issues with discontigious networks.

Let's walk through these different issues and I'll show you how to find and fix them. I'll use these two routers:

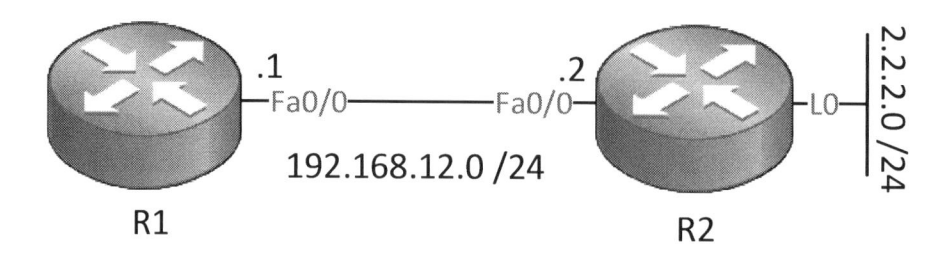

R1 is supposed to learn about 2.2.2.0 /24 but there's nothing in its routing table:

```
R1#show ip route rip
Codes: L - local, C - connected, S - static, R - RIP, M -
mobile, B - BGP
       D - EIGRP, EX - EIGRP external, O - OSPF, IA - OSPF inter
area
```

```
        N1 - OSPF NSSA external type 1, N2 - OSPF NSSA external
type 2
        E1 - OSPF external type 1, E2 - OSPF external type 2
        i - IS-IS, su - IS-IS summary, L1 - IS-IS level-1, L2 -
IS-IS level-2
        ia - IS-IS inter area, * - candidate default, U - per-
user static route
        o - ODR, P - periodic downloaded static route, H - NHRP,
l - LISP
        + - replicated route, % - next hop override

Gateway of last resort is not set
```

It's always a good idea to check on which interfaces RIP has been enabled or not:

```
R1#show ip protocols
*** IP Routing is NSF aware ***

Routing Protocol is "rip"
  Outgoing update filter list for all interfaces is not set
  Incoming update filter list for all interfaces is not set
  Sending updates every 30 seconds, next due in 0 seconds
  Invalid after 180 seconds, hold down 180, flushed after 240
  Redistributing: rip
  Default version control: send version 2, receive version 2
  Automatic network summarization is not in effect
  Maximum path: 4
  Routing for Networks:
    192.168.21.0
  Routing Information Sources:
    Gateway         Distance        Last Update
  Distance: (default is 120)
```

```
R2#show ip protocols
*** IP Routing is NSF aware ***

Routing Protocol is "rip"
  Outgoing update filter list for all interfaces is not set
  Incoming update filter list for all interfaces is not set
  Sending updates every 30 seconds, next due in 26 seconds
  Invalid after 180 seconds, hold down 180, flushed after 240
  Redistributing: rip
  Default version control: send version 2, receive version 2
    Interface              Send  Recv  Triggered RIP  Key-chain
    FastEthernet0/0        2     2
    Loopback0              2     2
  Automatic network summarization is not in effect
  Maximum path: 4
  Routing for Networks:
```

```
      2.0.0.0
      192.168.12.0
   Routing Information Sources:
      Gateway            Distance        Last Update
   Distance: (default is 120)
```

Show ip protocols is a quick way to check on which interfaces RIP has been enabled. As you can see, RIP is running on R1 and R2. Take a close look at the networks though...R1 has an incorrect network. Let's fix that:

```
R1(config)#router rip
R1(config-router)#no network 192.168.21.0
R1(config-router)#network 192.168.12.0
```

Let's see if that helped:

```
R1#show ip route rip
Codes: L - local, C - connected, S - static, R - RIP, M - mobile, B - BGP
       D - EIGRP, EX - EIGRP external, O - OSPF, IA - OSPF inter area
       N1 - OSPF NSSA external type 1, N2 - OSPF NSSA external type 2
       E1 - OSPF external type 1, E2 - OSPF external type 2
       i - IS-IS, su - IS-IS summary, L1 - IS-IS level-1, L2 - IS-IS level-2
       ia - IS-IS inter area, * - candidate default, U - per-user static route
       o - ODR, P - periodic downloaded static route, H - NHRP, l - LISP
       + - replicated route, % - next hop override

Gateway of last resort is not set

      2.0.0.0/24 is subnetted, 1 subnets
R        2.2.2.0 [120/1] via 192.168.12.2, 00:00:17, FastEthernet0/0
```

There we go, problem solved! **Lesson learned: Make sure the correct network commands have been used.**

Let's look at another problem, same two routers:

```
        .1                    .2
      —Fa0/0————————Fa0/0—        —L0—  2.2.2.0/24
          192.168.12.0 /24

         R1                      R2
```

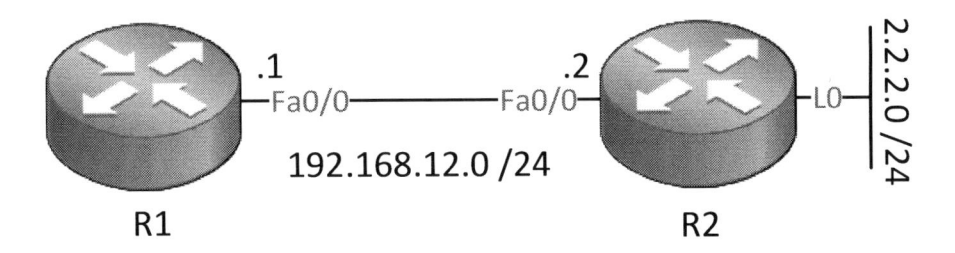

Just like the previous example, R1 is supposed to learn about 2.2.2.0 /24 but there's nothing in the routing table:

```
R1#show ip route rip
Codes: L - local, C - connected, S - static, R - RIP, M -
mobile, B - BGP
       D - EIGRP, EX - EIGRP external, O - OSPF, IA - OSPF inter
area
       N1 - OSPF NSSA external type 1, N2 - OSPF NSSA external
type 2
       E1 - OSPF external type 1, E2 - OSPF external type 2
       i - IS-IS, su - IS-IS summary, L1 - IS-IS level-1, L2 -
IS-IS level-2
       ia - IS-IS inter area, * - candidate default, U - per-
user static route
       o - ODR, P - periodic downloaded static route, H - NHRP,
l - LISP
       + - replicated route, % - next hop override

Gateway of last resort is not set
```

Let's see if the networks have been configured correctly:

```
R1#show ip protocols
*** IP Routing is NSF aware ***

Routing Protocol is "rip"
  Outgoing update filter list for all interfaces is not set
  Incoming update filter list for all interfaces is not set
  Sending updates every 30 seconds, next due in 18 seconds
  Invalid after 180 seconds, hold down 180, flushed after 240
  Redistributing: rip
  Default version control: send version 2, receive version 2
    Interface            Send  Recv  Triggered RIP  Key-chain
    FastEthernet0/0       2     2
  Automatic network summarization is not in effect
  Maximum path: 4
  Routing for Networks:
    192.168.12.0
  Routing Information Sources:
```

```
    Gateway           Distance        Last Update
    192.168.12.2         120          00:00:56
 Distance: (default is 120)
```

```
R2#show ip protocols
*** IP Routing is NSF aware ***

Routing Protocol is "rip"
  Outgoing update filter list for all interfaces is not set
  Incoming update filter list for all interfaces is not set
  Sending updates every 30 seconds, next due in 6 seconds
  Invalid after 180 seconds, hold down 180, flushed after 240
  Redistributing: rip
  Default version control: send version 2, receive version 2
    Interface              Send  Recv  Triggered RIP  Key-chain
    FastEthernet0/0         2     2
    Loopback0               2     2
  Automatic network summarization is not in effect
  Maximum path: 4
  Routing for Networks:
    2.0.0.0
    192.168.12.0
  Routing Information Sources:
    Gateway           Distance        Last Update
    192.168.12.1         120          00:00:03
  Distance: (default is 120)
```

No issues there, the correct networks are activated. Let's check R2 since that's the router that is supposed to advertise network 2.2.2.0 /24:

```
R2#show ip rip database
192.168.12.0/24      auto-summary
192.168.12.0/24      directly connected, FastEthernet0/0
```

The RIP database is a good place to check. If it's not in the database, it can't be advertised. R2 did have the correct network command so the network should be in its database. If you don't see it here, it has to be an interface-related problem. Let's check that:

```
R2#show ip interface brief | include Loopback0
Loopback0            2.2.2.2          YES manual administratively
down down
```

Here's the problem...the interface is down. RIP won't put a network in its database when the interface is not up/up. Let's fix it:

```
R2(config)#interface loopback 0
R2(config-if)#no shutdown
```

Take a look at the RIP database now:

```
R2#show ip rip database
2.0.0.0/8      auto-summary
2.2.2.0/24     directly connected, Loopback0
192.168.12.0/24     auto-summary
192.168.12.0/24     directly connected, FastEthernet0/0
```

There it is, now it can be advertised to R1. Let's check R1:

```
R1#show ip route rip | begin Gateway
Gateway of last resort is not set

     2.0.0.0/24 is subnetted, 1 subnets
R       2.2.2.0 [120/1] via 192.168.12.2, 00:00:19,
FastEthernet0/0
```

Problem solved! **Lesson learned: Make sure your interfaces are up and running.**

Onto the next problem:

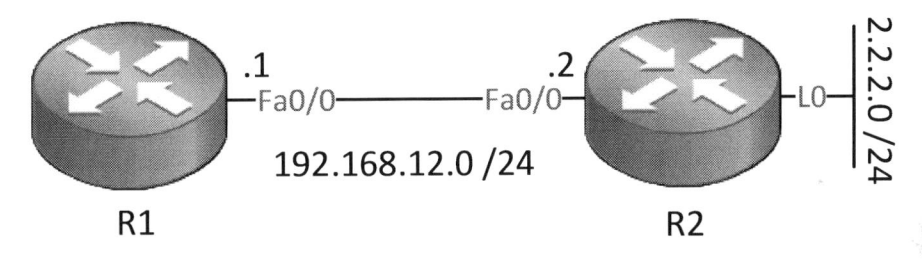

R1 ---Fa0/0--- 192.168.12.0 /24 ---Fa0/0--- R2 ---L0--- 2.2.2.0/24
.1   .2

Same issue, R1 is not learning 2.2.2.0 /24:

```
R1#show ip route rip | begin Gateway
Gateway of last resort is not set
```

It's empty...let's check show ip protocols again:

```
R1#show ip protocols
*** IP Routing is NSF aware ***

Routing Protocol is "rip"
  Outgoing update filter list for all interfaces is not set
  Incoming update filter list for all interfaces is not set
  Sending updates every 30 seconds, next due in 6 seconds
  Invalid after 180 seconds, hold down 180, flushed after 240
  Redistributing: rip
  Default version control: send version 2, receive version 2
    Interface           Send  Recv  Triggered RIP  Key-chain
    FastEthernet0/0      2     2
```

```
  Automatic network summarization is not in effect
  Maximum path: 4
  Routing for Networks:
    192.168.12.0
  Routing Information Sources:
    Gateway         Distance      Last Update
    192.168.12.2       120        00:46:14
  Distance: (default is 120)
```

```
R2#show ip protocols
*** IP Routing is NSF aware ***

Routing Protocol is "rip"
  Outgoing update filter list for all interfaces is not set
  Incoming update filter list for all interfaces is not set
  Sending updates every 30 seconds, next due in 23 seconds
  Invalid after 180 seconds, hold down 180, flushed after 240
  Redistributing: rip
  Default version control: send version 2, receive version 2
    Interface            Send  Recv  Triggered RIP  Key-chain
    Loopback0             2     2
  Automatic network summarization is not in effect
  Maximum path: 4
  Routing for Networks:
    2.0.0.0
    192.168.12.0
  Passive Interface(s):
    FastEthernet0/0
  Routing Information Sources:
    Gateway         Distance      Last Update
    192.168.12.1       120        00:49:15
  Distance: (default is 120)
```

The output of show ip protocols is very valuable for troubleshooting. You can see that the networks have been configured correctly but R2 has a passive interface. This prevents it from advertising anything. Let's fix it:

```
R2(config)#router rip
R2(config-router)#no passive-interface FastEthernet 0/0
```

Let's check R1:

```
R1#show ip route rip | begin Gateway
Gateway of last resort is not set

      2.0.0.0/24 is subnetted, 1 subnets
R        2.2.2.0 [120/1] via 192.168.12.2, 00:00:12,
FastEthernet0/0
```

Problem solved! ! **Lesson learned: Make sure interfaces that connect to other RIP routers are not configured as passive.**

The next problem can also be solved by taking a close look at show ip protocols, we'll use the same two routers:

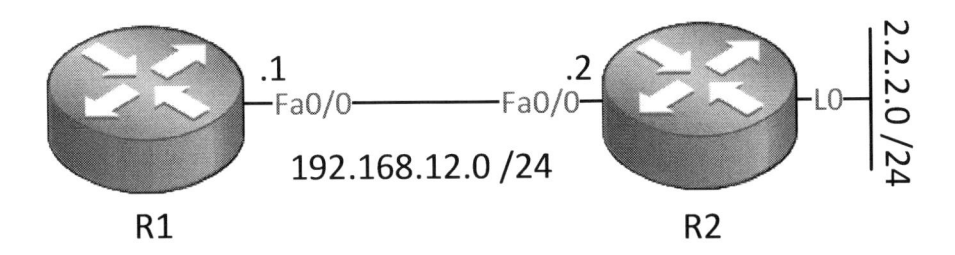

```
         .1              .2
    ─FaO/O────────FaO/O─          ─LO─  2.2.2.0/24
         192.168.12.0 /24
    R1                    R2
```

R1 isn't learning 2.2.2.0 /24:

```
R1#show ip route rip | begin Gateway
Gateway of last resort is not set
```

Let's compare show ip protocols:

```
R1#show ip protocols
*** IP Routing is NSF aware ***

Routing Protocol is "rip"
  Outgoing update filter list for all interfaces is not set
  Incoming update filter list for all interfaces is not set
  Sending updates every 30 seconds, next due in 14 seconds
  Invalid after 180 seconds, hold down 180, flushed after 240
  Redistributing: rip
  Default version control: send version 1, receive version 1
    Interface              Send  Recv  Triggered RIP  Key-chain
    FastEthernet0/0         1     1
  Automatic network summarization is not in effect
  Maximum path: 4
  Routing for Networks:
    192.168.12.0
  Routing Information Sources:
    Gateway         Distance        Last Update
    192.168.12.2         120        00:01:33
  Distance: (default is 120)
```

```
R2#show ip protocols
*** IP Routing is NSF aware ***

Routing Protocol is "rip"
  Outgoing update filter list for all interfaces is not set
  Incoming update filter list for all interfaces is not set
  Sending updates every 30 seconds, next due in 27 seconds
```

```
  Invalid after 180 seconds, hold down 180, flushed after 240
  Redistributing: rip
  Default version control: send version 2, receive version 2
    Interface             Send  Recv  Triggered RIP  Key-chain
    FastEthernet0/0        2     2
    Loopback0              2     2
  Automatic network summarization is not in effect
  Maximum path: 4
  Routing for Networks:
    2.0.0.0
    192.168.12.0
  Routing Information Sources:
    Gateway          Distance      Last Update
    192.168.12.1        120        01:03:49
  Distance: (default is 120)
```

If you look closely then you can see that we have a version mismatch. R1 is using RIP version 1 while R2 is using RIP version 2. Let's fix this:

```
R1(config)#router rip
R1(config-router)#version 2
```

This should fix the problem...

```
R1#show ip route rip | begin Gateway
Gateway of last resort is not set

     2.0.0.0/24 is subnetted, 1 subnets
R       2.2.2.0 [120/1] via 192.168.12.2, 00:00:20,
FastEthernet0/0
```

And it's fixed. **Lesson learned: Make sure you use the same RIP version on both sides.**

Let's look at a different issue...same two routers though:

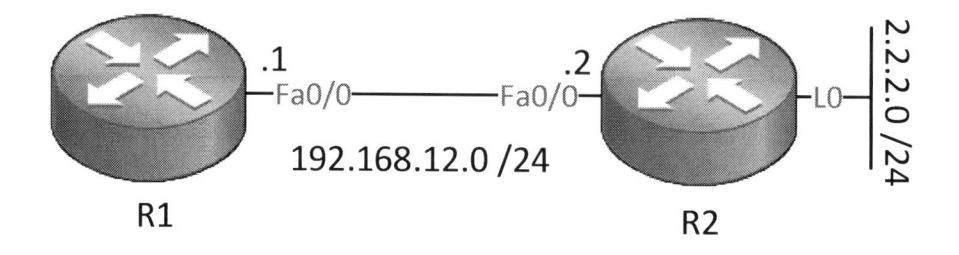

```
                .1                    .2
              -Fa0/0-            -Fa0/0-         -L0-   2.2.2.0/24
                    192.168.12.0 /24
            R1                              R2
```

Once again R1 is not learning 2.2.2.0 /24:

```
R1#show ip route rip | begin Gateway
Gateway of last resort is not set
```

Let's compare show ip protocols first:

```
R1#show ip protocols
*** IP Routing is NSF aware ***

Routing Protocol is "rip"
  Outgoing update filter list for all interfaces is not set
  Incoming update filter list for all interfaces is not set
  Sending updates every 30 seconds, next due in 22 seconds
  Invalid after 180 seconds, hold down 180, flushed after 240
  Redistributing: rip
  Default version control: send version 2, receive version 2
    Interface             Send  Recv  Triggered RIP  Key-chain
    FastEthernet0/0       2     2
  Automatic network summarization is not in effect
  Maximum path: 4
  Routing for Networks:
    192.168.12.0
  Routing Information Sources:
    Gateway           Distance        Last Update
    192.168.12.2         120          00:00:27
  Distance: (default is 120)
```

```
R2#show ip protocols
*** IP Routing is NSF aware ***

Routing Protocol is "rip"
  Outgoing update filter list for all interfaces is not set
  Incoming update filter list for all interfaces is not set
  Outgoing routes will have 15 added to metric
  Sending updates every 30 seconds, next due in 4 seconds
  Invalid after 180 seconds, hold down 180, flushed after 240
  Redistributing: rip
  Default version control: send version 2, receive version 2
    Interface             Send  Recv  Triggered RIP  Key-chain
    FastEthernet0/0       2     2
    Loopback0             2     2
  Automatic network summarization is not in effect
  Maximum path: 4
  Routing for Networks:
    2.0.0.0
    192.168.12.0
  Routing Information Sources:
    Gateway           Distance        Last Update
    192.168.12.1         120          00:00:34
  Distance: (default is 120)
```

Everything seems to be OK. Correct networks, same version, no passive interfaces. Let's check if the network is in the RIP database of R2:

103

```
R2#show ip rip database
2.0.0.0/8      auto-summary
2.2.2.0/24       directly connected, Loopback0
192.168.12.0/24     auto-summary
192.168.12.0/24      directly connected, FastEthernet0/0
```

It's in the RIP database. This might be a good moment to enable a debug:

```
R1#debug ip rip
RIP protocol debugging is on

RIP: received v2 update from 192.168.12.2 on FastEthernet0/0
     2.2.2.0/24 via 0.0.0.0 in 16 hops   (inaccessible)
```

There we go. R1 does receive an update but network 2.2.2.0 /24 has a hop count of 16. This can't be installed in the routing table. In large networks this problem might occur but for this example I used an offset-list:

```
R2(config)#router rip
R2(config-router)#no offset-list 0 out 15
```

This should fix the problem:

```
R1#
RIP: received v2 update from 192.168.12.2 on FastEthernet0/0
     2.2.2.0/24 via 0.0.0.0 in 1 hops
```

R1 now shows a hop count of 1, this can be installed:

```
R1#show ip route rip | begin Gateway
Gateway of last resort is not set

     2.0.0.0/24 is subnetted, 1 subnets
R       2.2.2.0 [120/1] via 192.168.12.2, 00:00:04,
FastEthernet0/0
```

There we go, problem solved. **Lesson learned: a hop count of 16 is unreachable for RIP. If the network is small, check for offset-lists that increased the metric.**

Onto the next issue...

```
                    .1                    .2
           ─FaO/O─────────FaO/O─              ─LO─  2.2.2.0/24
                  192.168.12.0 /24
           R1                        R2
```

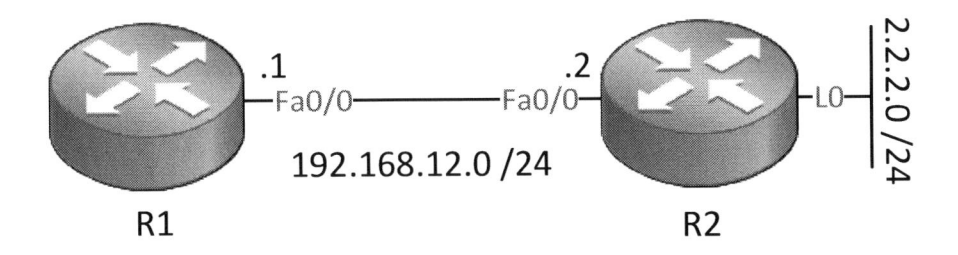

This is getting old but R1 once again can't learn 2.2.2.0 /24:

```
R1#show ip route rip | begin Gateway
Gateway of last resort is not set
```

Nothing here...let's check show ip protocols:

```
R1#show ip protocols
*** IP Routing is NSF aware ***

Routing Protocol is "rip"
  Outgoing update filter list for all interfaces is not set
  Incoming update filter list for all interfaces is not set
  Sending updates every 30 seconds, next due in 23 seconds
  Invalid after 180 seconds, hold down 180, flushed after 240
  Redistributing: rip
  Default version control: send version 2, receive version 2
    Interface            Send  Recv  Triggered RIP  Key-chain
    FastEthernet0/0      2     2                    MY_CHAIN
  Automatic network summarization is not in effect
  Maximum path: 4
  Routing for Networks:
    192.168.12.0
  Routing Information Sources:
    Gateway         Distance        Last Update
    192.168.12.2        120         00:01:01
  Distance: (default is 120)
```

```
R2#show ip protocols
*** IP Routing is NSF aware ***

Routing Protocol is "rip"
  Outgoing update filter list for all interfaces is not set
  Incoming update filter list for all interfaces is not set
  Sending updates every 30 seconds, next due in 12 seconds
  Invalid after 180 seconds, hold down 180, flushed after 240
  Redistributing: rip
  Default version control: send version 2, receive version 2
    Interface                Send  Recv  Triggered RIP  Key-chain
```

```
    FastEthernet0/0          2       2
    Loopback0                2       2
  Automatic network summarization is not in effect
  Maximum path: 4
  Routing for Networks:
    2.0.0.0
    192.168.12.0
  Routing Information Sources:
    Gateway           Distance      Last Update
    192.168.12.1      120           00:15:43
  Distance: (default is 120)
```

Everything is looking good. Let's enable a debug:

```
R1 + R2 #debug ip rip
RIP protocol debugging is on
```

You'll see this:

```
R2#
RIP: sending v2 update to 224.0.0.9 via FastEthernet0/0
(192.168.12.2)
RIP: build update entries
      2.2.2.0/24 via 0.0.0.0, metric 1, tag 0
```

R2 is sending the RIP update, no issues here so it's probably related to R1:

```
R1#
RIP: ignored v2 packet from 192.168.12.2 (invalid
authentication)
```

There we go, R1 is ignoring the RIP update because of an authentication mismatch. RIP authentication is done on the interface so let's check the differences:

```
R1#show run interface FastEthernet 0/0
Building configuration...

Current configuration : 171 bytes
!
interface FastEthernet0/0
 ip address 192.168.12.1 255.255.255.0
 ip rip authentication mode md5
 ip rip authentication key-chain MY_CHAIN
 duplex auto
 speed auto
end
```

```
R2#show run interface FastEthernet 0/0
Building configuration...
```

```
Current configuration : 97 bytes
!
interface FastEthernet0/0
 ip address 192.168.12.2 255.255.255.0
 duplex auto
 speed auto
end
```

There we go, R1 has authentication while R2 doesn't. Let's fix it:

```
R1(config)#interface FastEthernet 0/0
R1(config-if)#no ip rip authentication mode md5
R1(config-if)#no ip rip authentication key-chain MY_CHAIN
```

The "quick fix" is to disable authentication. This should do the job:

```
R1#show ip route rip | begin Gateway
Gateway of last resort is not set

     2.0.0.0/24 is subnetted, 1 subnets
R       2.2.2.0 [120/1] via 192.168.12.2, 00:00:15, FastEthernet0/0
```

Problem solved! **Lesson learned: Make sure you use the same authentication parameters on both sides.**

Next problem coming up!

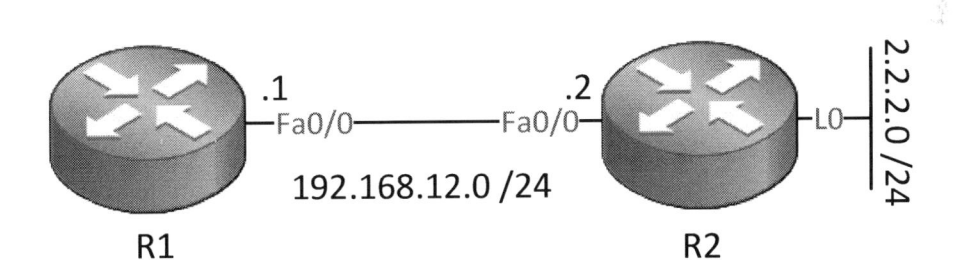

```
             .1              .2
         ─FaO/0────────FaO/0─         ─LO─  2.2.2.0/24
              192.168.12.0 /24
          R1                      R2
```

Same two routers, R1 isn't seeing the 2.2.2.0 /24 prefix:

```
R1#show ip route rip | begin Gateway
Gateway of last resort is not set
```

Show ip protocols is a good place to start:

```
R1#show ip protocols
*** IP Routing is NSF aware ***
```

107

```
Routing Protocol is "rip"
  Outgoing update filter list for all interfaces is not set
  Incoming update filter list for all interfaces is not set
    FastEthernet0/0 filtered by 1 (per-user), default is not set
  Sending updates every 30 seconds, next due in 26 seconds
  Invalid after 180 seconds, hold down 180, flushed after 240
  Redistributing: rip
  Default version control: send version 2, receive version 2
    Interface             Send  Recv  Triggered RIP  Key-chain
    FastEthernet0/0       2     2
  Automatic network summarization is not in effect
  Maximum path: 4
  Routing for Networks:
    192.168.12.0
  Routing Information Sources:
    Gateway         Distance        Last Update
    192.168.12.2    120             00:01:16
  Distance: (default is 120)
```

```
R2#show ip protocols
*** IP Routing is NSF aware ***

Routing Protocol is "rip"
  Outgoing update filter list for all interfaces is not set
  Incoming update filter list for all interfaces is not set
  Sending updates every 30 seconds, next due in 27 seconds
  Invalid after 180 seconds, hold down 180, flushed after 240
  Redistributing: rip
  Default version control: send version 2, receive version 2
    Interface             Send  Recv  Triggered RIP  Key-chain
    FastEthernet0/0       2     2
    Loopback0             2     2
  Automatic network summarization is not in effect
  Maximum path: 4
  Routing for Networks:
    2.0.0.0
    192.168.12.0
  Routing Information Sources:
    Gateway         Distance        Last Update
    192.168.12.1    120             00:24:34
  Distance: (default is 120)
```

This is a sneaky one...take a close look at R1. You can see that there's a filter on interface FastEthernet 0/0. Let me show you what the configuration of R1 looks like:

```
R1#show run | section rip
router rip
 version 2
 network 192.168.12.0
 distribute-list 1 in FastEthernet0/0
```

```
no auto-summary
```

I've added a distribute-list that uses access-list 1 inbound. Here's what the access-list looks like:

```
R1#show access-lists 1
Standard IP access list 1
    10 deny    any (10 matches)
```

R1 won't allow any RIP updates now. We can remove the access-list or edit it:

```
R1(config)#ip access-list standard 1
R1(config-std-nacl)#1 permit 2.2.2.0 0.0.0.255
```

This should do the job...

```
R1#show access-lists 1
Standard IP access list 1
    1 permit 2.2.2.0, wildcard bits 0.0.0.255 (1 match)
    10 deny    any (12 matches)
```

You can see we now have a match, let's see if its in the routing table:

```
R1#show ip route rip | begin Gateway
Gateway of last resort is not set

     2.0.0.0/24 is subnetted, 1 subnets
R       2.2.2.0 [120/1] via 192.168.12.2, 00:00:19, FastEthernet0/0
```

There it is! **Lesson learned: Make sure there are no filters in- or outbound preventing RIP updates from being installed or advertised.**

There are two more RIP scenarios, these use a different topology. Let's check it out:

192.168.123.0 /24

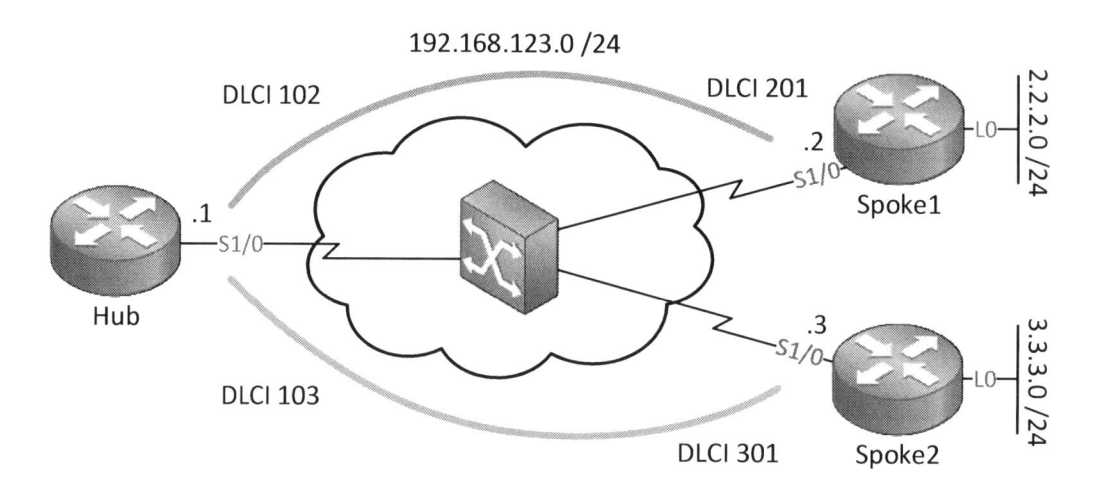

We have a hub and spoke topology with 3 routers. The two spoke routers have a loopback interface. The problem is that the two spoke routers are not learning each others networks:

```
Spoke1#show ip route rip
```

```
Spoke2#show ip route rip
```

It would be a good idea to check show ip protocols, see if the networks are advertised. This frame-relay hub and spoke topology should ring a bell though...split horizon could be an issue. Let's see if the hub has learned anything:

```
Hub#show ip route rip
     2.0.0.0/24 is subnetted, 1 subnets
R       2.2.2.0 [120/1] via 192.168.123.2, 00:00:25, Serial1/0
     3.0.0.0/24 is subnetted, 1 subnets
R       3.3.3.0 [120/1] via 192.168.123.3, 00:00:08, Serial1/0
```

The hub did learn these networks. Is split horizon the issue here?

```
Hub#show ip interface Serial 1/0 | include Split
  Split horizon is enabled
```

Sure is, let's get rid of it!

```
Hub(config)#interface Serial 1/0
Hub(config-if)#no ip split-horizon
```

Did it solve our issue?

```
Spoke2#show ip route rip
     2.0.0.0/24 is subnetted, 1 subnets
R        2.2.2.0 [120/2] via 192.168.123.2, 00:00:01, Serial1/0
```

```
Spoke1#show ip route rip
     3.0.0.0/24 is subnetted, 1 subnets
R        3.3.3.0 [120/2] via 192.168.123.3, 00:00:11, Serial1/0
```

Sure is, the spoke routers learned about each others network. Keep in mind that split horizon is *disabled* by default on physical serial interfaces. **Lesson learned: Make sure split horizon isn't enabled in hub and spoke topologies.**

Last but not least, there is a possible summarization problem:

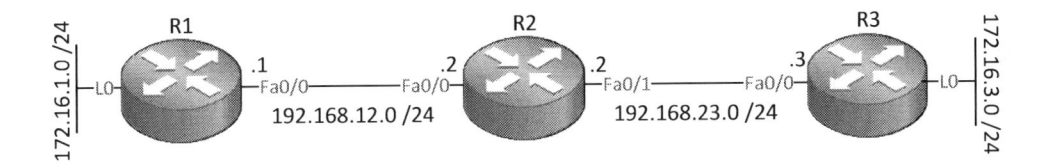

R2 is able to reach 172.16.1.0 /24 and 172.16.3.0 /24 but sometimes packets don't make it to their destination. Since R2 does know how to reach these networks, it's best to take a look at its routing table:

```
R2#show ip route rip
R    172.16.0.0/16 [120/1] via 192.168.23.3, 00:00:13,
FastEthernet0/1
                  [120/1] via 192.168.12.1, 00:00:15,
FastEthernet0/0
```

R2 sees a single entry for 172.16.0.0 /16 and thinks it can reach this network through 192.168.23.3 or 192.168.12.1. The problem in this scenario is that the 172.16.x.0 /24 networks have been summarized to the 172.16.0.0 /16 classful network. It seems RIP is behaving classful instead of classless. Let's verify this:

```
R1#show ip protocols | include summ
   Automatic network summarization is in effect
```

```
R3#show ip protocols | include summ
   Automatic network summarization is in effect
```

R1 and R3 are configured for auto-summarization. Let's disable this:

```
R1(config)#router rip
R1(config-router)#no auto-summary
```

```
R3(config)#router rip
R3(config-router)#no auto-summary
```

Now take a look at the routing table of R2:

```
R2#show ip route rip
     172.16.0.0/24 is subnetted, 2 subnets
R       172.16.1.0 [120/1] via 192.168.12.1, 00:00:00,
FastEthernet0/0
R       172.16.3.0 [120/1] via 192.168.23.3, 00:00:00,
FastEthernet0/1
```

R1 and R3 now advertise their networks with the correct subnet mask so R2 knows where to send its packets to. **Lesson learned: in case of discontigious networks, disable auto-summarization.**

That's all I have for you on RIP troubleshooting! It's not likely that you will see RIP on networks nowadays but in case you do, you now know the most common issues and how to troubleshoot them.

In the next chapter we'll take a look at EIGRP..

5. Troubleshooting EIGRP

In this chapter we'll take a look at Cisco's EIGRP routing protocol. EIGRP is an advanced distance vector routing protocol that has to establish a neighbor relationship before updates are sent. Because of this the first thing we'll have to do is check if the neighbor adjacency is working properly. If this is the case we can continue by checking if networks are being advertised or not. In this chapter I'll show you everything that can go wrong with EIGRP, how to fix it and in what order. Let's get started with the neighbor adjacency!

There are a number of items that cause problems with EIGRP neighbor adjacencies:

- **Uncommon subnet**: EIGRP neighbors with IP addresses that are not in the same subnet.
- **K value mismatch**: By default bandwidth and delay are enabled for the metric calculation. We can enable load and reliability as well but we have to do it on all EIGRP routers.
- **AS mismatch**: The autonomous system number has to match on both EIGRP routers in order to form a neighbor adjacency.
- **Layer 2 issues**: EIGRP works on layer 3 of the OSI-model. If layer 1 and 2 are not working properly we'll have issues with forming a neighbor adjacency.
- **Access-list issues**: It's possible that someone created an access-list that filters out multicast traffic. EIGRP by default uses 224.0.0.10 to communicate with other EIGRP neighbors.
- **NBMA**: Non Broadcast Multi Access networks like frame-relay will not allow broadcast or multicast traffic by default. This can prevent EIGRP from forming EIGRP neighbor adjacencies.

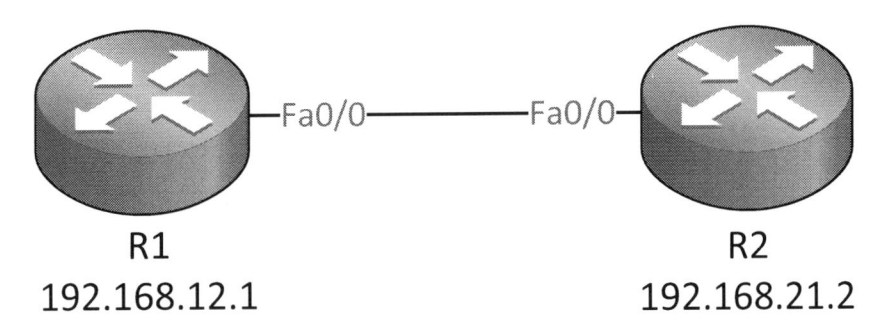

R1 —Fa0/0———Fa0/0— R2

R1
192.168.12.1

R2
192.168.21.2

```
R1(config)#interface f0/0
R1(config-if)#ip address 192.168.12.1 255.255.255.0
R1(config-if)#router eigrp 12
R1(config-router)#network 192.168.12.0
```

```
R2(config)#interface f0/0
R2(config-if)#ip address 192.168.21.2 255.255.255.0
```

```
R2(config)#router eigrp 12
R2(config-router)#network 192.168.21.0
```

The **uncommon subnet** error is easy to spot. In the example above we have 2 routers and you can see I configured a different subnet on each interface.

After enabling EIGRP the following errors pops up:

```
R1# IP-EIGRP(Default-IP-Routing-Table:12): Neighbor 192.168.21.2
not on common subnet for FastEthernet0/0
```

```
R2# IP-EIGRP(Default-IP-Routing-Table:12): Neighbor 192.168.12.1
not on common subnet for FastEthernet0/0
```

Both routers complain that they are not on the same subnet.

```
R2(config-router)#interface f0/0
R2(config-if)#ip address 192.168.12.2 255.25
R2(config)#router eigrp 12
R2(config-router)#no network 192.168.21.0
R2(config-router)#network 192.168.12.0
```

I'll change the IP address on R2 and make sure the correct network command is configured for EIGRP.

```
R1# %DUAL-5-NBRCHANGE: IP-EIGRP(0) 12: Ncighbor 192.168.12.2
(FastEthernet0/0) is up: new adjacency
```

```
R2# %DUAL-5-NBRCHANGE: IP-EIGRP(0) 12: Neighbor 192.168.12.1
(FastEthernet0/0) is up: new adjacency
```

Voila! We now have an EIGRP neighbor adjacency.

```
R1#show ip eigrp neighbors
IP-EIGRP neighbors for process 12
H    Address              Interface       Hold Uptime     SRTT
RTO  Q   Seq
                                          (sec)           (ms)
Cnt  Num
0    192.168.12.2         Fa0/0           13   00:05:15   3
200  0   3
```

```
R2#show ip eigrp neighbors
IP-EIGRP neighbors for process 12
H    Address              Interface       Hold Uptime     SRTT
RTO  Q   Seq
                                          (sec)           (ms)
Cnt  Num
```

```
0    192.168.12.1              Fa0/0              11 00:05:32 1263
5000  0  3
```

We can verify this by using the show ip eigrp neighbors command. **Lesson learned: Make sure both routers are on the same subnet.**

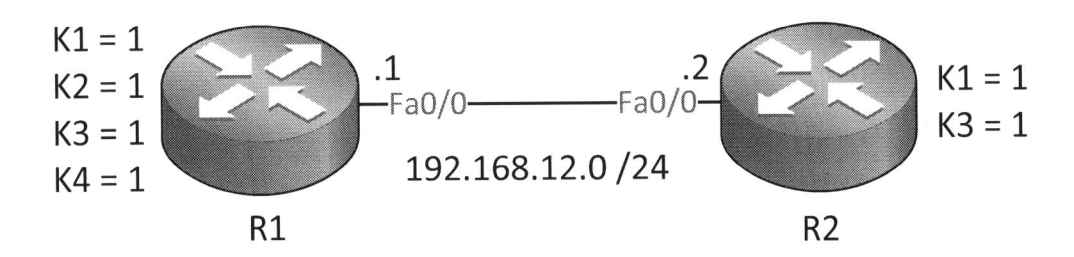

```
K1 = 1                    .1              .2
K2 = 1         R1 —Fa0/0————Fa0/0— R2        K1 = 1
K3 = 1                                          K3 = 1
K4 = 1         192.168.12.0 /24
```

This time the IP addresses are correct but we are using different K values on both sides. R1 has enabled bandwidth, delay, load and reliability. R2 is only using bandwidth and delay.

```
R1# %DUAL-5-NBRCHANGE: IP-EIGRP(0) 12: Neighbor 192.168.12.2
(FastEthernet0/0) is down: K-value mismatch
```

```
R1# %DUAL-5-NBRCHANGE: IP-EIGRP(0) 12: Neighbor 192.168.12.2
(FastEthernet0/0) is down: Interface Goodbye received
```

This error is easy to spot because your console will give you the "K-value mismatch" error on both routers.

```
R1#show run | section eigrp
router eigrp 12
 network 192.168.12.0
 metric weights 0 1 1 1 1 0
 auto-summary
```

We can verify our configuration by looking at both routers. You can see the K values were changed on R1.

```
R2(config)#router eigrp 12
R2(config-router)#metric weights 0 1 1 1 1 0
```

We'll make sure the K values are the same on both routers, I'll change R2.

```
R1# %DUAL-5-NBRCHANGE: IP-EIGRP(0) 12: Neighbor 192.168.12.2
(FastEthernet0/0) is up: new adjacency
```

```
R2# %DUAL-5-NBRCHANGE: IP-EIGRP(0) 12: Neighbor 192.168.12.1
(FastEthernet0/0) is up: new adjacency
```

After changing the K values we have an EIGRP neighbor adjacency.

```
R1#show ip eigrp neighbors
IP-EIGRP neighbors for process 12
H   Address                 Interface       Hold Uptime    SRTT
RTO   Q   Seq
                                            (sec)          (ms)
Cnt Num
0   192.168.12.2            Fa0/0           13 00:02:11    13
200   0   6
```

```
R2#show ip eigrp neighbors
IP-EIGRP neighbors for process 12
H   Address                 Interface       Hold Uptime    SRTT
RTO   Q   Seq
                                            (sec)          (ms)
Cnt Num
0   192.168.12.1            Fa0/0           13 00:02:42    19
200   0   6
```

Another problem solved! **Lesson learned: Make sure the K-values are the same on all EIGRP routers within the same autonomous system.** Let's continue with the next error...

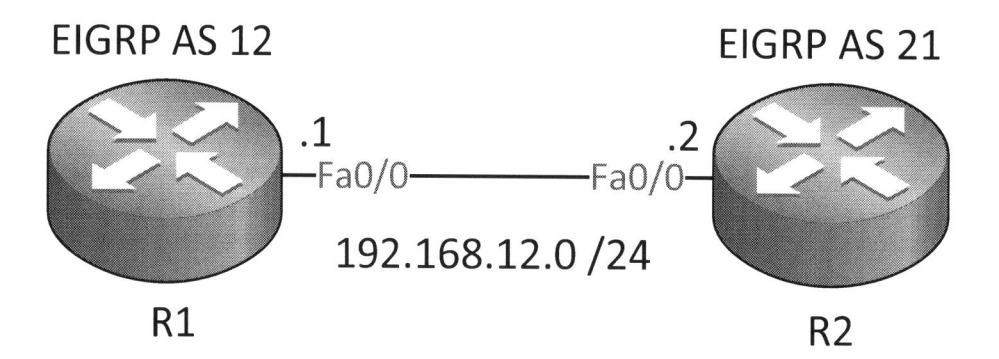

EIGRP AS 12   EIGRP AS 21

```
        .1                      .2
      Fa0/0 ─────────────── Fa0/0
            192.168.12.0 /24
   R1                              R2
```

Here's another example of a typical Monday morning problem. There's a mismatch in the AS number. When we configure EIGRP we have to type in an AS number. Unlike OSPF (which uses a process ID) this number has to be the same on both routers.

```
R1#show ip eigrp neighbors
IP-EIGRP neighbors for process 12
```

```
R2#show ip eigrp neighbors
IP-EIGRP neighbors for process 21
```

Unlike the other EIGRP configuration mistakes this one doesn't produce an error message. We can use show ip eigrp neighbors and see that there are no neighbors. Use your eagle eyes to spot for differences and you'll quickly see that we are not using the same AS number.

```
R1#show run | section eigrp
router eigrp 12
 network 192.168.12.0
 auto-summary
```

```
R2#show run | section eigrp
router eigrp 21
 network 192.168.12.0
 auto-summary
```

I can also take a quick look at the running configuration and I'll see the same thing.

```
R2(config)#no router eigrp 21

router eigrp 12
 network 192.168.12.0
 metric weights 0 1 1 1 1 0
 auto-summary
```

Let's change the AS number on R2.

```
R1# %DUAL-5-NBRCHANGE: IP-EIGRP(0) 12: Neighbor 192.168.12.2
(FastEthernet0/0) is up: new adjacency
```

```
R2# %DUAL-5-NBRCHANGE: IP-EIGRP(0) 12: Neighbor 192.168.12.1
(FastEthernet0/0) is up: new adjacency
```

After changing the AS number life is good. **Lesson learned: Make sure the AS number is the same if you want an EIGRP neighbor adjacency.**

```
R1#show ip eigrp neighbors
IP-EIGRP neighbors for process 12
H    Address              Interface       Hold Uptime    SRTT
RTO  Q   Seq
                                          (sec)          (ms)
Cnt  Num
0    192.168.12.2         Fa0/0           11   00:01:44  13
200  0   3
```

```
R2#show ip eigrp neighbors
IP-EIGRP neighbors for process 12
H    Address              Interface       Hold Uptime    SRTT
RTO  Q   Seq
                                          (sec)          (ms)
Cnt  Num
```

117

```
0    192.168.12.1            Fa0/0                 12 00:01:53     7
200   0    9
```

What if I only have access to one of the routers? That will be a challenge but it's possible to debug the AS number from the incoming EIGRP packets. If you want to see how this is done you can take a look at the following lab I created:

http://gns3vault.com/EIGRP/eigrp-debug-as-number.html

Last but not least...if you checked the AS number, K values, IP addresses and you still don't have a working EIGRP neighbor adjacency then you should think about security. Maybe an access-list is blocking EIGRP and/or multicast traffic.

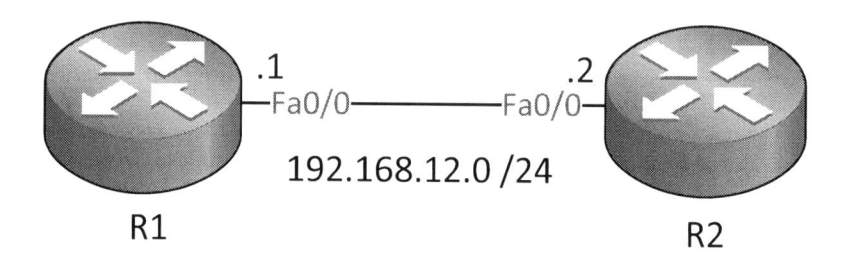

Once again two EIGRP routers and no neighbor adjacency. What is going on?

```
R1#show ip eigrp neighbors
IP-EIGRP neighbors for process 12
```

```
R2#show ip eigrp neighbors
IP-EIGRP neighbors for process 12
```

We see that there are no neighbors...

```
R1#show ip protocols
Routing Protocol is "eigrp 12"
  Outgoing update filter list for all interfaces is not set
  Incoming update filter list for all interfaces is not set
  Default networks flagged in outgoing updates
  Default networks accepted from incoming updates
  EIGRP metric weight K1=1, K2=0, K3=1, K4=0, K5=0
  EIGRP maximum hopcount 100
  EIGRP maximum metric variance 1
  Redistributing: eigrp 12
  EIGRP NSF-aware route hold timer is 240s
  Automatic network summarization is in effect
  Maximum path: 4
  Routing for Networks:
    192.168.12.0
  Routing Information Sources:
    Gateway         Distance      Last Update
```

```
  Distance: internal 90 external 170
```

```
R2#show ip protocols
Routing Protocol is "eigrp 12"
  Outgoing update filter list for all interfaces is not set
  Incoming update filter list for all interfaces is not set
  Default networks flagged in outgoing updates
  Default networks accepted from incoming updates
  EIGRP metric weight K1=1, K2=0, K3=1, K4=0, K5=0
  EIGRP maximum hopcount 100
  EIGRP maximum metric variance 1
  Redistributing: eigrp 12
  EIGRP NSF-aware route hold timer is 240s
  Automatic network summarization is in effect
  Maximum path: 4
  Routing for Networks:
    192.168.12.0
  Passive Interface(s):
    FastEthernet0/0
  Routing Information Sources:
    Gateway         Distance      Last Update
  Distance: internal 90 external 170
```

If you look at the output of show ip protocols you can see that the network has been advertised correctly. If you look closely on R2 you can see that we have a passive interface, let's get rid of it!

```
R2(config)#router eigrp 12
R2(config-router)#no passive-interface fastEthernet 0/0
```

Another misconfiguration bites the dust...

```
R1#show ip eigrp neighbors
IP-EIGRP neighbors for process 12
H    Address              Interface      Hold Uptime    SRTT
RTO  Q   Seq
                                         (sec)          (ms)
Cnt  Num
0    192.168.12.2         Fa0/0          13  00:05:23   24
200  0   6
```

```
R2#show ip eigrp neighbors
IP-EIGRP neighbors for process 12
H    Address              Interface      Hold Uptime    SRTT
RTO  Q   Seq
                                         (sec)          (ms)
Cnt  Num
0    192.168.12.1         Fa0/0          14  00:05:39   20
200  0   6
```

There we go! Problem solved! **Lesson learned: Don't enable passive interface if you want to establish an EIGRP neighbor adjacency.**

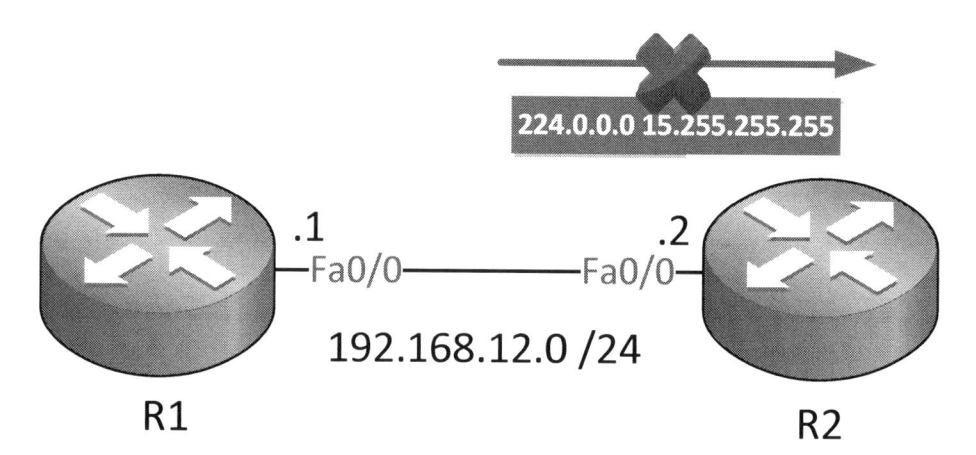

In the example above I have the same 2 routers but this time someone decided it was a good idea to configure an access-list on R2 that blocks all incoming multicast traffic.

```
R1# %DUAL-5-NBRCHANGE: IP-EIGRP(0) 12: Neighbor 192.168.12.2
(FastEthernet0/0) is down: retry limit exceeded
%DUAL-5-NBRCHANGE: IP-EIGRP(0) 12: Neighbor 192.168.12.2
(FastEthernet0/0) is up: new adjacency
%DUAL-5-NBRCHANGE: IP-EIGRP(0) 12: Neighbor 192.168.12.2
(FastEthernet0/0) is down: retry limit exceeded
%DUAL-5-NBRCHANGE: IP-EIGRP(0) 12: Neighbor 192.168.12.2
(FastEthernet0/0) is up: new adjacency
```

This is where things might become confusing. On R1 you can see that it believes it has established an EIGRP neighbor adjacency with R2. This happens because we are still **receiving** EIGRP packets from R2.

```
R1#debug eigrp neighbors
EIGRP Neighbors debugging is on
EIGRP: Retransmission retry limit exceeded
EIGRP: Holdtime expired
```

We can do a **debug eigrp neighbors** to see what is going on. Apparently R1 is not getting a response back from its hello messages, the holdtime expires and it will drop the EIGRP neighbor adjacency.

```
R1#ping 224.0.0.10

Type escape sequence to abort.
Sending 1, 100-byte ICMP Echos to 224.0.0.10, timeout is 2
seconds:
.
```

A quick way to test connectivity is to send a ping to the 224.0.0.10 multicast address that EIGRP uses. You can see we don't get a response from this ping. It's a good idea to check if there are access-lists in the network.

```
R2#show ip interface fa0/0 | include access list
  Outgoing access list is not set
  Inbound  access list is BLOCKMULTICAST
```

Bingo! We found something...

```
R2#show ip access-lists
Extended IP access list BLOCKMULTICAST
    10 deny ip any 224.0.0.0 15.255.255.255 (536 matches)
    20 permit ip any any (468 matches)
```

This access-list is blocking all multicast traffic. Let's punch a hole in it so EIGRP is allowed.

```
R2(config)#ip access-list extended BLOCKMULTICAST
R2(config-ext-nacl)#5 permit ip any host 224.0.0.10
```

We can create a specific statement that will allow EIGRP traffic.

```
R2#show access-lists
Extended IP access list BLOCKMULTICAST
    5 permit ip any host 224.0.0.10 (27 matches)
    10 deny ip any 224.0.0.0 15.255.255.255 (569 matches)
    20 permit ip any any (501 matches)
```

You can see our EIGRP traffic matches the statement I just created.

```
R1# %DUAL-5-NBRCHANGE: IP-EIGRP(0) 12: Neighbor 192.168.12.2
(FastEthernet0/0) is up: new adjacency
```

```
R2# %DUAL-5-NBRCHANGE: IP-EIGRP(0) 12: Neighbor 192.168.12.1
(FastEthernet0/0) is up: new adjacency
```

Both routers now show a working EIGRP neighbor adjacency.

```
R1#ping 224.0.0.10

Type escape sequence to abort.
Sending 1, 100-byte ICMP Echos to 224.0.0.10, timeout is 2
seconds:

Reply to request 0 from 192.168.12.2, 24 ms
```

The ping that I just tried is now working. **Lesson learned: Don't block**

EIGRP packets!

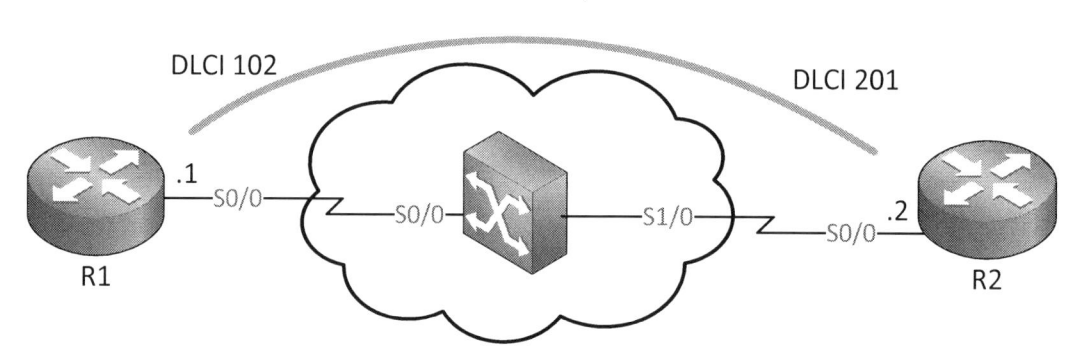

One more issue I want to share with you that can prevent EIGRP from becoming neighbors. In the picture above we have a frame-relay network and there's one PVC between R1 and R2. Here is the relevant configuration:

```
R1#
interface Serial0/0
 ip address 192.168.12.1 255.255.255.0
 encapsulation frame-relay
 serial restart-delay 0
 frame-relay map ip 192.168.12.2 102
 no frame-relay inverse-arp

router eigrp 12
 network 192.168.12.0
 auto-summary
```

```
R2#
interface Serial0/0
 ip address 192.168.12.2 255.255.255.0
 encapsulation frame-relay
 serial restart-delay 0
 frame-relay map ip 192.168.12.1 201
 no frame-relay inverse-arp

router eigrp 12
 network 192.168.12.0
 auto-summary
```

Both routers are configured for frame-relay and EIGRP has been configured.

```
R1#show ip eigrp neighbors
IP-EIGRP neighbors for process 12
```

```
R2#show ip eigrp neighbors
IP-EIGRP neighbors for process 12
```

You can see that there are no neighbors...that's not good! Can I ping the other side?

```
R1#ping 192.168.12.2

Type escape sequence to abort.
Sending 5, 100-byte ICMP Echos to 192.168.12.2, timeout is 2
seconds:
!!!!!
Success rate is 100 percent (5/5), round-trip min/avg/max =
4/8/24 ms
```

Sending a ping is no problem so we can assume the frame-relay PVC is working. EIGRP however uses multicast and frame-relay by default is NBMA. Can we ping the 224.0.0.10 EIGRP multicast address?

```
R1#ping 224.0.0.10

Type escape sequence to abort.
Sending 1, 100-byte ICMP Echos to 224.0.0.10, timeout is 2
seconds:
.
```

No response here, at least we now know that unicast traffic is working and multicast doesn't work. Frame-relay can be configured for point-to-point or point-to-multipoint. A physical interface is always a frame-relay point-to-multipoint interface and those require frame-relay maps, let's check it out:

```
R1#show frame-relay map
Serial0/0 (up): ip 192.168.12.2 dlci 102(0x66,0x1860), static,
          CISCO, status defined, active
```

```
R2#show frame-relay map
Serial0/0 (up): ip 192.168.12.1 dlci 201(0xC9,0x3090), static,
          CISCO, status defined, active
```

We can see both routers have a DLCI-to-IP mapping so they know how to reach each other. I can see they keyword **"static"** which also reveals to me that this mapping was configured by someone and not learned through Inverse ARP (otherwise you see "dynamic"). I don't see the **"broadcast"** keyword which is required to forward broadcast or multicast traffic. At this moment we have 2 options to fix this problem:

- Configure EIGRP to use unicast traffic instead of multicast.

- Check the frame-relay configuration and make sure multicast traffic can be forwarded.

Let's do the EIGRP unicast configuration first:

```
R1(config)#router eigrp 12
R1(config-router)#neighbor 192.168.12.2 serial 0/0
```

```
R2(config)#router eigrp 12
R2(config-router)#neighbor 192.168.12.1 serial 0/0
```

We require the **neighbor** command for the EIGRP configuration. As soon as you type in these commands and hit enter you'll see this:

```
R1#
%DUAL-5-NBRCHANGE: IP-EIGRP(0) 12: Neighbor 192.168.12.2
(Serial0/0) is up: new adjacency
```

```
R2#
%DUAL-5-NBRCHANGE: IP-EIGRP(0) 12: Neighbor 192.168.12.1
(Serial0/0) is up: new adjacency
```

Problem solved! Now let's try the other method where we send multicast traffic down the frame-relay PVC:

```
R1(config)#router eigrp 12
R1(config-router)#no neighbor 192.168.12.2 serial 0/0
```

```
R2(config)#router eigrp 12
R2(config-router)#no neighbor 192.168.12.1 serial 0/0
```

If it ain't broke…don't fix it…not this time! Time to hammer down the EIGRP neighbor adjacency.

```
R1(config)#interface serial 0/0
R1(config-if)#frame-relay map ip 192.168.12.2 102 broadcast
```

```
R2(config)#interface serial 0/0
R2(config-if)#frame-relay map ip 192.168.12.1 201 broadcast
```

Broadcast is the magic keyword here. This will allow broadcast and multicast traffic.

```
R1#
%DUAL-5-NBRCHANGE: IP-EIGRP(0) 12: Neighbor 192.168.12.2
(Serial0/0) is up: new adjacency
```

```
R2#
%DUAL-5-NBRCHANGE: IP-EIGRP(0) 12: Neighbor 192.168.12.1
(Serial0/0) is up: new adjacency
```

After changing the frame-relay map configuration we have an EIGRP neighbor adjacency! That's all there is to it. **Lesson learned: Check if your frame-relay network supports broadcast or not. Configure EIGRP to use unicast or change your frame-relay configuration to support broadcast traffic.**

Excellent! You have now seen the most common errors that can cause EIGRP not to form an EIGRP neighbor adjacency. If you want to get some practice right now you might want to try this lab that teaches you how to solve all the different EIGRP neighbor adjacency issues:

http://gns3vault.com/Troubleshooting/eigrp-neighbor-troubleshooting.html

Now we can continue with troubleshooting route advertisements. Most of the time you are expecting to see a certain network in the routing table but it's not there. I'll show you a number of things that could go wrong with EIGRP and how to fix them, here are the most common errors:

- Someone configured a distribute-list so routing information is being filtered.
- Auto-summarization has been configured or someone created a manual summary.
- Split-horizon is preventing the advertisement of routing information.
- Redistribution has been configured but information from EIGRP is not being used.
- Redistribution has been configured but no EIGRP external routes are showing up.

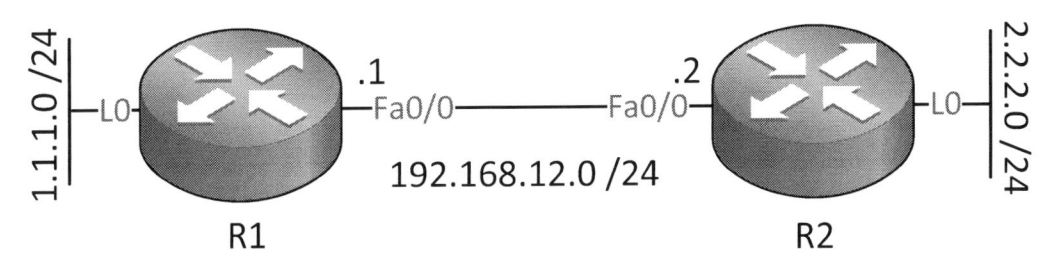

Let's start with a simple topology. R1 and R2 are running EIGRP and each router has a loopback interface. Here's the configuration of both routers:

```
R1(config)#router eigrp 12
R1(config-router)#no auto-summary
R1(config-router)#network 1.1.1.0 0.0.0.255
R1(config-router)#network 192.168.12.0 0.0.0.255
```

```
R2(config)#router eigrp 12
R2(config-router)#no auto-summary
R2(config-router)#network 2.2.2.0 0.0.0.255
R2(config-router)#network 192.168.12.0 0.0.0.255
```

Everything is working fine until a couple of weeks later one of the users is complaining that they are unable to reach the 2.2.2.0 /24 network from behind R1. You take a look at the routing table on R1 and this is what you see:

```
R1#show ip route

Gateway of last resort is not set

C    192.168.12.0/24 is directly connected, FastEthernet0/0
     1.0.0.0/24 is subnetted, 1 subnets
C       1.1.1.0 is directly connected, Loopback0
```

For some reason you don't see network 2.2.2.0 /24 in the routing table.

```
R1#show ip protocols | include filter
  Outgoing update filter list for all interfaces is not set
  Incoming update filter list for all interfaces is not set
```

I can see no distribute lists have been configured on R1.

```
R2#show ip route

Gateway of last resort is not set

C    192.168.12.0/24 is directly connected, FastEthernet0/0
     1.0.0.0/24 is subnetted, 1 subnets
D       1.1.1.0 [90/156160] via 192.168.12.1, 00:14:01, FastEthernet0/0
     2.0.0.0/24 is subnetted, 1 subnets
C       2.2.2.0 is directly connected, Loopback0
```

R2 does have network 1.1.1.0 /24 in its routing table. Let's do a quick debug to see what is going on.

```
R2#debug ip eigrp
IP-EIGRP Route Events debugging is on
IP-EIGRP(Default-IP-Routing-Table:12): 2.2.2.0/24 - denied by distribute list
```

A debug quickly shows us what is going on. It make tight a while before you see this message or you can reset the EIGRP neighbor adjacency to speed things up. As you can see network 2.2.2.0 /24 is being denied because of a distribute list.

```
R2#show ip protocols | include filter
  Outgoing update filter list for all interfaces is 1
  Incoming update filter list for all interfaces is not set
```

Another quick method of checking this is using the **show ip protocols** command.

```
R2#show run | section eigrp
router eigrp 12
 network 2.2.2.0 0.0.0.255
 network 192.168.12.0
 distribute-list 1 out
 no auto-summary
```

Using show run might have been quicker to spot the distribute-list in this case.

```
R2#show access-lists
Standard IP access list 1
    10 deny   2.2.2.0, wildcard bits 0.0.0.255 (5 matches)
    20 permit any (5 matches)
```

Here's the access-list causing us trouble.

```
R2(config)#router eigrp 12
R2(config-router)#no distribute-list 1 out
```

Let's get rid of the distribute-list.

```
R1#show ip route

Gateway of last resort is not set

C    192.168.12.0/24 is directly connected, FastEthernet0/0
     1.0.0.0/24 is subnetted, 1 subnets
C       1.1.1.0 is directly connected, Loopback0
     2.0.0.0/24 is subnetted, 1 subnets
D       2.2.2.0 [90/156160] via 192.168.12.2, 00:00:13,
FastEthernet0/0
```

Problem solved! **Lesson learned: If the network commands are correct, check if you have a distribute-list that is preventing prefixes from being advertised or installed in the routing table.**

Keep in mind distribute-lists can be configured **inbound** or **outbound** just like an access-list.

127

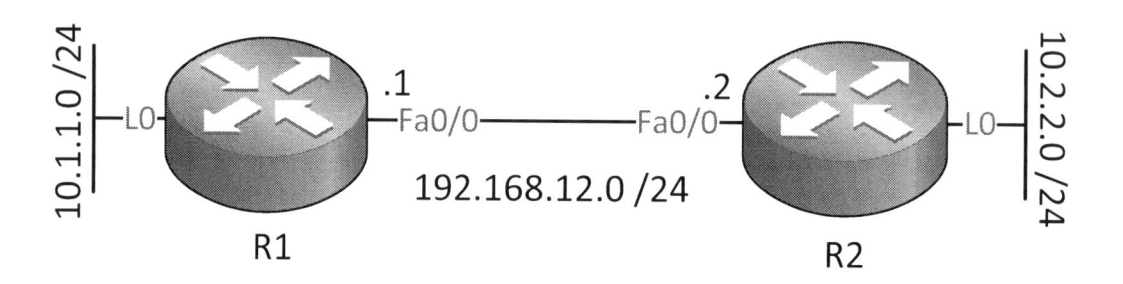

Onto the next scenario, same 2 routers but different networks on the loopbacks, here's the configuration:

```
R1(config)#router eigrp 12
R1(config-router)#network 192.168.12.0
R1(config-router)#network 10.0.0.0
```

```
R2(config)#router eigrp 12
R2(config-router)#network 192.168.12.0
R2(config-router)#network 10.0.0.0
```

It's a pretty basic configuration as you can see.

```
R1#show ip route

Gateway of last resort is not set

C       192.168.12.0/24 is directly connected, FastEthernet0/0
        10.0.0.0/8 is variably subnetted, 2 subnets, 2 masks
C          10.1.1.0/24 is directly connected, Loopback0
D          10.0.0.0/8 is a summary, 00:00:07, Null0
```

```
R2#show ip route

Gateway of last resort is not set

C       192.168.12.0/24 is directly connected, FastEthernet0/0
        10.0.0.0/8 is variably subnetted, 2 subnets, 2 masks
C          10.2.2.0/24 is directly connected, Loopback0
D          10.0.0.0/8 is a summary, 00:00:15, Null0
```

Looking at the routing tables, I don't see network 10.1.1.0 /24 or 10.2.2.0 /24. I do see an entry for the 10.0.0.0/8 network pointing to the null0 interface. This entry only shows up when summarization is configured and it's used to prevent routing loops.

```
R2#debug ip eigrp
IP-EIGRP Route Events debugging is on
```

Let's enable a debug and see what we can find.

```
R2#clear ip eigrp 12 neighbors
```

I'll do a reset of the EIGRP neighbor adjacency to speed things up, keep in mind this is probably not the best thing to do on a production network until you know what's wrong but it does help to speed things up.

```
R2#
IP-EIGRP(Default-IP-Routing-Table:12): 192.168.12.0/24 - do
advertise out FastEthernet0/0
IP-EIGRP(Default-IP-Routing-Table:12): 10.2.2.0/24 - don't
advertise out FastEthernet0/0
IP-EIGRP(Default-IP-Routing-Table:12): 10.0.0.0/8 - do advertise
out FastEthernet0/0
```

Here's our answer. The debug tells us that 10.2.2.0 /24 should not be advertised but 10.0.0.0 /8 has to be advertised (a summary). This can happen because of 2 reasons:

- Summarization was configured by someone.
- Auto-summary is enabled for EIGRP.

```
R1#show run | section eigrp
router eigrp 12
 network 10.0.0.0
 network 192.168.12.0
 auto-summary
```

```
R2#show run | section eigrp
router eigrp 12
 network 10.0.0.0
 network 192.168.12.0
 auto-summary
```

As you can see **auto-summary** is enabled for EIGRP. Depending on the IOS version this is enabled or disabled by default.

```
R1(config)#router eigrp 12
R1(config-router)#no auto-summary
```

```
R2(config)#router eigrp 12
R2(config-router)#no auto-summary
```

Disabling auto-summarization should do the trick.

```
R1#show ip route

C    192.168.12.0/24 is directly connected, FastEthernet0/0
```

```
         10.0.0.0/24 is subnetted, 2 subnets
D        10.2.2.0 [90/156160] via 192.168.12.2, 00:00:22,
FastEthernet0/0
C        10.1.1.0 is directly connected, Loopback0
```

```
R2#show ip route

C     192.168.12.0/24 is directly connected, FastEthernet0/0
      10.0.0.0/24 is subnetted, 2 subnets
C        10.2.2.0 is directly connected, Loopback0
D        10.1.1.0 [90/156160] via 192.168.12.1, 00:16:24,
FastEthernet0/0
```

Now we see both networks appearing in the routing table. **Lesson learned: If EIGRP auto-summary is enabled you might end up with discontigous networks.**

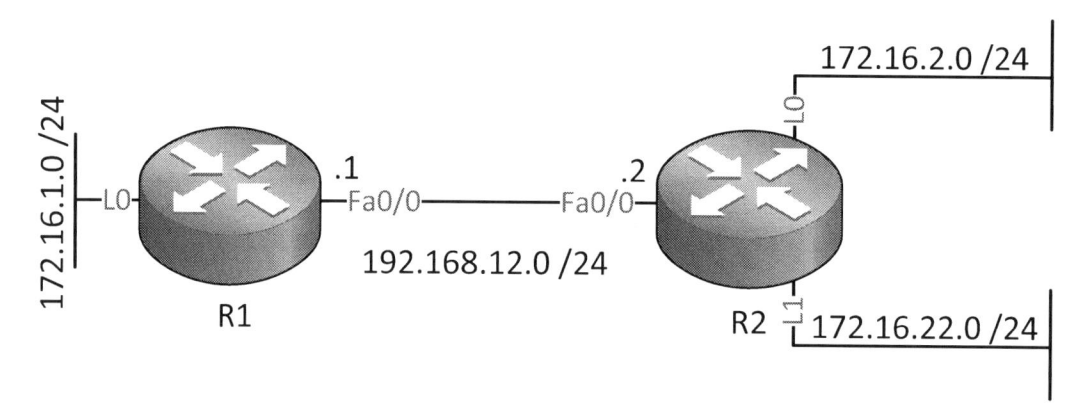

Let me show you another issue that can arise with summarization. In the example above we have 2 routers but different networks. R1 has network 172.16.1.0 /24 on a loopback interface and R2 has network 172.16.2.0 /24 and 172.16.22.0 /24 on its loopback interfaces. Let me show you the EIGRP configuration of both routers:

```
R1#
router eigrp 12
 network 172.16.1.0 0.0.0.255
 network 192.168.12.0
 auto-summary
```

```
R2#
router eigrp 12
 network 172.16.2.0 0.0.0.255
 network 172.16.22.0 0.0.0.255
 network 192.168.12.0
 no auto-summary
```

You can see that all networks are advertised. Note that R1 has auto-summary enabled and R2 has auto-summary disabled.

```
R2#
interface FastEthernet0/0
ip summary-address eigrp 12 172.16.0.0 255.255.0.0 5
```

Someone configured a summary on R2 and is sending it towards R1. The summary that was created is 172.16.0.0 /16.

```
R1#show ip route

C    192.168.12.0/24 is directly connected, FastEthernet0/0
     172.16.0.0/16 is variably subnetted, 2 subnets, 2 masks
D       172.16.0.0/16 is a summary, 00:30:07, Null0
C       172.16.1.0/24 is directly connected, Loopback0
```

However if I look at the routing table of R1 it doesn't show up. We do see an entry for the 172.16.0.0 /16 network but it's pointing to the null0 interface...not towards R2. What is going on here?

```
R2#debug ip eigrp
IP-EIGRP Route Events debugging is on
```

```
R2#clear ip eigrp 12 neighbors
```

Let's do a debug on R2 to see if the summary is being advertised. I'll do a clear ip eigrp neighbors too just to speed things up.

```
R2#
IP-EIGRP(Default-IP-Routing-Table:12): 192.168.12.0/24 - do
advertise out FastEthernet0/0
IP-EIGRP(Default-IP-Routing-Table:12): 172.16.2.0/24 - don't
advertise out FastEthernet0/0
IP-EIGRP(Default-IP-Routing-Table:12): 172.16.22.0/24 - don't
advertise out FastEthernet0/0
IP-EIGRP(Default-IP-Routing-Table:12): 172.16.0.0/16 - do
advertise out FastEthernet0/0
```

Looking at the debug we can see that R2 is working properly. It's advertising the 172.16.0.0 /16 summary route as it should. This means the problem has to be at R1.

```
R1#debug ip eigrp
IP-EIGRP Route Events debugging is on
```

Let's debug R1.

```
R1#
IP-EIGRP(Default-IP-Routing-Table:12): Processing incoming
UPDATE packet
IP-EIGRP(Default-IP-Routing-Table:12): Int 172.16.0.0/16 M
156160 - 25600 130560 SM 128256 - 256 128000
IP-EIGRP(Default-IP-Routing-Table:12): route installed for
172.16.0.0   (Summary)
IP-EIGRP(Default-IP-Routing-Table:12): 172.16.0.0/16 routing
table not updated thru 192.168.12.2
```

We can see that R1 receives the summary route from R2 but decides not to use it.

```
R1#show ip eigrp topology 172.16.0.0
IP-EIGRP (AS 12): Topology entry for 172.16.0.0/16
  State is Passive, Query origin flag is 1, 1 Successor(s), FD
is 128256
  Routing Descriptor Blocks:
  0.0.0.0 (Null0), from 0.0.0.0, Send flag is 0x0
      Composite metric is (128256/0), Route is Internal
      Vector metric:
        Minimum bandwidth is 10000000 Kbit
        Total delay is 5000 microseconds
        Reliability is 255/255
        Load is 1/255
        Minimum MTU is 1514
        Hop count is 0
  192.168.12.2 (FastEthernet0/0), from 192.168.12.2, Send flag
is 0x0
      Composite metric is (156160/128256), Route is Internal
      Vector metric:
        Minimum bandwidth is 100000 Kbit
        Total delay is 5100 microseconds
        Reliability is 255/255
        Load is 1/255
        Minimum MTU is 1500
        Hop count is 1
```

This is a good moment to check the EIGRP topology table. You can see that it does have the 172.16.0.0 /16 summary from R2 in its EIGRP topology table but R1 decides not to use it because the entry to the null0 interface is a better path.

```
R1(config)#router eigrp 12
R1(config-router)#no auto-summary
```

The solution is that we need to get rid of the null0 entry in the routing table. The only way to do this is by disabling auto summarization.

```
R1#show ip route

C      192.168.12.0/24 is directly connected, FastEthernet0/0
       172.16.0.0/16 is variably subnetted, 2 subnets, 2 masks
D         172.16.0.0/16 [90/156160] via 192.168.12.2, 00:00:51,
FastEthernet0/0
C         172.16.1.0/24 is directly connected, Loopback0
```

There we go. Disabling auto summarization removes the null0 entry and now the summary of R2 can be installed...problem solved! **Lesson learned: EIGRP auto-summary creates an entry to the null0 interface which might prevent the installation of summaries you receive from neighbor routers.**

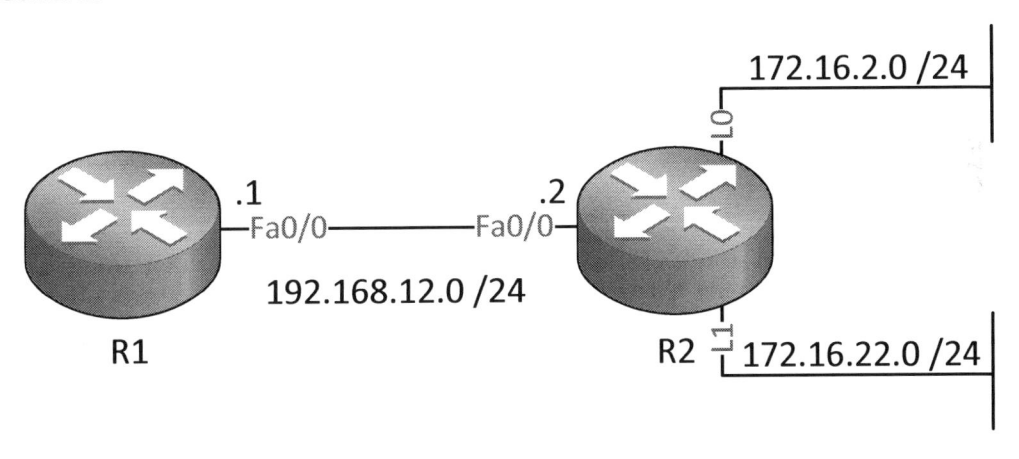

There is one more issue with summarization that I want to demonstrate. We are using the topology you see above and this is the EIGRP configuration of both routers.

```
R1#
router eigrp 12
 network 192.168.12.0
 no auto-summary
```

```
R2#
router eigrp 12
 network 172.16.2.0 0.0.0.255
 network 172.16.22.0 0.0.0.255
 network 192.168.12.0
 no auto-summary
```

All networks are advertised and auto summarization is disabled on both routers.

```
R2#
interface FastEthernet0/0
 ip summary-address eigrp 12 172.16.0.0 255.255.0.0 5
```

A summary has been configured on R2 and should be advertised towards R1.

```
R1#show ip route

C    192.168.12.0/24 is directly connected, FastEthernet0/0
```

Unfortunately I'm not seeing anything on R1. Let's check R2 to see what is wrong.

```
R2#debug ip eigrp
IP-EIGRP Route Events debugging is on

R2#clear ip eigrp 12 neighbors
```

When it comes to troubleshooting networking not Google but Debug and show commands are your friends.

```
R2#
IP-EIGRP(Default-IP-Routing-Table:12): 192.168.12.0/24 - do
advertise out FastEthernet0/0
```

Hmm this is the only network that R2 is advertising.

```
R2#show ip route

C    192.168.12.0/24 is directly connected, FastEthernet0/0
```

One of the **golden rules of routing**: You can't advertise what you don't have. Apparently R2 only knows about network 192.168.12.0 /24.

```
R2#show ip interface brief
Interface              IP-Address      OK? Method Status
Protocol
FastEthernet0/0        192.168.12.2    YES manual up
up
Loopback0              172.16.2.2      YES manual
administratively down down
Loopback1              172.16.22.22    YES manual
administratively down down
```

Uhoh...this looks like a Friday afternoon error! Someone left a shutdown command on the loopback interfaces.

```
R2(config)#interface loopback 0
R2(config-if)#no shutdown
R2(config)#interface loopback 1
R2(config-if)#no shutdown
```

Let's enable the interfaces.

```
R2#
IP-EIGRP(Default-IP-Routing-Table:12): 172.16.2.0/24 - don't
advertise out FastEthernet0/0
IP-EIGRP(Default-IP-Routing-Table:12): 172.16.22.0/24 - don't
advertise out FastEthernet0/0
IP-EIGRP(Default-IP-Routing-Table:12): 172.16.0.0/16 - do
advertise out FastEthernet0/0
```

Now we see that the summary is being advertised.

```
R1#show ip route | include 172.16.0.0
D    172.16.0.0/16 [90/156160] via 192.168.12.2, 00:09:39,
FastEthernet0/0
```

Now we see the summary in the routing table of R1, problem solved! **Lesson learned: You can't advertise wat you don't have in your routing table.**

> *The last problem might be simple but there's an important lesson you should not forget: In order for a summary route to be advertised at least one prefix that falls within the summary range has to be in the routing table of the advertising router!*

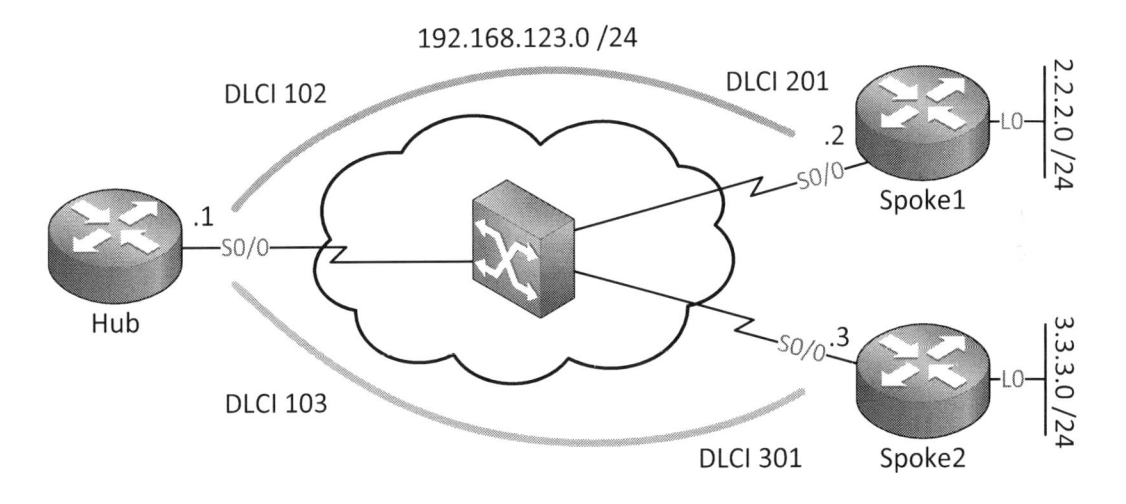

Let's take a look at another topology. In the picture above we have a frame-relay hub and spoke topology. Spoke1 and Spoke2 each have a loopback interface which we will advertise in EIGRP. Here's the relevant configuration of all routers:

```
Hub(config)#router eigrp 123
Hub(config-router)#no auto-summary
Hub(config-router)#network 192.168.123.0
```

```
Spoke1(config-if)#router eigrp 123
Spoke1(config-router)#no auto-summary
Spoke1(config-router)#network 192.168.123.0
Spoke1(config-router)#network 2.2.2.0 0.0.0.255
```

```
Spoke2(config)#router eigrp 123
Spoke2(config-router)#no auto-summary
Spoke2(config-router)#network 192.168.123.0
Spoke2(config-router)#network 3.3.3.0 0.0.0.255
```

As you can see all networks are advertised.

```
Hub#show ip route

C    192.168.123.0/24 is directly connected, Serial0/0
     2.0.0.0/24 is subnetted, 1 subnets
D       2.2.2.0 [90/2297856] via 192.168.123.2, 00:00:11, Serial0/0
     3.0.0.0/24 is subnetted, 1 subnets
D       3.3.3.0 [90/2297856] via 192.168.123.3, 00:00:03, Serial0/0
```

Our hub router sees the networks of the 2 spoke routers.

```
Spoke1#show ip route

C    192.168.123.0/24 is directly connected, Serial0/0
     2.0.0.0/24 is subnetted, 1 subnets
C       2.2.2.0 is directly connected, Loopback0
```

```
Spoke2#show ip route

C    192.168.123.0/24 is directly connected, Serial0/0
     3.0.0.0/24 is subnetted, 1 subnets
C       3.3.3.0 is directly connected, Loopback0
```

Unfortunately our spoke routers don't see anything…

```
Hub#debug ip eigrp
IP-EIGRP Route Events debugging is on
```

It seems the Hub router doesn't advertise the networks it learns from the spoke routers. Let's enable a debug to see what is going on.

```
Hub#clear ip eigrp 123 neighbors
```

I'll reset the EIGRP neighbor adjacencies to speed things up.

```
R1# processing incoming UPDATE packet
```

```
IP-EIGRP(Default-IP-Routing-Table:123): Processing incoming
UPDATE packet
IP-EIGRP(Default-IP-Routing-Table:123): Int 3.3.3.0/24 metric
2297856 - 1657856 640000
IP-EIGRP(Default-IP-Routing-Table:123): Processing incoming
UPDATE packet
IP-EIGRP(Default-IP-Routing-Table:123): Int 2.2.2.0/24 M 2297856
- 1657856 640000 SM 128256 - 256 128000
IP-EIGRP(Default-IP-Routing-Table:123): route installed for
2.2.2.0  ()
IP-EIGRP(Default-IP-Routing-Table:123): 192.168.123.0/24 - do
advertise out Serial0/0
```

In the debug we can see that our Hub router learns about network 2.2.2.0 /24 and 3.3.3.0 /24 but only advertises network 192.168.123.0 /24 to the spoke routers. **Split horizon** is preventing the advertisements from one spoke router to another. (If you learn something on an interface...don't advertise it out of the same interface again).

```
Hub(config)#interface serial 0/0
Hub(config-if)#no ip split-horizon eigrp 123
```

Let's disable split horizon on the serial interface of the Hub router.

```
Hub#
IP-EIGRP(Default-IP-Routing-Table:123): 192.168.123.0/24 - do
advertise out Serial0/0
IP-EIGRP(Default-IP-Routing-Table:123): 3.3.3.0/24 - do
advertise out Serial0/0
IP-EIGRP(Default-IP-Routing-Table:123): 2.2.2.0/24 - do
advertise out Serial0/0
```

Now we can see that the Hub router does advertise all networks.

```
Spoke1#show ip route

C    192.168.123.0/24 is directly connected, Serial0/0
     2.0.0.0/24 is subnetted, 1 subnets
C       2.2.2.0 is directly connected, Loopback0
     3.0.0.0/24 is subnetted, 1 subnets
D       3.3.3.0 [90/2809856] via 192.168.123.1, 00:16:02,
Serial0/0
```

```
Spoke2#show ip route

C    192.168.123.0/24 is directly connected, Serial0/0
     2.0.0.0/24 is subnetted, 1 subnets
D       2.2.2.0 [90/2809856] via 192.168.123.1, 00:16:33,
Serial0/0
     3.0.0.0/24 is subnetted, 1 subnets
```

```
C        3.3.3.0 is directly connected, Loopback0
```

The spoke routers can now learn about each other's networks since split horizon has been disabled. This is looking good but we are not done yet. Lesson learned: RIP and EIGRP are distance vector routing protocols and use split horizon. **Split horizon prevents the advertisement of a prefix out of the interface where we learned it on.**

```
Spoke1#ping 3.3.3.3

Type escape sequence to abort.
Sending 5, 100-byte ICMP Echos to 3.3.3.3, timeout is 2 seconds:
.....
Success rate is 0 percent (0/5)
```

```
Spoke2#ping 2.2.2.2

Type escape sequence to abort.
Sending 5, 100-byte ICMP Echos to 2.2.2.2, timeout is 2 seconds:
.....
Success rate is 0 percent (0/5)
```

Even though the networks show up in the routing tables I'm unable to ping from one spoke router to another. This is not an EIGRP problem but it's related to frame-relay....we still have to fix it.

When Spoke1 sends an IP packet to Spoke2 the IP packet looks like this:

Source: 192.168.123.2	Destination: 3.3.3.3

Let's think like a router for the moment and see what is happening here. First we need to check if Spoke1 knows where to send 3.3.3.3 to:

```
Spoke1#show ip route 3.3.3.3
Routing entry for 3.3.3.0/24
  Known via "eigrp 123", distance 90, metric 2809856, type internal
  Redistributing via eigrp 123
  Last update from 192.168.123.1 on Serial0/0, 00:38:10 ago
  Routing Descriptor Blocks:
  * 192.168.123.1, from 192.168.123.1, 00:38:10 ago, via Serial0/0
      Route metric is 2809856, traffic share count is 1
      Total delay is 45000 microseconds, minimum bandwidth is 1544 Kbit
      Reliability 255/255, minimum MTU 1500 bytes
```

```
        Loading 1/255, Hops 2
```

There's an entry for 3.3.3.3 and the next hop IP address is 192.168.123.1 (Hub router). Are we able to reach 192.168.123.1?

```
Spoke1#ping 192.168.123.1

Type escape sequence to abort.
Sending 5, 100-byte ICMP Echos to 192.168.123.1, timeout is 2
seconds:
!!!!!
Success rate is 100 percent (5/5), round-trip min/avg/max =
1/4/8 ms
```

No problem at all, it seems Spoke1 is able to forward packets meant for network 3.3.3.0 /24. Let's go to the Hub router.

```
Hub#ping 3.3.3.3

Type escape sequence to abort.
Sending 5, 100-byte ICMP Echos to 3.3.3.3, timeout is 2 seconds:
!!!!!
Success rate is 100 percent (5/5), round-trip min/avg/max =
4/4/4 ms
```

The Hub router has no issues sending traffic to network 3.3.3.0 /24 so at this moment we can draw the conclusion that the problem must be at router Spoke2.

Source: 192.168.123.2	Destination: 3.3.3.3

This is the IP packet that router Spoke2 receives, when it responds it will create a new IP packet that looks like this:

Source: 3.3.3.3	Destination: 192.168.123.2

Is spoke2 able to reach IP address 192.168.123.2? Time to find out!

```
Spoke2#ping 192.168.123.2

Type escape sequence to abort.
```

```
Sending 5, 100-byte ICMP Echos to 192.168.123.2, timeout is 2
seconds:
.....
Success rate is 0 percent (0/5)
```

Now we know the problem...Spoke2 is unable to reach IP address 192.168.123.2.

```
Spoke2#show ip route | include 192.168.123.0
C    192.168.123.0/24 is directly connected, Serial0/0
```

If we look at the routing table of Spoke2 we can see that network 192.168.123.0 /24 is directly connected. From a layer 3 perspective we don't have any issues. Time to move down the OSI model and check layer 2...or maybe in between layer 2 and 3.

```
Spoke2#show frame-relay map
Serial0/0 (up): ip 192.168.123.1 dlci 301(0x12D,0x48D0),
dynamic,
          broadcast,, status defined, active
```

Frame-relay uses Inverse ARP to bind layer 2 (DLCI) to layer 3 (IP address). You can see that there is no mapping for IP address 192.168.123.2.

```
Spoke2(config)#int s0/0
Spoke2(config-if)#frame-relay map ip 192.168.123.2 301
```

Let's add the frame-relay map ourselves.

```
Spoke2#show frame-relay map
Serial0/0 (up): ip 192.168.123.1 dlci 301(0x12D,0x48D0),
dynamic,
          broadcast,, status defined, active
Serial0/0 (up): ip 192.168.123.2 dlci 301(0x12D,0x48D0), static,
          CISCO, status defined, active
```

Now router Spoke2 knows how to reach router Spoke1.

```
Spoke1#ping 3.3.3.3

Type escape sequence to abort.
Sending 5, 100-byte ICMP Echos to 3.3.3.3, timeout is 2 seconds:
!!!!!
Success rate is 100 percent (5/5), round-trip min/avg/max =
8/10/16 ms
```

Finally router Spoke1 is able to ping router Spoke2's loopback interface. When we try to ping from router Spoke2 to router Spoke1's loopback interface we'll have the same issue so we'll add a frame-relay map statement there as well:

```
Spoke1(config)#int s0/0
Spoke1(config-if)#frame-relay map ip 192.168.123.3 201
```

```
Spoke1#show frame-relay map
Serial0/0 (up): ip 192.168.123.1 dlci 201(0xC9,0x3090), dynamic,
          broadcast,, status defined, active
Serial0/0 (up): ip 192.168.123.3 dlci 201(0xC9,0x3090), static,
          CISCO, status defined, active
```

Now we have an extra frame-relay mapping on router Spoke1.

```
Spoke2#ping 2.2.2.2

Type escape sequence to abort.
Sending 5, 100-byte ICMP Echos to 2.2.2.2, timeout is 2 seconds:
!!!!!
Success rate is 100 percent (5/5), round-trip min/avg/max =
8/8/8 ms
```

And our ping is successful! **Lesson learned: Make sure the next hop IP address is reachable and if needed add additional frame-relay map statements.**

We just got a little sidetracked from EIGRP to solving frame-relay problems but that's what network engineers do…sometimes troubleshooting is a deadly cocktail of multiple protocols. Another method of dealing with split-horizon is changing the point-to-multipoint configuration to a point-to-point configuration.

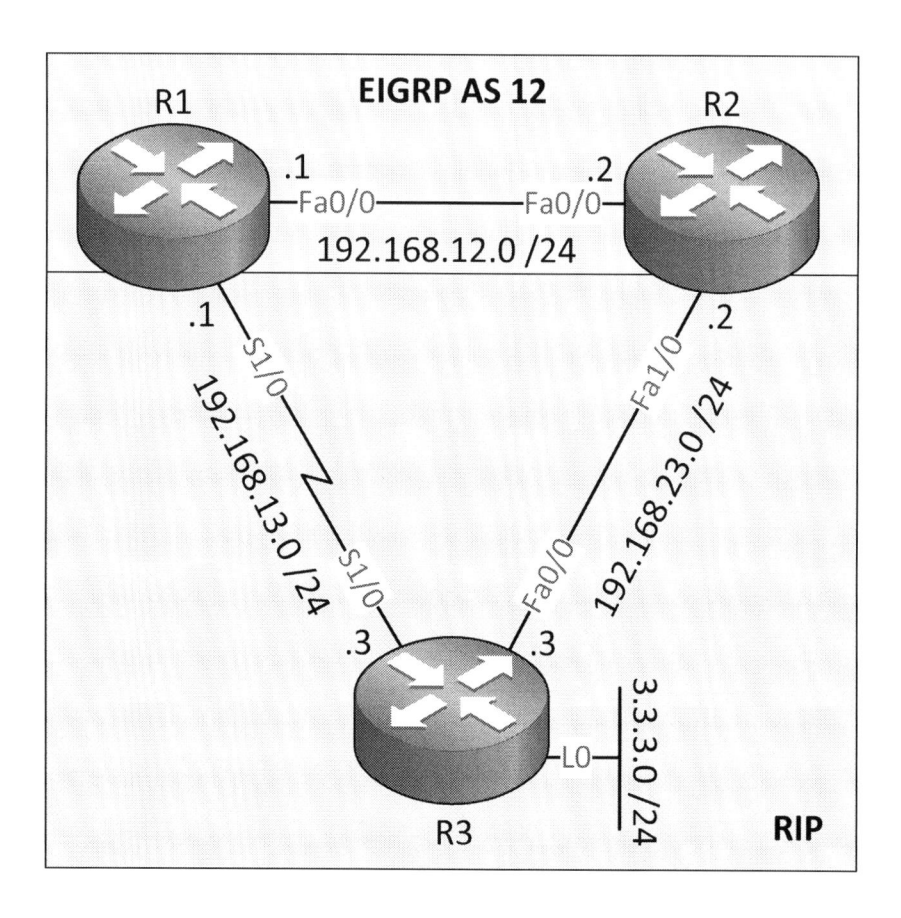

Here's a totally different scenario for you. In the picture above R1 and R2 are running EIGRP AS 12. All routers are running RIP. R3 has a loopback interface with network 3.3.3.0 /24 that will be advertised in RIP. R2 is going to redistribute this network into EIGRP AS 12.

Here are the EIGRP and RIP configurations of all routers:

```
R1#
router eigrp 12
 network 192.168.12.0
 no auto-summary
!
router rip
 version 2
 network 192.168.13.0
 no auto-summary
```

```
R2#
router eigrp 12
 redistribute rip metric 1 1 1 1 1500
 network 192.168.12.0
```

```
 no auto-summary
!
router rip
 version 2
 redistribute eigrp 12 metric 5
 network 192.168.23.0
 no auto-summary
```

```
R3#
 router rip
 version 2
 network 3.0.0.0
 network 192.168.13.0
 network 192.168.23.0
 no auto-summary
```

Note that R2 has been configured for redistribution between EIGRP AS 12 and RIP. How does this influence our routing selections?

```
R1#show ip route 3.3.3.0
Routing entry for 3.3.3.0/24
  Known via "rip", distance 120, metric 1
  Redistributing via rip
  Last update from 192.168.13.3 on Serial1/0, 00:00:06 ago
  Routing Descriptor Blocks:
  * 192.168.13.3, from 192.168.13.3, 00:00:06 ago, via Serial1/0
      Route metric is 1, traffic share count is 1
```

R1 is sending traffic towards network 3.3.3.0 /24 using the serial link between R1 and R3. It would have been better if we would use the link between R1 and R2 because using the FastEthernet links is faster than the serial link.

```
R1#show ip eigrp topology 3.3.3.0 255.255.255.0
IP-EIGRP (AS 12): Topology entry for 3.3.3.0/24
  State is Passive, Query origin flag is 1, 0 Successor(s), FD is 4294967295
  Routing Descriptor Blocks:
  192.168.12.2 (FastEthernet0/0), from 192.168.12.2, Send flag is 0x0
      Composite metric is (2560002816/2560000256), Route is External
```

We can look at the EIGRP topology table and see that R1 did learn about network 3.3.3.0 /24 through EIGRP from R2. So why are not we using this information instead of RIP?
The problem here is that EIGRP external routes has an AD (administrative distance) of 170 while RIP has an AD of 120.

```
R1(config)#router rip
R1(config-router)#distance 175 192.168.13.3 0.0.0.0
```

We can fix this problem by changing the AD. In the example above I'm setting the AD to 175 for all RIP routes that we learn from IP address 192.168.13.3 (R3).

```
R1#show ip route 3.3.3.0
Routing entry for 3.3.3.0/24
  Known via "eigrp 12", distance 170, metric 2560002816, type external
    Redistributing via eigrp 12
    Last update from 192.168.12.2 on FastEthernet0/0, 00:17:53 ago
```

```
R1#show ip route | include 3.3.3.0
D EX    3.3.3.0 [170/2560002816] via 192.168.12.2, 00:18:46, FastEthernet0/0
```

Since the AD of EIGRP external (170) is lower than the AD of my RIP routes (175) R1 will install the EIGRP external information. We are now using the FastEthernet links to get to network 3.3.3.0 /24...problem solved! **Lesson learned: Change the administrative distance to change traffic patterns but be aware; In more complex topologies this can also cause routing loops.**

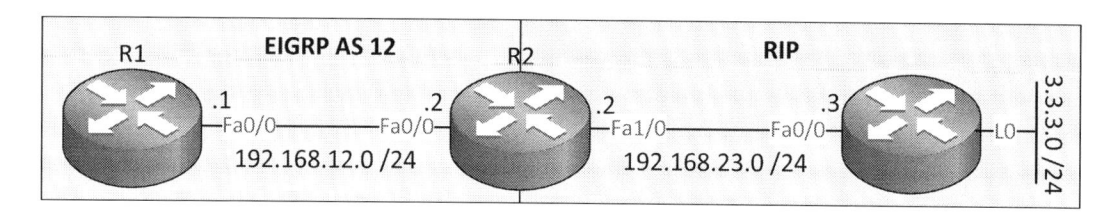

I have another redistribution situation for you. There are 3 routers and R2 is the router performing the redistribution between EIGRP AS 12 and RIP. Here are the configurations:

```
R1#
router eigrp 12
 network 192.168.12.0
 no auto-summary
```

```
R2#
router eigrp 12
 redistribute rip
 network 192.168.12.0
 no auto-summary
!
router rip
 version 2
 redistribute eigrp 12 metric 1
```

```
 network 192.168.23.0
 no auto-summary
```

```
router rip
 version 2
 network 3.0.0.0
 network 192.168.23.0
 no auto-summary
```

As you can see R1 is running EIGRP, R2 is running RIP and EIGRP and is doing redistribution, R3 is only running RIP.

```
R1#show ip route

C    192.168.12.0/24 is directly connected, FastEthernet0/0
```

However when I look at the routing table of R1 I'm expecting to see some redistributed routes. Unfortunately there's nothing here. What's going on?

```
R2#show ip route rip
     3.0.0.0/24 is subnetted, 1 subnets
R       3.3.3.0 [120/1] via 192.168.23.3, 00:00:23,
FastEthernet1/0
```

R2 is the router performing the redistribution and we can see that it has learned network 3.3.3.0 /24 through RIP. It should be redistributing this network into EIGRP.

```
R2#show ip eigrp topology 3.3.3.0 255.255.255.0
% IP-EIGRP (AS 12): Route not in topology table
```

Hmm network 3.3.3.0 /24 is not in the EIGRP topology table of R2 even though we configured redistribution, let's check the redistribution configuration:

```
R2#
router eigrp 12
 redistribute rip
 network 192.168.12.0
 no auto-summary
```

We do have the redistribute rip command but there's no **default seed metric**. If you don't specify a metric then the default seed metric will be **infinite**. In other words it's unreachable.

```
R2(config)#router eigrp 12
R2(config-router)#default-metric 1500 100 255 1 1500
```

Let's configure a default seed metric. You need to specify the bandwidth, delay, load and reliability yourself. I just used some random values.

```
R2#show ip eigrp topology 3.3.3.0 255.255.255.0
IP-EIGRP (AS 12): Topology entry for 3.3.3.0/24
  State is Passive, Query origin flag is 1, 1 Successor(s), FD
is 1732096
  Routing Descriptor Blocks:
  192.168.23.3, from Redistributed, Send flag is 0x0
      Composite metric is (1732096/0), Route is External
```

Now we see the 3.3.3.0 /24 network in the EIGRP topology table of R2.

```
R1#show ip route | include 3.3.3.0
D EX    3.3.3.0 [170/1734656] via 192.168.12.2, 00:04:08,
FastEthernet0/0
```

And as a result it can be advertised to R1…problem solved! **Lesson learned: When you redistribute something into EIGRP you need to configure seed metrics.**

This is the end of the EIGRP chapter! You now should have a better understanding about what could possibly go wrong with EIGRP and how to fix it. If you want to get some practice you can take a look at my all-in-one EIGRP troubleshooting lab. It's not easy (it's maybe even a bit above CCNP level) but it will be VERY helpful if you do it by yourself, you can find it here:

http://gns3vault.com/Troubleshooting/eigrp-troubleshooting.html

6. Troubleshooting OSPF

This chapter covers OSPF and all the different things that could possibly go wrong. OSPF is unlike EIGRP a link-state protocol but what they share in common is that both routing protocols establish a neighbor adjacency before exchanging routing information. In the case of OSPF we are exchanging LSA's (Link State Advertisement) in order to build the LSDB (Link State Database). The best information from the LSDB will be copied to the routing table.

In this chapter we'll start with troubleshooting the OSPF neighbor adjacency. Once we have a working OSPF neighbor adjacency we can look at other issues like missing routes.

```
R1#
%OSPF-5-ADJCHG: Process 1, Nbr 192.168.12.2 on FastEthernet0/0
from LOADING to FULL, Loading Done
```

```
R1#show ip ospf neighbor

Neighbor ID      Pri    State            Dead Time     Address
Interface
192.168.12.2      1     FULL/BDR         00:00:39      192.168.12.2
FastEthernet0/0
```

When looking at the OSPF neighbor adjacency this is what we are looking for. It should say **full**. Anything else and we know OSPF is busy getting to the full state or its hanging.

If the OSPF neighbor adjacency isn't full we are looking at one of the following states:

- There's no OSPF neighbor at all.
- It's stuck in ATTEMPT.
- It's stuck in INIT.
- It's stuck in 2-WAY.
- It's stuck in EXSTART/EXCHANGE.
- It's stuck in LOADING.

Let's get started and look at all the different things that could go wrong with the OSPF neighbor adjacency!

```
                    OSPF AREA 0
          .1                        .2
         —Fa0/0—————————Fa0/0—
              192.168.12.0 /24
         R1                              R2
```

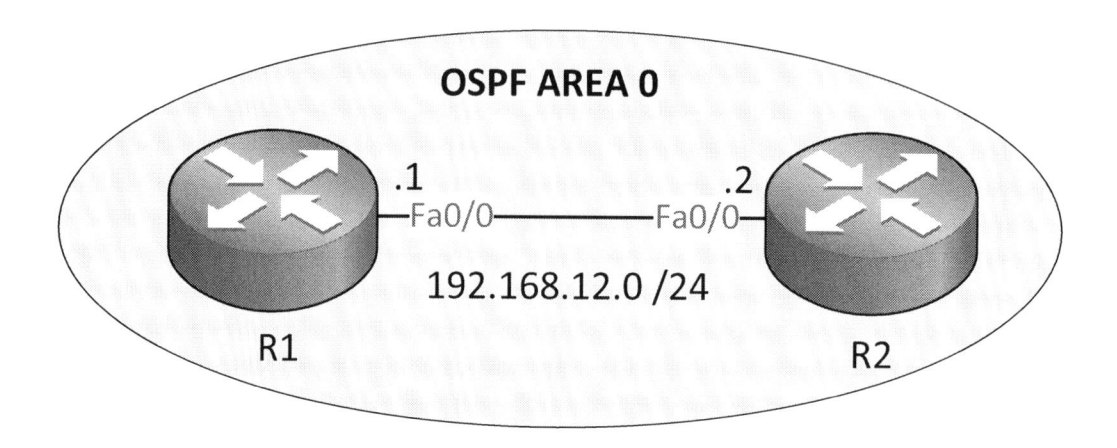

We'll start with some scenarios where OSPF doesn't have a neighbor at all. In the example above we have 2 routers.

```
R1#show ip ospf neighbor
R1#
```

As you can see we don't have any OSPF neighbors...so what could be wrong?

```
R1#show ip ospf interface fastEthernet 0/0
%OSPF: OSPF not enabled on FastEthernet0/0
```

```
R2#show ip ospf interface fastEthernet 0/0
FastEthernet0/0 is up, line protocol is up
  Internet Address 192.168.12.2/24, Area 0
  Process ID 1, Router ID 192.168.12.2, Network Type BROADCAST,
Cost: 1
```

I could just look at the running-configuration and see what's wrong but I want to show you some other useful OSPF commands. First I'll use the **show ip ospf interface** command. We can see the OSPF is not enabled on the FastEthernet 0/0 interface of R1 but it's running on R2.

```
R1#show run | section ospf
router ospf 1
 log-adjacency-changes
 network 192.168.21.0 0.0.0.255 area 0
```

Someone made a mistake with the network command and typed in the wrong network address...silly mistake but stuff like this happens.

```
R1(config)#router ospf 1
R1(config-router)#no network 192.168.21.0 0.0.0.255 area 0
```

```
R1(config-router)#network 192.168.12.0 0.0.0.255 area 0
```

Configuring the correct network address and wildcard should do the job.

```
R1#show ip ospf neighbor

Neighbor ID      Pri    State         Dead Time    Address
Interface
192.168.12.2      1     FULL/DR       00:00:31     192.168.12.2
FastEthernet0/0
```

Problem solved, we now have a working OSPF neighbor adjacency. This was an easy one to get you started...**Lesson learned: Make sure you have the configured the correct network address, wildcard bits and area.**

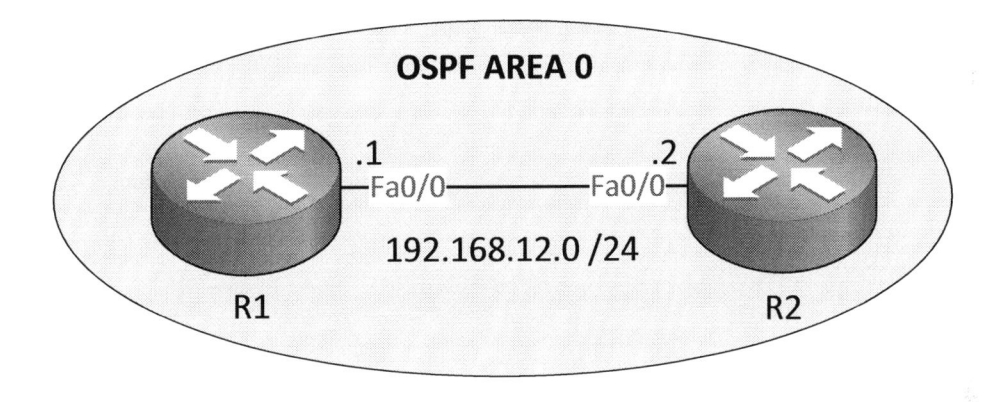

OSPF AREA 0

R1 —Fa0/0— .1 ———— .2 —Fa0/0— R2
192.168.12.0 /24

On to the next issue...same 2 routers but we have a different problem.

```
R1#show ip ospf neighbor

R1#
```

As you can see there is no OSPF neighbor.

```
R1#show ip ospf interface fastEthernet 0/0
FastEthernet0/0 is up, line protocol is up
  Internet Address 192.168.12.1/24, Area 0
  Process ID 1, Router ID 192.168.12.1, Network Type BROADCAST,
Cost: 1
  Transmit Delay is 1 sec, State WAITING, Priority 1
  No designated router on this network
  No backup designated router on this network
  Timer intervals configured, Hello 10, Dead 40, Wait 40,
Retransmit 5
    oob-resync timeout 40
  No Hellos (Passive interface)
```

```
R2#show ip ospf interface fastEthernet 0/0
FastEthernet0/0 is up, line protocol is up
  Internet Address 192.168.12.2/24, Area 0
  Process ID 1, Router ID 192.168.12.2, Network Type BROADCAST,
Cost: 1
  Transmit Delay is 1 sec, State DR, Priority 1
  Designated Router (ID) 192.168.12.2, Interface address
192.168.12.2
  No backup designated router on this network
  Timer intervals configured, Hello 10, Dead 40, Wait 40,
Retransmit 5
    oob-resync timeout 40
    Hello due in 00:00:01
```

OSPF has been enabled on the interface of both routers so we know that the correct network type was used. However if you look closely at R1 you can see that it says **"No Hellos (Passive Interface)"**. If you configure passive interface then the network on the interface will still be advertised but it won't send any OSPF hello packets. This way it's impossible to form an OSPF neighbor adjacency.

```
R1#show run | section ospf
router ospf 1
 log-adjacency-changes
 passive-interface FastEthernet0/0
 network 192.168.12.0 0.0.0.255 area 0
```

There's our problem.

```
R1(config)#router ospf 1
R1(config-router)#no passive-interface fastEthernet 0/0
```

Let's get rid of the passive interface.

```
R1#show ip ospf neighbor

Neighbor ID      Pri   State        Dead Time    Address
Interface
192.168.12.2      1    FULL/DR      00:00:31     192.168.12.2
FastEthernet0/0
```

Now we have a working OSPF neighbor adjacency...problem solved! **Lesson learned: Make sure OSPF is sending hello packets on an interface because otherwise you won't be able to become neighbors.**

OSPF AREA 0

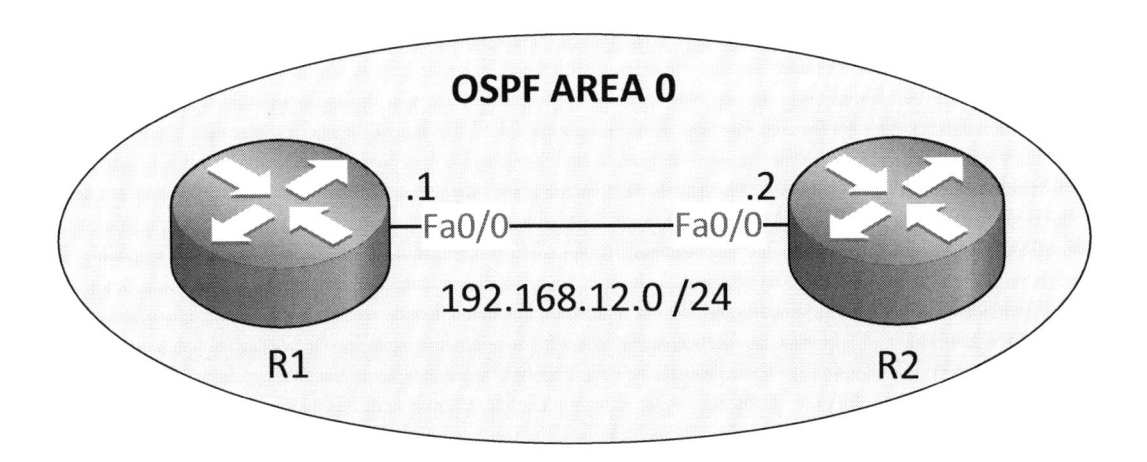

R1 .1 —Fa0/0———Fa0/0— .2 R2
192.168.12.0 /24

Next scenario...same routers, different problem.

```
R1#show ip ospf neighbor

Neighbor ID     Pri   State           Dead Time   Address
Interface
192.168.12.2    1     INIT/DROTHER    00:00:31    192.168.12.2
FastEthernet0/0
```

```
R2#show ip ospf neighbor

R2#
```

Interesting...R1 is showing our OSPF neighbor to be in the INIT state while R2 is showing nothing.

```
R1#show ip ospf interface fastEthernet 0/0
FastEthernet0/0 is up, line protocol is up
  Internet Address 192.168.12.1/24, Area 0
  Process ID 1, Router ID 192.168.12.1, Network Type BROADCAST,
Cost: 1
```

```
R2#show ip ospf interface fastEthernet 0/0
FastEthernet0/0 is up, line protocol is up
  Internet Address 192.168.12.2/24, Area 0
  Process ID 1, Router ID 192.168.12.2, Network Type BROADCAST,
Cost: 1
```

OSPF has been configured properly on both interfaces as we can see in the example above.

Since R1 is showing the INIT state we can draw the conclusion that it's receiving something from R2. R2 isn't showing anything so it's probably not receiving anything from R1. OSPF uses **hello** packets to establish the OSPF neighbor adjacency and these are sent using the **224.0.0.5** multicast address.

```
R1#ping 224.0.0.5

Type escape sequence to abort.
Sending 1, 100-byte ICMP Echos to 224.0.0.5, timeout is 2
seconds:
.
```

```
R2#ping 224.0.0.5

Type escape sequence to abort.
Sending 1, 100-byte ICMP Echos to 224.0.0.5, timeout is 2
seconds:
.
```

It's a good idea to check if we can ping the multicast address that OSPF uses for the hello packets. We can see the R1 and R2 both don't receive a response.

```
R1#ping 192.168.12.2

Type escape sequence to abort.
Sending 5, 100-byte ICMP Echos to 192.168.12.2, timeout is 2
seconds:
!!!!!
Success rate is 100 percent (5/5), round-trip min/avg/max =
4/5/8 ms
```

```
R2#ping 192.168.12.1

Type escape sequence to abort.
Sending 5, 100-byte ICMP Echos to 192.168.12.1, timeout is 2
seconds:
!!!!!
Success rate is 100 percent (5/5), round-trip min/avg/max =
4/4/8 ms
```

Pinging the IP addresses of each other is no problem however. So what could cause an issue with sending and receiving OSPF multicast traffic? How about an access-list?

```
R1#show ip interface fastEthernet 0/0 | include access list
  Outgoing access list is not set
  Inbound  access list is not set
```

```
R2#show ip interface fastEthernet 0/0 | include access list
  Outgoing access list is not set
  Inbound  access list is BLOCKSTUFF
```

We are onto something. R2 has an inbound access-list called BLOCKSTUFF.

```
R2#show access-lists
Extended IP access list BLOCKSTUFF
    10 permit tcp any any
    20 permit udp any any
    30 permit icmp any any (45 matches)
```

The access-list is only permitting TCP, UDP and ICMP traffic. OSPF doesn't use TCP or UDP and it's being dropped by this access-list because of the **implicit deny any.** You don't see it but there's always a deny any at the bottom of an access-list.

```
R2(config)#ip access-list extended BLOCKSTUFF
R2(config-ext-nacl)#5 permit ospf any any
```

```
R2#show access-lists
Extended IP access list BLOCKSTUFF
    5 permit ospf any any (12 matches)
    10 permit tcp any any
    20 permit udp any any
    30 permit icmp any any (45 matches)
```

Let's edit the access-list so OSPF traffic is allowed. You can see it's matching traffic.

```
R1#show ip ospf neighbor

Neighbor ID     Pri   State         Dead Time    Address
Interface
192.168.12.2    1     FULL/DR       00:00:37     192.168.12.2
FastEthernet0/0
```

Problem solved, it's now showing FULL.

```
R1#ping 224.0.0.5

Type escape sequence to abort.
Sending 1, 100-byte ICMP Echos to 224.0.0.5, timeout is 2
seconds:

Reply to request 0 from 192.168.12.2, 16 ms
```

```
R2#ping 224.0.0.5

Type escape sequence to abort.
Sending 1, 100-byte ICMP Echos to 224.0.0.5, timeout is 2
seconds:

Reply to request 0 from 192.168.12.1, 4 ms
```

In case you were wondering, it's now possible to ping to the 224.0.0.5 OSPF multicast address. You'll see the reply from the other side. **Lesson learned: Don't block OSPF multicast addresses 224.0.0.5 and 224.0.0.6 (DR/BDR).**

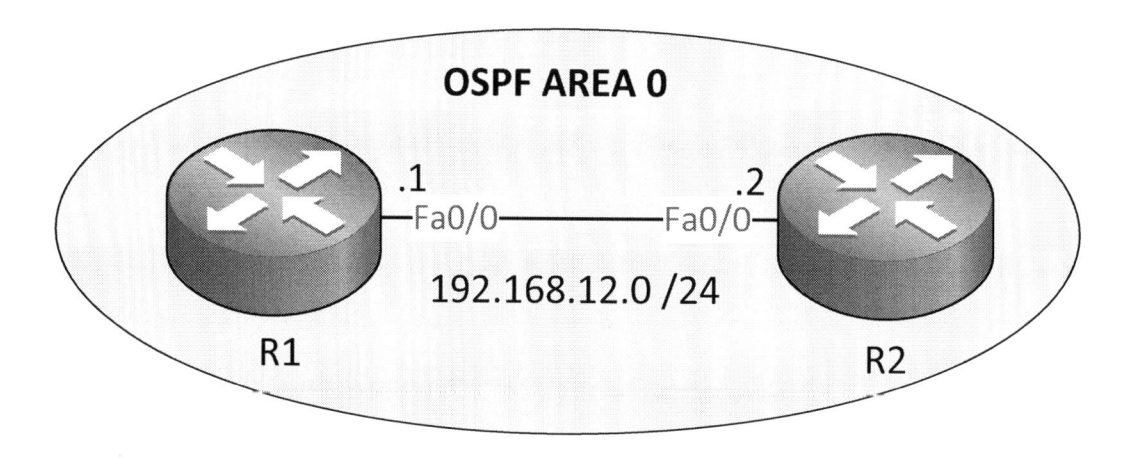

There's more to explore! Same scenario different issue:

```
R1#show ip ospf neighbor
```

```
R2#show ip ospf neighbor
```

```
R1#show ip ospf interface fastEthernet 0/0
FastEthernet0/0 is up, line protocol is up
  Internet Address 192.168.12.1/24, Area 0
  Process ID 1, Router ID 192.168.12.1, Network Type BROADCAST,
Cost: 1
```

```
R2#show ip ospf interface fastEthernet 0/0
FastEthernet0/0 is up, line protocol is up
  Internet Address 192.168.12.2/25, Area 0
  Process ID 1, Router ID 192.168.12.2, Network Type BROADCAST,
Cost: 1
```

There are no OSPF neighbors but we do see that OSPF has been enabled on the interface.

```
R1#ping 224.0.0.5

Type escape sequence to abort.
Sending 1, 100-byte ICMP Echos to 224.0.0.5, timeout is 2
seconds:

Reply to request 0 from 192.168.12.2, 16 ms
```

```
R2#ping 224.0.0.5

Type escape sequence to abort.
Sending 1, 100-byte ICMP Echos to 224.0.0.5, timeout is 2
seconds:

Reply to request 0 from 192.168.12.1, 4 ms
```

I can ping the multicast addresses so that's fine too.

This might be a good moment to enable a debug to see what is going on:

```
R1#debug ip ospf hello
OSPF hello events debugging is on
```

This is a very useful debug to see what is going on behind the scenes.

```
R1#clear ip ospf process
Reset ALL OSPF processes? [no]: yes
```

I'll reset the OSPF process to speed things up. Keep in mind you can also reset just 1 OSPF neighbor which is a better idea if this was a production network.

```
R1#
OSPF: Mismatched hello parameters from 192.168.12.2
OSPF: Dead R 40 C 40, Hello R 10 C 10  Mask R 255.255.255.128 C
255.255.255.0
```

Now we have something to work with. R1 says it received a hello packet but we have **mismatched hello parameters.** The **R** stands for what we **received** and the **C** stands for what we have **configured**.

You can see that there is a mismatch in the subnet mask. R1 is configured with subnet mask 255.255.255.0 while R2 has subnet mask 255.255.255.128. OSPF will only compare the subnet mask when you are using the **broadcast** network type.

```
R1#show ip ospf interface fastEthernet 0/0
FastEthernet0/0 is up, line protocol is up
  Internet Address 192.168.12.1/24, Area 0
  Process ID 1, Router ID 192.168.12.1, Network Type BROADCAST,
Cost: 1
```

```
R2#show ip ospf interface fastEthernet 0/0
FastEthernet0/0 is up, line protocol is up
  Internet Address 192.168.12.2/25, Area 0
  Process ID 1, Router ID 192.168.12.2, Network Type BROADCAST,
Cost: 1
```

I can use the show ip ospf interface command to check the network type, you can see it's broadcast.

```
R1#show run interface fastEthernet 0/0
Building configuration...

Current configuration : 97 bytes
!
interface FastEthernet0/0
 ip address 192.168.12.1 255.255.255.0
 duplex auto
 speed auto
```

```
R2#show run interface fastEthernet 0/0
Building configuration...

Current configuration : 130 bytes
!
interface FastEthernet0/0
 ip address 192.168.12.2 255.255.255.128
 duplex auto
 speed auto
```

Here you can see that R2 has a different subnet mask, let's fix it!

```
R2(config)#interface fastEthernet 0/0
R2(config-if)#ip address 192.168.12.2 255.255.255.0
```

Easy enough...

```
R1#
%OSPF-5-ADJCHG: Process 1, Nbr 192.168.12.2 on FastEthernet0/0
from LOADING to FULL, Loading Done
```

```
R2#
%OSPF-5-ADJCHG: Process 1, Nbr 192.168.12.1 on FastEthernet0/0
from LOADING to FULL, Loading Done
```

And as you can see we now have a working OSPF neighbor adjacency ☺
Lesson learned: Make sure you use the same subnet mask on routers that are directly connected to each other.

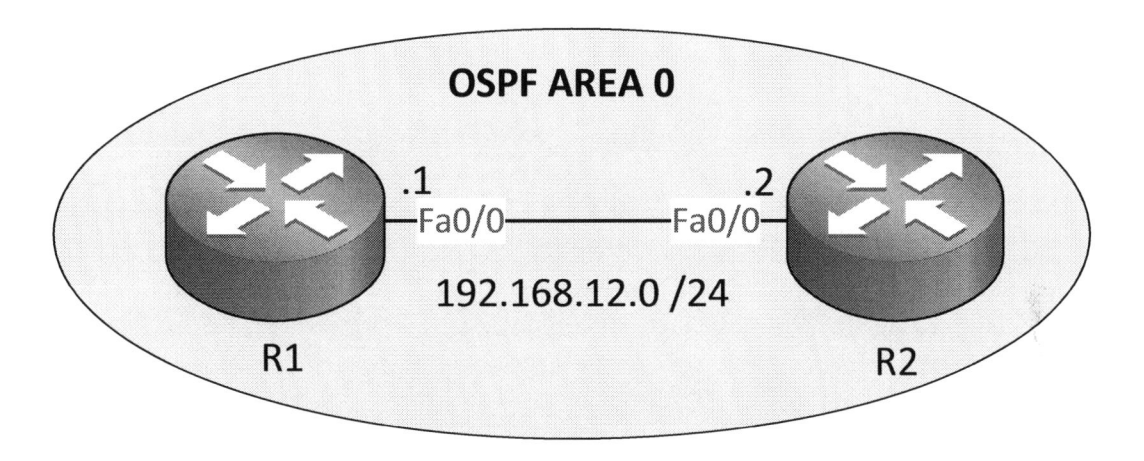

OSPF AREA 0

R1 .1 Fa0/0 ———— Fa0/0 .2 R2
192.168.12.0 /24

Let's continue with the next error. Same topology and I'm having another issue with the hello packets. I'm going to jump straight to the debug portion:

```
R1#debug ip ospf hello
OSPF hello events debugging is on
R1#
OSPF: Send hello to 224.0.0.5 area 0 on FastEthernet0/0 from
192.168.12.1
OSPF: Rcv hello from 192.168.12.2 area 0 from FastEthernet0/0
192.168.12.2
OSPF: Mismatched hello parameters from 192.168.12.2
OSPF: Dead R 11 C 24, Hello R 10 C 6   Mask R 255.255.255.0 C
255.255.255.0
```

This issue is similar to the last scenario. There are a number of things that have to match in the hello packet in order to become OSPF neighbors. The **dead interval** on R1 is configured for 24 seconds and on R2 for 11 seconds. The **hello interval** is configured for 10 seconds on R2 and 6 seconds on R1. Let's make sure these are the same:

```
R1(config)#interface fastEthernet 0/0
R1(config-if)#ip ospf hello-interval 10
R1(config-if)#ip ospf dead-interval 11
```

We need to change it on the interface level.

```
R1#show ip ospf neighbor

Neighbor ID     Pri   State         Dead Time   Address
Interface
192.168.12.2     1    FULL/DR       00:00:04    192.168.12.2
FastEthernet0/0
```

This fixes our problem; we now have a working OSPF neighbor adjacency.

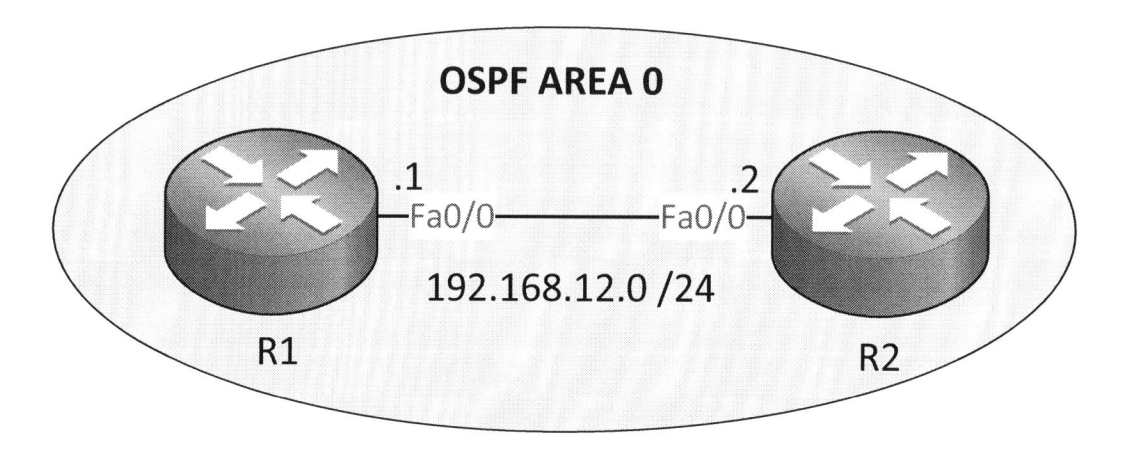

OSPF AREA 0

R1 —.1 Fa0/0————Fa0/0 .2— R2
192.168.12.0 /24

Another issue we might have to deal with is authentication. OSPF offers 3 methods for authentication:

- No authentication
- Plaintext
- MD5 authentication

```
R1#show ip ospf neighbor
```

```
R2#show ip ospf neighbor
```

You can see that we don't have any OSPF neighbors. I'm going to jump straight into the debug:

```
R1#debug ip ospf adj
OSPF adjacency events debugging is on
OSPF: Rcv pkt from 192.168.12.2, FastEthernet0/0 : Mismatch
Authentication type. Input packet specified type 2, we use type
0
```

Debug ip ospf adj will help me solve this issue. It says we are receiving a packet with type 2 authentication while we use type 0. This is what it means:

- **Type 0**: no authentication.
- **Type 1**: plaintext authentication.
- **Type 2**: MD5 authentication.

This means R1 is configured for no authentication while R2 is using MD5 authentication.

```
R2#show ip ospf interface fastEthernet 0/0 | include authentication
  Message digest authentication enabled
```

We can also look at the OSPF information per interface to see if authentication is enabled or not.

```
R2#show run interface fastEthernet 0/0 | include ospf
 ip ospf authentication message-digest
 ip ospf message-digest-key 1 md5 MYKEY
```

This is what R2 has configured on the interface.

```
R1(config)#interface FastEthernet0/0
R1(config-if)#ip ospf authentication message-digest
R1(config-if)#ip ospf message-digest-key 1 md5 MYKEY
```

We'll copy and paste it to R1.

```
R1#show ip ospf neighbor

Neighbor ID Pri   State         Dead Time   Address        Interface
192.168.12.2  1   FULL/DR       00:00:34    192.168.12.2   FastEthernet0/0
```

Problem solved!

In case you are wondering...this is what you will see if you have the wrong password on one of your routers:

```
R1(config)#interface FastEthernet0/0
R1(config-if)#no ip ospf message-digest-key 1 md5 MYKEY
R1(config-if)#ip ospf message-digest-key 1 md5 WRONGKEY
```

First we'll swap the key.

```
R1#debug ip ospf adj
OSPF adjacency events debugging is on
OSPF: Rcv pkt from 192.168.12.2, FastEthernet0/0 : Mismatch
Authentication Key - Message Digest Key 1
```

161

Our debug is nice enough to tell us we are using the wrong key between our routers.

Lesson learned: Make sure you use the same OSPF authentication type and password between routers.

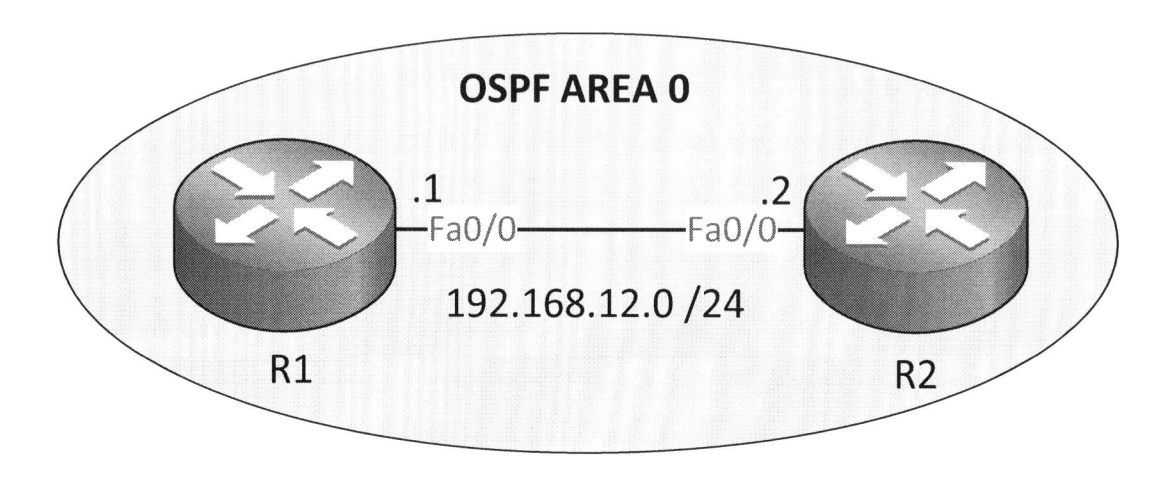

```
                    OSPF AREA 0
        .1                          .2
      —Fa0/0——————————Fa0/0—
   R1    192.168.12.0 /24        R2
```

What else could go wrong? Seems like there's no end to OSPF neighbor adjacency-related issues! Same scenario...different problem:

```
R1#show ip ospf neighbor
```

```
R2#show ip ospf neighbor
```

I'm not seeing any OSPF neighbors.

```
R1# %OSPF-4-ERRRCV: Received invalid packet: mismatch area ID,
from backbone area must be virtual-link but not found from
192.168.12.2, FastEthernet0/0
```

I'm seeing this message on one of my routers however. The message is self-explanatory, seems we have a mismatch in the area number.

```
R1#show ip ospf interface fastEthernet 0/0 | include Area
   Internet Address 192.168.12.1/24, Area 1
```

```
R2#show ip ospf interface fastEthernet 0/0 | include Area
   Internet Address 192.168.12.2/24, Area 0
```

R1 is configured for area 1 while R2 is configured for area 0. Time to fix this!

```
R1#show run | section ospf
```

```
router ospf 1
 log-adjacency-changes
 network 192.168.12.0 0.0.0.255 area 1
```

```
R1(config)#router ospf 1
R1(config-router)#no network 192.168.12.0 0.0.0.255 area 1
R1(config-router)#network 192.168.12.0 0.0.0.255 area 0
```

We'll change the network command so we are using the correct area number.

```
R1#show ip ospf neighbor

Neighbor ID Pri   State           Dead Time   Address
Interface
192.168.12.2  1   FULL/DR         00:00:31    192.168.12.2
FastEthernet0/0
```

Problem solved! **Lesson learned: Make sure your OSPF routers agree on the same area number.**

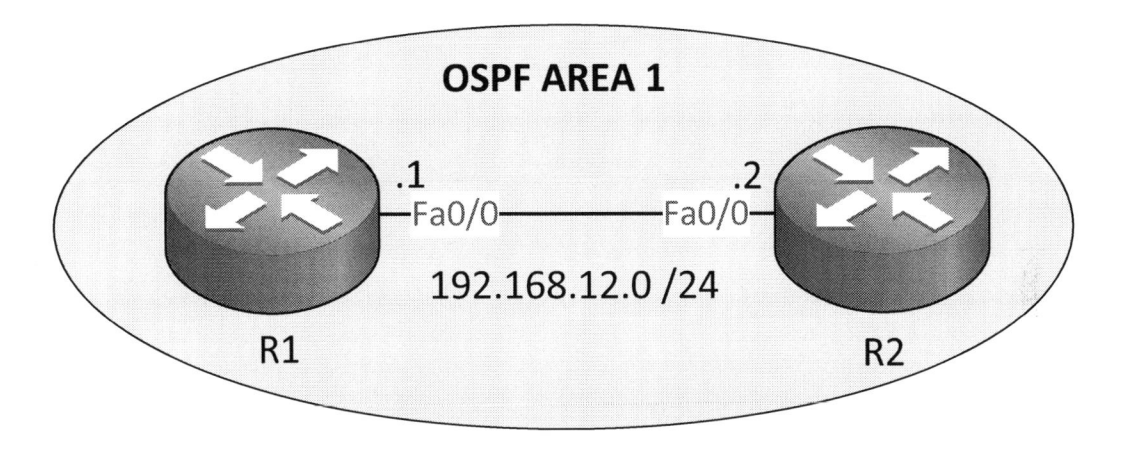

The picture above is slightly different compared to what you have seen before. This time R1 and R2 are in area 1.

```
R1#show ip ospf neighbor
```

```
R2#show ip ospf neighbor
```

What a surprise...no neighbors! Let's dive into the debug:

```
R1#debug ip ospf hello
OSPF hello events debugging is on
```

163

```
OSPF: Rcv hello from 192.168.12.2 area 1 from FastEthernet0/0
192.168.12.2
OSPF: Hello from 192.168.12.2 with mismatched Stub/Transit area
option bits
```

Hmm interesting. There is a mismatch in the **stub/transit area option**. OSPF has different area types and both routes have to agree on the area type (stub, nssa, totally stub and totally nssa).

```
R1#show ip protocols | include area
  Number of areas in this router is 1. 1 normal 0 stub 0 nssa
    192.168.12.0 0.0.0.255 area 1
```

R1 seems to be configured to use a normal area.

```
R2#show ip protocols | include area
  Number of areas in this router is 1. 0 normal 1 stub 0 nssa
    192.168.12.0 0.0.0.255 area 1
```

R2 seems to be configured to use a stub area. A mismatch in the area type means we can't establish an OSPF neighbor adjacency.

```
R2#show running-config | section ospf
router ospf 1
 log-adjacency-changes
 area 1 stub
 network 192.168.12.0 0.0.0.255 area 1
 permit ospf any any
```

Here you can see that R2 has the **area 1 stub** command, let's get rid of it.

```
R2(config)#router ospf 1
R2(config-router)#no area 1 stub
```

We'll change area 1 into a normal area for R2.

```
R1# %OSPF-5-ADJCHG: Process 1, Nbr 192.168.12.2 on
FastEthernet0/0 from LOADING to FULL, Loading Done
```

```
R2# %OSPF-5-ADJCHG: Process 1, Nbr 192.168.12.1 on
FastEthernet0/0 from LOADING to FULL, Loading Done
```

R1 and R2 live happily ever after...**Lesson learned: Make sure your OSPF routers use the same area type.**

How to Master CCNP TSHOOT

💡 *Most people have learned that OSPF always requires at least area 0 (the backbone area). It's perfectly fine to configure single area OSPF and to use a different area number. Only when you connect different OSPF areas to each other you'll need a backbone area.*

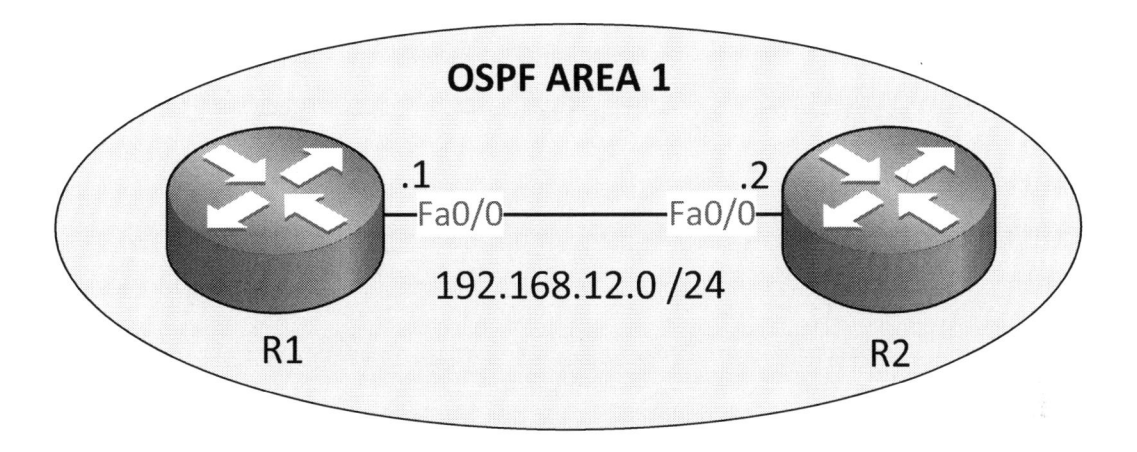

OSPF AREA 1

R1 .1 —Fa0/0———Fa0/0— .2 R2
192.168.12.0 /24

Here's another interesting scenario to look at that might be confusing at first. I'll show you the OSPF configuration of both routers:

```
R1#show run | section router ospf
router ospf 1
 log-adjacency-changes
 network 192.168.12.0 0.0.0.255 area 0
```

```
R2#show run | section router ospf
router ospf 1
 log-adjacency-changes
 network 192.168.12.0 0.0.0.255 area 0
```

As you can see it's a simple configuration.

```
R1#show ip ospf neighbor

Neighbor ID     Pri   State           Dead Time   Address         Interface
192.168.12.2     0    2WAY/DROTHER    00:00:36    192.168.12.2    FastEthernet0/0
```

```
R2#show ip ospf neighbor

Neighbor ID     Pri   State           Dead Time   Address         Interface
192.168.12.1     0    2WAY/DROTHER    00:00:30    192.168.12.1    FastEthernet0/0
```

165

We don't have a blank OSPF neighbor table but we do see that both routers are stuck in the 2WAY state. Besides focusing your eyes looking for the word "FULL" there are 2 things you should look at in this show command:

- Both routers show each other as **DROTHER**.
- The **priority** for both routers is 0.

On a multi-access network like Ethernet OSPF will do a DR/BDR election if the network type is **broadcast** or **non-broadcast**.

Let's verify the network type:

```
R1#show ip ospf interface | include Network Type
  Process ID 1, Router ID 192.168.12.1, Network Type BROADCAST,
Cost: 1
```

```
R2#show ip ospf interface | include Network Type
  Process ID 1, Router ID 192.168.12.2, Network Type BROADCAST,
Cost: 1
```

Both interfaces are configured for the broadcast network type. This is the default for Ethernet interfaces. This means we have a DR/BDR election but both routers are configured for priority 0 which means they won't participate in the DR/BDR election. This is the reason they are stuck in the 2WAY state. Let's fix it:

```
R1(config)#interface fastEthernet 0/0
R1(config-if)#ip ospf priority 1
```

I'll change the priority on one of the routers.

```
R1#show ip ospf neighbor

Neighbor ID   Pri   State         Dead Time   Address
Interface
192.168.12.2  0     FULL/DROTHER  00:00:38    192.168.12.2
FastEthernet0/0
```

```
R2#show ip ospf neighbor

Neighbor ID   Pri   State         Dead Time   Address
Interface
192.168.12.1  1     FULL/DR       00:00:37    192.168.12.1
FastEthernet0/0
```

Now we have a working OSPF neighbor adjacency. You can see R1 has been elected for the DR because it has a priority of 1. **Lesson learned: The broadcast and non-broadcast network types require a DR/BDR election. Make sure one of the routers gets elected.**

How to Master CCNP TSHOOT

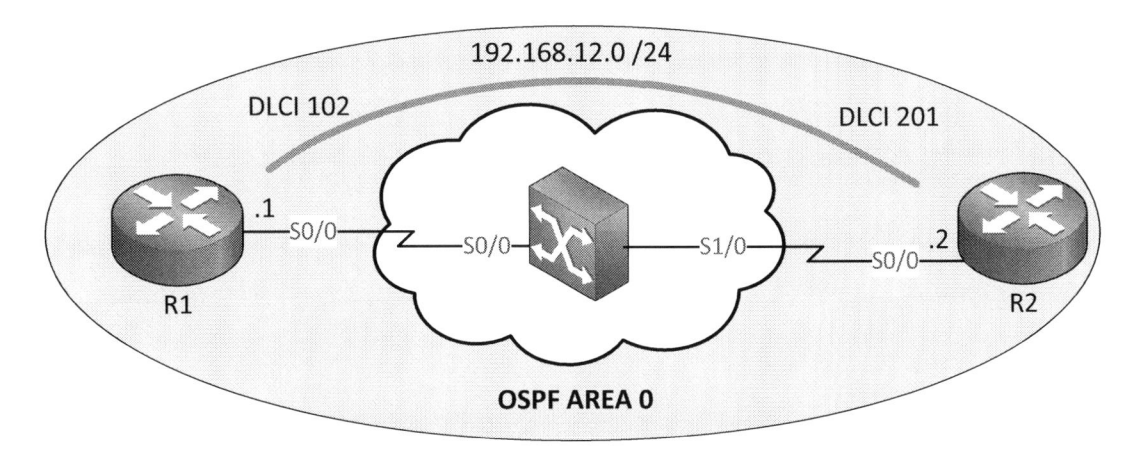

Here's a different scenario for us to troubleshoot. We have 2 routers connected to each other running frame-relay. For some reason OSPF isn't establishing the neighbor adjacency. Here's the relevant OSPF configuration:

```
R1#show run | section ospf
router ospf 1
 log-adjacency-changes
 network 192.168.12.0 0.0.0.255 area 0
R2#show run | section ospf
router ospf 1
 log-adjacency-changes
 network 192.168.12.0 0.0.0.255 area 0
```

It's just a basic OSPF configuration and you can see that the network command looks fine.

```
R1#show ip ospf neighbor
```

```
R2#show ip ospf neighbor
```

Unfortunately we do not have a working OSPF neighbor adjacency. Let's see if we have connectivity:

```
R1#ping 192.168.12.2

Type escape sequence to abort.
Sending 5, 100-byte ICMP Echos to 192.168.12.2, timeout is 2 seconds:
!!!!!
Success rate is 100 percent (5/5), round-trip min/avg/max = 4/10/36 ms
```

I can ping the other side without issues.

167

```
R1#ping 224.0.0.5

Type escape sequence to abort.
Sending 1, 100-byte ICMP Echos to 224.0.0.5, timeout is 2
seconds:

Reply to request 0 from 192.168.12.2, 8 ms
```

I'm also able to ping the OSPF multicast address. This proves that broadcast capabilities for frame-relay have been enabled. I can verify this by looking at the frame-relay maps:

```
R1#show frame-relay map
Serial0/0 (up): ip 192.168.12.2 dlci 102(0x66,0x1860), dynamic,
          broadcast,, status defined, active
```

```
R2#show frame-relay map
Serial0/0 (up): ip 192.168.12.1 dlci 201(0xC9,0x3090), dynamic,
          broadcast,, status defined, active
```

The keyword **broadcast** means we can send broadcast and multicast traffic down the PVC.

If you studied CCNP ROUTE you might recall that OSPF has different network types:

- Broadcast
- Non-Broadcast
- Point-to-Multipoint
- Point-to-Multipoint Non-Broadcast
- Point-to-Point

What OSPF network type is default for a frame-relay interface?

```
R1#show ip ospf interface serial 0/0 | include Network Type
   Process ID 1, Router ID 192.168.12.1, Network Type
NON_BROADCAST, Cost: 64
```

```
R2#show ip ospf interface serial 0/0 | include Network Type
   Process ID 1, Router ID 192.168.12.2, Network Type
NON_BROADCAST, Cost: 64
```

Here's food for thought. The default network type is **Non-Broadcast**. This means OSPF expects us to configure the neighbors ourselves! Let's do it:

```
R1(config)#router ospf 1
R1(config-router)#neighbor 192.168.12.2
```

```
R2(config)#router ospf 1
```

```
R2(config-router)#neighbor 192.168.12.1
```

I'll configure the neighbors myself.

```
R1#
%OSPF-5-ADJCHG: Process 1, Nbr 192.168.12.2 on Serial0/0 from
LOADING to FULL, Loading Done
```

```
R2#
%OSPF-5-ADJCHG: Process 1, Nbr 192.168.12.1 on Serial0/0 from
LOADING to FULL, Loading Done
```

As soon as I do this our OSPF neighbor adjacency is working! Any other way to fix this? Of course it's also possible to change the OSPF network type, let me give you an example:

```
R1(config)#router ospf 1
R1(config-router)#no neighbor 192.168.12.2
```

```
R2(config)#router ospf 1
R2(config-router)#no neighbor 192.168.12.1
```

First I'll remove the OSPF neighbor commands.

```
R1(config)#interface serial 0/0
R1(config-if)#ip ospf network broadcast
```

```
R2(config)#interface serial 0/0
R2(config-if)#ip ospf network broadcast
```

In my example I'll change the network type to broadcast.

```
R1#show ip ospf neighbor

Neighbor ID      Pri   State         Dead Time   Address
Interface
192.168.12.2      1    FULL/DR       00:00:36    192.168.12.2
Serial0/0
```

```
R2#show ip ospf neighbor

Neighbor ID      Pri   State         Dead Time   Address
Interface
192.168.12.1      1    FULL/BDR      00:00:34    192.168.12.1
Serial0/0
```

This also fixes my OSPF over frame-relay issue.
Lesson learned: Make sure you understand all the OSPF network types and their requirements.

These are all the issues I wanted to show you with the OSPF neighbor adjacency. There's quite some stuff that could go wrong but you've seen that I mostly used the same commands to spot these errors:

- Show ip ospf neighbors.
- Show ip ospf interface
- Show ip protocols
- Debug ip ospf adj
- Debug ip ospf hello

If you want to get some practice yourself you can take a look at the following lab I created. It's one big lab with OSPF routers that have issues with establishing the neighbor adjacency. You should be able to fix these issues after reading this chapter!

http://gns3vault.com/Troubleshooting/ospf-neighbor-troubleshooting.html

Now we have a working OSPF neighbor adjacency we can look at some of the other things that could go wrong with OSPF. Most of the times you are expecting to see something in the routing table while it's not there or you see something different than what you are expecting. Let's get started and walk through the different scenarios together.

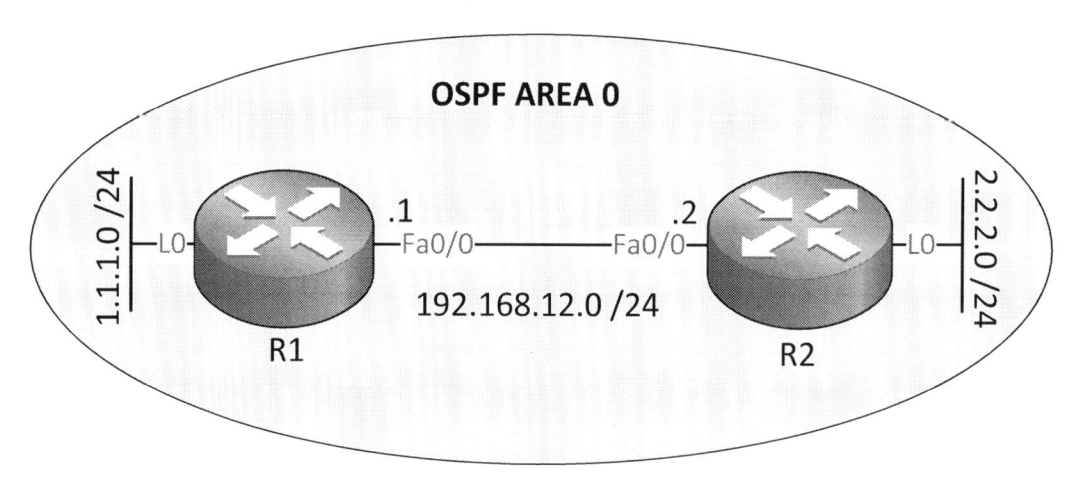

Let's start with an easy scenario. 2 routers running single area OSPF and each router has a loopback interface advertised in OSPF. Here's the output of the routing tables:

```
R1#show ip route

C    192.168.12.0/24 is directly connected, FastEthernet0/0
     10.0.0.0/8 is variably subnetted, 2 subnets, 2 masks
O       10.2.2.2/32 [110/2] via 192.168.12.2, 00:00:14,
FastEthernet0/0
C       10.1.1.0/24 is directly connected, Loopback0
R2#show ip route
```

```
C    192.168.12.0/24 is directly connected, FastEthernet0/0
     10.0.0.0/24 is subnetted, 1 subnets
C       10.2.2.0 is directly connected, Loopback0
```

We can see that R1 has learned about network 10.2.2.0 /24 from R2 but there's nothing in the routing table of R2. What's going on?

```
R1#show ip ospf interface loopback 0
%OSPF: OSPF not enabled on Loopback0
```

```
R2#show ip ospf interface loopback 0
Loopback0 is up, line protocol is up
  Internet Address 10.2.2.2/24, Area 0
  Process ID 1, Router ID 10.2.2.2, Network Type LOOPBACK, Cost: 1
  Loopback interface is treated as a stub Host
```

We can see that OSPF is not enabled on the loopback0 interface of R1, so what networks are we advertising then?

```
R1#show ip protocols | begin Networks
  Routing for Networks:
    10.10.1.1 0.0.0.0 area 0
    192.168.12.0 0.0.0.255 area 0
```

Looks like we are advertising network 10.10.1.0 /24 but this network is not configured on any interface...network 10.1.1.0 /24 is configured on the loopback0 interface of R1.

```
R1#show run | section router ospf
router ospf 1
 log-adjacency-changes
 network 10.10.1.1 0.0.0.0 area 0
 network 192.168.12.0 0.0.0.255 area 0
```

Here you can see the wrong network command, let's get rid of it.

```
R1(config)#router ospf 1
R1(config-router)#no network 10.10.1.1 0.0.0.0 area 0
R1(config-router)#network 10.1.1.0 0.0.0.255 area 0
```

We'll make sure we have the correct network command configured here.

```
R2#show ip route | include 10.1.1.
O       10.1.1.1/32 [110/2] via 192.168.12.1, 00:01:29, FastEthernet0/0
```

Problem solved! This issue might sound a bit lame but using the wrong network statements is something that happens all the time. Especially if we are using smaller subnets (like /27 or /28 or something) people tend to make errors with the wildcard masks.

Lesson learned: Make sure you configure the correct network address, wildcard bits and area.

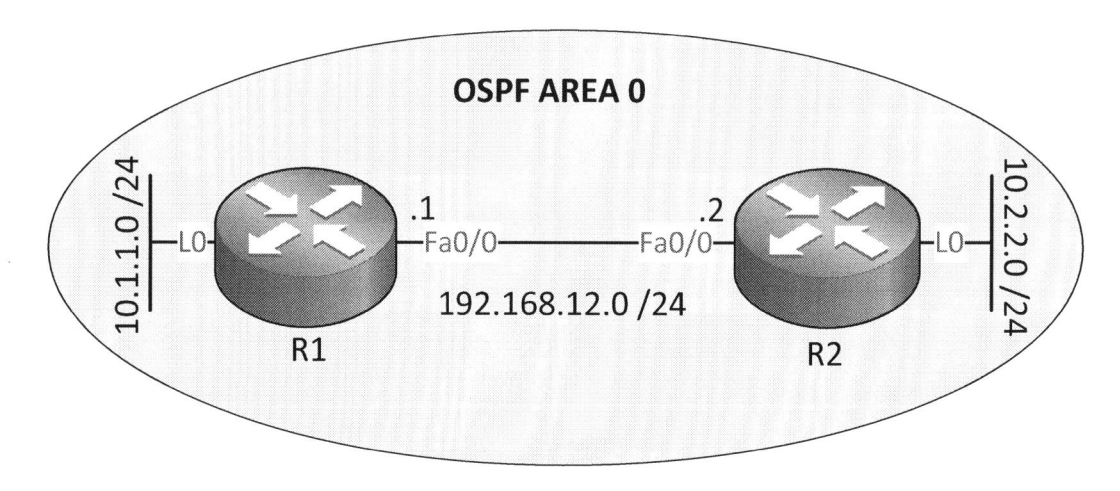

On to to the next scenario. Same 2 routers but another issue. Here are the routing tables:

```
R1#show ip route

C     192.168.12.0/24 is directly connected, FastEthernet0/0
      10.0.0.0/8 is variably subnetted, 2 subnets, 2 masks
O        10.2.2.2/32 [110/2] via 192.168.12.2, 00:00:14,
FastEthernet0/0
```

```
R2#show ip route

C     192.168.12.0/24 is directly connected, FastEthernet0/0
      10.0.0.0/24 is subnetted, 1 subnets
C        10.2.2.0 is directly connected, Loopback0
```

Once again R2 has not learned about network 10.1.1.0 /24. Note that R1 doesn't have network 10.1.1.0 /24 in its routing table as directly connected.

```
R1#show ip protocols | begin Networks
  Routing for Networks:
    10.1.1.0 0.0.0.255 area 0
    192.168.12.0 0.0.0.255 area 0
```

We can verify that R1 is using the correct network command. Since R1 doesn't even have the network in its routing table we can assume that something is wrong with the interface.

```
R1#show ip interface brief
Interface              IP-Address      OK? Method Status                Protocol
FastEthernet0/0        192.168.12.1    YES manual up                    up
Loopback0              10.1.1.1        YES manual administratively down down
```

Seems someone had a TGIF moment (Thank God It's Friday) and forgot to do a "no shutdown" on the interface.

```
R1(config)#interface loopback 0
R1(config-if)#no shutdown
```

Let's bring the interface back to the land of the living.

```
R2#show ip route | include 10.1.1
O       10.1.1.1/32 [110/2] via 192.168.12.1, 00:00:32, FastEthernet0/0
```

And now it shows up in the routing table of R2. **Lesson learned: You can not advertise what you don't have!**

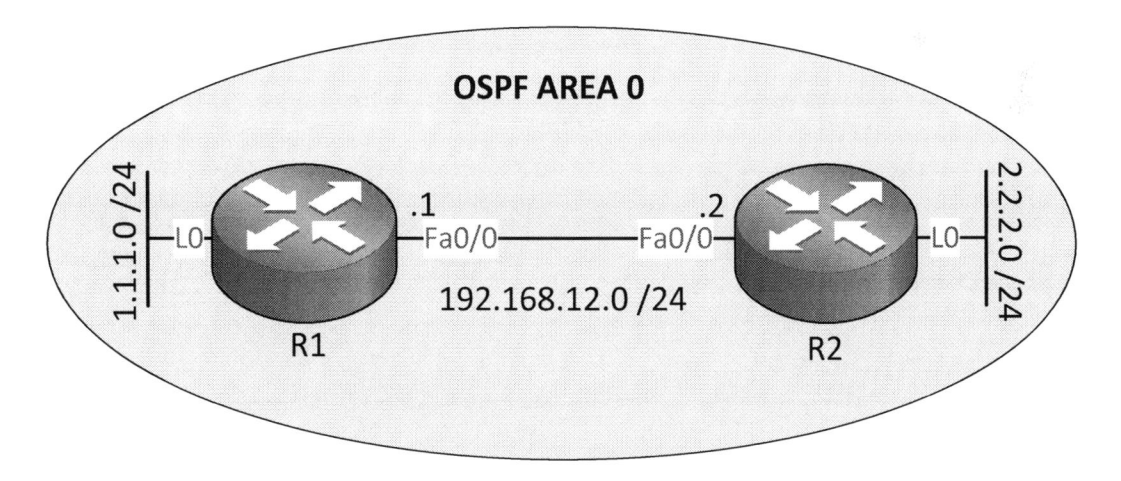

New issue! Single area, same 2 routers…we would like to have "full connectivity" but something is off…here is the output of the routing tables:

```
R1#show ip route ospf
```

```
R2#show ip route ospf
```

173

```
        1.0.0.0/32 is subnetted, 1 subnets
O       1.1.1.1 [110/2] via 192.168.12.1, 00:08:46,
FastEthernet0/0
```

R1 doesn't show any OSPF routes, R2 does...let's find out what is going wrong:

```
R2#show ip protocols
Routing Protocol is "ospf 1"
  Outgoing update filter list for all interfaces is not set
  Incoming update filter list for all interfaces is not set
  Router ID 2.2.2.2
  Number of areas in this router is 1. 1 normal 0 stub 0 nssa
  Maximum path: 4
  Routing for Networks:
    2.2.2.0 0.0.0.255 area 0
    192.168.12.0 0.0.0.255 area 0
```

I can take a quick look at R2 to confirm that it's indeed advertising the correct network(s) which is the case.

```
R1#show ip protocols
Routing Protocol is "ospf 1"
  Outgoing update filter list for all interfaces is not set
  Incoming update filter list for all interfaces is 1
  Router ID 1.1.1.1
  Number of areas in this router is 1. 1 normal 0 stub 0 nssa
  Maximum path: 4
  Routing for Networks:
    1.1.1.0 0.0.0.255 area 0
    192.168.12.0 0.0.0.255 area 0
 Reference bandwidth unit is 100 mbps
  Routing Information Sources:
    Gateway         Distance      Last Update
    2.2.2.2              110      00:07:23
    192.168.12.2         110      00:24:54
  Distance: (default is 110)
```

The output of R1 is more interesting...you can see that it has an inbound distribute-list configured.

```
R1#show access-lists
Standard IP access list 1
    10 deny   2.2.2.0, wildcard bits 0.0.0.255 (2 matches)
    20 permit any
```

Here's our problem.

Let's get rid of the distribute-list.

```
R1(config)#router ospf 1
R1(config-router)#no distribute-list 1 in
```

This will disable it.

```
R1#show ip route ospf
*Mar  1 01:48:39.683: %SYS-5-CONFIG_I: Configured from console
by console
     2.0.0.0/32 is subnetted, 1 subnets
O    2.2.2.2 [110/2] via 192.168.12.2, 00:00:24,
FastEthernet0/0
```

Problem solved! **Lesson learned: Be aware of distribute-lists that prevent the advertising and/or installing of prefixes in the routing table.**

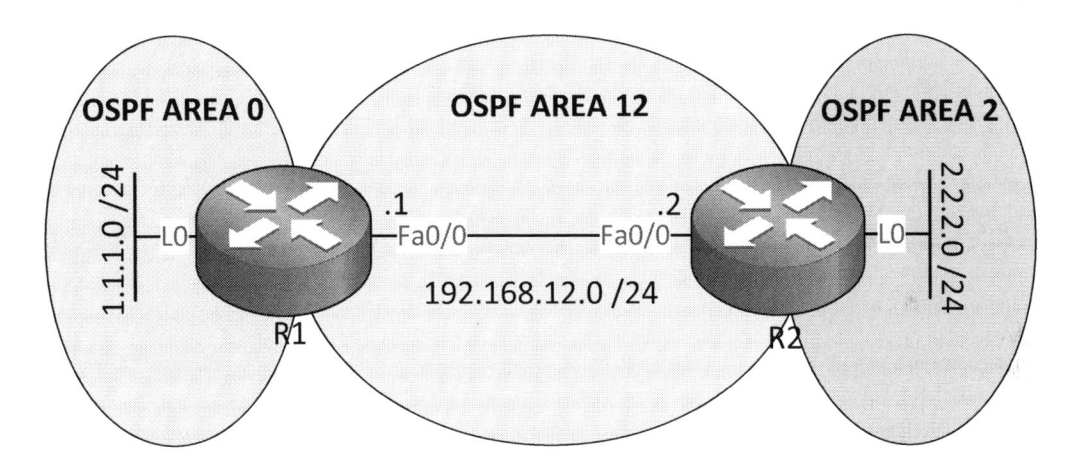

Let's look at some more advanced OSPF issues. In the picture above we have R1 and R2 but this time we have a multi-area OSPF configuration. Here's the OSPF configuration of both routers:

```
R1#show run | section router ospf
router ospf 1
 log-adjacency-changes
 area 12 virtual-link 192.168.12.2
 network 1.1.1.0 0.0.0.255 area 0
 network 192.168.12.0 0.0.0.255 area 12
```

```
R2#show run | section ospf
router ospf 1
 log-adjacency-changes
 area 12 virtual-link 192.168.12.1
 network 2.2.2.0 0.0.0.255 area 2
```

175

```
network 192.168.12.0 0.0.0.255 area 12
```

As you can see all networks have been advertised. Area 2 is not directly connected to area 0 so a virtual link has been created.

```
R1#show ip route

C    192.168.12.0/24 is directly connected, FastEthernet0/0
     1.0.0.0/24 is subnetted, 1 subnets
C       1.1.1.0 is directly connected, Loopback0
```

```
R2#show ip route

C    192.168.12.0/24 is directly connected, FastEthernet0/0
     1.0.0.0/32 is subnetted, 1 subnets
O IA    1.1.1.1 [110/2] via 192.168.12.1, 00:07:34, FastEthernet0/0
     2.0.0.0/24 is subnetted, 1 subnets
C       2.2.2.0 is directly connected, Loopback0
```

R1 however didn't learn about network 2.2.2.0 /24 from R2 but R2 did learn about network 1.1.1.0 /24.

It's best to start with the virtual link here:

```
R1#show ip ospf virtual-links
Virtual Link OSPF_VL1 to router 192.168.12.2 is down
```

```
R2#show ip ospf virtual-links
Virtual Link OSPF_VL0 to router 192.168.12.1 is down
```

Hmm this doesn't look good. The virtual link is down. Note the IP addresses that we see here, those are the IP addresses that are configured on the FastEthernet interfaces of both routers.

```
R1#show ip ospf neighbor

Neighbor ID   Pri   State         Dead Time    Address        Interface
2.2.2.2        1    FULL/DR       00:00:31     192.168.12.2   FastEthernet0/0
```

```
R2#show ip ospf neighbor

Neighbor ID   Pri   State         Dead Time    Address        Interface
1.1.1.1        1    FULL/BDR      00:00:38     192.168.12.1   FastEthernet0/0
```

Whenever we configure a virtual link we need to configure the **OSPF router ID** of the other side, not the IP address of the other side!

```
R1#show run | incl virtual-link
  area 12 virtual-link 192.168.12.2
```

```
R2#show run | incl virtual-link
  area 12 virtual-link 192.168.12.1
```

Here's the error so let's correct it.

```
R1(config)#router ospf 1
R1(config-router)#no area 12 virtual-link 192.168.12.2
R1(config-router)#area 12 virtual-link 2.2.2.2
```

```
R2(config)#router ospf 1
R2(config-router)#no area 12 virtual-link 192.168.12.1
R2(config-router)#area 12 virtual-link 1.1.1.1
```

This is what the virtual link should look like, configured between the OSPF router IDs.

```
R1# %OSPF-5-ADJCHG: Process 1, Nbr 2.2.2.2 on OSPF_VL2 from
LOADING to FULL, Loading Done
```

```
R2# OSPF-5-ADJCHG: Process 1, Nbr 1.1.1.1 on OSPF_VL1 from
LOADING to FULL, Loading Done
```

Right after typing in the correct commands you'll see this message on your console.

```
R1#show ip route ospf
     2.0.0.0/32 is subnetted, 1 subnets
O IA    2.2.2.2 [110/2] via 192.168.12.2, 00:01:38,
FastEthernet0/0
```

Now we see the OSPF entry for network 2.2.2.0 /24. Problem solved!

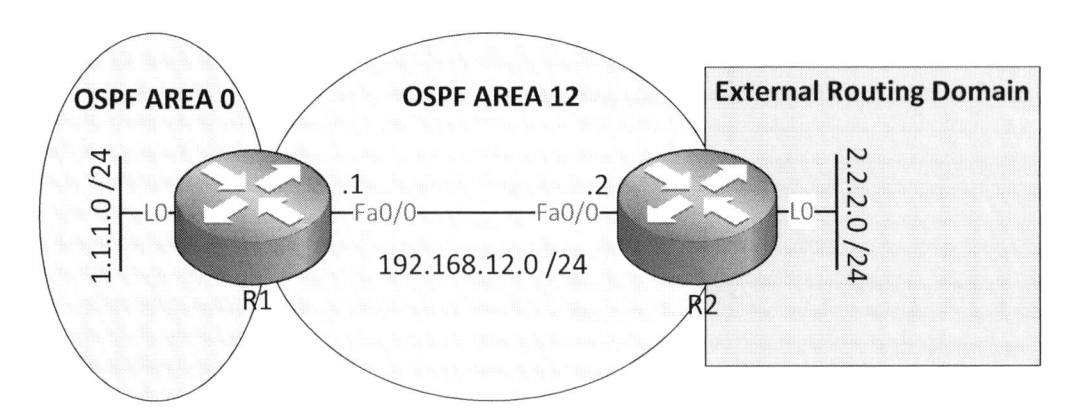

OSPF Area 0 / OSPF Area 12 / External Routing Domain

```
         OSPF AREA 0          OSPF AREA 12         External Routing Domain
                              .1          .2
           1.1.1.0/24 -L0-  -Fa0/0------Fa0/0-  -L0- 2.2.2.0/24
                       R1    192.168.12.0 /24   R2
```

Let's take a look at another issue. Same routers but there's an "external routing domain". This could be another routing protocol like RIP or EIGRP, it's something that we will redistribute into OSPF. R2 will redistribute network 2.2.2.0 /24 into OSPF but for some reason it's not showing up on R1. To keep things exciting I'm not going to show you the OSPF configuration of both routers ;)

```
R1#show ip route

C    192.168.12.0/24 is directly connected, FastEthernet0/0
     1.0.0.0/24 is subnetted, 1 subnets
C       1.1.1.0 is directly connected, Loopback0
```

I'm not seeing network 2.2.2.0 /24 on R1 so let's take a look at R2.

```
R2#show ip route | include 2.2.2
C       2.2.2.0 is directly connected, Loopback0
```

I can see the network is in the routing table of R2 as directly connected.

```
R2#show ip protocols
Routing Protocol is "ospf 1"
  Outgoing update filter list for all interfaces is not set
  Incoming update filter list for all interfaces is not set
  Router ID 2.2.2.2
  It is an autonomous system boundary router
  Redistributing External Routes from,
    connected, includes subnets in redistribution
```

I can see R2 has been configured to redistribute directly connected networks. This should include network 2.2.2.0 /24 from the loopback0 interface.

```
R2#show ip ospf database external

            OSPF Router with ID (2.2.2.2) (Process ID 1)
```

However I don't find anything in the OSPF database? What could be a possible reason for this? If you remember CCNP ROUTE you might recall the rules of the different OSPF area types. Let's find out what kind of area this is!

```
R2#show ip protocols | include areas
  Number of areas in this router is 1. 0 normal 1 stub 0 nssa
```

Ahhh that explains, it's a stub area! Stub areas do not allow LSA type 5 (external routes). We can either turn this area into a normal area or a NSSA. Let's turn it into a NSSA...

```
R1(config)#router ospf 1
R1(config-router)#no area 12 stub
R1(config-router)#area 12 nssa
```

```
R2(config)#router ospf 1
R2(config-router)#no area 12 stub
R2(config-router)#area 12 nssa
```

I'll change the area type on both routers. The NSSA area allows external routes by using LSA type 7.

```
R2#show ip ospf database nssa-external

            OSPF Router with ID (2.2.2.2) (Process ID 1)

              Type-7 AS External Link States (Area 12)

  LS age: 122
  Options: (No TOS-capability, Type 7/5 translation, DC)
  LS Type: AS External Link
  Link State ID: 2.2.2.0 (External Network Number )
  Advertising Router: 2.2.2.2
  LS Seq Number: 80000001
  Checksum: 0xB759
  Length: 36
  Network Mask: /24
```

We can now find network 2.2.2.0 /24 in the OSPF database of R2.

```
R1#show ip route | include 2.2.2
O N2    2.2.2.0 [110/20] via 192.168.12.2, 00:03:35,
FastEthernet0/0
```

Because of this R1 can now learn this network...problem solved!

Lesson learned: Stub areas do not allow external prefixes (LSA Type 5). Either change the area to NSSA or stop redistributing.

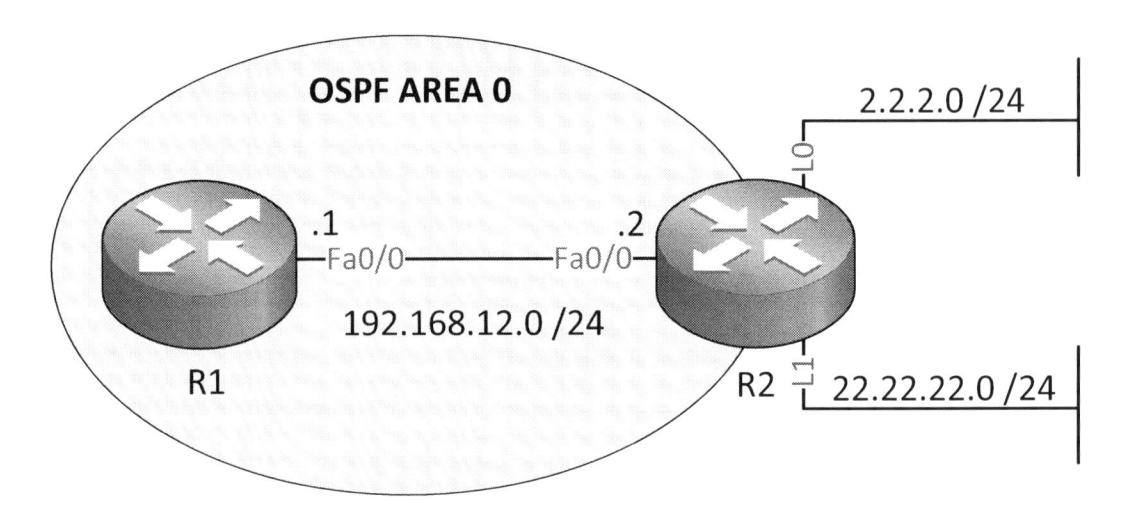

OSPF AREA 0 diagram: R1 (Fa0/0 .1) — 192.168.12.0 /24 — (Fa0/0 .2) R2, with R2 L0 to 2.2.2.0/24 and R2 L1 to 22.22.22.0/24.

Next scenario, this one is about OSPF default routes. In the picture above we have R1 and R2 and the 192.168.12.0 /24 network has been advertised in OSPF. The loopback interfaces of R2 are not advertised in OSPF but we are using a default route so R1 can reach them. Here are the OSPF configurations:

```
R1#show run | section router ospf
router ospf 1
 log-adjacency-changes
 network 192.168.12.0 0.0.0.255 area 0
```

```
R2#show run | section router ospf
router ospf 1
 log-adjacency-changes
 network 192.168.12.0 0.0.0.255 area 0
 default-information originate
```

As you can see R2 has the **default-information originate** command to advertise a default route.

```
R1#show ip route

C    192.168.12.0/24 is directly connected, FastEthernet0/0
```

Unfortunately I'm not seeing a default route on R1. What could be the issue? Let's check R2:

```
R2#show ip route

C    192.168.12.0/24 is directly connected, FastEthernet0/0
     2.0.0.0/24 is subnetted, 1 subnets
C       2.2.2.0 is directly connected, Loopback0
     22.0.0.0/24 is subnetted, 1 subnets
```

```
C       22.22.22.0 is directly connected, Loopback1
```

I'm not seeing a default route in R2's routing table.

In order for OSPF to advertise a default route I have 2 options:

1. Make sure you have the default route in your routing table (you can't advertise what you don't have).
2. Use the default-information originate **always** command. This will advertise the default route even if you don't have one yourself.

```
R2(config)#ip route 0.0.0.0 0.0.0.0 null 0
```

This is the first method of solving the problem. I'll create a default route on R2, normally you'll point this default route to your ISP router but in my case there's no other router. I'll point the default route to the null0 interface and it will be installed in the routing table.

```
R1#show ip route ospf
O*E2 0.0.0.0/0 [110/1] via 192.168.12.2, 00:01:02,
FastEthernet0/0
```

You can see that this works.

```
R2(config)#no ip route 0.0.0.0 0.0.0.0 null 0
R2(config)#router ospf 1
R2(config-router)#default-information originate always
```

This is the second method, I'll get rid of the default route and use the default-information originate always command.

```
R1#show ip route ospf
O*E2 0.0.0.0/0 [110/1] via 192.168.12.2, 00:00:38,
FastEthernet0/0
```

There's my default route...problem solved! **Lesson learned: If you want to advertise a default route with OSPF you need to have a default route in your routing table or use the "always" keyword.**

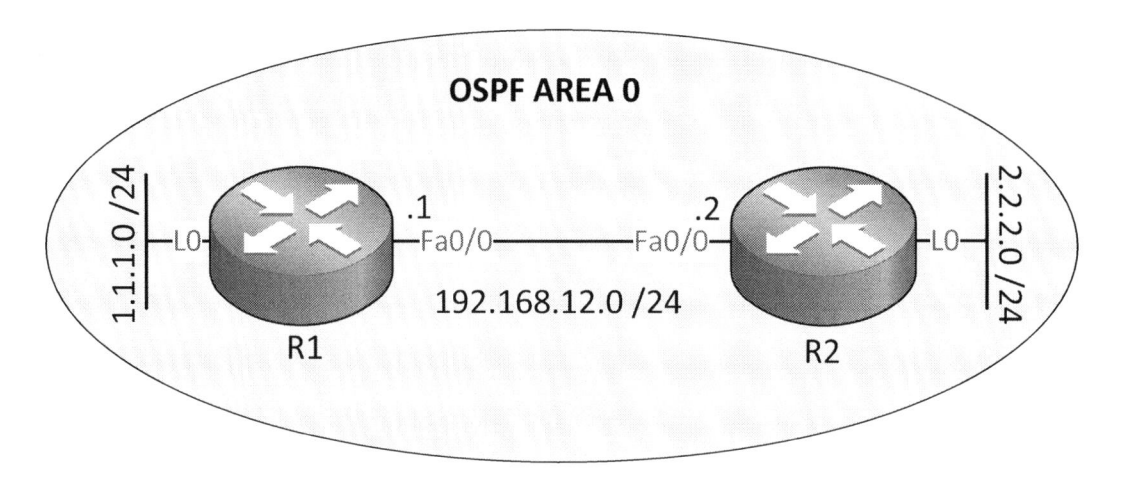

The next scenario is a little trickier…same 2 routers, everything in area 0. Here are the OSPF configurations:

```
R1#show run | section router ospf
router ospf 1
 log-adjacency-changes
 network 1.1.1.0 0.0.0.255 area 0
 network 192.168.12.0 0.0.0.255 area 0
```

```
R2#show run | section router ospf
router ospf 1
 log-adjacency-changes
 network 2.2.2.0 0.0.0.255 area 0
 network 192.168.12.0 0.0.0.255 area 0
```

Nothing special here, all networks are advertised and we are using a single area.

```
R1#show ip route

C    192.168.12.0/24 is directly connected, FastEthernet0/0
     1.0.0.0/24 is subnetted, 1 subnets
C       1.1.1.0 is directly connected, Loopback0
```

```
R2#show ip route

C    192.168.12.0/24 is directly connected, FastEthernet0/0
     2.0.0.0/24 is subnetted, 1 subnets
C       2.2.2.0 is directly connected, Loopback0
```

Alas…empty routing tables! At least no OSPF information…The network commands are looking good so this might be a good moment to dive in the OSPF LSDB.

Let's check the OSPF router IDs first:

```
R1#show ip ospf neighbor

Neighbor ID     Pri   State          Dead Time   Address         Interface
192.168.12.2    0     FULL/  -       00:00:30    192.168.12.2    FastEthernet0/0
```

```
R2#show ip ospf neighbor

Neighbor ID     Pri   State          Dead Time   Address         Interface
1.1.1.1         1     FULL/BDR       00:00:32    192.168.12.1    FastEthernet0/0
```

Here I can see the OSPF router IDs. If you look closely at the output above you can already see something funky is going on. The state is full but R1 didn't elect a DR/BDR and R2 elected R1 as a BDR.

```
R1#show ip ospf database router 192.168.12.2

        OSPF Router with ID (1.1.1.1) (Process ID 1)

                Router Link States (Area 0)

  Adv Router is not-reachable
  LS age: 527
  Options: (No TOS-capability, DC)
  LS Type: Router Links
  Link State ID: 192.168.12.2
  Advertising Router: 192.168.12.2
  LS Seq Number: 80000003
  Checksum: 0x1E1C
  Length: 48
  Number of Links: 2

    Link connected to: a Stub Network
      (Link ID) Network/subnet number: 2.2.2.2
      (Link Data) Network Mask: 255.255.255.255
      Number of TOS metrics: 0
        TOS 0 Metrics: 1

    Link connected to: a Transit Network
      (Link ID) Designated Router address: 192.168.12.2
      (Link Data) Router Interface address: 192.168.12.2
      Number of TOS metrics: 0
        TOS 0 Metrics: 1
```

I can use the **show ip ospf database router** command to lookup information from a particular OSPF neighbor. R1 is telling me **adv router is not-**

reachable. That doesn't sound good.

```
R2#show ip ospf database router 1.1.1.1

            OSPF Router with ID (192.168.12.2) (Process ID 1)

                Router Link States (Area 0)

  Adv Router is not-reachable
  LS age: 776
  Options: (No TOS-capability, DC)
  LS Type: Router Links
  Link State ID: 1.1.1.1
  Advertising Router: 1.1.1.1
  LS Seq Number: 80000003
  Checksum: 0xE8B7
  Length: 60
  Number of Links: 3

    Link connected to: a Stub Network
     (Link ID) Network/subnet number: 1.1.1.1
     (Link Data) Network Mask: 255.255.255.255
      Number of TOS metrics: 0
       TOS 0 Metrics: 1

    Link connected to: another Router (point-to-point)
     (Link ID) Neighboring Router ID: 192.168.12.2
     (Link Data) Router Interface address: 192.168.12.1
      Number of TOS metrics: 0
       TOS 0 Metrics: 1

    Link connected to: a Stub Network
     (Link ID) Network/subnet number: 192.168.12.0
     (Link Data) Network Mask: 255.255.255.0
      Number of TOS metrics: 0
       TOS 0 Metrics: 1
```

R2 is also telling me that R1 is not-reachable and if you look closely you can see that it sees the link as **point-to-point**. We don't see this in the output on R1. This probably means that R1 and R2 are using a different OSPF network type which results in a difference in the LSDB. This will prevent our routers from installing routes into the routing table!

```
R1#show ip ospf interface fastEthernet 0/0 | include Network
Type
  Process ID 1, Router ID 1.1.1.1, Network Type POINT_TO_POINT,
Cost: 1
```

```
R2#show ip ospf interface fastEthernet 0/0 | include Network
Type
  Process ID 1, Router ID 192.168.12.2, Network Type BROADCAST,
Cost: 1
```

Now we are onto something. The network type is different...broadcast on R2 and point-to-point on R1. We did manage to establish an OSPF neighbor adjacency with this but it does cause a difference in the LSDB.

Let's fix it:

```
R1(config)#interface fa0/0
R1(config-if)#ip ospf network broadcast
```

Change the network type on R1 should do the trick.

```
R1#show ip route ospf
     2.0.0.0/32 is subnetted, 1 subnets
O       2.2.2.2 [110/2] via 192.168.12.2, 00:00:18,
FastEthernet0/0
```

```
R2#show ip route ospf
     1.0.0.0/32 is subnetted, 1 subnets
O       1.1.1.1 [110/2] via 192.168.12.1, 00:00:49,
FastEthernet0/0
```

Finally the "O" is appearing in our routing tables...problem solved! **Lesson learned: Make sure you use the correct OSPF network type on both routers.**

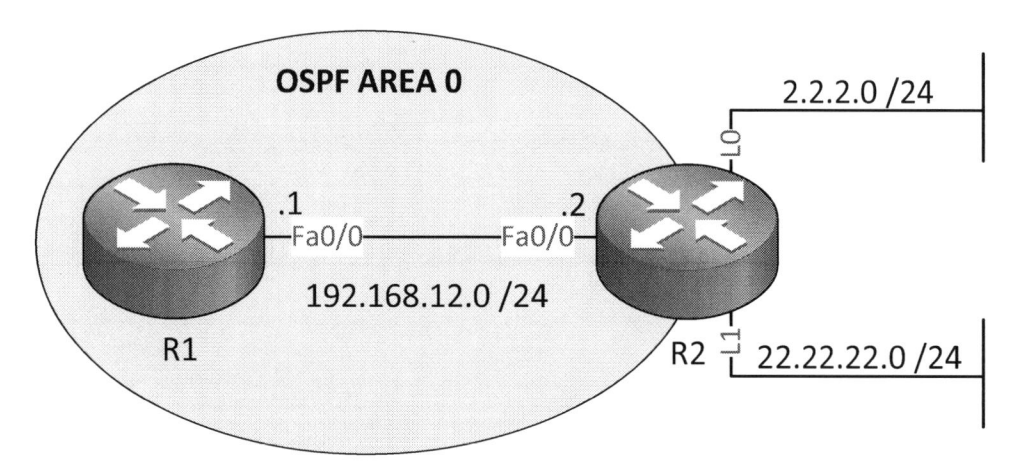

In this scenario we have configured OSPF between R1 and R2 but not all networks are advertised. The loopback interfaces of R2 are redistributed into OSPF. Here's the configuration of both routers:

```
R1#show run | section router ospf
router ospf 1
 log-adjacency-changes
 network 192.168.12.0 0.0.0.255 area 0
```

```
R2#show run | section router ospf
router ospf 1
 log-adjacency-changes
 redistribute connected
 network 192.168.12.0 0.0.0.255 area 0
```

You can see the redistribute connected command on R2 that should redistribute the networks on the loopback interfaces into OSPF.

```
R1#show ip route

C    192.168.12.0/24 is directly connected, FastEthernet0/0
```

However I'm not seeing anything here...

```
R1#show ip protocols | include filter
  Outgoing update filter list for all interfaces is not set
  Incoming update filter list for all interfaces is not set
```

```
R2#show ip protocols | include filter
  Outgoing update filter list for all interfaces is not set
  Incoming update filter list for all interfaces is not set
```

Normally it would be a good idea to check if there's a distribute list, there's no such thing here.

```
R2#show run | include redistribute
 redistribute connected
```

They key to this problem is this command; it's something you should memorize. If you type in **redistribute connected** OSPF will only redistribute **classful** networks.

```
R2(config)#router ospf 1
R2(config-router)#redistribute connected subnets
```

I need to add the **subnets** keyword to make it redistribute subnets of major networks.

```
R1#show ip route ospf
     2.0.0.0/24 is subnetted, 1 subnets
O E2    2.2.2.0 [110/20] via 192.168.12.2, 00:00:52,
FastEthernet0/0
```

```
        22.0.0.0/24 is subnetted, 1 subnets
O E2    22.22.22.0 [110/20] via 192.168.12.2, 00:00:51,
FastEthernet0/0
```

There we go; our routing table has been filled. Problem solved**! Lesson learned: Add the "subnets" keyword when using redistribution or only classful networks are redistributed.**

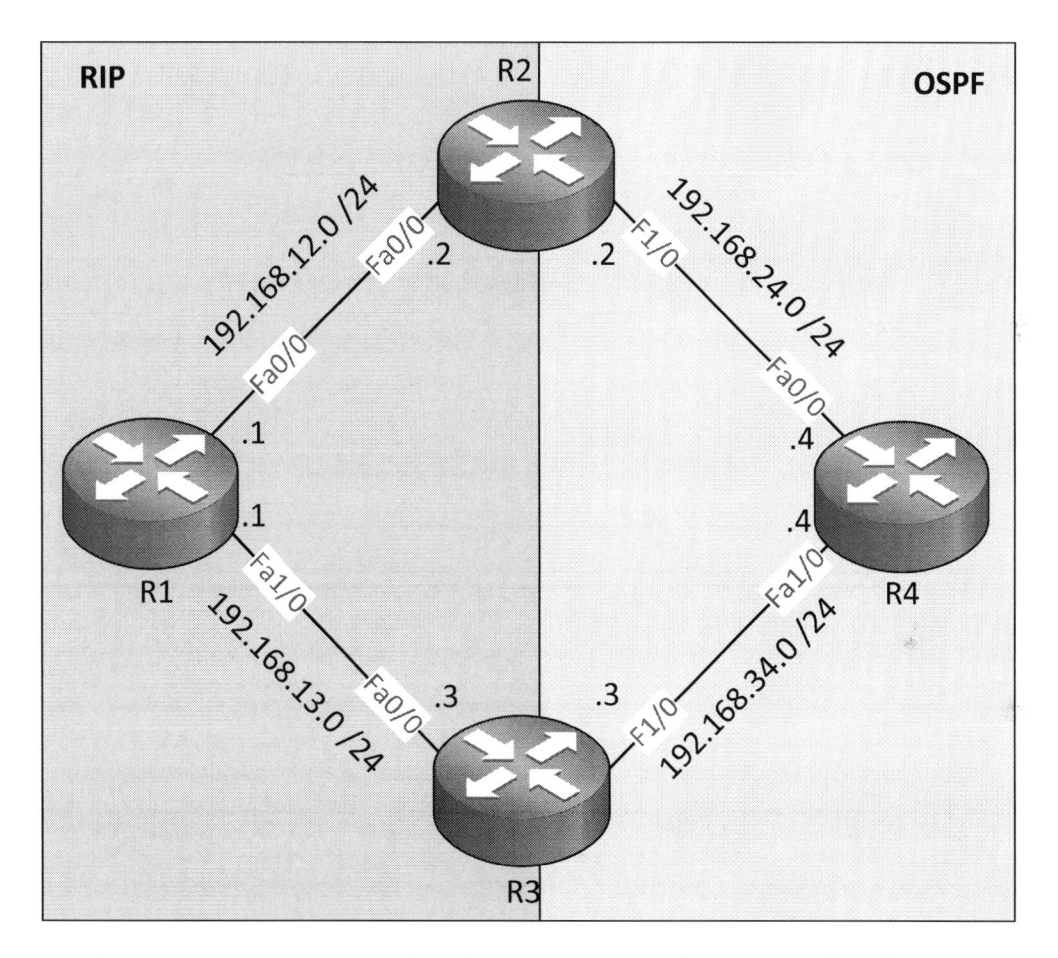

Here's a more interesting redistribution scenario for you. Redistribution can be complex and there are multiple solutions how you can solve redistribution issues. In the topology above we have 4 routers. On the left side we are running RIP and on the right side we are running OSPF. Redistribution has been configured between RIP and OSPF on router R2 and R3. Let's start by looking at the routing tables of each router:

```
R1#show ip route rip
R    192.168.24.0/24 [120/1] via 192.168.13.3, 00:00:09,
FastEthernet1/0
                    [120/1] via 192.168.12.2, 00:00:05,
FastEthernet0/0
```

187

```
R      192.168.34.0/24 [120/1] via 192.168.13.3, 00:00:09,
FastEthernet1/0
                       [120/1] via 192.168.12.2, 00:00:05,
FastEthernet0/0
```

R1 is only running RIP and we can see the prefixes that it has learned. If you look closely you can see something is weird:

- 192.168.24.0/24 can be reached through R2 and R3 but if we look at the topology picture we can clearly see that the path through R2 is shorter. The hop count is 1 for both paths.
- The same thing applies for prefix 192.168.34.0/24.

```
R2#show ip route
Codes: C - connected, S - static, R - RIP, M - mobile, B - BGP
       D - EIGRP, EX - EIGRP external, O - OSPF, IA - OSPF inter
area
       N1 - OSPF NSSA external type 1, N2 - OSPF NSSA external
type 2
       E1 - OSPF external type 1, E2 - OSPF external type 2
       i - IS-IS, su - IS-IS summary, L1 - IS-IS level-1, L2 -
IS-IS level-2
       ia - IS-IS inter area, * - candidate default, U - per-
user static route
       o - ODR, P - periodic downloaded static route

Gateway of last resort is not set

C    192.168.12.0/24 is directly connected, FastEthernet0/0
O E2 192.168.13.0/24 [110/1] via 192.168.24.4, 00:32:21,
FastEthernet1/0
C    192.168.24.0/24 is directly connected, FastEthernet1/0
O    192.168.34.0/24 [110/2] via 192.168.24.4, 00:32:21,
FastEthernet1/0
```

R2 is running OSPF and RIP and here's the routing table. Something is strange however:

- 192.168.13.0/24 has been learned as an OSPF external prefix and traffic is sent through R4 to get there. If you look at the picture you can see that it would be better to send it to R1.

```
R3#show ip route
Codes: C - connected, S - static, R - RIP, M - mobile, B - BGP
       D - EIGRP, EX - EIGRP external, O - OSPF, IA - OSPF inter
area
       N1 - OSPF NSSA external type 1, N2 - OSPF NSSA external
type 2
       E1 - OSPF external type 1, E2 - OSPF external type 2
       i - IS-IS, su - IS-IS summary, L1 - IS-IS level-1, L2 -
IS-IS level-2
```

```
        ia - IS-IS inter area, * - candidate default, U - per-
user static route
       o - ODR, P - periodic downloaded static route

Gateway of last resort is not set

O E2 192.168.12.0/24 [110/1] via 192.168.34.4, 00:36:06,
FastEthernet1/0
C    192.168.13.0/24 is directly connected, FastEthernet0/0
O    192.168.24.0/24 [110/2] via 192.168.34.4, 00:36:06,
FastEthernet1/0
C    192.168.34.0/24 is directly connected, FastEthernet1/0
```

R3 is similar to R2. This router wants to send traffic for 192.168.12.0/24 towards R4 while the link through R1 would be a better choice.

```
R4#show ip route ospf
O E2 192.168.12.0/24 [110/1] via 192.168.24.2, 00:46:31,
FastEthernet0/0
O E2 192.168.13.0/24 [110/1] via 192.168.34.3, 00:46:31,
FastEthernet1/0
```

R4 looks fine. It has learned about network 192.168.12.0/24 and 192.168.13.0/24.

In this topology we have **suboptimal routing**. Before we start smashing in commands it's wise to think about what is going on here:

- OSPF and RIP both don't make a difference between internal and external prefixes when it comes to the administrative distance. They only care about the path with the lowest metric.
    - Example: R2 has installed 192.168.13.0/24 because the OSPF external has a better administrative distance (110) compared to RIP (120). The same thing applies for prefix 192.168.12.0/24 on R3.
    - EIGRP "protects" itself against this because the administrative distance for EIGRP external prefixes is 170 compared to 90 for the internal prefixes.
- The reason that R1 sees two paths to 192.168.24.0/24 and 192.168.34.0/24 is because the hop count is both 1.

```
R2#show run | section rip
router rip
 version 2
 redistribute ospf 1 metric 1
 network 192.168.12.0
 no auto-summary
R3#show run | section rip
router rip
 version 2
```

```
 redistribute ospf 1 metric 1
 network 192.168.13.0
 no auto-summary
```

We can see that everything from OSPF is redistributed into RIP with a hop count of 1.

```
R2#show run | section ospf
router ospf 1
 log-adjacency-changes
 redistribute rip metric 1 subnets
 network 192.168.24.0 0.0.0.255 area 0
```

```
R3#show run | section ospf
router ospf 1
 log-adjacency-changes
 redistribute rip metric 1 subnets
 network 192.168.34.0 0.0.0.255 area 0
```

And all RIP prefixes are redistributed into OSPF with a cost of 1. In this scenario we can adapt OSPF so it will make a difference between the administrative distance of internal and external prefixes.

```
R2(config)#router ospf 1
R2(config-router)#distance ospf external 130
```

```
R3(config)#router ospf 1
R3(config-router)#distance ospf external 130
```

```
R4(config)#router ospf 1
R4(config-router)#distance ospf external 130
```

We'll change this on all OSPF routers. The administrative distance for external OSPF prefixes is now 130.
Does this make a difference? You bet! Let's take a look:

```
R2#show ip route

C    192.168.12.0/24 is directly connected, FastEthernet0/0
R    192.168.13.0/24 [120/1] via 192.168.12.1, 00:00:17,
FastEthernet0/0
C    192.168.24.0/24 is directly connected, FastEthernet1/0
O    192.168.34.0/24 [110/2] via 192.168.24.4, 00:02:39,
FastEthernet1/0
```

R2 now prefers the RIP entry for network 192.168.13.0/24. This is because the AD for RIP is 120 compared to OSPF external which is now 130.

```
R3#show ip route
```

```
R     192.168.12.0/24 [120/1] via 192.168.13.1, 00:00:10,
FastEthernet0/0
C     192.168.13.0/24 is directly connected, FastEthernet0/0
O     192.168.24.0/24 [110/2] via 192.168.34.4, 00:03:07,
FastEthernet1/0
C     192.168.34.0/24 is directly connected, FastEthernet1/0
```

R3 now prefers the RIP entry for network 192.168.12.0/24. This is because the AD for RIP is 120 compared to OSPF external which is now 130.

The routing tables of R2 and R3 are now looking good. Because of these changes something changed on R4 however:

```
R4#show ip route ospf
O E2 192.168.12.0/24 [130/1] via 192.168.34.3, 00:06:36,
FastEthernet1/0
                    [130/1] via 192.168.24.2, 00:06:36,
FastEthernet0/0
O E2 192.168.13.0/24 [130/1] via 192.168.34.3, 00:06:36,
FastEthernet1/0
                    [130/1] via 192.168.24.2, 00:06:36,
FastEthernet0/0
```

Network 192.168.12.0/24 can be reached through both R2 and R3. The best path however would be through R2. Network 192.168.13.0/24 can also be reached through both R2 and R3 but the best path is to go through R3.

This happens because R2 and R3 both have network 192.168.12.0/24 and 192.168.13.0/24 in their routing table and they are redistributing it into OSPF with a cost of 1. We can fix this by playing with the metric of OSPF.

If we want to make sure that R4 picks the best path for 192.168.12.0 /24 we need to make sure that R2 has a lower cost than R3. We can do the same thing for 192.168.13.0 /24 and make sure R3 has the lowest cost path.

```
R2(config)#route-map RIP2OSPF permit 10
R2(config-route-map)#match ip address 1
R2(config-route-map)#set metric 10
R2(config-route-map)#exit
R2(config)#route-map RIP2OSPF permit 20
```

```
R2(config)#access-list 1 permit 192.168.13.0 0.0.0.255
```

This will be the route-map for R2. Whenever something matches access-list 1 it will set the metric to 10. Access-list 1 matches network 192.168.13.0/24. All other traffic will match (permit 20) but I don't need any set commands.

```
R2(config)#router ospf 1
```

```
R2(config-router)#redistribute rip subnets metric 1 route-map
RIP2OSPF
```

Don't forget to activate it by adding it to the redistribution command.

```
R4#show ip route ospf
O E2 192.168.12.0/24 [130/1] via 192.168.34.3, 00:00:16,
FastEthernet1/0
                    [130/1] via 192.168.24.2, 00:00:16,
FastEthernet0/0
O E2 192.168.13.0/24 [130/1] via 192.168.34.3, 00:00:16,
FastEthernet1/0
```

We can see its working. R4 only has a single entry now for network 192.168.13.0/24 through R3.

```
R4#show ip ospf database | include 192.168.13.0
192.168.13.0      192.168.24.2     117           0x80000005 0x007933
0
192.168.13.0      192.168.34.3     830           0x80000007 0x00CED9
0
```

In the OSPF database we'll still find the entry from R2. This is good because if R3 fails we still have a backup path through R2.

```
R3(config)#route-map RIP2OSPF permit 10
R3(config-route-map)#match ip address 1
R3(config-route-map)#set metric 10
R3(config-route-map)#exit
R3(config-route-map)#route-map RIP2OSPF permit 20
```

```
R3(config)#access-list 1 permit 192.168.12.0 0.0.0.255
```

We'll create a similar route-map on R3 for network 192.168.12.0/24. I want to make sure R4 uses R2 as the primary path to reach this network.

```
R3(config)#router ospf 1
R3(config-router)#redistribute rip metric 1 subnets route-map
RIP2OSPF
```

Activate it and wait till the magic happens...

```
R4#show ip route ospf
O E2 192.168.12.0/24 [130/1] via 192.168.24.2, 00:00:30,
FastEthernet0/0
O E2 192.168.13.0/24 [130/1] via 192.168.34.3, 00:08:24,
FastEthernet1/0
```

Excellent! R4 is now using the most optimal path to reach network

192.168.12.0 /24.

```
R4#show ip ospf database | include 192.168.12.0
192.168.12.0    192.168.24.2    575         0x8000000D 0x001A94
0
192.168.12.0    192.168.34.3    101         0x80000003 0x003C68
0
```

And we have a backup path through R3 in case R2 goes down.

At this moment everything looks fine on the "OSPF side".

```
R1#show ip route rip
R    192.168.24.0/24 [120/1] via 192.168.13.3, 00:00:05,
FastEthernet1/0
                     [120/1] via 192.168.12.2, 00:00:04,
FastEthernet0/0
R    192.168.34.0/24 [120/1] via 192.168.13.3, 00:00:05,
FastEthernet1/0
                     [120/1] via 192.168.12.2, 00:00:04,
FastEthernet0/0
```

R1 however still has a similar issue like R4 did. It's using both R2 and R3 for network 192.168.24.0/24 and 192.168.34.0/24. We'll play with the hop count to fix this.

```
R2(config)#route-map OSPF2RIP permit 10
R2(config-route-map)#match ip address 2
R2(config-route-map)#set metric 10
R2(config-route-map)#exit
R2(config)#route-map OSPF2RIP permit 20
R2(config-route-map)#exit

R2(config)#access-list 2 permit 192.168.34.0 0.0.0.255

R2(config)#router rip
R2(config-router)#redistribute ospf 1 route-map OSPF2RIP
```

First we'll create a route-map on R2 that will set the hop count to 10 for network 192.168.34.0/24.

```
R3(config)#route-map OSPF2RIP permit 10
R3(config-route-map)#match ip address 2
R3(config-route-map)#set metric 10
R3(config-route-map)#exit
R3(config)#route-map OSPF2RIP permit 20
R3(config-route-map)#exit

R3(config)#access-list 2 permit 192.168.24.0 0.0.0.255
```

```
R3(config)#router rip
R3(config-router)#redistribute ospf 1 route-map OSPF2RIP
```

We'll create the same route-map on R3 that will set the hop count to 10 for network 192.168.24.0/24.

```
R1#show ip route rip
R     192.168.24.0/24 [120/1] via 192.168.12.2, 00:00:14,
FastEthernet0/0
R     192.168.34.0/24 [120/1] via 192.168.13.3, 00:00:04,
FastEthernet1/0
```

R1 is now using the most optimal path to reach these networks. Looks like we are done here!

Lesson learned: Use the administrative distance to prevent or allow the installation of prefixes in your routing table(s) and use the metric to select the best path.

If you want to see if you could solve a similar issue yourself you can try the following OSPF to RIP redistribution lab:

http://gns3vault.com/Troubleshooting/ospf-rip-redistribution-ad-troubleshooting.html

Redistribution is *not* easy and there are multiple ways to solve issues.

Make sure you are very familiar with routing protocols, administrative distance and path selection.

Think about a solution first before implementing it.

OSPF AREA 0 — OSPF AREA 2

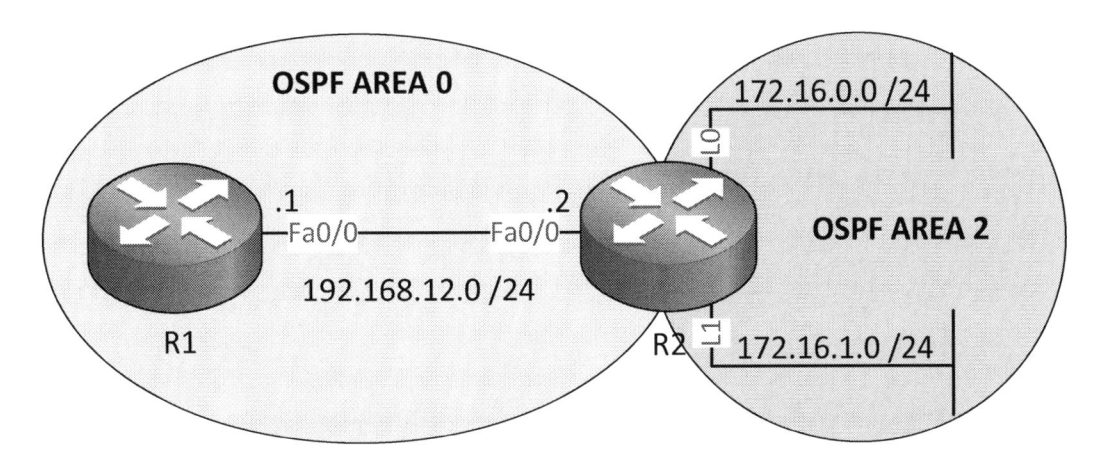

This example is about OSPF summarization. R2 is supposed to summarize network 172.16.0.0 /24 and 172.16.1.0 /24 and advertise it to R1.

```
R1#show run | section router ospf
router ospf 1
 log-adjacency-changes
 network 192.168.12.0 0.0.0.255 area 0
R2#show run | section router ospf
router ospf 1
 log-adjacency-changes
 summary-address 172.16.0.0 255.255.0.0
 network 172.16.0.0 0.0.255.255 area 2
 network 192.168.12.0 0.0.0.255 area 0
```

The network engineer that configured R1 and R2 expects to see network 172.16.0.0 /26 in the routing table of R1.

```
R1#show ip route ospf
     172.16.0.0/32 is subnetted, 2 subnets
O IA    172.16.0.2 [110/2] via 192.168.12.2, 00:01:25, FastEthernet0/0
O IA    172.16.1.2 [110/2] via 192.168.12.2, 00:01:25, FastEthernet0/0
```

But the summary isn't working; we still see the 2 separate networks. What went wrong here?

```
R2#show run | section router ospf
router ospf 1
 log-adjacency-changes
 summary-address 172.16.0.0 255.255.0.0
```

The issue lies in this command.

OSPF has 2 commands for summarization:

- Area range: inter-area routes (LSA type 3)
- Summary-address: external routes (LSA type 5

```
R2(config)#router ospf 1
R2(config-router)#no summary-address 172.16.0.0 255.255.0.0
R2(config-router)#area 2 range 172.16.0.0 255.255.0.0
```

Using the correct command will solve our problem.

```
R1#show ip route ospf
O IA 172.16.0.0/16 [110/2] via 192.168.12.2, 00:00:47,
FastEthernet0/0
```

Now we see the summary in the routing table of R1...problem solved! **Lesson learned: Use the correct command for OSPF summarization.**

You made it to the end of the OSPF chapter! There's quite some stuff that could go wrong with OSPF and it's a core topic of CCNP so make sure you are very familiar with it. If you want some practice you can take a look at the following "all-in-one" OSPF lab that I created:

http://gns3vault.com/Troubleshooting/ospf-troubleshooting.html

It's similar to the EIGRP troubleshooting lab and quite a challenge, you'll learn a lot if you do it yourself!

7. Troubleshooting BGP

BGP is a complex routing protocol and there are many things that could go possibly wrong. Besides being complex it's also completely different compared to our IGPs (OSPF and EIGRP). In this chapter we'll start with troubleshooting BGP neighbor adjacencies and once that's working we'll look at issues with route advertisements that should or should not show up!

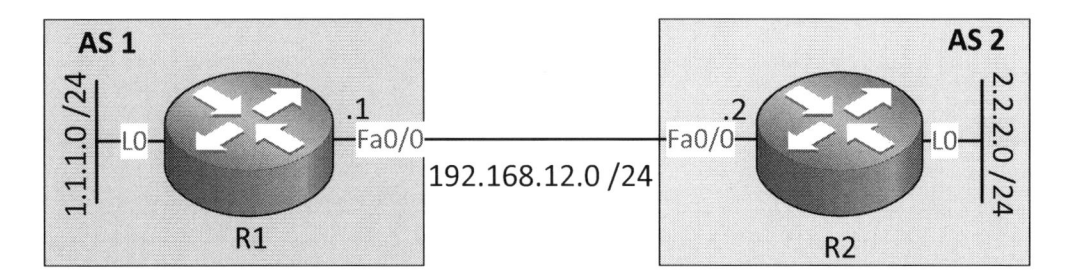

We'll start with some easy scenarios. Two BGP routers which are connected and configured for EBGP. Unfortunately we are seeing this when check the BGP neighbor adjacency:

```
R1#show ip bgp summary
BGP router identifier 192.168.12.1, local AS number 1
BGP table version is 1, main routing table version 1

Neighbor        V    AS MsgRcvd MsgSent   TblVer  InQ OutQ
Up/Down   State/PfxRcd
192.168.12.2    4    2       8       8        0    0    0
00:00:06 Active
```

```
R2#show ip bgp summary
BGP router identifier 192.168.12.2, local AS number 2
BGP table version is 1, main routing table version 1

Neighbor        V    AS MsgRcvd MsgSent   TblVer  InQ OutQ
Up/Down   State/PfxRcd
192.168.12.1    4    1       8       8        0    0    0
00:00:59 Active
```

When 2 EBGP routers that are directly connected do not form a working BGP neighbor adjacency there could be a number of things that are wrong:

- Layer 2 down preventing us from reaching the other side.
- Layer 3 issue: wrong IP address on one of the routers.
- Access-list blocking TCP port 179 (BGP).
- Wrong IP address configured for BGP neighbor router.

We can use the **show ip bgp summary** command to check the IP addresses of the routers, these seem to match.

```
R1#ping 192.168.12.2

Type escape sequence to abort.
Sending 5, 100-byte ICMP Echos to 192.168.12.2, timeout is 2
seconds:
.....
Success rate is 0 percent (0/5)
```

I can do a quick ping and I'll see that I'm unable to reach the other side.

```
R1#show ip int brief
Interface               IP-Address      OK? Method Status
Protocol
FastEthernet0/0         192.168.12.1    YES manual up    up
```

```
R2#show ip int brief
Interface               IP-Address      OK? Method Status
Protocol
FastEthernet0/0         192.168.12.2    YES manual
administratively down down
```

We'll check the interfaces and find out that someone left a shutdown command on the interface (DOH!).

```
R2(config)#interface fa0/0
R2(config-if)#no shutdown
```

Awake the interface...

```
R1# %BGP-5-ADJCHANGE: neighbor 192.168.12.2 Up
```

```
R2# %BGP-5-ADJCHANGE: neighbor 192.168.12.1 Up
```

That's what we like to see. Our BGP neighbor adjacency is established...told you this one would be easy ;) **Lesson learned: Make sure your interfaces are up and running.**

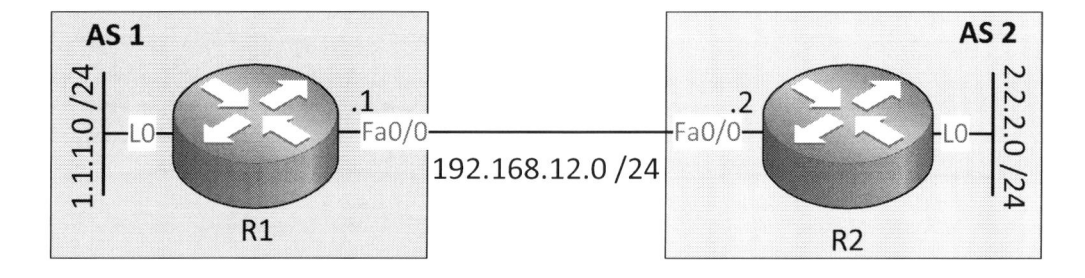

The next scenario is similar but slightly different. We are using the same routers and AS numbers but this time the BGP neighbor adjacency has to be

200

established between the loopback interfaces.

Let me show you what the BGP configuration looks like:

```
R1#show run | section bgp
router bgp 1
 no synchronization
 bgp log-neighbor-changes
 neighbor 2.2.2.2 remote-as 2
 no auto-summary
```

```
R2#show run | section bgp
router bgp 2
 no synchronization
 bgp log-neighbor-changes
 neighbor 1.1.1.1 remote-as 1
 no auto-summary
```

Here's the BGP configuration, you can see that we are using the loopback interfaces to establish a BGP neighbor adjacency.

```
R1#show ip bgp summary
BGP router identifier 192.168.12.1, local AS number 1
BGP table version is 1, main routing table version 1

Neighbor        V    AS MsgRcvd MsgSent   TblVer  InQ OutQ
Up/Down   State/PfxRcd
2.2.2.2         4     2       0       0        0    0    0 never
Idle
```

```
R2#show ip bgp summary
BGP router identifier 192.168.12.2, local AS number 2
BGP table version is 1, main routing table version 1

Neighbor        V    AS MsgRcvd MsgSent   TblVer  InQ OutQ
Up/Down   State/PfxRcd
1.1.1.1         4     1       0       0        0    0    0 never
Idle
```

Both routers show their BGP neighbor as idle. There are a number of things we have to check here:

- Is the IP address of the BGP neighbor **reachable**? We are not using the directly connected links so we might have routing issues.
- The **TTL of IP packets that we use for external BGP is 1**. This works for directly connected networks but if it's not directly connected we need to change this behavior.
- By default BGP will **source** its updates from the IP address that is closest to the BGP neighbor. In our example that's the FastEthernet interface. This is something we'll have to change.

```
R1#show ip route

C    192.168.12.0/24 is directly connected, FastEthernet0/0
```

```
R2#show ip route

C    192.168.12.0/24 is directly connected, FastEthernet0/0
```

We'll start with the routing. Both routers only know about their directly connected networks. In order to reach each other's loopback interfaces we'll use static routing.

```
R1(config)#ip route 2.2.2.2 255.255.255.255 192.168.12.2
```

```
R2(config)#ip route 1.1.1.1 255.255.255.255 192.168.12.1
```

Two static routes should do the job.

```
R1#ping 2.2.2.2 source loopback 0

Type escape sequence to abort.
Sending 5, 100-byte ICMP Echos to 2.2.2.2, timeout is 2 seconds:
Packet sent with a source address of 1.1.1.1
!!!!!
Success rate is 100 percent (5/5), round-trip min/avg/max = 4/4/4 ms
```

Sending a ping to IP address 2.2.2.2 and sourcing it from my own loopback interface proves that both routers know how to reach each other's loopback interface.

```
R1(config-router)#neighbor 2.2.2.2 ebgp-multihop 2
```

```
R2(config-router)#neighbor 1.1.1.1 ebgp-multihop 2
```

The **ebgp-multihop** command changes the TTL to 2.

```
R2#debug ip bgp
BGP debugging is on for address family: IPv4 Unicast
```

```
R2#
BGPNSF state: 1.1.1.1 went from nsf_not_active to nsf_not_active
BGP: 1.1.1.1 went from Active to Idle
BGP: 1.1.1.1 went from Idle to Active
BGP: 1.1.1.1 open active delayed 31810ms (35000ms max, 28% jitter)
BGP: 1.1.1.1 open active, local address 192.168.12.2
BGP: 1.1.1.1 open failed: Connection refused by remote host, open active delayed 34480ms (35000ms max, 28% jitter)
```

We can enable a debug to see the progress. You can clearly see that R2 is using IP address 192.168.12.2 and that R1 is refusing the connection.

```
R1(config-router)#neighbor 2.2.2.2 update-source loopback 0
```

```
R2(config-router)#neighbor 1.1.1.1 update-source loopback 0
```

Use the **update-source** command to change the source IP address for the BGP updates.

```
R1#
%BGP-5-ADJCHANGE: neighbor 2.2.2.2 Up
```

```
R2#
%BGP-5-ADJCHANGE: neighbor 1.1.1.1 Up
```

There goes! A working BGP neighbor adjacency ☺ Lesson learned: BGP routers don't have to establish a neighbor adjacency using the directly connected interfaces. **Make sure the BGP routers can reach each other, that BGP packets are sourced from the correct interface and in case of EBGP don't forget to use the multihop command.**

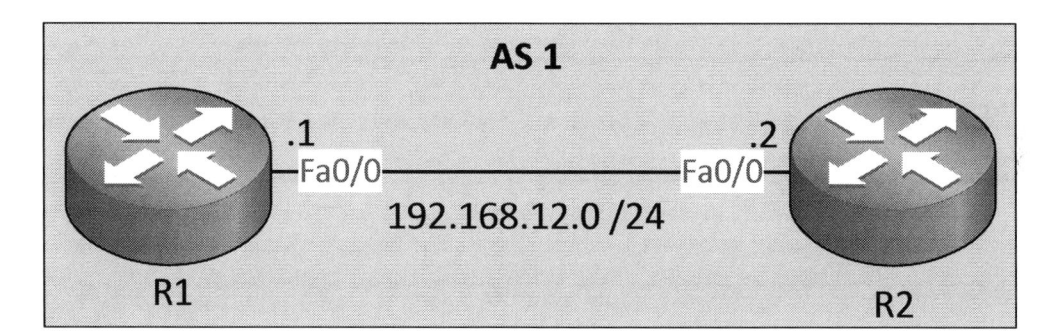

We'll continue by looking at some IBGP issues. Two routers in the same AS and here's the configuration:

```
R1#show run | section bgp
router bgp 1
 no synchronization
 bgp log-neighbor-changes
 neighbor 192.168.12.2 remote-as 1
 no auto-summary
```

```
R2#show run | section bgp
router bgp 1
 no synchronization
```

203

```
bgp log-neighbor-changes
neighbor 192.168.12.1 remote-as 1
no auto-summary
```

Plain and simple. The routers use the directly connected IP addresses for the BGP neighbor adjacency.

```
R1#show ip bgp summary
BGP router identifier 192.168.12.1, local AS number 1
BGP table version is 1, main routing table version 1

Neighbor        V    AS MsgRcvd MsgSent   TblVer  InQ OutQ
Up/Down   State/PfxRcd
192.168.12.2    4     1      46      46        0    0    0
00:05:24 Active
```

```
R2#show ip bgp summary
BGP router identifier 192.168.12.2, local AS number 1
BGP table version is 1, main routing table version 1

Neighbor        V    AS MsgRcvd MsgSent   TblVer  InQ OutQ
Up/Down   State/PfxRcd
192.168.12.1    4     1      46      46        0    0    0
00:05:30 Active
```

Too bad...we are not becoming neighbors. What could possibly be wrong? We are using the directly connected interfaces so there's not that much that could go wrong except for L2/L2 issues.

```
R1#ping 192.168.12.2

Type escape sequence to abort.
Sending 5, 100-byte ICMP Echos to 192.168.12.2, timeout is 2 seconds:
!!!!!
Success rate is 100 percent (5/5), round-trip min/avg/max = 4/4/4 ms
```

Sending a ping from one router to the other proves that L2 and L3 are working fine. What about L3? We could have issues with the transport layer.

```
R1#telnet 192.168.12.2 179
Trying 192.168.12.2, 179 ...
% Destination unreachable; gateway or host down
```

```
R2#telnet 192.168.12.1 179
Trying 192.168.12.1, 179 ...
```

I'm unable to connect to TCP port 179 from both routers. This should ring a bell, maybe something is blocking BGP ?

```
R1#show ip interface fastEthernet 0/0 | include access
  Outgoing access list is not set
  Inbound  access list is not set
```

```
R2#show ip interface fastEthernet 0/0 | include access
  Outgoing access list is not set
  Inbound  access list is 100
```

Dang! It's the security team...

```
R2#show ip access-lists
Extended IP access list 100
    10 deny tcp any eq bgp any (293 matches)
    15 deny tcp any any eq bgp (153 matches)
    20 permit ip any any (109 matches)
```

Someone decided it was a good idea to "secure" BGP and block it with an access-list.

```
R2(config)#interface fastEthernet 0/0
R2(config-if)#no ip access-group 100 in
```

Let's get rid of the access-list.

```
R1# %BGP-5-ADJCHANGE: neighbor 192.168.12.2 Up
```

```
R2# %BGP-5-ADJCHANGE: neighbor 192.168.12.1 Up
```

That's what we are looking for!

Lesson learned: Don't block BGP TCP port 179.

AS 1

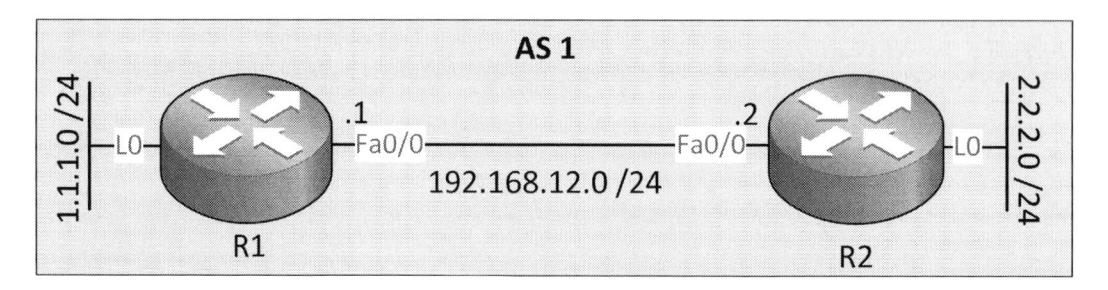

R1 — Lo 1.1.1.0/24 — Fa0/0 .1 — 192.168.12.0/24 — Fa0/0 .2 — R2 — Lo 2.2.2.0/24

Next IBGP issue. This one is similar to the EBGP situation earlier...we are using the loopback interfaces to establish the BGP neighbor adjacency, here are the configurations:

```
R1#show run | section router bgp
router bgp 1
 no synchronization
 bgp log-neighbor-changes
 neighbor 2.2.2.2 remote-as 1
  no auto-summary
```

```
R1#show run | section router bgp
router bgp 1
 no synchronization
 bgp log-neighbor-changes
 neighbor 2.2.2.2 remote-as 1
  no auto-summary
```

Nothing special, IBGP and we are using the loopback interfaces.

```
R1#show ip bgp summary | begin Neighbor
Neighbor     V    AS MsgRcvd MsgSent    TblVer   InQ OutQ
Up/Down   State/PfxRcd
2.2.2.2      4     1       0       0         0     0    0 never
Active
```

```
R2#show ip bgp summary | begin Neighbor
Neighbor     V    AS MsgRcvd MsgSent    TblVer   InQ OutQ
Up/Down   State/PfxRcd
1.1.1.1      4     1       0       0         0     0    0 never
Active
```

No luck here...no neighbors. Let's first check if the routers can reach each other's loopback interfaces:

```
R1#show ip route

C    192.168.12.0/24 is directly connected, FastEthernet0/0
     1.0.0.0/24 is subnetted, 1 subnets
C       1.1.1.0 is directly connected, Loopback0
```

```
R2#show ip route

C    192.168.12.0/24 is directly connected, FastEthernet0/0
     2.0.0.0/24 is subnetted, 1 subnets
C       2.2.2.0 is directly connected, Loopback0
```

A quick look at the routing table shows us that this is not the case. We could fix this with a static route or an IGP.
Normally we use an IGP for IBGP to advertise the loopback interfaces, let's use OSPF:

```
R1(config)#router ospf 1
R1(config-router)#network 1.1.1.0 0.0.0.255 area 0
R1(config-router)#network 192.168.12.0 0.0.0.255 area 0
```

```
R2(config)#router ospf 1
R2(config-router)#network 192.168.12.0 0.0.0.255 area 0
R2(config-router)#network 2.2.2.0 0.0.0.255 area 0
```

Smashing in the correct OSPF commands should do the job!

```
R1#ping 2.2.2.2 source loopback 0

Type escape sequence to abort.
Sending 5, 100-byte ICMP Echos to 2.2.2.2, timeout is 2 seconds:
Packet sent with a source address of 1.1.1.1
!!!!!
Success rate is 100 percent (5/5), round-trip min/avg/max = 4/4/4 ms
```

A quick ping to check if the routers know how to reach each other's networks is successful.

```
R1#show ip bgp summary | begin Neighbor
Neighbor        V    AS MsgRcvd MsgSent   TblVer  InQ OutQ
Up/Down  State/PfxRcd
2.2.2.2         4     1       0       0        0    0    0 never
Active
```

```
R2#show ip bgp summary | begin Neighbor
Neighbor        V    AS MsgRcvd MsgSent   TblVer  InQ OutQ
Up/Down  State/PfxRcd
1.1.1.1         4     1       0       0        0    0    0 never
Active
```

Still no BGP neighbor adjacency though...

```
R1#debug ip bgp
BGP debugging is on for address family: IPv4 Unicast
```

```
BGP: 2.2.2.2 open active, local address 192.168.12.1
BGP: 2.2.2.2 open failed: Connection refused by remote host,
open active delayed 32957ms (35000ms max, 28% jitter)
```

```
R2#debug ip bgp
BGP debugging is on for address family: IPv4 Unicast
BGP: 1.1.1.1 open active, local address 192.168.12.2
BGP: 1.1.1.1 open failed: Connection refused by remote host,
open active delayed 32957ms (35000ms max, 28% jitter)
```

A debug shows up that the connection is refused and it also shows us the local IP address that is used for BGP. Seems someone forgot to add the update-source command so let's fix it!

```
R1(config)#router bgp 1
R1(config-router)#neighbor 2.2.2.2 update-source loopback 0
```

```
R2(config)#router bgp 1
R2(config-router)#neighbor 1.1.1.1 update-source loopback 0
```

Just like EBGP we have to set the correct source for our BGP packets.

```
R1# BGP-5-ADJCHANGE: neighbor 2.2.2.2 Up
```

```
R2# BGP-5-ADJCHANGE: neighbor 1.1.1.1 Up
```

Problem solved! The only difference with EBGP is that we don't have to change the TTL with the ebgp-multihop command. **Lesson learned: Its common practice to configure IBGP between loopback interfaces. Make sure these loopbacks are reachable and that the BGP updates are sourced from the loopback interface.**

These are all the BGP neighbor adjacency related issues I wanted to show you. There are not as many things that could go wrong here as with OSPF or EIGRP.

If you want to do some BGP neighbor adjacency troubleshooting yourself, take a look at this lab:

http://gns3vault.com/Troubleshooting/bgp-neighbor-troubleshooting.html

We'll continue by looking at troubleshooting BGP route advertisements. All routers will have working BGP neighbor adjacencies.

How to Master CCNP TSHOOT

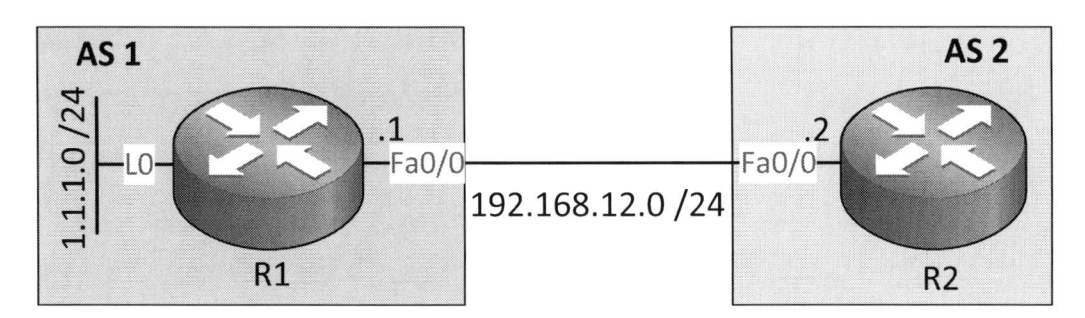

```
          AS 1                                                    AS 2
   1.1.1.0/24
         L0         .1                        .2
                  Fa0/0                      Fa0/0
                         192.168.12.0 /24
          R1                                                      R2
```

Here's a new scenario for you. R1 and R2 are in different autonomous systems. We are trying to advertise network 1.1.1.0 /24 from R1 to R2 but it's not showing up on R2. Here are the configurations:

```
R1#show run | section bgp
 no synchronization
 bgp log-neighbor-changes
 network 1.1.1.0
 neighbor 192.168.12.2 remote-as 2
 no auto-summary
```

```
R2#show run | section bgp
router bgp 2
 no synchronization
 bgp log-neighbor-changes
 neighbor 192.168.12.1 remote-as 1
 no auto-summary
```

At first sight there seems to be nothing wrong here.

```
R2#show ip bgp summary
BGP router identifier 192.168.12.2, local AS number 2
BGP table version is 1, main routing table version 1

Neighbor        V    AS MsgRcvd MsgSent    TblVer  InQ OutQ Up/Down
State/PfxRcd
192.168.12.1 4       1       4       4         1    0    0 00:01:26
0
```

However R2 didn't learn any prefixes from R1.

```
R1#show ip protocols | include filter
  Outgoing update filter list for all interfaces is not set
  Incoming update filter list for all interfaces is not set
```

```
R2#show ip protocols | include filter
  Outgoing update filter list for all interfaces is not set
  Incoming update filter list for all interfaces is not set
```

209

Maybe there's a distribute-list but that's not the case here. This means we'll have to check our network commands.

```
R1#show run | section router bgp
router bgp 1
 no synchronization
 bgp log-neighbor-changes
 network 1.1.1.0
 neighbor 192.168.12.2 remote-as 2
 no auto-summary
```

The problem is the network command, it works differently for BGP vs our IGPs. If we configure a network command for BGP it has to be an **exact match**. In this case I forgot to add the subnet mask…

```
R1(config)#router bgp 1
R1(config-router)#network 1.1.1.0 mask 255.255.255.0
```

I have to make sure I type the correct subnet mask.

```
R2#show ip bgp summary | begin Neighbor
Neighbor        V    AS MsgRcvd MsgSent   TblVer  InQ OutQ Up/Down State/PfxRcd
192.168.12.1 4      1       9       8       2    0    0 00:05:15 1
```

```
R2#show ip route bgp
      1.0.0.0/24 is subnetted, 1 subnets
B        1.1.1.0 [20/0] via 192.168.12.1, 00:01:08
```

Now you can see we learned the prefix and R2 installs it in the routing table…problem solved! **Lesson learned: Type in the exact correct subnet mask…BGP is picky!**

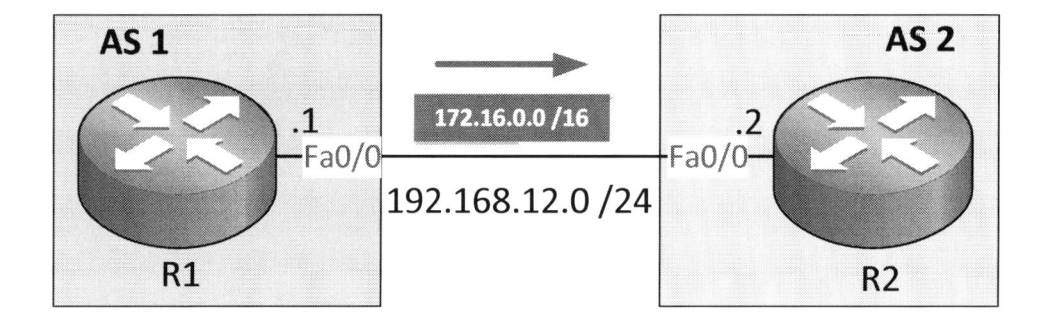

Let's move onto the next scenario. The network engineer from AS1 wants to advertise a summary to AS 2. The network engineer from AS 2 is complaining however that he's not receiving anything…let's find out what is going wrong!

```
R1#show run | section router bgp
router bgp 1
 no synchronization
 bgp log-neighbor-changes
 aggregate-address 172.16.0.0 255.255.0.0
 neighbor 192.168.12.2 remote-as 2
 no auto-summary
```

```
R2#show run | section router bgp
router bgp 2
 no synchronization
 bgp log-neighbor-changes
 neighbor 192.168.12.1 remote-as 1
 no auto-summary
```

Here's the configuration. You can see the **aggregate-address** command on R1 for network 172.16.0.0 /16.

```
R2#show ip bgp summary | begin Neighbor
Neighbor      V    AS MsgRcvd MsgSent   TblVer  InQ OutQ Up/Down
State/PfxRcd
192.168.12.1  4     1      21      19        3    0    0 00:16:21
0
```

Too bad...no prefixes have been received by R2. There are two things I could check here:

- See if a distribute-list is blocking prefixes like I did in the previous example.
- See what R1 has in its routing table (can't advertise what I don't have!).

Let's start with the routing table of R1 since I think by now you know what a distribute-list looks like ☺

```
R1#show ip route

C    192.168.12.0/24 is directly connected, FastEthernet0/0
     1.0.0.0/24 is subnetted, 1 subnets
C       1.1.1.0 is directly connected, Loopback0
```

There's nothing here that looks even close to 172.16.0.0 /16. If we want to advertise a summary we have to put something in the routing table of R1 first. Let me show you the different options:

```
R1(config)#interface loopback 0
R1(config-if)#ip address 172.16.0.1 255.255.255.0
R1(config-if)#exit
R1(config)#router bgp 1
R1(config-router)#network 172.16.0.0 mask 255.255.255.0
```

This is **option 1**: I'll create a loopback0 interface and configure an IP address that falls within the range of the aggregate-address command.

```
R2#show ip route bgp
     172.16.0.0/16 is variably subnetted, 2 subnets, 2 masks
B       172.16.0.0/24 [20/0] via 192.168.12.1, 00:01:25
B       172.16.0.0/16 [20/0] via 192.168.12.1, 00:01:25
```

Now we see the summary in the routing table of R2. By default it will still advertise the other prefixes. If you don't want this you need to use the **aggregate-address summary-only** command!

Let me show you option 2 of advertising the summary:

```
R1(config)#ip route 172.16.0.0 255.255.0.0 null 0
R1(config)#router bgp 1
R1(config-router)#network 172.16.0.0 mask 255.255.0.0
```

First we'll put the 172.16.0.0 /16 network in the routing table by creating a static route and pointing it to the null0 interface. Secondly I'll use a network command for BGP to advertise this network.

```
R2#show ip route bgp
B     172.16.0.0/16 [20/0] via 192.168.12.1, 00:00:45
```

Now it shows up on R2! Problem solved! **Lesson learned: You can't advertise what you don't have. Create a static route and point it to the null0 interface to create a loopback interface that has a prefix that falls within the summary address range.**

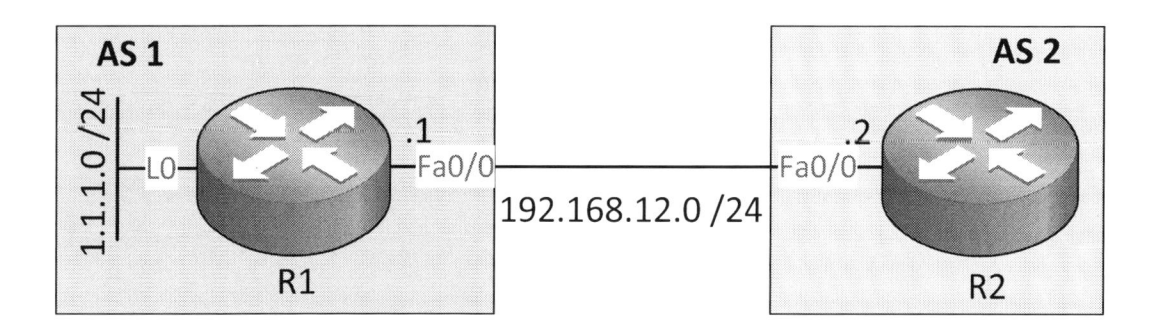

Onto the next scenario. You are working as a network engineer for AS 1 and one day you get a phone call from the network engineer at AS 2 asking you why you are advertising a summary for 1.0.0.0 /8.

You have no idea what the hell he is talking about so you decide to check your router.

```
R2#show ip route bgp
B    1.0.0.0/8 [20/0] via 192.168.12.1, 00:02:15
```

This is what the network engineer on R2 is seeing.

```
R1#show ip bgp 1.0.0.0
BGP routing table entry for 1.0.0.0/8, version 3
Paths: (1 available, best #1, table Default-IP-Routing-Table)
  Advertised to update-groups:
    1
  Local
    0.0.0.0 from 0.0.0.0 (1.1.1.1)
      Origin incomplete, metric 0, localpref 100, weight 32768,
valid, sourced, best
```

We can see that we have network 1.0.0.0 /8 in the BGP table of R1. Let's check its routing table.

```
R1#show ip route 1.0.0.0
Routing entry for 1.0.0.0/24, 1 known subnets
  Attached (1 connections)
  Redistributing via bgp 1
  Advertised by bgp 1

C       1.1.1.0 is directly connected, Loopback0
```

Network 1.1.1.0 /24 is configured on the loopback interface but it's in the BGP table as 1.0.0.0 /8. This could mean only 1 thing....**summarization**.

```
R1#show ip protocols
Routing Protocol is "bgp 1"
  Outgoing update filter list for all interfaces is not set
  Incoming update filter list for all interfaces is not set
  IGP synchronization is disabled
  Automatic route summarization is enabled
```

A quick look at show ip protocols reveals that automatic summarization is enabled. Let's disable it:

```
R1(config)#router bgp 1
R1(config-router)#no auto-summary
```

We'll disable it on R1.

```
R2#show ip route bgp
     1.0.0.0/24 is subnetted, 1 subnets
```

213

```
B        1.1.1.0 [20/0] via 192.168.12.1, 00:00:20
```

Now we see 1.1.1.0 /24 on R2...problem solved! **Lesson learned: If you see classful networks in your BGP table you might have auto-summary enabled.**

Some of the problems I've been showing you could be resolved easily by just looking and/or comparing the output of a "show run". This might be true but keep in mind that you don't always have access to ALL routers in the network so maybe there's no way to compare configurations. There could be a switch or another router in between the devices you are trying to troubleshooting that are causing issues. Using the appropriate show and debug commands will show you exactly what your router is doing and what it is advertising to other routers.

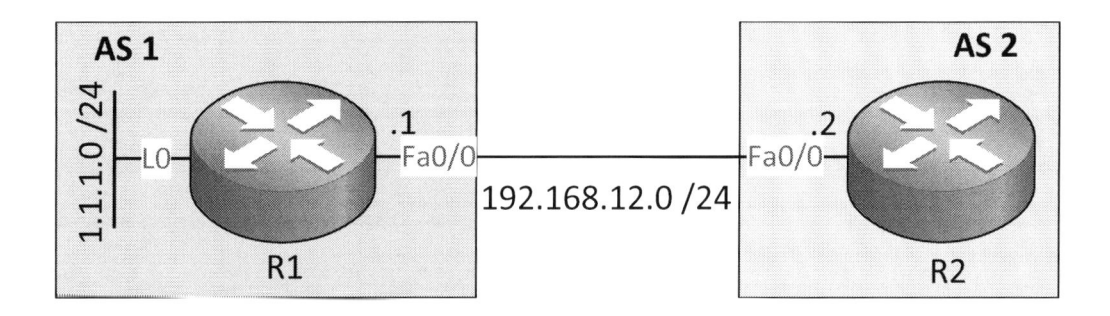

Same topology, different problem. The people from AS 2 are complaining that they are not receiving anything from AS 1. To keep it interesting I'm not going to show you the configurations ;)

```
R2#show ip bgp summary | begin Neighbor
Neighbor      V    AS MsgRcvd MsgSent    TblVer  InQ OutQ Up/Down State/PfxRcd
192.168.12.1  4    1     51      48        1      0   0   00:08:51 0
```

For starters, we can see that R2 is not receiving any prefixes.

```
R1#show ip protocols | include filter
  Outgoing update filter list for all interfaces is not set
  Incoming update filter list for all interfaces is not set
```

I can also verify that R1 doesn't have any distribute-lists.

```
R1#show ip bgp 1.1.1.0
BGP routing table entry for 1.1.1.0/24, version 4
Paths: (1 available, best #1, table Default-IP-Routing-Table)
  Not advertised to any peer
  Local
    0.0.0.0 from 0.0.0.0 (1.1.1.1)
      Origin incomplete, metric 0, localpref 100, weight 32768,
valid, sourced, best
```

I can confirm that R1 does have network 1.1.1.0 /24 in its routing table so why is it not advertising this to R2?

Let's see if R1 has configured anything special for its neighbor R2:

```
R1#show ip bgp neighbors 192.168.12.2
BGP neighbor is 192.168.12.2,  remote AS 2, external link
  BGP version 4, remote router ID 192.168.12.2
  BGP state = Established, up for 00:03:34
  Last read 00:00:33, last write 00:00:33, hold time is 180,
keepalive interval is 60 seconds
  Neighbor capabilities:
    Route refresh: advertised and received(old & new)
    Address family IPv4 Unicast: advertised and received
  Message statistics:
    InQ depth is 0
    OutQ depth is 0
                         Sent       Rcvd
    Opens:                 11         11
    Notifications:          0          0
    Updates:                7          0
    Keepalives:            85         86
    Route Refresh:          0          0
    Total:                103         97
  Default minimum time between advertisement runs is 30 seconds

 For address family: IPv4 Unicast
  BGP table version 3, neighbor version 3/0
 Output queue size : 0
  Index 1, Offset 0, Mask 0x2
  1 update-group member
  Outbound path policy configured
  Route map for outgoing advertisements is NEIGHBORS
                         Sent       Rcvd
    Prefix activity:     ----       ----
    Prefixes Current:       0          0
    Prefixes Total:         0          0
    Implicit Withdraw:      0          0
    Explicit Withdraw:      0          0
    Used as bestpath:     n/a          0
    Used as multipath:    n/a          0
```

I will use the **show ip bgp neighbors** command to see detailed information of R2. We can see that a route-map has been applied to R2 and it's called "NEIGHBORS". Keep in mind that besides distribute-lists we can use also use route-maps for BGP filtering.

```
R1# show route-map
route-map NEIGHBORS, permit, sequence 10
  Match clauses:
    ip address prefix-lists: PREFIXES
  Set clauses:
  Policy routing matches: 0 packets, 0 bytes
```

There's only a match statement for prefix-list "PREFIXES".

```
R1#show ip prefix-list
ip prefix-list PREFIXES: 1 entries
    seq 5 deny 1.1.1.0/24
```

There's our troublemaker...its denying network 1.1.1.0 /24!

```
R1(config)#router bgp 1
R1(config-router)#no neighbor 192.168.12.2 route-map NEIGHBORS out
```

We'll get rid of the route-map...

```
R2#show ip route bgp
     1.0.0.0/24 is subnetted, 1 subnets
B       1.1.1.0 [20/0] via 192.168.12.1, 00:00:03
```

And finally R2 has learned about this prefix...problem solved! **Lesson learned: Make sure there are no route-maps blocking the advertisement of prefixes.**

> *BGP can be slow sometimes especially when you are waiting for results as you are doing labs. "clear ip bgp *" is a good way to speed it up...just don't do it on routers in a production network* ☺

216

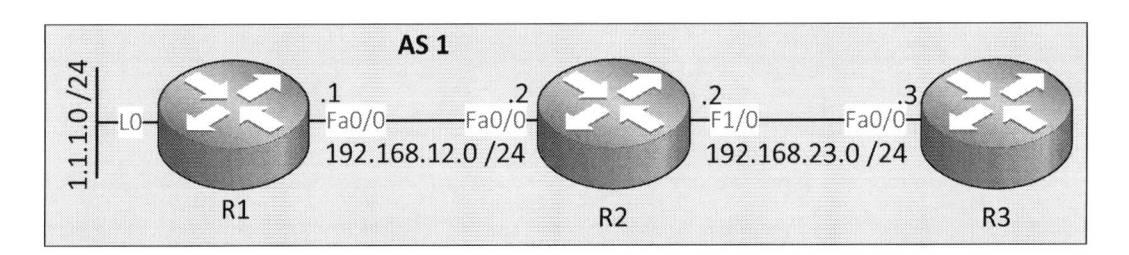

Finally a third contestant enters the arena to demonstrate a new issue. R1 is advertising network 1.1.1.0 /24 but R3 is not learning about this network. Here are the configurations:

```
R1#show run | section router bgp
router bgp 1
 no synchronization
 bgp log-neighbor-changes
 network 1.1.1.0 mask 255.255.255.0
 neighbor 192.168.12.2 remote-as 1
 no auto-summary
```

```
R2#show run | section router bgp
router bgp 1
 no synchronization
 bgp log-neighbor-changes
 neighbor 192.168.12.1 remote-as 1
 neighbor 192.168.23.3 remote-as 1
 no auto-summary
```

```
R3#show run | section router bgp
router bgp 1
 no synchronization
 bgp log-neighbor-changes
 neighbor 192.168.23.2 remote-as 1
 no auto-summary
```

The neighbor adjacencies have been configured, R1 is advertising network 1.1.1.0 /24.

```
R2#show ip route bgp
      1.0.0.0/24 is subnetted, 1 subnets
B        1.1.1.0 [200/0] via 192.168.12.1, 00:00:23
```

```
R3#show ip route bgp
```

We can see network 1.1.1.0 /24 in the routing table of R2 but it's not showing up on R3.

Technically there is no problem. If you look closely at the BGP configuration of all three routers you can see there is only a BGP neighbor adjacency between R1 & R2 and between R2 & R3. Because of **IBGP split horizon** R2 does not forward network 1.1.1.0 /24 towards R3. In order to fix this we need to configure R1 and R3 to become neighbors.

```
R1(config)#ip route 192.168.23.3 255.255.255.255 192.168.12.2
```

```
R3(config)#ip route 192.168.12.1 255.255.255.255 192.168.23.2
```

If I'm going to configure the BGP neighbor adjacency between R1 and R3 I'll need to make sure they can reach each other. I can use a static route or an IGP...to keep things easy I'll use a static route this time.

```
R1(config)#router bgp 1
R1(config-router)#neighbor 192.168.23.3 remote-as 1
```

```
R3(config)#router bgp 1
R3(config-router)#neighbor 192.168.12.1 remote-as 1
```

Configure the correct BGP neighbor commands...

```
R3#show ip route bgp
     1.0.0.0/24 is subnetted, 1 subnets
B       1.1.1.0 [200/0] via 192.168.12.1, 00:00:08
```

And R3 has access to network 1.1.1.0 /24!

Lesson learned: IBGP neighbor adjacencies have to be full mesh! Another solution would be by using a route-reflector or confederation.

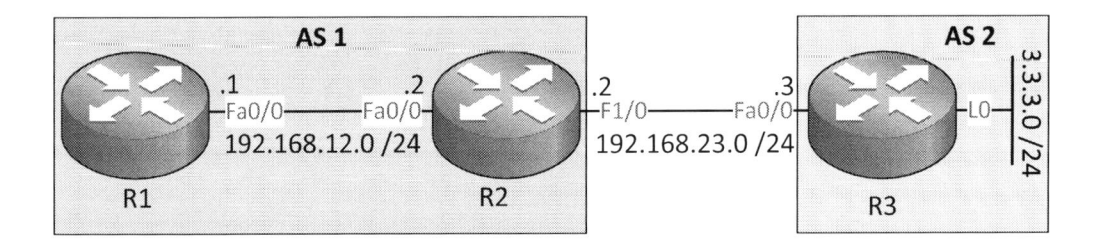

Here's a new scenario for you. R3 is advertising network 3.3.3.0 /24 through EBGP and R2 installs it in the routing table. R1 however doesn't have this network in its routing table. Here are the configurations:

```
R1#show run | section router bgp
router bgp 1
 no synchronization
 bgp log-neighbor-changes
 neighbor 192.168.12.2 remote-as 1
 no auto-summary
```

```
R2#show run | section router bgp
router bgp 1
 no synchronization
 bgp log-neighbor-changes
 neighbor 192.168.12.1 remote-as 1
```

```
 neighbor 192.168.23.3 remote-as 2
 no auto-summary
```

```
R3#show run | section router bgp
router bgp 2
 no synchronization
 bgp log-neighbor-changes
 network 3.3.3.0 mask 255.255.255.0
 neighbor 192.168.23.2 remote-as 1
 no auto-summary
```

Here are the configurations. To keep things easy I'm using the physical interface IP addresses to configure the BGP neighbor adjacencies.

```
R2#show ip route bgp
     3.0.0.0/24 is subnetted, 1 subnets
B       3.3.3.0 [20/0] via 192.168.23.3, 00:09:37
```

We can verify that network 3.3.3.0 /24 is in the routing table of R2.

```
R1#show ip route bgp
```

There's nothing in the routing table of R1 however. The first thing we should check is if it's the BGP table or not.

```
R1#show ip bgp
BGP table version is 1, local router ID is 192.168.12.1
Status codes: s suppressed, d damped, h history, * valid, >
best, i - internal,
              r RIB-failure, S Stale
Origin codes: i - IGP, e - EGP, ? - incomplete

   Network            Next Hop          Metric LocPrf Weight Path
* i3.3.3.0/24         192.168.23.3           0    100      0 2 i
```

We can see it's in the BGP table and the * indicates that this is a valid route. However I don't see the > symbol which indicates the best path. For some reason BGP is unable to install this entry in the routing table. Take a close look at the next hop IP address (192.168.23.3). Is this IP address reachable?

```
R1#show ip route 192.168.23.3
% Network not in table
```

R1 has no idea how to reach 192.168.23.3 so our next hop is unreachable. There are 2 ways how we can deal with this issue:

- Use a static route or IGP to make this next hop IP address reachable.

- Change the next hop IP address.

We'll change the next hop IP address since I think you've seen enough static routes and IGPs so far.

```
R2(config)#router bgp 1
R2(config-router)#neighbor 192.168.12.1 next-hop-self
```

This command will change the next hop IP address to the IP address of R2.

```
R1#show ip bgp
BGP table version is 2, local router ID is 192.168.12.1
Status codes: s suppressed, d damped, h history, * valid, > best, i - internal,
           r RIB-failure, S Stale
Origin codes: i - IGP, e - EGP, ? - incomplete

   Network          Next Hop            Metric LocPrf Weight Path
*>i3.3.3.0/24       192.168.12.2             0    100      0 2 i
```

You can see the > symbol that indicates that this path has been selected as the best one. The next hop IP address is now 192.168.12.2.

```
R1#show ip route bgp
     3.0.0.0/24 is subnetted, 1 subnets
B       3.3.3.0 [200/0] via 192.168.12.2, 00:10:52
```

Hooray! It's in the routing table now. Are we done now? If my goal was to make this show up in the routing table then we are now finished...there's another issue however.

```
R1#ping 3.3.3.3

Type escape sequence to abort.
Sending 5, 100-byte ICMP Echos to 3.3.3.3, timeout is 2 seconds:
.....
Success rate is 0 percent (0/5)
```

My ping is unsuccessful. R1 and R2 both have network 3.3.3.0 /24 in their routing table so we know that *they* know where to forward the IP packets to. Let's take a look at R3:

```
R3#show ip route

     3.0.0.0/24 is subnetted, 1 subnets
C       3.3.3.0 is directly connected, Loopback0
C    192.168.23.0/24 is directly connected, FastEthernet0/0
```

R3 will receive an IP packet with destination 3.3.3.3 and source 192.168.12.1. You can see in the routing table that it has no idea where to send IP packets meant for 192.168.12.1. Let's change that:

```
R2(config)#router bgp 1
R2(config-router)#network 192.168.12.0 mask 255.255.255.0
```

We'll advertise network 192.168.12.0 /24 on R2.

```
R3#show ip route bgp
B    192.168.12.0/24 [20/0] via 192.168.23.2, 00:00:33
```

Now R3 knows where to send traffic for 192.168.12.0 /24 to.

```
R1#ping 3.3.3.3

Type escape sequence to abort.
Sending 5, 100-byte ICMP Echos to 3.3.3.3, timeout is 2 seconds:
!!!!!
Success rate is 100 percent (5/5), round-trip min/avg/max = 4/11/28 ms
```

Problem solved! **Lesson learned: Make sure the next hop IP address is reachable so routes can be installed in the routing table and that all required networks are reachable.**

These are all the BGP issues I wanted to show you so you made it to the end of this chapter. Of course I have something for you to chew on so you can take a look at the following lab:

http://gns3vault.com/Troubleshooting/bgp-troubleshooting.html

8. Troubleshooting Network Services

In this chapter we will look at troubleshooting NAT (Network Address Translation) / PAT (Port Address Translation), DHCP and FHRPs (First Hop Redundancy Protocols). NAT/PAT can be troublesome, not because the configuration is so difficult (it can be!) but mostly because you could encounter routing issues since you are changing IP addresses. In the second part of this chapter we'll look at the most common DHCP issues and finally we'll close the chapter with some FHRP issues. Let's troubleshooting some translations first!

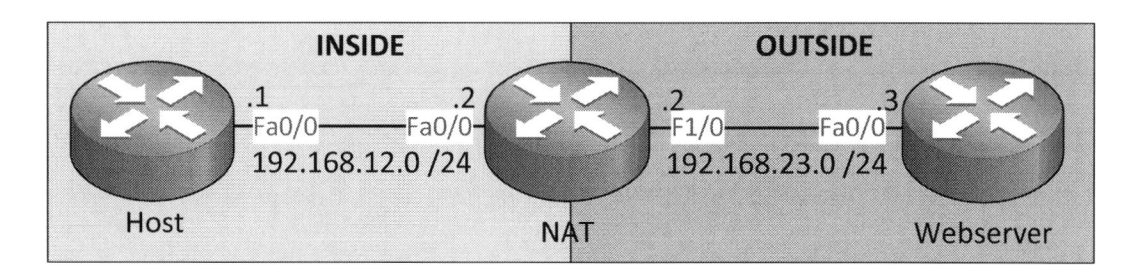

In this scenario we have 3 devices. The router on the left side is called "Host" and this is supposed to be a computer on our LAN. If you have played with my labs or read my other books then you'll know I like to use routers as host devices. The device on the right side is supposed to be some webserver, something on the Internet that we are trying to reach on the Internet. In the middle we'll find our router that is configured for NAT and/or PAT.

Users from our LAN are complaining that they are unable to reach anything on the Internet. They have confirmed that their IP address and default gateway is OK. Let's take a look at the NAT router:

```
NAT#ping 192.168.23.3

Type escape sequence to abort.
Sending 5, 100-byte ICMP Echos to 192.168.23.3, timeout is 2 seconds:
!!!!!
Success rate is 100 percent (5/5), round-trip min/avg/max = 4/4/8 ms
```

It's not a bad idea to check if the NAT router can reach the webserver by trying a simple ping. If it doesn't work you at least know that you have routing issues or that the webserver is down (or maybe just blocking ICMP traffic).

```
NAT#telnet 192.168.23.3 80
Trying 192.168.23.3, 80 ... Open
```

Because it's a webserver it's better to try and connect to TCP port 80. You can see that this is working so routing between the NAT router and the webserver plus connecting to the TCP port is no problem.

```
NAT#show ip nat translations
Pro Inside global      Inside local       Outside local
Outside global
icmp 192.168.23.2:1    192.168.12.2:1     192.168.12.1:1
192.168.12.1:1
```

We can use the **show ip nat translations** to see if anything is going on. We see that the NAT router is translating something but it doesn't look quite right if you look closely. The outside local and global IP addresses refer to the IP address on the inside. Let's take a look at the configuration...

```
NAT#show ip nat statistics
Total active translations: 0 (0 static, 0 dynamic; 0 extended)
Outside interfaces:
  FastEthernet0/0
Inside interfaces:
  FastEthernet1/0
Hits: 5  Misses: 0
CEF Translated packets: 0, CEF Punted packets: 0
Expired translations: 1
Dynamic mappings:
-- Inside Source
[Id: 1] access-list 1 interface FastEthernet1/0 refcount 0
Queued Packets: 0
```

Show ip nat statistics is a nice command to verify your configuration. You can see that the inside and outside interfaces have been swapped. FastEthernet 0/0 should be the inside and FastEthernet 1/0 should be the outside.

```
NAT(config)#interface fastEthernet 0/0
NAT(config-if)#ip nat inside
NAT(config)#interface fastEthernet 1/0
NAT(config-if)#ip nat outside
```

Let's change it so we have the correct inside and outside interfaces.

```
Host#ping 192.168.23.3

Type escape sequence to abort.
Sending 5, 100-byte ICMP Echos to 192.168.23.3, timeout is 2 seconds:
!!!!!
Success rate is 100 percent (5/5), round-trip min/avg/max = 8/9/16 ms
```

Traffic from the host to the webserver is now working!

```
NAT#show ip nat translations
Pro Inside global      Inside local       Outside local
Outside global
icmp 192.168.23.2:5    192.168.12.1:5     192.168.23.3:5
192.168.23.3:5
```

In case you are wondering, this is what the NAT translation table should look like. The **inside local** IP address is our inside host. The **inside global** IP address is what we have configured on the outside of our NAT router (FastEthernet 1/0). The outside **local and global** IP address is our webserver...problem solved! **Lesson learned: Make sure you have the correct inside and outside interfaces.**

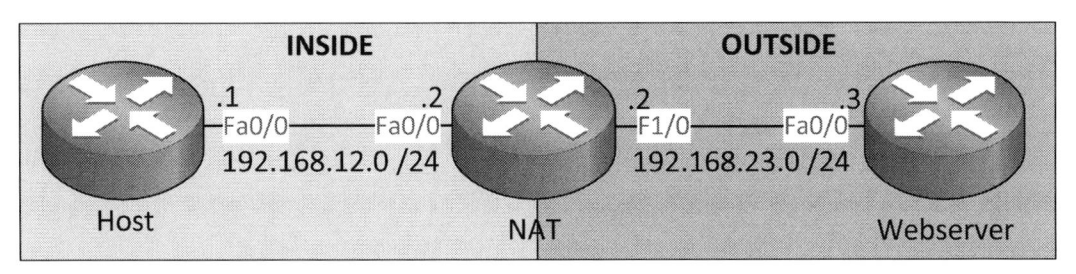

```
                INSIDE              |              OUTSIDE
        .1                .2        |        .2                .3
       Fa0/0           Fa0/0        |       F1/0             Fa0/0
       192.168.12.0 /24             |      192.168.23.0 /24
       Host                  NAT                        Webserver
```

Same topology, different problem! Once again users from the inside are complaining that they are unable to reach the webserver. Let's check out our NAT router:

```
NAT#show ip nat translations
```

First I'll check if the router is translating *anything*. As you can see it's kinda quiet...nothing is going on!

```
NAT#show ip nat statistics
Total active translations: 0 (0 static, 0 dynamic; 0 extended)
Outside interfaces:
  FastEthernet1/0
Inside interfaces:
  FastEthernet0/0
Hits: 0  Misses: 0
CEF Translated packets: 0, CEF Punted packets: 0
Expired translations: 0
Dynamic mappings:
-- Inside Source
[Id: 1] access-list 1 interface FastEthernet1/0 refcount 0
Queued Packets: 0
```

We can verify that the inside and outside interfaces have been configured correctly. There are no translations going on however. The inside source has been defined by using access-list 1. Let's take a closer look at this ACL:

```
Standard IP access list 1
    10 permit 0.0.0.0, wildcard bits 255.255.255.0
```

Ahh look...seems someone messed up the ACL! Let's fix it:

```
NAT(config)#no access-list 1
NAT(config)#access-list 1 permit 192.168.12.0 0.0.0.255
```

We'll create the ACL so it matches on 192.168.12.0/24.

```
Host#ping 192.168.23.3

Type escape sequence to abort.
Sending 5, 100-byte ICMP Echos to 192.168.23.3, timeout is 2
seconds:
!!!!!
Success rate is 100 percent (5/5), round-trip min/avg/max =
8/8/12 ms
```

We can now reach the webserver from our host.

```
NAT#show ip nat statistics
Total active translations: 1 (0 static, 1 dynamic; 1 extended)
Outside interfaces:
  FastEthernet1/0
Inside interfaces:
  FastEthernet0/0
Hits: 4  Misses: 1
CEF Translated packets: 5, CEF Punted packets: 0
Expired translations: 0
Dynamic mappings:
-- Inside Source
[Id: 1] access-list 1 interface FastEthernet1/0 refcount 1
Queued Packets: 0
```

I'm seeing hits if I look at the NAT statistics.

```
NAT#show ip nat translations
Pro Inside global      Inside local       Outside local
Outside global
icmp 192.168.23.2:10   192.168.12.1:10    192.168.23.3:10
192.168.23.3:10
```

And I'm seeing the translation...problem solved! **Lesson learned: Make sure you use the correct access-list to match your inside hosts.**

In the next part of this chapter we'll look at DHCP issues.

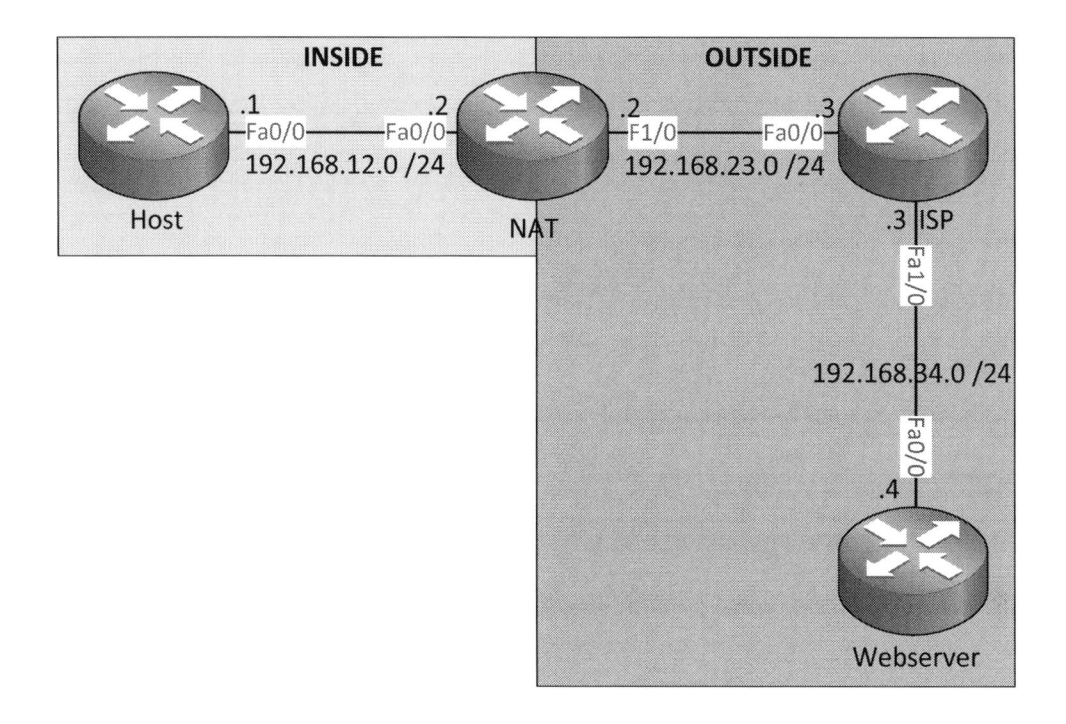

Here's a new scenario for you, let me explain it first:

- The green area is our LAN so it's our NAT inside.
- The red area is the Internet so it's our NAT outside.
- The host is supposed to be a computer that has 192.168.12.2 as its default gateway.
- Our NAT router is connected to an ISP router.
- The ISP router has assigned us subnet 172.16.1.0 /24 that we are going to use for NAT translation.
- BGP has been configured between the NAT and ISP router for reachability to network 192.168.34.0 /24.
- The webserver is supposed to be something that is listening on TCP port 80 and is using 192.168.34.3 as its default gateway.

Users from our LAN however are complaining that they are unable to reach the webserver. Let's verify our NAT configuration:

```
NAT#show ip nat translations
Pro Inside global      Inside local      Outside local
Outside global
icmp 172.16.1.1:5      192.168.12.1:5    192.168.34.4:5
192.168.34.4:5
```

We can verify that translation is working:

- Inside local is the IP address of our host.
- Inside global is one of the IP addresses from our 172.16.1.0/24 subnet.

227

- Outside local and global is the IP address of our webserver.

This translation is looking good to me because all the IP addresses are correct.

```
NAT#show ip route | include 192.168.34.0
B    192.168.34.0/24 [20/0] via 192.168.23.3, 00:13:48
```

We can see that the NAT router has learned how to reach network 192.168.34.0 /24 through BGP.

```
NAT#telnet 192.168.34.4 80
Trying 192.168.34.4, 80 ... Open
```

Our NAT router can reach the webserver so connectivity is not the problem. There is one important thing to keep in mind however. The IP packet that the NAT router produces looks like this:

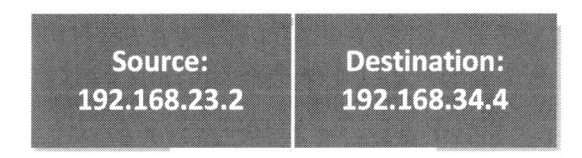

Source:	Destination:
192.168.23.2	192.168.34.4

The destination IP address is our webserver and reaching it is no problem. The source IP address is 192.168.23.2 and since we got a response we know that the ISP router knows how to reach the 192.168.23.0 /24 subnet. This makes sense because the 192.168.23.0 /24 subnet is directly connected to the ISP router.

However if we send a ping from the host device it is being translated because of NAT to an IP address in the 172.16.1.0 /24 subnet. The IP packet will look like this:

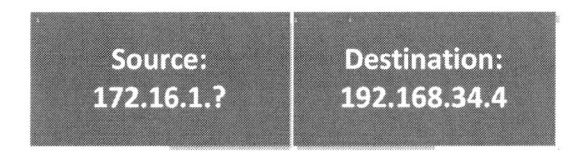

Source:	Destination:
172.16.1.?	192.168.34.4

This is what happens when this IP packet leaves the NAT router and is sent to the ISP router:

1. The ISP router receives the IP packet and will check its routing table if it knows where to send traffic for network 192.168.34.0 /24.
2. The 192.168.34.0 /24 network is directly connected for the ISP router so it will do an ARP request for the MAC address of the webserver, receives the ARP reply and it can forward the IP packet to the webserver.
3. The webserver wants to respond and it will create a new IP packet with destination IP address 172.16.1.something.

4. Because the webserver has the ISP router as its default gateway it will send the IP packet to the ISP router.
5. The ISP router has to do a routing table lookup to see if it knows where network 172.16.1.0 /24 is located.
6. The ISP router has no idea where 172.16.1.0 /24 is and will drop the IP packet.

If this were a real production network you wouldn't have access to the ISP router. Because this is a lab we do have access so let's do a nice debug!

```
ISP#debug ip packet 1
IP packet debugging is on for access list 1
ISP#conf t
ISP(config)#access-list 1 permit host 192.168.34.4
```

First I'll enable debugging of IP packets and I'll use an access-list that matches the webserver's IP address.

```
Host#ping 192.168.34.4

Type escape sequence to abort.
Sending 5, 100-byte ICMP Echos to 192.168.34.4, timeout is 2 seconds:
.....
Success rate is 0 percent (0/5)
```

Next step is that we will generate some traffic from the host device.

```
ISP# IP: s=192.168.34.4 (FastEthernet1/0), d=172.16.1.1, len 100, unroutable
```

This is what the ISP router will produce. It tells us that it has no idea where to send the IP packet for 172.16.1.1 to...it is unroutable and will be forwarded to IP packet heaven.

So how do we solve this issue? The ISP router requires network 172.16.1.0 /24 in its routing table. Since we are already running BGP we can use it to advertise this network from our NAT router:

```
NAT(config)#ip route 172.16.1.0 255.255.255.0 null 0
NAT(config)#router bgp 1
NAT(config-router)#network 172.16.1.0 mask 255.255.255.0
```

First I'll create a static rule that points network 172.16.1.0 /24 to the null0 interface. I'm doing this because it's impossible to advertise what you don't have.

Next step is to advertise this network in BGP.

```
Host#ping 192.168.34.4

Type escape sequence to abort.
Sending 5, 100-byte ICMP Echos to 192.168.34.4, timeout is 2
seconds:
!!!!!
Success rate is 100 percent (5/5), round-trip min/avg/max =
12/16/24 ms
```

My pings are now working…problem solved!

Lesson learned: Make sure your routers know how to reach the translated networks.

That's all that I wanted to teach you about NAT/PAT troubleshooting. We'll continue this chapter by looking at some DHCP-related problems.

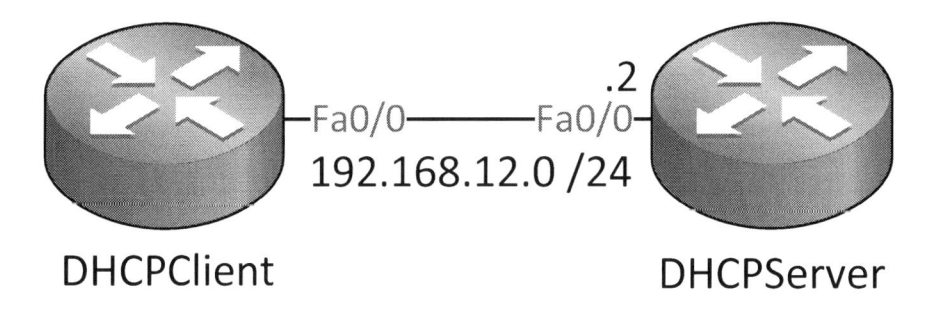

```
          Fa0/0 ———— Fa0/0   .2
              192.168.12.0 /24

       DHCPClient              DHCPServer
```

We'll start with a simple scenario. The router on the left side is our DHCP Client and the router on the right side will be our DHCP Server. The Client however is not receiving any IP addresses…what could be wrong?

```
DHCPClient#show ip interface brief
Interface               IP-Address      OK? Method Status
Protocol
FastEthernet0/0         unassigned      YES DHCP   up
up
```

First I'll verify if the interface on the DHCP client is up/up and that it has been configured for DHCP, this is indeed the case.

```
DHCPServer#show ip interface brief
Interface               IP-Address      OK? Method Status
Protocol
FastEthernet0/0         192.168.12.2    YES manual up
up
```

I also want to make sure the interface on the DHCP server is up/up and that it has an IP address. This looks fine to me...

```
DHCPClient#debug dhcp detail
DHCP client activity debugging is on (detailed)
```

If I want to be absolutely sure that the client is not the issue I can enable **debug dhcp detail** to see if the DHCP client is sending DHCP discover messages.

```
DHCPClient# Hostname: DHCPClient
DHCP: new entry. add to queue, interface FastEthernet0/0
DHCP: SDiscover attempt # 1 for entry:
Temp IP addr: 0.0.0.0  for peer on Interface: FastEthernet0/0
Temp  sub net mask: 0.0.0.0
DHCP Lease server: 0.0.0.0, state: 1 Selecting
DHCP transaction id: 289
Lease: 0 secs,  Renewal: 0 secs,  Rebind: 0 secs
Next timer fires after: 00:00:04
Retry count: 1   Client-ID: cisco-cc00.1ab0.0000-Fa0/0
Client-ID hex dump: 636973636F2D636330302E316162302E
                    303030302D4661302F30
```

You'll see some debug output like above. This proves that my DHCP client is sending DHCP Discover messages; the client doesn't seem to be the problem here.

```
DHCPServer#show ip dhcp pool

Pool MYPOOL :
 Utilization mark (high/low)    : 100 / 0
 Subnet size (first/next)       : 0 / 0
 Total addresses                : 254
 Leased addresses               : 0
 Pending event                  : none
 1 subnet is currently in the pool :
 Current index        IP address range                        Leased addresses
 192.168.12.1         192.168.12.1      - 192.168.12.254      0
```

We'll use the **show ip dhcp pool** command to check if there is a DHCP pool. You can see that we do have a DHCP pool called "MYPOOL" and it's configured for the 192.168.12.0 /24 subnet. This is looking fine to me.

```
DHCPServer#show ip dhcp server statistics
Memory usage         8754
Address pools        1
Database agents      0
Automatic bindings   0
Manual bindings      0
```

```
Expired bindings         0
Malformed messages       0
Secure arp entries       0

Message                  Received
BOOTREQUEST              0
DHCPDISCOVER             0
DHCPREQUEST              0
DHCPDECLINE              0
DHCPRELEASE              0
DHCPINFORM               0

Message                  Sent
BOOTREPLY                0
DHCPOFFER                0
DHCPACK                  0
DHCPNAK                  0
```

We can use **show ip dhcp server statistics** to see if the DHCP server is doing anything. You can see that it's not doing anything…what could this mean?

```
DHCPServer#show ip sockets
Proto    Remote        Port      Local        Port  In Out Stat TTY
OutputIF
```

This is a command you probably don't see every day. **Show ip sockets** shows us on which ports the router is listening. As you can see it's not listening on any ports…if I don't see port 67 here (DHCP) it means that the DHCP service has been disabled.

```
DHCPServer(config)#service dhcp
```

Let's enable the service.

```
DHCPServer#show ip sockets
Proto    Remote        Port      Local        Port  In Out Stat TTY
OutputIF
  17   0.0.0.0           0   192.168.12.2      67    0   0 2211   0
```

That's better! Now we see the router is listening on port 67, this means the DHCP service is active.

```
DHCPClient# %DHCP-6-ADDRESS_ASSIGN: Interface FastEthernet0/0
assigned DHCP address 192.168.12.1, mask 255.255.255.0, hostname
DHCPClient
```

As soon as the DHCP service is running you can see the client receives an IP address through DHCP…problem solved**! Lesson learned: If everything is OK, make sure the DHCP service is running.**

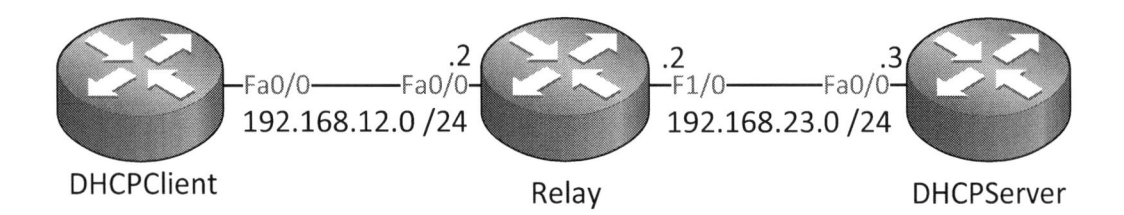

```
                         .2              .2              .3
        ─Fa0/0──────Fa0/0─        ─F1/0──────Fa0/0─
          192.168.12.0 /24          192.168.23.0 /24

        DHCPClient              Relay              DHCPServer
```

Let's try something else! Take a look at the scenario above. We have 3 routers; the router on the left side is configured as a DHCP client for its FastEthernet 0/0 interface. The router on the right side is configured as a DHCP server. Keep in mind that DHCP discover messages from clients are broadcasted and not forwarded by routers. This is why we require the **ip helper** command on the router in the middle called relay. The problem in this scenario is that the client is not receiving any IP addresses through DHCP...

```
DHCPClient#show ip int brief
%SYS-5-CONFIG_I: Configured from console by consoleef
Interface                  IP-Address      OK? Method Status
Protocol
FastEthernet0/0            unassigned      YES DHCP   up
up
```

First we'll verify that the interface has been configured for DHCP. We can see this by using the show ip interface brief command.

```
DHCPClient(config)#interface fastEthernet 0/0
DHCPClient(config-if)#shutdown
DHCPClient(config-if)#no shutdown
```

I'm going to bounce the interface up and down as a quick check to see if it will send a DHCP Discover message.

```
DHCPServer#show ip dhcp server statistics
Memory usage            23054
Address pools           1
Database agents         0
Automatic bindings      1
Manual bindings         0
Expired bindings        0
Malformed messages      0
Secure arp entries      0

Message                 Received
BOOTREQUEST             0
DHCPDISCOVER            12
DHCPREQUEST             0
DHCPDECLINE             0
DHCPRELEASE             0
```

233

DHCPINFORM	0
Message	Sent
BOOTREPLY	0
DHCPOFFER	**12**
DHCPACK	0
DHCPNAK	0

We can see that the DHCP Discover messages are received at the DHCP server. This means that the router in the middle has been configured with IP helper otherwise I wouldn't even receive these messages. DHCP offer messages have been sent but I don't see any DHCPACK (Acknowledgment) messages. This gives me a clue that something is going on...

```
DHCPServer#debug ip dhcp server packet
```

Let's enable a debug to see what is going on.

```
DHCPServer# DHCPD: DHCPDISCOVER received from client
0063.6973.636f.2d63.6330.302e.3139.3632.2e30.3030.302d.4661.302f
.30 through relay 192.168.12.2.
DHCPD: Sending DHCPOFFER to client
0063.6973.636f.2d63.6330.302e.3139.3632.2e30.3030.302d.4661.302f
.30 (192.168.12.2).
DHCPD: unicasting BOOTREPLY for client cc00.1962.0000 to relay
192.168.12.2.
```

We can see that our DHCP server is trying to reach IP address 192.168.12.2, this is the FastEthernet 0/0 interface of our router in the middle. Does the DHCP server know how to reach this IP address?

```
DHCPServer#show ip route 192.168.12.0
% Network not in table
```

As you can see it's not in the routing table, this means that IP packets with destination 192.168.12.2 will be dropped.

```
DHCPServer#debug ip packet
IP packet debugging is on
```

To prove this we can enable a debug...

```
DHCPServer#
IP: tableid=0, s=192.168.12.2 (FastEthernet0/0), d=192.168.23.3
(FastEthernet0/0), routed via RIB
IP: s=192.168.12.2 (FastEthernet0/0), d=192.168.23.3
(FastEthernet0/0), len 604, rcvd 3
IP: s=192.168.23.3 (local), d=192.168.12.2, len 328, unroutable
```

Here you can see that destination IP address 192.168.12.2 is unroutable and as a result the IP packet will be dropped. Let's fix this problem.

```
DHCPServer(config)#ip route 192.168.12.0 255.255.255.0
192.168.23.2
```

We'll add this static route to fix our connectivity issue.

```
DHCPClient# %DHCP-6-ADDRESS_ASSIGN: Interface FastEthernet0/0
assigned DHCP address 192.168.12.1, mask 255.255.255.0, hostname
DHCPClient
```

After a while you should see the client gets an IP address through DHCP.

```
DHCPServer# DHCPD: DHCPDISCOVER received from client
0063.6973.636f.2d63.6330.302e.3139.3632.2e30.3030.302d.4661.302f
.30 through relay 192.168.12.2.
DHCPD: Allocate an address without class information
(192.168.12.0)
DHCPD: Sending DHCPOFFER to client
0063.6973.636f.2d63.6330.302e.3139.3632.2e30.3030.302d.4661.302f
.30 (192.168.12.4).
DHCPD: unicasting BOOTREPLY for client cc00.1962.0000 to relay
192.168.12.2.
DHCPD: DHCPREQUEST received from client
0063.6973.636f.2d63.6330.302e.3139.3632.2e30.3030.302d.4661.302f
.30.
DHCPD: No default domain to append - abort update
DHCPD: Sending DHCPACK to client
0063.6973.636f.2d63.6330.302e.3139.3632.2e30.3030.302d.4661.302f
.30 (192.168.12.4).
DHCPD: unicasting BOOTREPLY for client cc00.1962.0000 to relay
192.168.12.2.
```

If you left "debug ip dhcp server packet" enabled you'll see the whole DHCP process:

1. DHCP Discover
2. DHCP Offer
3. DHCP Request
4. DHCP ACK

That's it...problem solved! **Lesson learned: If you use IP helper make sure the DHCP server knows how to reach the subnet where the client is located.**

The last part of this chapter will cover some issue with FHRPs, we'll start with VRRP!

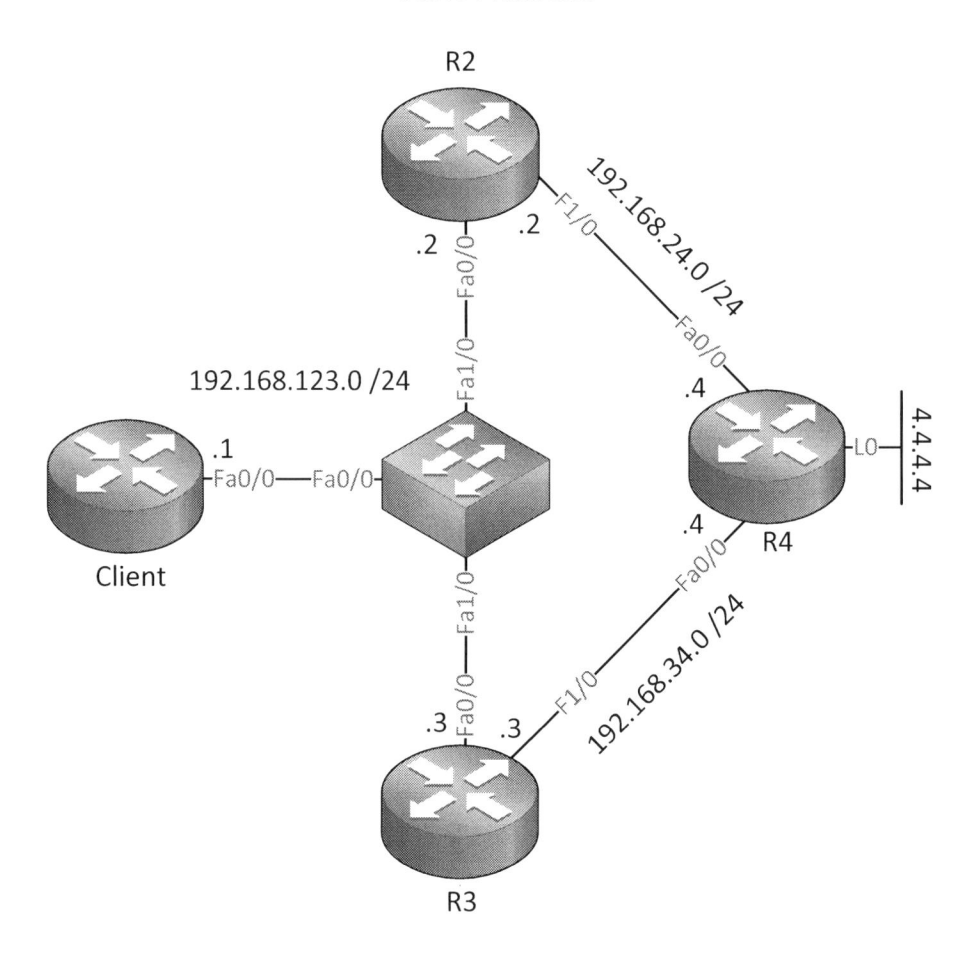

In the scenario above we have an issue with HSRP. Let me explain the topology first. On the left side there's a client (I used a router so we can recreate it in GNS3) that uses a virtual IP address as its default gateway. R2 and R3 are configured for HSRP. On the right side there's a router that has IP address 4.4.4.4 on a loopback0 interface. Unfortunately our client is unable to ping 4.4.4.4. What is going on here?

```
Client#ping 4.4.4.4

Type escape sequence to abort.
Sending 5, 100-byte ICMP Echos to 4.4.4.4, timeout is 2 seconds:
U.U.U
Success rate is 0 percent (0/5)
```

First I'll send a ping from the client to IP address 4.4.4.4. You can see the **U (unreachable)** so we know that we are getting a response from a default gateway.

```
Client#show ip route
Default gateway is 192.168.123.254
```

```
Host            Gateway              Last Use    Total Uses
Interface
ICMP redirect cache is empty
```

The routing table has been disabled on this client router (no ip routing) but you can see a default gateway has been configured. Let's see if this IP address is reachable.

```
Client#ping 192.168.123.254

Type escape sequence to abort.
Sending 5, 100-byte ICMP Echos to 192.168.123.254, timeout is 2 seconds:
!!!!!
Success rate is 100 percent (5/5), round-trip min/avg/max = 4/4/4 ms
```

Reaching the default gateway is no issue so we can move our focus to R2 or R3.

```
R2#show standby
FastEthernet0/0 - Group 1
  State is Standby
    1 state change, last state change 00:08:34
  Virtual IP address is 192.168.123.254
  Active virtual MAC address is 0000.0c07.ac01
    Local virtual MAC address is 0000.0c07.ac01 (v1 default)
  Hello time 3 sec, hold time 10 sec
    Next hello sent in 1.916 secs
  Preemption disabled
  Active router is 192.168.123.3, priority 90 (expires in 8.464 sec)
  Standby router is local
  Priority 100 (default 100)
    Track interface FastEthernet1/0 state Up decrement 10
  IP redundancy name is "hsrp-Fa0/0-1" (default)
```

```
R3#show standby
FastEthernet0/0 - Group 1
  State is Active
    2 state changes, last state change 00:14:44
  Virtual IP address is 192.168.123.254
  Active virtual MAC address is 0000.0c07.ac01
    Local virtual MAC address is 0000.0c07.ac01 (v1 default)
  Hello time 3 sec, hold time 10 sec
    Next hello sent in 0.616 secs
  Preemption disabled
  Active router is local
  Standby router is 192.168.123.2, priority 100 (expires in 8.084 sec)
```

```
    Priority 90 (default 100)
      Track interface FastEthernet1/0 state Down decrement 10
    IP redundancy name is "hsrp-Fa0/0-1" (default)
```

We can use the **show standby** command to verify that R3 is the active HSRP router. Let's verify if it can reach IP address 4.4.4.4.

```
R3#ping 4.4.4.4

Type escape sequence to abort.
Sending 5, 100-byte ICMP Echos to 4.4.4.4, timeout is 2 seconds:
.....
Success rate is 0 percent (0/5)
```

Too bad...it can't reach it.

```
R3#show ip route
Codes: C - connected, S - static, R - RIP, M - mobile, B - BGP
       D - EIGRP, EX - EIGRP external, O - OSPF, IA - OSPF inter area
       N1 - OSPF NSSA external type 1, N2 - OSPF NSSA external type 2
       E1 - OSPF external type 1, E2 - OSPF external type 2
       i - IS-IS, su - IS-IS summary, L1 - IS-IS level-1, L2 - IS-IS level-2
       ia - IS-IS inter area, * - candidate default, U - per-user static route
       o - ODR, P - periodic downloaded static route

Gateway of last resort is not set

C    192.168.123.0/24 is directly connected, FastEthernet0/0
```

It's not in the routing table and if you look closely you can see that FastEthernet1/0 is not in the routing table as directly connected, this indicates that something is wrong with this interface.

```
R3#show ip interface brief
Interface              IP-Address      OK? Method Status    Protocol
FastEthernet0/0        192.168.123.3   YES manual up        up
FastEthernet1/0        192.168.34.3    YES manual administratively down down
```

There we go...the interface is down.

```
R3(config)#interface fastEthernet 1/0
R3(config-if)#no shutdown
```

Let's bring it back to the land of the living.

```
R3#ping 4.4.4.4

Type escape sequence to abort.
Sending 5, 100-byte ICMP Echos to 4.4.4.4, timeout is 2 seconds:
!!!!!
Success rate is 100 percent (5/5), round-trip min/avg/max =
4/4/8 ms
```

There we go, it's now working.

```
Client#ping 4.4.4.4

Type escape sequence to abort.
Sending 5, 100-byte ICMP Echos to 4.4.4.4, timeout is 2 seconds:
!!!!!
Success rate is 100 percent (5/5), round-trip min/avg/max =
8/8/12 ms
```

Problem solved...the client can now ping 4.4.4.4! There's one thing left though...we are using HSRP so our default gateway isn't a single point of failure but in this case R3 had a link failure...shouldn't R2 take over?

```
R2#show standby | begin Preemption
  Preemption disabled
  Active router is 192.168.123.3, priority 100 (expires in 8.692 sec)
  Standby router is local
  Priority 100 (default 100)
    Track interface FastEthernet1/0 state Up decrement 10
  IP redundancy name is "hsrp-Fa0/0-1" (default)
```

```
R3#show standby | begin Preemption
  Preemption disabled
  Active router is local
  Standby router is 192.168.123.2, priority 100 (expires in 8.700 sec)
  Priority 100 (default 100)
    Track interface FastEthernet1/0 state Up decrement 10
  IP redundancy name is "hsrp-Fa0/0-1" (default)
```

Interface tracking has been enabled and you can see that the priority should decrement by 10 if interface FastEthernet1/0 goes down. This means that normally R2 should take over but **preemption is disabled** by default for HSRP.

```
R2(config)#interface fastEthernet 0/0
R2(config-if)#standby 1 preempt
```

239

```
R3(config)#interface fastEthernet 0/0
R3(config-if)#standby 1 preempt
```

Before we bring out the champagne and celebrate our troubleshooting victory we should make sure this issue doesn't occur anymore in the future. We'll enable preemption on both routers, now are done! **Lesson learned: Make sure preemption is enabled for HSRP if you use interface tracking.**

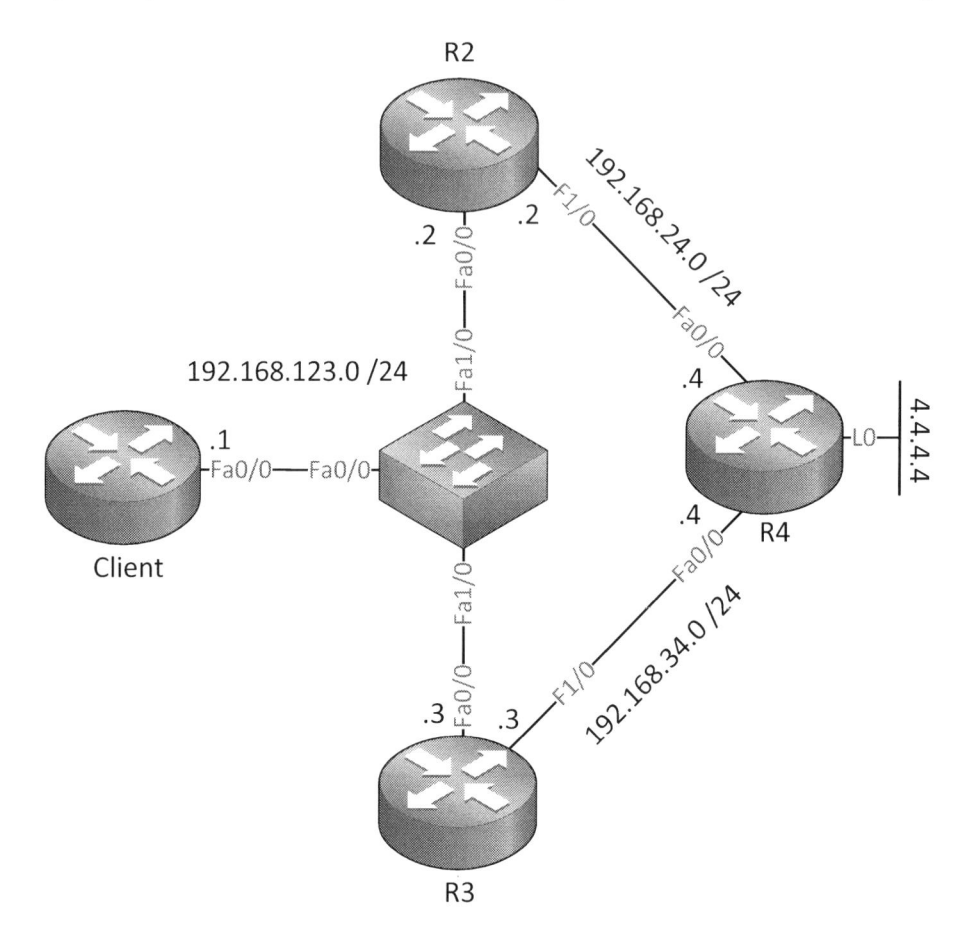

Here's the same topology but this time we are using VRRP instead of HSRP. The problem is different however; the client is complaining that not all IP packets are making it to 4.4.4.4.

```
Client#ping 4.4.4.4

Type escape sequence to abort.
Sending 5, 100-byte ICMP Echos to 4.4.4.4, timeout is 2 seconds:
U.!!!
Success rate is 60 percent (3/5), round-trip min/avg/max =
8/13/20 ms
```

Some of the IP packets are not arriving at 4.4.4.4.

```
Client#show ip route
Default gateway is 192.168.123.254

Host              Gateway            Last Use     Total Uses
Interface
ICMP redirect cache is empty
```

The gateway IP address is 192.168.123.254.

```
Client#ping 192.168.123.254

Type escape sequence to abort.
Sending 5, 100-byte ICMP Echos to 192.168.123.254, timeout is 2
seconds:
!!!!!
Success rate is 100 percent (5/5), round-trip min/avg/max =
4/7/20 ms
```

Pinging the gateway address is no problem.

```
R2#ping 4.4.4.4

Type escape sequence to abort.
Sending 5, 100-byte ICMP Echos to 4.4.4.4, timeout is 2 seconds:
.....
Success rate is 0 percent (0/5)
```

```
R3#ping 4.4.4.4

Type escape sequence to abort.
Sending 5, 100-byte ICMP Echos to 4.4.4.4, timeout is 2 seconds:
!!!!!
Success rate is 100 percent (5/5), round-trip min/avg/max =
4/7/20 ms
```

R2 is unable to reach 4.4.4.4 but R3 has no issues. Before we continue checking why R2 is unable to reach 4.4.4.4 we'll take a look at the VRRP configuration to see which router is the master.

```
R2#show vrrp
FastEthernet0/0 - Group 1
  State is Master
  Virtual IP address is 192.168.123.254
  Virtual MAC address is 0000.5e00.0101
  Advertisement interval is 1.000 sec
  Preemption enabled
  Priority is 100
  Authentication MD5, key-string "WRONGPASS"
```

```
  Master Router is 192.168.123.2 (local), priority is 100
  Master Advertisement interval is 1.000 sec
  Master Down interval is 3.609 sec
```

```
R3#show vrrp
FastEthernet0/0 - Group 1
  State is Master
  Virtual IP address is 192.168.123.254
  Virtual MAC address is 0000.5e00.0101
  Advertisement interval is 1.000 sec
  Preemption enabled
  Priority is 100
  Authentication MD5, key-string "SECRET"
  Master Router is 192.168.123.3 (local), priority is 100
  Master Advertisement interval is 1.000 sec
  Master Down interval is 3.609 sec
```

The output of **show vrrp** is interesting. Both routers think they are active and if you look closely you can see why. Authentication has been enabled and there is a mismatch in the key-string. Since both routers are active half of the packets will end up at R2 and the rest at R3. This is why our client sees some packets arriving and others not. Let's fix our authentication:

```
R2(config)#interface fa0/0
R2(config-if)#vrrp 1 authentication md5 key-string SECRET
```

We'll make sure the key-string is the same.

```
R2# %VRRP-6-STATECHANGE: Fa0/0 Grp 1 state Master -> Backup
```

This message on the console of R2 is promising.

```
R2#show vrrp | include Master
  Master Router is 192.168.123.3, priority is 100
```

```
R3#show vrrp | include Master
  State is Master
  Master Router is 192.168.123.3 (local), priority is 100
```

R3 has been elected as the master router. Now let's find out why R2 was unable to reach 4.4.4.4 since this issue is fixed.

```
R2#show ip route
Codes: C - connected, S - static, R - RIP, M - mobile, B - BGP
       D - EIGRP, EX - EIGRP external, O - OSPF, IA - OSPF inter area
       N1 - OSPF NSSA external type 1, N2 - OSPF NSSA external type 2
       E1 - OSPF external type 1, E2 - OSPF external type 2
```

```
        i - IS-IS, su - IS-IS summary, L1 - IS-IS level-1, L2 -
IS-IS level-2
        ia - IS-IS inter area, * - candidate default, U -per-user
static
        o - ODR, P - periodic downloaded static route

Gateway of last resort is not set

C    192.168.123.0/24 is directly connected, FastEthernet0/0
```

Hmm R2 only shows a single entry in the routing table, something is wrong with FastEthernet 1/0.

```
R2#show ip interface brief
Interface              IP-Address       OK? Method Status
Protocol
FastEthernet0/0        192.168.123.2    YES NVRAM  up
up
FastEthernet1/0        192.168.24.2     YES NVRAM
administratively down down
```

Seems someone loves the shutdown command ☺. Keep in mind this could be anything else...access-lists blocking traffic between R2 and R4, port-security (if there was a switch in the middle), interfaces in err-disabled mode, wrong IP addresses and more. Check everything!

```
R2(config)#interface fastEthernet 1/0
R2(config-if)#no shutdown
```

We'll fix the interface.

```
Client#ping 4.4.4.4

Type escape sequence to abort.
Sending 5, 100-byte ICMP Echos to 4.4.4.4, timeout is 2 seconds:
!!!!!
Success rate is 100 percent (5/5), round-trip min/avg/max =
4/9/16 ms
```

Problem solved!

Lesson learned: Make sure the VRRP routers are able to reach each other.

That's all I have for you on network services so another chapter bites the dust. If you want to practice troubleshooting NAT/PAT, DHCP and our FHRPs you can take a look at the following labs:

http://gns3vault.com/Troubleshooting/nat-dynamic-troubleshooting.html

http://gns3vault.com/Troubleshooting/dhcp-troubleshooting.html

http://gns3vault.com/Troubleshooting/vrrp-troubleshooting.html

http://gns3vault.com/Troubleshooting/glbp-troubleshooting.html

http://gns3vault.com/Troubleshooting/hsrp-troubleshooting.html

Our next stop will be network management protocols!

9. Troubleshooting Network Management Protocols

In this chapter we'll take a look at some protocols like NTP, syslog and SNMP. These are all used to monitor the "health" of your network. When configured correctly they can be very useful...if they don't work, it might be really difficult to figure out when a certain event occurred on the network and what triggered it. Syslog and SNMP are both used to monitor the network, NTP is used to ensure that our logging information has the correct time and date.

We'll start with NTP, it's not a very difficult protocol but there are a couple of things that could go wrong with it:

- **NTP traffic filtered**: access-lists could block NTP traffic.
- **NTP Authentication issues**: NTP supports authentication, client and server need to use the same settings.
- **Time offset too high**: When the time offset between client/server is too large it will take a very long time to synchronize.
- **Stratum level too high**: The stratum level is between 1 (best) and 15 (worst). A stratum level of 16 is considered unusable.
- **NTP server source filter**: NTP servers can be configured to allow only clients from certain IP addresses.

Let's take a look at these issues. I'll use two routers for this:

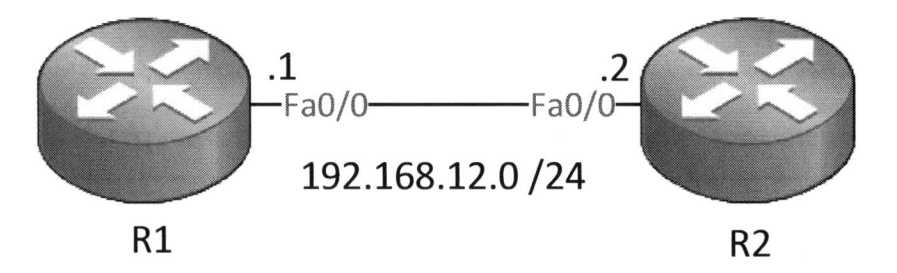

```
        .1              .2
R1 ──FaO/O──────FaO/O── R2
       192.168.12.0 /24
```

R1 will be our NTP client and R2 will be the NTP server. There are two useful commands that we should start with:

```
R1#show ntp status
Clock is unsynchronized, stratum 16, no reference clock
nominal freq is 250.0000 Hz, actual freq is 250.0000 Hz,
precision is 2**18
reference time is 00000000.00000000 (00:00:00.000 UTC Mon Jan 1 1900)
clock offset is 0.0000 msec, root delay is 0.00 msec
root dispersion is 0.00 msec, peer dispersion is 0.00 msec
```

```
R1#show ntp associations
```

```
      address          ref clock     st   when  poll reach  delay   offset
disp
 ~192.168.12.2         0.0.0.0       16    -    64    0     0.0     0.00
16000.
 * master (synced), # master (unsynced), + selected, - candidate, ~
configured
```

These tell us that R1 has 192.168.12.2 configured as the NTP server and it's currently not synchronized. Let's check if R1 is receiving NTP packets, this is best done with a debug:

```
R1#debug ntp packets
NTP packets debugging is on

NTP: xmit packet to 192.168.12.2:
 leap 3, mode 3, version 3, stratum 0, ppoll 64
 rtdel 0000 (0.000), rtdsp 10001 (1000.015), refid 00000000
(0.0.0.0)
 ref 00000000.00000000 (00:00:00.000 UTC Mon Jan 1 1900)
 org 00000000.00000000 (00:00:00.000 UTC Mon Jan 1 1900)
 rec 00000000.00000000 (00:00:00.000 UTC Mon Jan 1 1900)
 xmt C0295220.A6D7FB14 (01:04:32.651 UTC Fri Mar 1 2002)
```

This debug tells us that R1 is sending NTP packets but we are not receiving anything from the NTP server. Make sure NTP server is allowed to go through:

```
R1#show access-lists
Extended IP access list NO_TIME
    1 deny udp any any eq ntp (3 matches)
```

R1 uses UDP port 123, make sure it's not blocked:

```
R1(config)#interface FastEthernet 0/0
R1(config-if)#no ip access-group NO_TIME in
```

After removing the access-list, NTP will be able to use the NTP packets from the server:

```
R1#
NTP: rcv packet from 192.168.12.2 to 192.168.12.1 on
FastEthernet0/0:
 leap 0, mode 4, version 3, stratum 1, ppoll 64
 rtdel 0000 (0.000), rtdsp 0002 (0.031), refid 4C4F434C
(76.79.67.76)
 ref C02952FA.C3830714 (01:08:10.763 UTC Fri Mar 1 2002)
 org C0295320.A6D6D314 (01:08:48.651 UTC Fri Mar 1 2002)
```

Here's the end result:

```
R1#show ntp status
Clock is synchronized, stratum 2, reference is 192.168.12.2
nominal freq is 250.0000 Hz, actual freq is 250.0000 Hz,
precision is 2**18
reference time is C0295360.FAE093C8 (01:09:52.979 UTC Fri Mar 1
2002)
clock offset is 3.9974 msec, root delay is 47.78 msec
root dispersion is 15879.03 msec, peer dispersion is 15875.02
msec
```

The clock is now synchronized. Another issue you can spot with the debugging NTP is an authentication mismatch:

```
R1(config)#ntp server 192.168.12.2 key 1
R1(config)#ntp authentication-key 1 md5 MY_KEY
```

I'll configure R1 to only accepts NTP packets from the NTP server that are authenticated with a certain key. The NTP server however doesn't use any form of authentication. We can find this error with the following debug:

```
R1#debug ntp validity
NTP peer validity debugging is on
```

It will tell us:

```
R1#
NTP: packet from 192.168.12.2 failed validity tests 10
Authentication failed
```

Make sure your NTP authentication settings match on both sides.

When the time/date difference between the NTP server and NTP server is big, it will take a long time to sync. Right now the clocks look like this:

```
R1#show clock
.01:32:25.208 UTC Fri Mar 1 2002
```

```
R2#show clock
18:01:44.327 UTC Fri Jan 30 2015
```

Setting the clock on the NTP client to something close to the NTP server will speed up the sync process a lot:

```
R1#clock set 18:00:00 30 January 2015
```

In a few minutes, the clock on the NTP client should be synced.

Another issue with NTP is that the stratum level is limited, we can use values between 1 (best) and 15 (worst). If the NTP server has a stratum level of 15 then the NTP client won't be able to sync since 16 is considered unreachable.

Debugging the NTP packets on the client will reveal this:

```
R1#
NTP: rcv packet from 192.168.12.2 to 192.168.12.1 on
FastEthernet0/0:
 leap 0, mode 4, version 3, stratum 15, ppoll 1024
 rtdel 0000 (0.000), rtdsp 0002 (0.031), refid 7F7F0701
(127.127.7.1)
 ref D876471C.52EF5E3C (18:08:28.323 UTC Fri Jan 30 2015)
 org D876474C.7D0383EE (18:09:16.488 UTC Fri Jan 30 2015)
 rec D876474C.80123528 (18:09:16.500 UTC Fri Jan 30 2015)
 xmt D876474C.8312ABB8 (18:09:16.512 UTC Fri Jan 30 2015)
 inp D876474C.87424408 (18:09:16.528 UTC Fri Jan 30 2015)
```

R1 will never be able to synchronize itself since the NTP server is announcing itself as stratum 15. You can fix this by setting a lower NTP stratum value on your NTP server:

```
R2(config)#ntp master 2
```

I'll change it to stratum value 5.

This allows R1 to synchronize itself:

```
R1#show ntp status
Clock is synchronized, stratum 2, reference is 192.168.12.2
nominal freq is 250.0000 Hz, actual freq is 250.0000 Hz,
precision is 2**18
reference time is C0295360.FAE093C8 (01:09:52.979 UTC Fri Mar 1
2002)
clock offset is 3.9974 msec, root delay is 47.78 msec
root dispersion is 15879.03 msec, peer dispersion is 15875.02
msec
```

Last but not least, NTP servers can be configured to only allow NTP clients from certain IP addresses:

```
R2(config)#ntp access-group ?
  peer        Provide full access
  query-only  Allow only control queries
  serve       Provide server and query access
  serve-only  Provide only server access
```

For example I'll configure it to only allow IP address 1.1.1.1:

```
R2(config)#ntp access-group serve 1
R2(config)#access-list 1 permit 1.1.1.1
R2(config)#ip route 1.1.1.1 255.255.255.255 192.168.12.1
```

In this case, I need to make sure that the NTP client is sourcing its NTP packets from the correct IP address:

```
R1(config)#interface loopback 0
R1(config-if)#ip address 1.1.1.1 255.255.255.255

R1(config)#ntp source loopback0
```

The NTP source command will tell R1 to use IP address 1.1.1.1 from its loopback interface as the source of its NTP packets.

These are the most common NTP errors. Let's continue by looking at syslog.

The most common issue with syslog is that we are missing logging information. By default logging is only enabled for the console and not for external syslog servers.

There is one command that you can use to verify its configuration:

```
R1#show logging
Syslog logging: enabled (12 messages dropped, 1 messages rate-limited,
                0 flushes, 0 overruns, xml disabled, filtering disabled)

No Active Message Discriminator.



No Inactive Message Discriminator.

    Console logging: level debugging, 1482 messages logged, xml disabled,
                    filtering disabled
    Monitor logging: level debugging, 0 messages logged, xml disabled,
                    filtering disabled
    Buffer logging:  disabled, xml disabled,
                    filtering disabled
    Logging Exception size (4096 bytes)
    Count and timestamp logging messages: disabled
    Persistent logging: disabled

No active filter modules.

ESM: 0 messages dropped

    Trap logging: level informational, 41 message lines logged
```

249

This tells us that syslog is enabled for the console up to the debugging level. If you don't see everything on the console then someone maybe changed the logging level to a lower value. Here are the options:

```
R1(config)#logging console ?
  <0-7>           Logging severity level
  alerts          Immediate action needed           (severity=1)
  critical        Critical conditions               (severity=2)
  debugging       Debugging messages                (severity=7)
  discriminator   Establish MD-Console association
  emergencies     System is unusable                (severity=0)
  errors          Error conditions                  (severity=3)
  filtered        Enable filtered logging
  guaranteed      Guarantee console messages
  informational   Informational messages            (severity=6)
  notifications   Normal but significant conditions (severity=5)
  warnings        Warning conditions                (severity=4)
  xml             Enable logging in XML
  <cr>
```

The debugging level is the highest value (7) so it will show all syslog messages. If you don't see all messages, make sure it's set at the debugging level for the console.

By default, syslog information isn't sent to an external server. You have to configure this yourself:

```
R1(config)#logging host 192.168.12.2
```

This will send logging information for all severity levels to an external server at 192.168.12.2. Make sure this **traffic isn't blocked, syslog uses UDP port 514**.

Another common mistake is that syslog messages don't show up on telnet or SSH sessions. You can enable this with the **terminal monitor** command.

The next protocol we will discuss is SNMP version 2c and 3. Before you dive into the SNMP configuration, make sure your NMS (Network Management Server) is able to reach your device (SNMP Agent). SNMP uses UDP port 161 for messages and UDP port 162 for traps and informs. Make sure this traffic is allowed.

When it comes to SNMPv2c, there are a couple of common issues:

- **Incorrect community string:** The community string is like a password that is used so the NMS can read or write to the network device. If it doesn't match, SNMP won't work.
- **Access-list errors:** Access-lists can be to define which NMS is allowed to use the community-string. Make sure you use the correct IP address.

- **Index shuffles:** When new interfaces are added to the network device, the interface numbers might not match anymore.
- **Traps not sent:** If you want to send SNMP traps (or informs) then you'll need to configure this, it's not done automatically.

Here are the related SNMPv2c commands that you should verify in case SNMP doesn't work:

```
R1(config)#snmp-server community MY_COMMUNITY ro 1
R1(config)#access-list 1 permit host 192.168.1.1
```

Above we configured a community called MY_COMMUNITY with read-only access. We use access-list 1 to determine which device is allowed to use this community. Make sure the access-list has the correct permit statement(s). The following command ensures that the interface index remains the same:

```
R1(config)#snmp-server ifindex persist
```

And if you want to send SNMP traps, configure it like this:

```
R1(config)#snmp-server enable traps eigrp
R1(config)#snmp-server host 192.168.1.1 traps version 2c
MY_COMMUNITY
```

This will enable SNMP traps for EIGRP and it will be sent to a NMS on IP address 192.168.1.1 using community "MY_COMMUNITY". If you don't specify what traps you want, it will enable all traps.

SNMPv3 is quite different compared to version 2c, many changes have been made to security and authentication. There are a couple of SNMPv3 specific things you need to keep in mind when troubleshooting SNMPv3:

- **Nesting:** with SNMPv3 we create users that are nested in groups. The groups are nested in views that give access to certain MIBs on the network device. Make sure your user is in the correct group and that the view has correct view permissions.
- **Security Level:** SNMPv3 supports different security levels, this has to match on the network device and the NMS:
  - **noAuthNoPriv**
  - **authNoPriv**
  - **authPriv**
- **Security Parameters:** SNMPv3 offers multiple algorithms for hashing and encryption. Make sure you configure the same algorithms on the network device and the NMS.
- **Views configuration:** In the view we configure the objects that the NMS is allowed to access, make sure you configure the correct ones.

Let me show you a configuration example for what we discussed:

```
Router(config)#snmp-server user MY_USER MY_GROUP v3 auth md5
MY_PASSWORD priv aes 128 MY_PASSWORD
```

First we configure a user called MY_USER that belongs to a group called MY_GROUP. We use version 3 of SNMP. For authentication of this user we use MD5 and the password is "MY_PASSWORD". For encryption we use AES 128-bit and the same password. Make sure everything is the same on the network device and the NMS…

Now we configure the group:

```
Router(config)#snmp-server group MY_GROUP v3 priv read MY_VIEW
access 1
Router(config)#access-list 1 permit host 192.168.1.1
```

The group is called MY_GROUP and we use the authPriv security level. We also attach the group to a view called MY_VIEW. We also use an access-list, only a NMS using IP address 192.168.1.1 is allowed to use this group. Let's configure the view:

```
Router(config)#snmp-server view MY_VIEW system included
Router(config)#snmp-server view MY_VIEW cisco included
```

This view allows the NMS to only access objects in the MIB-II system group and all objects in the Cisco enterprise MIB. Make sure you add all objects that you need to access here.

User information doesn't show up in the configuration, if you want to see the users you have to use another command:

```
Router#show snmp user

User name: MY_USER
Engine ID: 800000090300001DA18B36D0
storage-type: nonvolatile          active
Authentication Protocol: MD5
Privacy Protocol: AES128
Group-name: MY_GROUP
```

This shows us our user account, it's authentication and encryption algorithms and tells us to which group it belongs.

That's all we have on network management protocols!

10. Troubleshooting IPv6

In this chapter we'll take a look at some IPv6 related issues. Some network engineers that don't have a lot of experience with IPv6 might feel uncomfortable when we talk about this protocol. The addresses look weird, there are no broadcasts anymore and most of us have read about it and did some labs but don't have a lot of "real world" experience yet (unless you work at an ISP). Although IPv6 and IPv4 are different, a lot of your experience with IPv4 can be applied to IPv6. For example most of the commands are the same:

Show ip route VS **show ipv6 route**

Show ip interfaces brief VS **show ipv6 interfaces brief**

Of course there are some very important differences between the two protocols but at the end of the day..."IP is a just a number" and OSPF is still OSPF...even though we are running version 3 (IPv6) instead of version 2 (IPv4). RIP is still RIP but now it's "next generation" ☺.

I'm exaggerating a bit and making it sound too simple but perhaps it helps to take some of the IPv6 anxiety away ;)

Here's a short overview with some of the important differences between IPv4 and IPv6:

	IPv4	IPv6
Address Resolution	ARP (Address Resolution Protocol)	ICMPv6 Neighbor Discovery
Secondary IP address	Possible.	You can use many different types of IPv6 addresses on a single interface.
Routing Protocols	Use IP address on the interface.	Use IPv6 link-local address on the interface.
Broadcast possible	Yes	No
Address Assignment	Static or DHCP.	Static, Autoconfiguration or DHCP.

It's impossible to cover everything that could go wrong with IPv6 into this troubleshooting chapter so we'll focus on the IPv6 specific sections and the topics that you might encounter on the CCNP TSHOOT exam. Having said that, let's get our hands dirty and look at our first scenario!

```
                    Fa0/0————Fa0/0
                        2001::/64
          R1                              R2
```

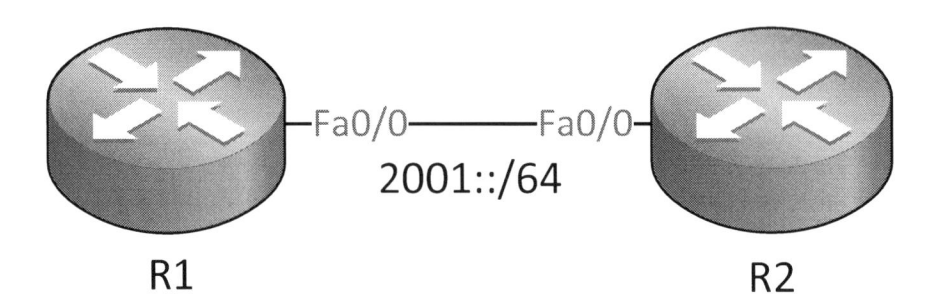

In the picture above we have two routers, R1 and R2. We only have IPv6 addresses and you can see that in between R1 and R2 we have configured the 2001::/64 prefix. R1 has been configured for **stateless Autoconfiguration** but for some reason it's not receiving an IPv6 address from R2. Let's find out what is wrong here shall we?

```
R1#show ipv6 interface fa0/0
FastEthernet0/0 is up, line protocol is up
  IPv6 is enabled, link-local address is FE80::CE00:29FF:FE35:0
```

We can verify that the FastEthernet 0/0 interface is operational and that IPv6 has been enabled.

```
R1#show ipv6 interface fa0/0 | include stateless
  Hosts use stateless autoconfig for addresses.
```

We should also check if the router has been configured for stateless Autoconfiguration. We can see this is the case.

At this moment we at least know that IPv6 has been enabled on R1 and that it is not receiving an IPv6 address through stateless Autoconfiguration. What is the next step of our plan?

```
R1#debug ipv6 nd
ICMP Neighbor Discovery events debugging is on
```

Stateless Autoconfiguration is a part of neighbor discovery. We'll enable a debug to see if anything is going on.

```
R1(config)#interface fa0/0
R1(config-if)#shutdown
R1(config-if)#no shutdown
```

I'll do a shutdown and no shutdown to restart the neighbor discovery.

```
R1#
ICMPv6-ND: Sending NS for FE80::CE00:29FF:FE35:0 on
FastEthernet0/0
%LINK-3-UPDOWN: Interface FastEthernet0/0, changed state to up
ICMPv6-ND: DAD: FE80::CE00:29FF:FE35:0 is unique.
ICMPv6-ND: Sending NA for FE80::CE00:29FF:FE35:0 on
FastEthernet0/0
ICMPv6-ND: Address FE80::CE00:29FF:FE35:0/10 is up on
FastEthernet0/0
%LINEPROTO-5-UPDOWN: Line protocol on Interface FastEthernet0/0,
changed state to up
ICMPv6-ND: Sending RS on FastEthernet0/0
ICMPv6-ND: Sending RS on FastEthernet0/0
ICMPv6-ND: Sending RS on FastEthernet0/0
```

In the debug we see that R1 is sending **RS (Router Solicitation)** messages. Unfortunately we are not receiving any response to these messages so it seems the issue is on R2.

```
R2#show ipv6 interface fa0/0
FastEthernet0/0 is up, line protocol is up
  IPv6 is enabled, link-local address is FE80::CE01:29FF:FE35:0
  Global unicast address(es):
    2001::12:2, subnet is 2001::/64
```

We can verify that R2 has a working FastEthernet 0/0 interface and that IPv6 address 2001::12:2 has been configured.

We know that R2 has a working IPv6 address and there are no issues with the interface. What prevents it from sending RA (Router Advertisements)? If you recall correctly, configuring an IPv6 address isn't enough to enable IPv6 features like routing protocols or router advertisements. We need to make sure **IPv6 unicast-routing is enabled**. Let's see if this is the case:

```
R2#show running-config | include unicast-routing
```

There's maybe another show command to verify it but this time I'm checking the running-configuration to see if IPv6 unicast-routing has been enabled, it seems to be disabled.

```
R2(config)#ipv6 unicast-routing
```

Let's enable it on R2.

```
R1#
ICMPv6-ND: Sending RA to FF02::1 on FastEthernet0/0
ICMPv6-ND:      MTU = 1500
ICMPv6-ND: Sending RA to FF02::1 on FastEthernet0/0
ICMPv6-ND:      MTU = 1500
```

```
ICMPv6-ND: Received RA from FE80::CE01:29FF:FE35:0 on
FastEthernet0/0
ICMPv6-ND: Sending NS for 2001::CE00:29FF:FE35:0 on
FastEthernet0/0
ICMPv6-ND: Autoconfiguring 2001::CE00:29FF:FE35:0 on
FastEthernet0/0
ICMPv6-ND: DAD: 2001::CE00:29FF:FE35:0 is unique.
ICMPv6-ND: Sending NA for 2001::CE00:29FF:FE35:0 on
FastEthernet0/0
ICMPv6-ND: Address 2001::CE00:29FF:FE35:0/64 is up on
FastEthernet0/0
ICMPv6-ND: Received RA from FE80::CE01:29FF:FE35:0 on
FastEthernet0/0
```

As soon as I enable unicast-routing on R2 you'll see some debug information on R1. It receives the router advertisement and it has configured itself with IPv6 address 2001::CE00:29FF:FE35:0.

```
R1#show ipv6 interface brief
FastEthernet0/0           [up/up]
    FE80::CE00:29FF:FE35:0
    2001::CE00:29FF:FE35:0
```

Here you can see our new IPv6 address on R1.

```
R1#ping 2001::12:2

Type escape sequence to abort.
Sending 5, 100-byte ICMP Echos to 2001::12:2, timeout is 2
seconds:
!!!!!
Success rate is 100 percent (5/5), round-trip min/avg/max =
4/6/16 ms
```

Problem solved! **Lesson learned: Make sure IPv6 unicast-routing is enabled if you want to use router advertisements or IPv6 routing protocols.**

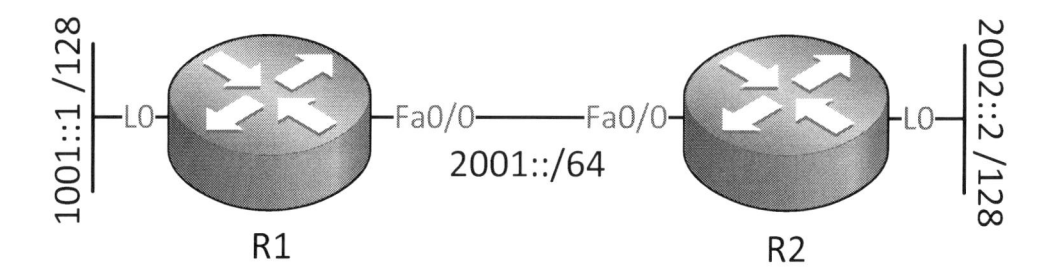

Let's look at another scenario. In the picture above we have 2 routers, each router has a loopback interface and IPv6 addresses have been configured on the loopback0 interfaces. RIPNG has been configured and we should have connectivity between the two loopback0 interfaces. Unfortunately R1 is not learning about network 2002::2/128. Let's find out why!

```
R1#show ipv6 route rip
IPv6 Routing Table - 5 entries
Codes: C - Connected, L - Local, S - Static, R - RIP, B - BGP
       U - Per-user Static route
       I1 - ISIS L1, I2 - ISIS L2, IA - ISIS interarea, IS -
ISIS summary
       O - OSPF intra, OI - OSPF inter, OE1 - OSPF ext 1, OE2 -
OSPF ext 2
       ON1 - OSPF NSSA ext 1, ON2 - OSPF NSSA ext 2
```

R1 hasn't learned any RIPNG routes.

```
R2#show ipv6 route rip
IPv6 Routing Table - 6 entries
Codes: C - Connected, L - Local, S - Static, R - RIP, B - BGP
       U - Per-user Static route
       I1 - ISIS L1, I2 - ISIS L2, IA - ISIS interarea, IS -
ISIS summary
       O - OSPF intra, OI - OSPF inter, OE1 - OSPF ext 1, OE2 -
OSPF ext 2
       ON1 - OSPF NSSA ext 1, ON2 - OSPF NSSA ext 2
R   1001::1/128 [120/2]
     via FE80::CE00:4DFF:FE47:0, FastEthernet0/0
```

R2 has learned about the loopback0 interface behind R1.

```
R1#show ipv6 interface brief
FastEthernet0/0            [up/up]
    FE80::CE00:4DFF:FE47:0
    2001:12::1
Loopback0                  [up/up]
    FE80::CE00:4DFF:FE47:0
    1001::1
```

```
R2#show ipv6 interface brief
FastEthernet0/0            [up/up]
    FE80::CE01:4DFF:FE47:0
    2001:12::2
Loopback0                  [up/up]
    FE80::CE01:4DFF:FE47:0
    2002::2
```

This scenario is a good example of how you can use your IPv4 skills to fix a IPv6 problem. First we'll see if there is anything in the routing table, if the interfaces are operational and if IPv6 addresses have been configured. This seems to be the case.

```
R1#show ipv6 protocols
IPv6 Routing Protocol is "connected"
IPv6 Routing Protocol is "static"
IPv6 Routing Protocol is "rip NEXTGEN"
  Interfaces:
    Loopback0
    FastEthernet0/0
  Redistribution:
    None
```

```
R2#show ipv6 protocols
IPv6 Routing Protocol is "connected"
IPv6 Routing Protocol is "static"
IPv6 Routing Protocol is "rip NEXTGEN"
  Interfaces:
    FastEthernet0/0
  Redistribution:
    None
```

We'll use show ipv6 protocols to see if all prefixes are advertised. You can see that RIPNG is not enabled on the loopback0 interface of R2, let's fix that!

```
R2(config)#interface loopback 0
R2(config-if)#ipv6 rip NEXTGEN enable
```

This is how we enable it.

```
R2#show ipv6 protocols
IPv6 Routing Protocol is "connected"
IPv6 Routing Protocol is "static"
IPv6 Routing Protocol is "rip NEXTGEN"
  Interfaces:
    Loopback0
    FastEthernet0/0
  Redistribution:
    None
```

Now we see that the loopback0 interface has joined RIPNG.

```
R1#show ipv6 route rip
IPv6 Routing Table - 6 entries
Codes: C - Connected, L - Local, S - Static, R - RIP, B - BGP
       U - Per-user Static route
       I1 - ISIS L1, I2 - ISIS L2, IA - ISIS interarea, IS -
ISIS summary
       O - OSPF intra, OI - OSPF inter, OE1 - OSPF ext 1, OE2 -
OSPF ext 2
       ON1 - OSPF NSSA ext 1, ON2 - OSPF NSSA ext 2
R    2002::2/128 [120/2]
```

```
    via FE80::CE01:4DFF:FE47:0, FastEthernet0/0
```

Now we see that 2002::2/128 is in the routing table of R1, problem solved! **Lesson learned: Make sure you activate RIPNG on all interfaces if they have prefixes that you want to see advertised.**

Troubleshooting this lab is pretty much the same as IPv4 RIP, here are the commands we used:

IPv6 Command	IPv4 Command
Show ipv6 route rip	Show ip route rip
Show ipv6 interface brief	Show ip interface brief
Show ipv6 protocols	Show ip protocols

If you are not sure what the IPv6 command is, just try the IPv4 equivalent and replace "ip" with "ipv6".

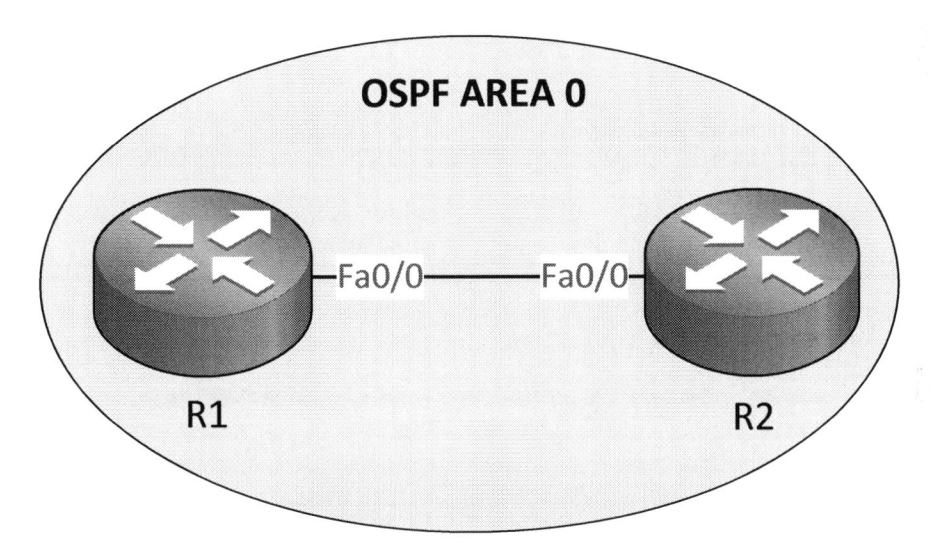

OSPF AREA 0

R1 —Fa0/0———Fa0/0— R2

Let's continue our IPv6 troubleshooting with some OSPFv3 issues. In the topology above we have 2 routers and there's only a single area. For some reason the two routers are unable to become OSPF neighbors, up to us to find out why!

```
R1#show ipv6 interface brief
FastEthernet0/0            [up/up]
    FE80::CE00:1BFF:FE29:0
```

```
R2#show ipv6 interface brief
FastEthernet0/0            [up/up]
    FE80::CE01:1BFF:FE29:0
```

First I'll see if IPv6 has been enabled on the interfaces. IPv6 routing protocols **use the link-local addresses for neighbor adjacency and next-hops**. We can see that both interfaces have a link-local IPv6 address and are active (up/up).

```
R1#ping FE80::CE01:1BFF:FE29:0
Output Interface: FastEthernet0/0
Type escape sequence to abort.
Sending 5, 100-byte ICMP Echos to FE80::CE01:1BFF:FE29:0,
timeout is 2 seconds:
Packet sent with a source address of FE80::CE00:1BFF:FE29:0
!!!!!
Success rate is 100 percent (5/5), round-trip min/avg/max =
0/4/8 ms
```

It's not a bad idea to check if they can ping each other, this seems to be the case.

```
R1#show ipv6 protocols
IPv6 Routing Protocol is "connected"
IPv6 Routing Protocol is "static"
IPv6 Routing Protocol is "ospf 1"
  Interfaces (Area 0):
    FastEthernet0/0
```

```
R2#show ipv6 protocols
IPv6 Routing Protocol is "connected"
IPv6 Routing Protocol is "static"
IPv6 Routing Protocol is "ospf 1"
  Interfaces (Area 0):
    FastEthernet0/0
```

Let's check if OSPF is active on the FastEthernet 0/0 interfaces, this seems to be the case.

```
R1#show ipv6 ospf neighbor
%OSPFv3: Router process 1 is INACTIVE, please configure a
router-id
```

```
R2#show ipv6 ospf neighbor
%OSPFv3: Router process 1 is INACTIVE, please configure a
router-id
```

We'll use **show ipv6 ospf neighbor** and we find out that the router-id has not been configured. OSPFv3 requires an IPv4 address-style router-ID and we need to configure it ourselves.

```
R1(config-rtr)#router-id ?
  A.B.C.D  OSPF router-id in IP address format
```

```
R1(config-rtr)#router-id 1.1.1.1
```

```
R2(config)#ipv6 router ospf 1
R2(config-rtr)#router-id 2.2.2.2
```

The router-ID has to be an IPv4 address format. I have no idea why they decided to do it this way for OSPFv3 but my best guess is someone got a bit nostalgic or something.

```
R1# %OSPFv3-5-ADJCHG: Process 1, Nbr 2.2.2.2 on FastEthernet0/0
from LOADING to FULL, Loading Done
```

```
R2# %OSPFv3-5-ADJCHG: Process 1, Nbr 1.1.1.1 on FastEthernet0/0
from LOADING to FULL, Loading Done
```

After configuring the router-ID we almost immediately see a message that the OSPFv3 neighbor adjacency has been established.

```
R1#show ipv6 ospf neighbor

Neighbor ID     Pri   State         Dead Time   Interface ID
Interface
2.2.2.2          1    FULL/DR       00:00:33    4
FastEthernet0/0
```

```
R2#show ipv6 ospf neighbor

Neighbor ID     Pri   State         Dead Time   Interface ID
Interface
1.1.1.1          1    FULL/BDR      00:00:31    4
FastEthernet0/0
```

Problem solved! **Lesson learned: Make sure you configure a router-ID for OSPFv3**.

OSPF AREA 0

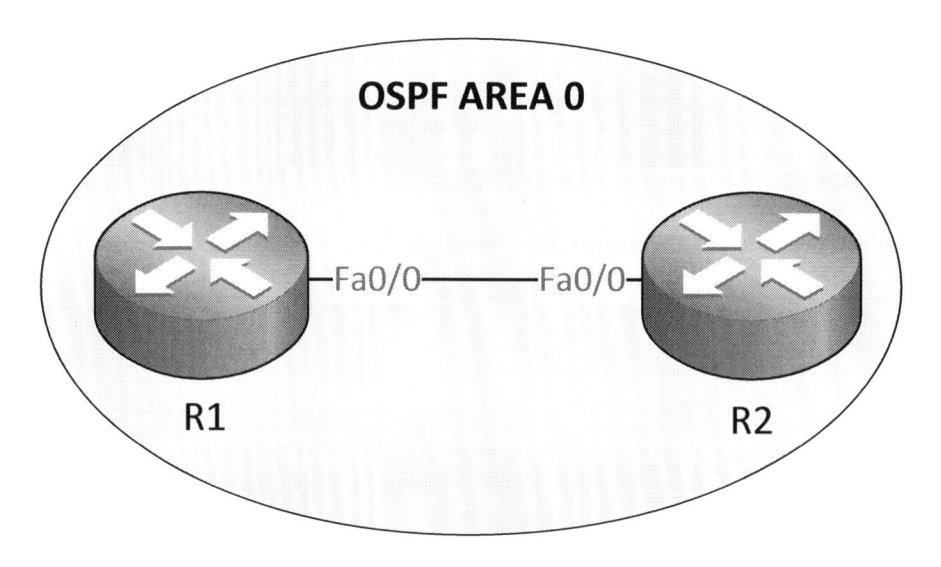

R1 —Fa0/0————Fa0/0— R2

Let's take another look at the same topology with another scenario. R1 and R2 are once again unable to form an OSPFv3 neighbor adjacency.

```
R1#show ipv6 interface brief
FastEthernet0/0            [up/up]
    FE80::CE00:1BFF:FE29:0
```

```
R2#show ipv6 interface brief
FastEthernet0/0            [up/up]
    FE80::CE01:1BFF:FE29:0
```

The interfaces and IPv6 addresses are fine.

```
R1#ping FE80::CE01:1BFF:FE29:0
Output Interface: FastEthernet0/0
Type escape sequence to abort.
Sending 5, 100-byte ICMP Echos to FE80::CE01:1BFF:FE29:0,
timeout is 2 seconds:
Packet sent with a source address of FE80::CE00:1BFF:FE29:0
!!!!!
Success rate is 100 percent (5/5), round-trip min/avg/max =
0/4/8 ms
```

Pinging each other is no issue.

```
R1#show ipv6 protocols
IPv6 Routing Protocol is "connected"
IPv6 Routing Protocol is "static"
IPv6 Routing Protocol is "ospf 1"
  Interfaces (Area 0):
    FastEthernet0/0
```

```
R2#show ipv6 protocols
IPv6 Routing Protocol is "connected"
IPv6 Routing Protocol is "static"
IPv6 Routing Protocol is "ospf 1"
  Interfaces (Area 0):
    FastEthernet0/0
```

OSPFv3 has been enabled on the interfaces.

```
R1#show ipv6 ospf neighbor
```

```
R2#show ipv6 ospf neighbor
```

Unfortunately we don't have any neighbors.

```
R1#debug ipv6 ospf hello
  OSPFv3 hello events debugging is on
```

Becoming OSPFv3 neighbors starts with a hello packet. Let's do a **debug ipv6 ospf hello**.

```
R1# OSPFv3: Mismatched hello parameters from
FE80::CE01:1BFF:FE29:0
    OSPFv3: Dead R 36 C 40, Hello R 9 C 10
    OSPFv3: Send hello to FF02::5 area 0 on FastEthernet0/0 from
FE80::CE
```

There we go; we see that there is a mismatch in the hello parameters. R1 is configured to send hello packets each 10 seconds and R2 is configured to send them every 9 seconds.

```
R1#show ipv6 ospf 1 interface fa0/0 | include intervals
  Timer intervals configured, Hello 10, Dead 40, Wait 40,
Retransmit 5
```

```
R2#show ipv6 ospf 1 interface fa0/0 | include intervals
  Timer intervals configured, Hello 9, Dead 36, Wait 36,
Retransmit 5
```

We can verify the timers by using the **show ipv6 ospf interface** command.

```
R2(config)#interface fa0/0
R2(config-if)#ipv6 ospf hello-interval 10
```

Let's change the hello timer back to 10 seconds.

```
R1# %OSPFv3-5-ADJCHG: Process 1, Nbr 2.2.2.2 on FastEthernet0/0
from LOADING to FULL, Loading Done
```

```
R2# %OSPFv3-5-ADJCHG: Process 1, Nbr 1.1.1.1 on FastEthernet0/0
from LOADING to FULL, Loading Done
```

After changing the hello timer back to the defaults you'll see this message appear on your consoles.

```
R1#show ipv6 ospf neighbor

Neighbor ID      Pri   State         Dead Time    Interface ID
Interface
2.2.2.2           1    FULL/DR       00:00:33     4
FastEthernet0/0
```

```
R2#show ipv6 ospf neighbor

Neighbor ID      Pri   State         Dead Time    Interface ID
Interface
1.1.1.1           1    FULL/BDR      00:00:31     4
FastEthernet0/0
```

Boomshakalaka our problem is solved!

Lesson Learned: OSPFv3 for IPv6 has the same requirements to form a neighbor adjacency as OSPFv2 for IPv4. Apply your "IPv4 OSPF" knowledge to solve neighbor adjacency issues.

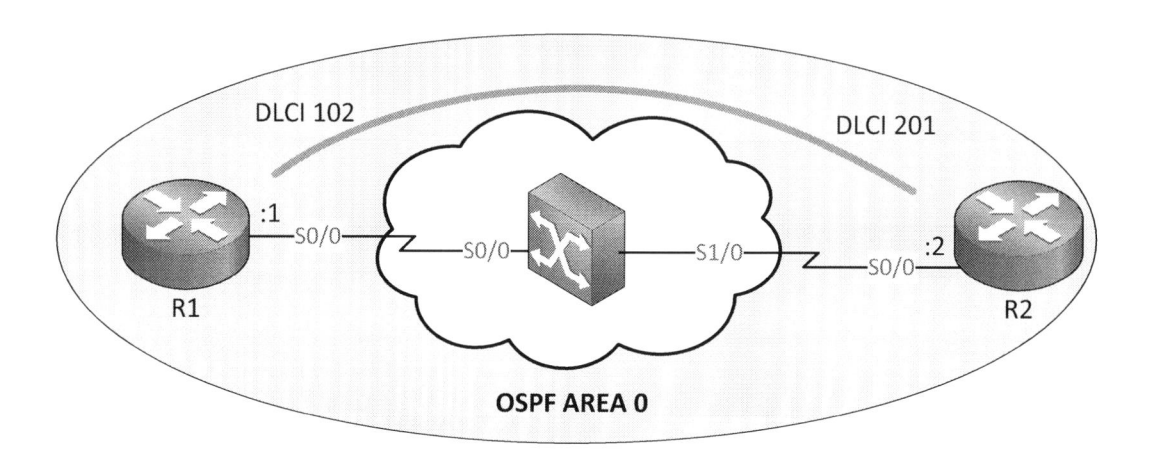

Here's something different for you. We are still working on troubleshooting OSPFv3 neighbor adjacencies. In the scenario above we have a frame-relay setup. There's a single PVC between R1 and R2. R1 has been configured to use

2001:12::1 and R2 is using 2001:12::2. For some reason the OSPFv3 neighbor adjacency is not working...let's troubleshoot!

What's the best place to start troubleshooting a problem like this? There are two options:

- Start in the middle of the OSI-model and dive into the OSPFv3 configuration right away.
- Start at the bottom of the OSI-model and check if the frame-relay configuration is properly configured.

Personally I like a structured approach and start at the bottom of the OSI model and work my way up. In this case that means we have to check if the interfaces are up, frame-relay encapsulation has been configured, if the PVC is working, if we have a valid frame-relay map, if we can ping each other and then move on to OSPFv3.

If you start at the bottom you'll find the problem eventually but it might be a bit more time-consuming sometimes.

Just to try something different I'll start in the middle of the OSI-model this time and we'll check the OSPFv3 configuration first.

```
R1#show ipv6 ospf neighbor
```

```
R2#show ipv6 ospf neighbor
```

I can confirm that there are no neighbor adjacencies.

```
R1#show ipv6 protocols
IPv6 Routing Protocol is "connected"
IPv6 Routing Protocol is "static"
IPv6 Routing Protocol is "ospf 1"
  Interfaces (Area 0):
    Serial0/0
```

```
R2#show ipv6 protocols
IPv6 Routing Protocol is "connected"
IPv6 Routing Protocol is "static"
IPv6 Routing Protocol is "ospf 1"
  Interfaces (Area 0):
    Serial0/0
```

You can see that OSPFv3 has been enabled for the serial 0/0 interfaces.

```
R1#show ipv6 ospf interface serial 0/0
Serial0/0 is up, line protocol is up
  Link Local Address FE80::9CD7:2EFF:FEF0:99FA, Interface ID 4
  Area 0, Process ID 1, Instance ID 0, Router ID 1.1.1.1
  Network Type NON_BROADCAST, Cost: 64
  Transmit Delay is 1 sec, State DR, Priority 1
  Designated Router (ID) 1.1.1.1, local address
FE80::9CD7:2EFF:FEF0:99FA
  No backup designated router on this network
  Timer intervals configured, Hello 30, Dead 120, Wait 120,
Retransmit 5
```

```
R2#show ipv6 ospf interface serial 0/0
Serial0/0 is up, line protocol is up
  Link Local Address FE80::9CD7:2EFF:FEF0:99FA, Interface ID 4
  Area 0, Process ID 1, Instance ID 0, Router ID 2.2.2.2
  Network Type NON_BROADCAST, Cost: 64
  Transmit Delay is 1 sec, State DR, Priority 1
  Designated Router (ID) 2.2.2.2, local address
FE80::9CD7:2EFF:FEF0:99FA
  No backup designated router on this network
  Timer intervals configured, Hello 30, Dead 120, Wait 120,
Retransmit 5
```

This is something that is worth a closer look. The network type and timer intervals match. The network type is "NON_BROADCAST" which means that we have to configure our neighbors ourselves. Has this been done?

```
R1#show ipv6 ospf neighbor
```

```
R2#show ipv6 ospf neighbor
```

I know it hasn't been configured because otherwise I would see them in the output above. Let's fix it…

```
R1#show ipv6 interface brief
Serial0/0                  [up/up]
    FE80::9CD8:2EFF:FEF0:99FA
```

```
R2#show ipv6 interface brief
Serial0/0                  [up/up]
    FE80::9CD7:2EFF:FEF0:99FA
```

Here you can see the link-local addresses that we need to use.

```
R1(config)#interface serial 0/0
R1(config-if)#ipv6 ospf neighbor FE80::9CD7:2EFF:FEF0:99FA
R2(config)#interface serial 0/0
```

```
R2(config-if)#ipv6 ospf neighbor FE80::9CD8:2EFF:FEF0:99FA
```

This is how we configure the neighbors ourselves. Keep in mind you need to use the link-local addresses for this.

```
R1#show ipv6 ospf neighbor

Neighbor ID     Pri   State            Dead Time   Interface ID
Interface
N/A              0    ATTEMPT/DROTHER 00:01:00     0
Serial0/0
```

```
R2#show ipv6 ospf neighbor

Neighbor ID     Pri   State            Dead Time   Interface ID
Interface
N/A              0    ATTEMPT/DROTHER 00:00:39     0
Serial0/0
```

Too bad...I want to see "FULL" but I'm only seeing "ATTEMPT" here. My OSPFv3 configuration looks fine to me so this would be a good moment to move down the OSI model.

```
R1#ping FE80::9CD7:2EFF:FEF0:99FA
Output Interface: Serial0/0
Type escape sequence to abort.
Sending 5, 100-byte ICMP Echos to FE80::9CD7:2EFF:FEF0:99FA,
timeout is 2 seconds:
Packet sent with a source address of FE80::9CD8:2EFF:FEF0:99FA
.....
Success rate is 0 percent (0/5)
```

I'm unable to ping between the link-local addresses. Now I know that layer 3 of the OSI-model is not working, let's dive deeper...

```
R1#show frame-relay map
```

```
R2#show frame-relay map
```

There seems to be no frame-relay map. We need this in order to bind the DLCI to the IPv6 addresses. Normally Inverse ARP takes care of this but not this time. It's probably disabled (or the interface is not operational).

```
R1#show frame-relay pvc | include ACTIVE
DLCI = 102, DLCI USAGE = UNUSED, PVC STATUS = ACTIVE, INTERFACE
= Serial0/0
```

```
R2#show frame-relay pvc | include ACTIVE
DLCI = 201, DLCI USAGE = UNUSED, PVC STATUS = ACTIVE, INTERFACE
= Serial0/0
```

We'll check if the PVC is operational and what the DLCI number is. It's active on both sides and you can see the DLCI numbers, let's create some frame-relay maps.

```
R1(config)#interface serial 0/0
R1(config-if)#frame-relay map ipv6 FE80::9CD7:2EFF:FEF0:99FA 102
```

```
R2(config)#interface serial 0/0
R2(config-if)#frame-relay map ipv6 FE80::9CD8:2EFF:FEF0:99FA 201
```

I'll map the link-local addresses to the DLCI numbers.

```
R1# %OSPFv3-5-ADJCHG: Process 1, Nbr 2.2.2.2 on Serial0/0 from
LOADING to FULL, Loading Done
```

```
R2# %OSPFv3-5-ADJCHG: Process 1, Nbr 1.1.1.1 on Serial0/0 from
LOADING to FULL, Loading Done
```

This is looking good!

```
R1#show ipv6 ospf neighbor

Neighbor ID     Pri    State          Dead Time    Interface ID
Interface
2.2.2.2         1      FULL/DR        00:01:47     4
Serial0/0
```

```
R2#show ipv6 ospf neighbor

Neighbor ID     Pri    State          Dead Time    Interface ID
Interface
1.1.1.1         1      FULL/BDR       00:01:58     4
Serial0/0
```

Problem solved!

Lesson learned: Check the OSPFv3 network type and configure the neighbors using the link-local addresses. Also make sure you have the correct frame-relay maps.

If I would have started at the bottom of the OSI-model I would have found out sooner that the frame-relay map wasn't there, verified IP connectivity and then moved on to OSPFv3. In this case it wouldn't have mattered much but sometimes one approach is faster than another. It takes time and experience in troubleshooting to know where to start and develop that "gut" feeling ☺.

How to Master CCNP TSHOOT

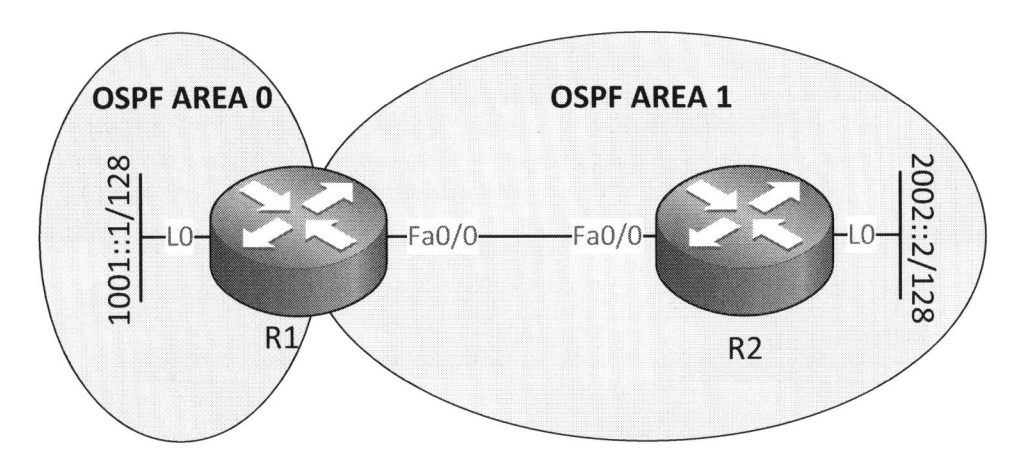

```
                OSPF AREA 0                    OSPF AREA 1
        1001::1/128                                              2002::2/128
                    L0──────Fa0/0────Fa0/0──────L0
                      R1                            R2
```

Onto the next OSPFv3 scenario for you: This time the neighbor adjacencies are working fine but users behind R1 are complaining that they are unable to reach network 2002::2/128. Up to us to troubleshoot this issue...

```
R1#show ipv6 ospf neighbor

Neighbor ID     Pri   State          Dead Time    Interface ID
Interface
2.2.2.2          1    FULL/DR        00:00:38     4
FastEthernet0/0
```

```
R2#show ipv6 ospf neighbor

Neighbor ID     Pri   State          Dead Time    Interface ID
Interface
1.1.1.1          1    FULL/BDR       00:00:36     4
FastEthernet0/0
```

The neighbor adjacency is working.

```
R1#show ipv6 route ospf
IPv6 Routing Table - 3 entries
Codes: C - Connected, L - Local, S - Static, R - RIP, B - BGP
       U - Per-user Static route
       I1 - ISIS L1, I2 - ISIS L2, IA - ISIS interarea, IS -
ISIS summary
       O - OSPF intra, OI - OSPF inter, OE1 - OSPF ext 1, OE2 -
OSPF ext 2
       ON1 - OSPF NSSA ext 1, ON2 - OSPF NSSA ext 2
```

I don't see network 2002::2/128 in the routing table of R1.

```
R2#show ipv6 route ospf
IPv6 Routing Table - 4 entries
```

271

```
Codes: C - Connected, L - Local, S - Static, R - RIP, B - BGP
       U - Per-user Static route
       I1 - ISIS L1, I2 - ISIS L2, IA - ISIS interarea, IS -
ISIS summary
       O - OSPF intra, OI - OSPF inter, OE1 - OSPF ext 1, OE2 -
OSPF ext 2
       ON1 - OSPF NSSA ext 1, ON2 - OSPF NSSA ext 2
OI   1001::1/128 [110/1]     via FE80::CE06:21FF:FED9:0,
FastEthernet0/0
```

R2 did learn about 1001::1/128. Let's check if R2 has OSPFv3 enabled on the loopback0 interface.

```
R2#show ipv6 protocols
IPv6 Routing Protocol is "connected"
IPv6 Routing Protocol is "static"
IPv6 Routing Protocol is "ospf 1"
  Interfaces (Area 1):
    FastEthernet0/0
  Interfaces (Area 12):
    Loopback0
```

There we go...you can see that OSPFv3 is enabled for the loopback0 interface but it has been configured for area 12...that's not right!

```
R2(config)#interface loopback 0
R2(config-if)#ipv6 ospf 1 area 1
```

Let's change the area from area 12 to area 1.

```
R1#show ipv6 route ospf
IPv6 Routing Table - 4 entries
Codes: C - Connected, L - Local, S - Static, R - RIP, B - BGP
       U - Per-user Static route
       I1 - ISIS L1, I2 - ISIS L2, IA - ISIS interarea, IS -
ISIS summary
       O - OSPF intra, OI - OSPF inter, OE1 - OSPF ext 1, OE2 -
OSPF ext 2
       ON1 - OSPF NSSA ext 1, ON2 - OSPF NSSA ext 2
O    2002::2/128 [110/1]     via FE80::CE07:21FF:FED9:0,
FastEthernet0/0
```

There we go...R1 has learned about 2002::2/128. Problem solved! Lesson learned: **Apply the same IPv4 OSPF troubleshooting techniques to OSPFv3 after the neighbor adjacency has been established.**

This scenario was also a good example of how OSPFv2 and OSPFv3 are very alike. The commands are almost the same and the troubleshooting techniques are the same.

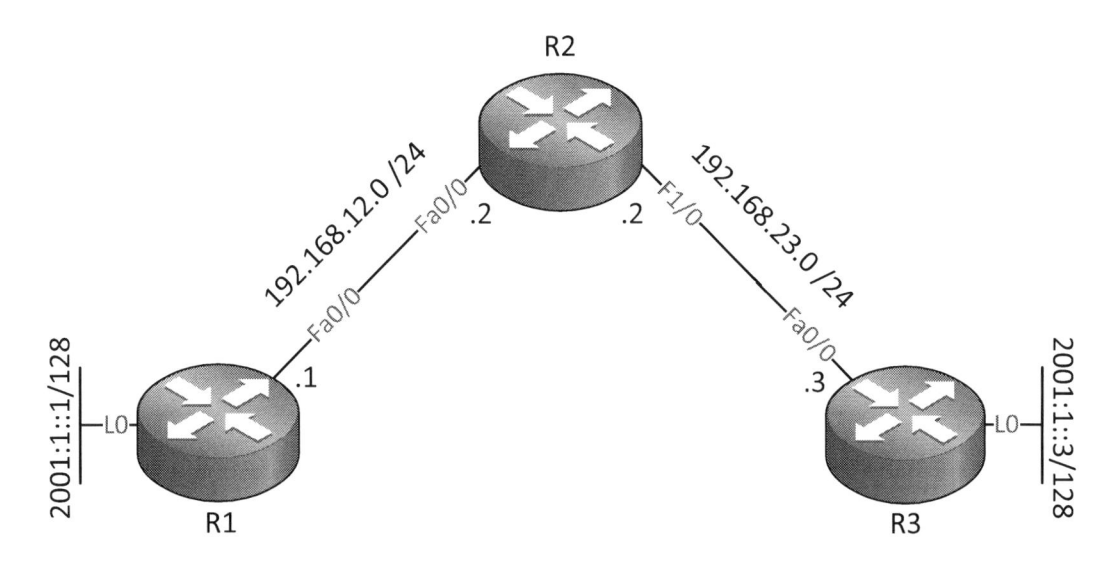

Here's something new for you. This scenario requires some more explanation. R1 and R3 each have a loopback0 interface with an IPv6 prefix on it. The FastEthernet interfaces of R1, R2 and R3 only have IPv4 addresses. The network engineer that designed this topology created an automatic 6to4 tunnel to establish connectivity between the two IPv6 networks. Of course this is not working so we'll have some fixing to do. This time I'll show you the tunnel configuration from the running-config:

```
R1#show running-config | begin Tunnel0
interface Tunnel0
 no ip address
 no ip redirects
 ipv6 address 2002:A0A:A01::1/64
 tunnel source FastEthernet0/0
 tunnel mode ipv6ip 6to4
```

```
R3#show running-config | begin Tunnel0
interface Tunnel0
 no ip address
 no ip redirects
 ipv6 address 2002:A14:1403::3/64
 tunnel source FastEthernet0/0
 tunnel mode ipv6ip 6to4
```

Here's the tunnel0 configuration of both routers.

```
R1#ping 2001:1::3

Type escape sequence to abort.
Sending 5, 100-byte ICMP Echos to 2001:1::3, timeout is 2 seconds:
.....
```

273

```
Success rate is 0 percent (0/5)
```

```
R3#ping 2001:1::1

Type escape sequence to abort.
Sending 5, 100-byte ICMP Echos to 2001:1::1, timeout is 2
seconds:
.....
Success rate is 0 percent (0/5)
```

A quick ping shows us that we can't ping the IPv6 addresses on the loopback interfaces. So where should we start troubleshooting?

```
R1#ping 192.168.23.3 source fastEthernet 0/0

Type escape sequence to abort.
Sending 5, 100-byte ICMP Echos to 192.168.23.3, timeout is 2
seconds:
Packet sent with a source address of 192.168.12.1
!!!!!
Success rate is 100 percent (5/5), round-trip min/avg/max =
4/8/12 ms
```

The tunnel0 interfaces are sourced from the FastEthernet 0/0 interfaces of R1 and R3. By sending a ping from R1 to R3 between the FastEthernet 0/0 interfaces I know that IPv4 routing is no issue.

```
R1#show ipv6 interface brief
FastEthernet0/0            [up/up]
Loopback0                  [up/up]
    FE80::CE09:25FF:FEB0:0
    2001:1::1
Tunnel0                    [up/up]
    FE80::C0A8:C01
    2002:A0A:A01::1
```

```
R3#show ipv6 interface brief
FastEthernet0/0            [up/up]
Loopback0                  [up/up]
    FE80::CE0B:25FF:FEB0:0
    2001:1::3
Tunnel0                    [up/up]
    FE80::C0A8:1703
    2002:A14:1403::3
```

Taking a quick look at the interfaces tells us that the IPv6 addresses on the loopback0 interfaces have been configured correctly and that the interfaces are up and running. You can also see the IPv6 addresses on the Tunnel0 interfaces. What does the 2002:A0A:A01::1 and 2002:A14:1403::3 mean?

Keep in mind that the tunnel mode is **automatic** 6to4. The "automatic" part means that the tunnel destination IP is not configured statically but within the IPv6 address. 2002::/16 is the range that is reserved for tunnels.

```
R1#ping 2002:A14:1403::3

Type escape sequence to abort.
Sending 5, 100-byte ICMP Echos to 2002:A14:1403::3, timeout is 2
seconds:
.....
Success rate is 0 percent (0/5)
```

```
R3#ping 2002:A0A:A01::1

Type escape sequence to abort.
Sending 5, 100-byte ICMP Echos to 2002:A0A:A01::1, timeout is 2
seconds:
.....
Success rate is 0 percent (0/5)
```

We are unable to ping the IPv6 addresses on the tunnel0 interfaces. This could mean that 2002:A0A:A01::1 and 2002:A14:1403::3 are not correct or that my routing is not working.

The tunnel should be built between IP address 192.168.12.1 and 192.168.23.3. If you want you can manually calculate from decimal to hexadecimal but there's an easier method!

```
R1(config)#ipv6 general-prefix IAMLAZY 6to4 fastEthernet 0/0
```

We can let our router do the calculation from decimal to hexadecimal for us.

```
R1#show ipv6 general-prefix
IPv6 Prefix IAMLAZY, acquired via 6to4
  2002:C0A8:C01::/48
```

There you go, the IPv6 address should be in this range 2002:C0A8:C01/48 so 2002:A0A:A01::1/64 is incorrect.

```
R1(config)#interface tunnel 0
R1(config-if)#no ipv6 address 2002:A0A:A01::1/64
R1(config-if)#ipv6 address 2002:C0A8:C01::1/64
```

We'll remove the old IPv6 address and configure a new one in the 2002:C0A8:C01/48 range.

```
R3(config)#ipv6 general-prefix IAMLAZY 6to4 FastEthernet 0/0
```

Let's calculate the correct prefix on R3 as well.

275

```
R3#show ipv6 general-prefix
IPv6 Prefix IAMLAZY, acquired via 6to4
  2002:C0A8:1703::/48
```

The correct prefix is 2002:C0A8:1703::/48 so 2002:A14:1403::3 is not going to work.

```
R3(config-if)#no ipv6 address 2002:A14:1403::3/64
R3(config-if)#ipv6 address 2002:C0A8:1703::3/64
```

We'll remove the IPv6 address and configure another one that falls within the 2002:A14:1403::3 range.

Now we know that the IPv6 addresses on the tunnel0 interfaces are correct. Next step is to check our routing to see if R1 and R3 know how to reach each other's IPv6 addresses.

```
R1#show ipv6 route
IPv6 Routing Table - 7 entries
Codes: C - Connected, L - Local, S - Static, R - RIP, B - BGP
       U - Per-user Static route
       I1 - ISIS L1, I2 - ISIS L2, IA - ISIS interarea, IS -
ISIS summary
       O - OSPF intra, OI - OSPF inter, OE1 - OSPF ext 1, OE2 -
OSPF ext 2
       ON1 - OSPF NSSA ext 1, ON2 - OSPF NSSA ext 2
LC  2001:1::1/128 [0/0]
    via ::, Loopback0
S   2001:1::3/128 [1/0]
    via 2002:A14:1403::3
S   2002::/16 [1/0]
    via ::, Tunnel0
C   2002:C0A8:C01::/64 [0/0]
    via ::, Tunnel0
L   2002:C0A8:C01::1/128 [0/0]
    via ::, Tunnel0
L   FE80::/10 [0/0]
    via ::, Null0
L   FF00::/8 [0/0]
    via ::, Null0
```

There are two static routes here. The 2001:1::3/128 points to the loopback0 interface of R3 but the next hop IPv6 address is 2002:A14:1403::3. This next hop is incorrect so we'll have to change it. The static route for 2002::/16 to the tunnel0 interface is fine. This prefix is reserved for tunneling and we need it because the router will do a recursive routing looking when it tries to reach 2001:1::3/128.

```
R1(config)#no ipv6 route 2001:1::3/128 2002:A14:1403::3
```

```
R1(config)#ipv6 route 2001:1::3/128   2002:C0A8:1703::3
```

We'll remove the old static route and create a new one with the correct next hop.

```
R3#show ipv6 route
*Mar  1 01:20:11.827: %SYS-5-CONFIG_I: Configured from console
by console
IPv6 Routing Table - 7 entries
Codes: C - Connected, L - Local, S - Static, R - RIP, B - BGP
       U - Per-user Static route
       I1 - ISIS L1, I2 - ISIS L2, IA - ISIS interarea, IS -
ISIS summary
       O - OSPF intra, OI - OSPF inter, OE1 - OSPF ext 1, OE2 -
OSPF ext 2
       ON1 - OSPF NSSA ext 1, ON2 - OSPF NSSA ext 2
S   2001:1::1/128 [1/0]
     via 2002:A0A:A01::1
LC  2001:1::3/128 [0/0]
     via ::, Loopback0
S   2002::/16 [1/0]
     via ::, Tunnel0
C   2002:C0A8:1703::/64 [0/0]
     via ::, Tunnel0
L   2002:C0A8:1703::3/128 [0/0]
     via ::, Tunnel0
L   FE80::/10 [0/0]
     via ::, Null0
L   FF00::/8 [0/0]
     via ::, Null0
```

R3 has the same issue. The static route with 2002::/16 to the tunnel0 interface is fine but 2001:1::1/128 has the old (and wrong) next hop.

```
R3(config)#no ipv6 route 2001:1::1/128 2002:A0A:A01::1
R3(config)#ipv6 route 2001:1::1/128 2002:C0A8:C01::1
```

We'll correct the static route.

```
R3#ping 2001:1::1 source loopback 0

Type escape sequence to abort.
Sending 5, 100-byte ICMP Echos to 2001:1::1, timeout is 2
seconds:
Packet sent with a source address of 2001:1::3
!!!!!
Success rate is 100 percent (5/5), round-trip min/avg/max =
8/8/8 ms
```

There we go! A ping between the loopback0 interfaces of R1 and R3 proves that they know how to reach each other's prefixes...problem solved! **Lesson learned: Make sure you use the correct 6to4 tunnel IPv6 addresses.**

I have one more IPv6 problem for you and it's about redistribution. Here's the topology:

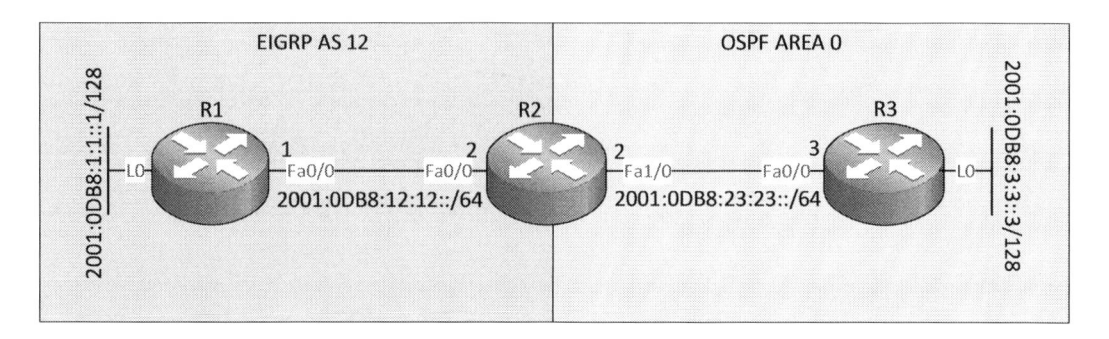

R1 and R2 are configured to use EIGRP, R2 and R3 use OSPF. R2 is redistributing between the two routing protocols. The problem is that R1 is unable to reach 2001:0DB8:23:23::/64 and R3 is unable to reach 2001:0DB8:12:12::/64. Everything else is reachable...

Let's check some routing tables, see what we are dealing with:

```
R1#show ipv6 route eigrp

EX   2001:DB8:3:3::3/128 [170/1757696]
     via FE80::C002:17FF:FE28:0, FastEthernet0/0
```

```
R2#show ipv6 route

D    2001:DB8:1:1::1/128 [90/409600]
     via FE80::C001:18FF:FEB0:0, FastEthernet0/0
O    2001:DB8:3:3::3/128 [110/10]
     via FE80::C003:FFF:FE10:0, FastEthernet0/1
```

```
R3#show ipv6 route ospf

OE2  2001:DB8:1:1::1/128 [110/20]
     via FE80::C002:17FF:FE28:1, FastEthernet0/0
```

Looking at these routing tables, we can see that R1 knows how to reach the loopback of R3 and vice versa. Since we have something in the routing table, we know that the EIGRP and OSPF neighbor adjacencies are working. There are a couple of reasons why we miss something in the routing table:

- **Networks are not configured:** Keep in mind that IPv6 routing protocols use their link-local IPv6 addresses for the neighbor adjacency.

- **Filtering**: Route filtering could filter some of the prefixes.
- **Redistribution**: Configuration errors with redistribution could cause issues.

Let's check if those two networks are configured correctly, you could check the addresses or a quick ping:

```
R2#show ipv6 interface brief
FastEthernet0/0            [up/up]
    FE80::C002:17FF:FE28:0
    2001:DB8:12:12::2
FastEthernet0/1            [up/up]
    FE80::C002:17FF:FE28:1
    2001:DB8:23:23::2
```

```
R2#ping 2001:0DB8:12:12::1

Type escape sequence to abort.
Sending 5, 100-byte ICMP Echos to 2001:DB8:12:12::1, timeout is 2 seconds:
!!!!!
Success rate is 100 percent (5/5), round-trip min/avg/max = 8/15/28 ms
```

```
R2#ping 2001:0DB8:23:23::3

Type escape sequence to abort.
Sending 5, 100-byte ICMP Echos to 2001:DB8:23:23::3, timeout is 2 seconds:
!!!!!
Success rate is 100 percent (5/5), round-trip min/avg/max = 4/13/28 ms
```

It seems that these networks are configured and the pings are working. What about filtering? Normally I'd like to use specific show commands but in this case, checking the EIGRP and OSPF configs would be easier:

```
R1#show run | section ipv6 router
ipv6 router eigrp 12
 router-id 1.1.1.1
 no shutdown
```

```
R2#show run | section ipv6 router
ipv6 router eigrp 12
 router-id 2.2.2.2
 no shutdown
 redistribute ospf 1 metric 1500 100 255 1 1500
ipv6 router ospf 1
 router-id 2.2.2.2
 log-adjacency-changes
```

```
 redistribute eigrp 12
```

```
R3#show run | section ipv6 router
ipv6 router ospf 1
 router-id 3.3.3.3
 log-adjacency-changes
```

These configurations are pretty straight-forward. There are no filters and no route-maps attached to the redistribution config, everything is looking good. So what's the issue here?

Redistribution for IPv6 works a little bit different compared to IPv4. When you redistribute with IPv4, all networks that are advertised in your routing protocols will be redistributed...that includes the directly connected networks.

With IPv6, networks that are directly connected and advertised in your routing protocols are NOT redistributed by default...this is something we have to enable ourselves. Let me show you what I mean:

```
R2(config)#ipv6 router eigrp 12
R2(config-rtr)#redistribute ospf 1 metric 1500 100 255 1 1500
include-connected

R2(config)#ipv6 router ospf 1
R2(config-rtr)#redistribute eigrp 12 include-connected
```

We need to add the **include-connected** keyword when we want to redistribute the directly connected networks that are advertised in our routing protocol. Let's see the result of this:

```
R1#show ipv6 route eigrp

EX  2001:DB8:3:3::3/128 [170/1757696]
     via FE80::C002:17FF:FE28:0, FastEthernet0/0
EX  2001:DB8:23:23::/64 [170/1757696]
     via FE80::C002:17FF:FE28:0, FastEthernet0/0
```

```
R3#show ipv6 route ospf

OE2  2001:DB8:1:1::1/128 [110/20]
      via FE80::C002:17FF:FE28:1, FastEthernet0/0
OE2  2001:DB8:12:12::/64 [110/20]
      via FE80::C002:17FF:FE28:1, FastEthernet0/0
```

R1 and R3 are now able to learn about the 2001:DB8:23:23::/64 and 2001:DB8:12:12::/64 networks...problem solved. **Lesson learned: IPv6 redistribution behaves a bit different than IPv4 redistribution.**

This is the end of the troubleshooting IPv6 chapter. I could easily write a complete book on IPv6 troubleshooting but I decided to focus mostly on the "IPv6" specific areas. Most of your IPv4 knowledge can be applied to IPv6 but you have to be familiar with some of the new stuff like autoconfiguration and the different tunneling techniques.

If you want to practice your IPv6 skills to see if you are ready for the future, take a look at the following lab that teaches you all the IPv6 troubleshooting skills you need to master for CCNP TSHOOT:

http://gns3vault.com/Troubleshooting/ipv6-troubleshooting.html

11. Troubleshooting Full Labs

Here you are...you made it to the final chapter. However before we are done with troubleshooting there's one final battle awaiting you.

In the previous chapters I have showed you how to troubleshoot all the different protocols one-by-one but in real life we have production networks where we have a mix of all those protocols.

In this chapter I'm going to walk you through a full lab that is based on the official Cisco CCNP TSHOOT topology. This lab is "broken" so that we have something to fix.

The official Cisco CCNP TSHOOT topology can be found here:

https://learningnetwork.cisco.com/thread/10965

I recreated this topology in GNS3 as best as I could. Cisco released the topology pictures but without any configurations. I recreated the configurations so it will probably be 95% the same as what you might encounter on the exam. You can find my GNS3 topology right here:

http://gns3vault.com/Faq/ccnp-tshoot-gns3-topology.html

Let's troubleshoot one of those full labs! Before you continue reading I would highly suggest first giving this full lab a try yourself. If you get stuck you can continue reading and see *how* and *why* I solve it. Here's the lab we are going to fix:

http://gns3vault.com/Troubleshooting/ccnp-tshoot-troubleshooting-1.html

Enough talking, let's get labbing!

Its Monday morning 8 AM. You slept great and there's a lovely croissant and cup of coffee waiting for you. Suddenly the phone rings...it's your colleague!

His voice sounds like he's in panic. There are users complaining that they can't access the network and he is unable to solve the problems by himself...he seriously needs your help.

You throw your croissant out of the window...it's time to show what a network troubleshooting rockstar looks like! ;)

The first thing you do is grab a copy of the network diagram. You want to know the layer2 and layer3 topology so you don't have to do everything off top of your head.

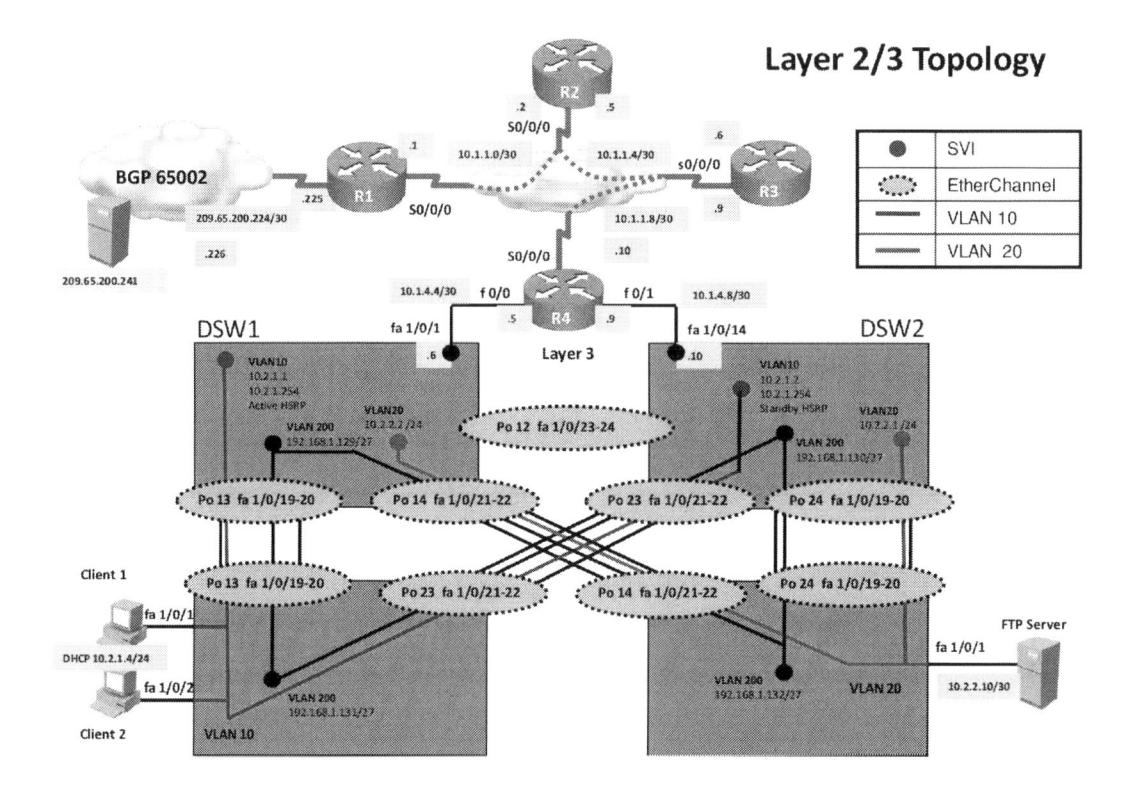

IPv4 Layer 3 Topology

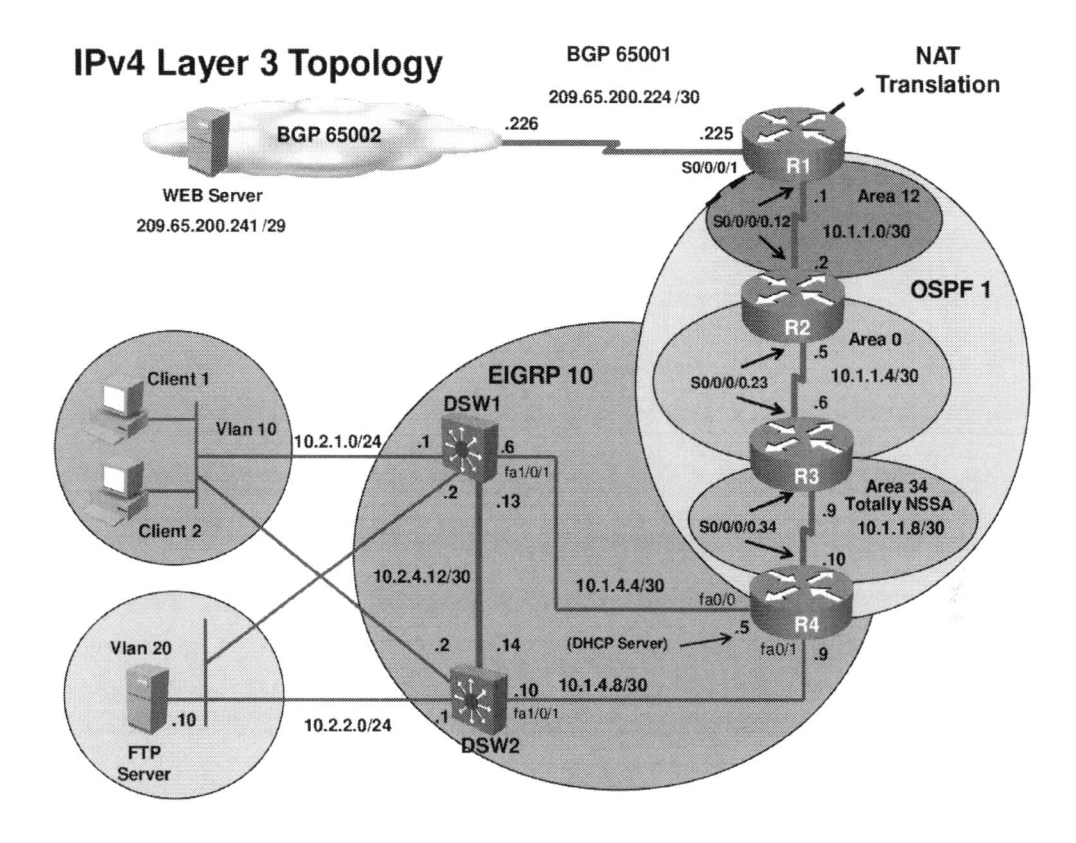

Then you open your helpdesk application and you'll find the following troubleshooting tickets waiting for you:

- **Ticket #1**: One of the users was working on Client1 but he's complaining that there is no connectivity. He left a comment that he saw a message on the windows taskbar that said something like "no network connectivity". One of your colleagues looked into the problem and told you it had probably something to do with DHCP.

- **Ticket #2**: After fixing the issue with Client1 you receive another ticket that users from VLAN 10 are complaining that they are unable to connect to the FTP server.

- **Ticket #3**: Your users are happy that they can connect to the FTP server but they are still unable to reach the webserver.

- **Ticket #4**: The IPv6 team left a ticket for you that they are unable to reach 2026::12:/122 from DSW1 or DSW2.

You decide to start with ticket #1. "no network connectivity" probably has something to do with the client not receiving an IP address.

285

To solve this problem there are a number of devices we might have to check:

- DHCP server: The pool could be misconfigured, DHCP might not be running, maybe some of the interfaces are not working.
- Client: Maybe the client is configured to use a static IP address.
- ASW1, DSW1 and/or DSW2: These are devices that are in between our client and the DHCP server.

The ticket told us that client1 has an issue but didn't tell us anything about other clients in VLAN 10 like client2. We can take a quick look if client2 can get a DHCP lease or not. If this is the case then we at least know the DHCP server is fine.

```
Client2#show ip interface brief
Interface              IP-Address      OK? Method Status    Protocol
FastEthernet0/0        unassigned      YES DHCP   up        up
```

It seems client2 has the same issue, lucky for us nobody reported this issue yet.

```
Client1#show ip interface brief
Interface              IP-Address      OK? Method Status    Protocol
FastEthernet0/0        unassigned      YES DHCP   up        up
```

Client1 is configured for DHCP so to me this machine is looking good. If this were a real computer you might want to check other settings like the firewall. We will move our focus to the DHCP server.

```
R4#show ip dhcp server statistics
Memory usage         23235
Address pools        1
Database agents      0
Automatic bindings   0
Manual bindings      0
Expired bindings     0
Malformed messages   0
Secure arp entries   0

Message              Received
BOOTREQUEST          0
DHCPDISCOVER         0
DHCPREQUEST          0
DHCPDECLINE          0
DHCPRELEASE          0
DHCPINFORM           0
```

```
Message                      Sent
BOOTREPLY                    0
DHCPOFFER                    0
DHCPACK                      0
DHCPNAK                      0
```

First I'll check if the DHCP server has received and sent any DHCP related messages. This doesn't seem to be the case but doesn't have to be an issue. Maybe the router was rebooted and hasn't received any DHCP discover messages since then. I do see that there is a DHCP pool.

```
R4#show processes | include DHCP
  42 Mwe 6155B92C           0          43       0 5496/6000      0
DHCPD Timer
 131 Mwe 61D4112C         1948       10172   19110568/12000      0
DHCPD Receive
 150 Msi 61563C34            4          91      43 5124/6000     0
DHCPD Database
```

This router doesn't support the "show ip sockets" command so I'll take a look at the running processes. The DHCP service is running so we know this is not the issue.

```
R4#show ip dhcp pool

Pool VLAN10 :
 Utilization mark (high/low)    : 100 / 0
 Subnet size (first/next)       : 0 / 0
 Total addresses                : 254
 Leased addresses               : 0
 Pending event                  : none
 1 subnet is currently in the pool :
 Current index         IP address range                      Leased addresses
 10.2.10.1             10.2.10.1        - 10.2.10.254        0
```

We'll take a look at the pool. The first thing that I notice is that the address range is incorrect. This pool is configured to use 10.2.10.0 /24 but VLAN 10 is using 10.2.1.0 /24. Let's fix this:

```
R4(config)#ip dhcp pool VLAN10
R4(dhcp-config)#network 10.2.1.0 /24
```

This is looking better. The DHCP configuration itself is looking good now to me.

```
R4#ping 10.1.4.6

Type escape sequence to abort.
Sending 5, 100-byte ICMP Echos to 10.1.4.6, timeout is 2 seconds:
```

```
!!!!!
Success rate is 100 percent (5/5), round-trip min/avg/max =
4/4/8 ms

R4#ping 10.1.4.10

Type escape sequence to abort.
Sending 5, 100-byte ICMP Echos to 10.1.4.10, timeout is 2
seconds:
!!!!!
Success rate is 100 percent (5/5), round-trip min/avg/max =
1/3/4 ms
```

I haven't checked connectivity from R4 to DSW1 and DSW2. To test this I'll do a quick ping to DSW1 and DSW2. This is working fine so to me R4 is 100% operational when it comes to DHCP. This means we'll have to move our focus to the switches in between the client and R4. I'll start with ASW1.

```
ASW1#show ip int brief | include FastEthernet1/4
FastEthernet1/4            unassigned      YES unset  up
up
```

First we'll check the interface that is connected to client1. It seems to be up/up.

```
ASW1#show interfaces fa1/4 switchport
Name: Fa1/4
Switchport: Enabled
Administrative Mode: static access
Operational Mode: static access
Administrative Trunking Encapsulation: dot1q
Operational Trunking Encapsulation: native
Negotiation of Trunking: Disabled
Access Mode VLAN: 200 (VLAN0200)
Trunking Native Mode VLAN: 1 (default)
Trunking VLANs Enabled: ALL
Trunking VLANs Active: 200
Protected: false
Priority for untagged frames: 0
Override vlan tag priority: FALSE
Voice VLAN: none
Appliance trust: none
```

Here's something wrong. The interface is in access mode which is good but it has been assigned to VLAN 200. Client1 should be in VLAN 10.

```
ASW1(config)#interface f1/4
ASW1(config-if)#switchport access vlan 10
```

We'll put the interface in VLAN 10. Now this probably doesn't fix this error since client1 isn't the only device that didn't get an IP address through DHCP. Client2 was also having issues. We need to verify connectivity from ASW1 to DSW1 and DSW2.

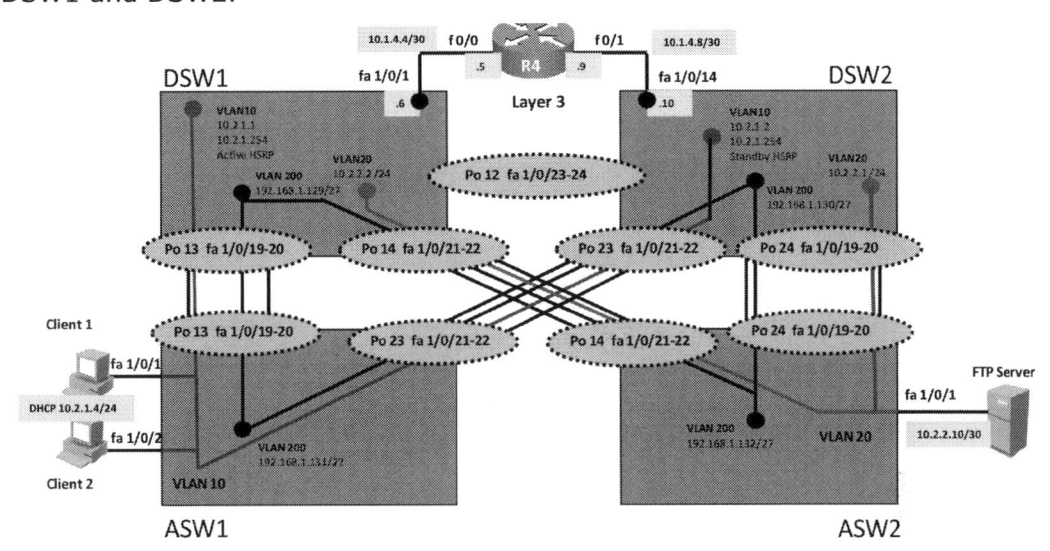

This is the area of the topology where I will focus on. Client1 is connected to ASW1 and is in VLAN 10. VLAN 10 is configured on ASW1, ASW2, DSW1 and DSW3. R4 is our DHCP server but it's not directly connected to VLAN 10, it's in another subnet. This means that DSW1 and DSW2 require the IP helper command so that DHCP discover messages can be relayed to the the DHCP server. This is what we'll have to check:

- Is VLAN 10 configured and operational on all switches? Even if only ASW1 and DSW1 would work, I still want to have redundancy so we'll check DSW2 too.
- Is IP helper configured on DSW1 and DSW2 for VLAN 10?

We'll start with IP helper. It's only a single command so if this is the issue we'll save a lot of time by not having to check all the interfaces between the switches.

```
DSW1#show ip interface vlan 10 | include Helper
  Helper address is not set
```

```
DSW2#show ip interface vlan 10 | include Helper
  Helper address is not set
```

That's not looking good. DSW1 and DSW2 don't have IP helper configured.

Let's fix it:

```
DSW1(config)#interface vlan 10
DSW1(config-if)#ip helper-address 10.1.4.5
```

```
DSW2(config)#int vlan 10
DSW2(config-if)#ip helper-address 10.1.4.9
```

This is how we configure IP helper. This would be a good moment to check if the clients are receiving IP addresses through DHCP.

```
Client2#show ip interface brief
Interface              IP-Address       OK? Method Status
Protocol
FastEthernet0/0        unassigned       YES DHCP   up
up
```

```
Client1#show ip interface brief
Interface              IP-Address       OK? Method Status
Protocol
FastEthernet0/0        unassigned       YES DHCP   up
up
```

Still no DHCP action. This looks like one of those Mondays where everything goes wrong...we'll have to check all the interfaces between the switches.

```
ASW1#show etherchannel summary
Flags:  D - down         P - in port-channel
        I - stand-alone  s - suspended
        R - Layer3       S - Layer2
        U - in use
Group Port-channel  Ports
-----+------------+------------------------------------------
1     Po1(SU)      Fa1/2(P)    Fa1/3(P)
2     Po2(SU)      Fa1/10(P)   Fa1/11(P)
```

In between the switches we are using etherchannels. We can see that port-channel 1 and 2 are up and running. This doesn't tell me anything about the VLANS though.

```
ASW1#show vlan-switch id 10

VLAN Name                            Status    Ports
---- ------------------------------- --------- ----------------
10   VLAN0010                        active    Fa1/4, Fa1/5
```

I can see that VLAN 10 is operational. Interface Fa1/4 and Fa1/5 are assigned to it.

```
ASW1#show interfaces po1 trunk

Port       Mode              Encapsulation    Status           Native vlan
Po1        on                802.1q           trunking         1

Port       Vlans allowed on trunk
Po1        1-9,11-4094

Port       Vlans allowed and active in management domain
Po1        1,20,200

Port       Vlans in spanning tree forwarding state and not pruned
Po1        1,200
```

```
ASW1#show interfaces po2 trunk

Port       Mode              Encapsulation    Status           Native vlan
Po2        on                802.1q           trunking         1

Port       Vlans allowed on trunk
Po2        1-9,11-4094

Port       Vlans allowed and active in management domain
Po2        1,20,200

Port       Vlans in spanning tree forwarding state and not pruned
Po2        1,20
```

Now we are onto something! When we look at the trunk information of the Etherchannels we can see that VLAN 10 is not active. Let's add it to the trunks:

```
ASW1(config)#interface po1
ASW1(config-if)#switchport trunk allowed vlan add 10

ASW1(config)#interface po2
ASW1(config-if)#switchport trunk allowed vlan add 10
```

This will add VLAN 10 to the etherchannels. Let's check the other switches as well.

```
DSW1#show etherchannel summary
Flags:  D - down         P - in port-channel
        I - stand-alone  s - suspended
        R - Layer3       S - Layer2
        U - in use
Group  Port-channel  Ports
------+-------------+-----------------------------------------------
1      Po1(SU)       Fa1/2(P)    Fa1/3(P)
3      Po3(SU)       Fa1/4(P)    Fa1/5(P)
5      Po5(SU)       Fa1/8(P)    Fa1/9(P)
```

```
DSW2#show etherchannel summary
Flags:  D - down          P - in port-channel
        I - stand-alone   s - suspended
        R - Layer3        S - Layer2
        U - in use
Group  Port-channel  Ports
-----+-------------+--------------------------------------------
--------------
2      Po2(SU)       Fa1/10(P)   Fa1/11(P)
3      Po3(SU)       Fa1/4(P)    Fa1/5(P)
4      Po4(SU)       Fa1/6(P)    Fa1/7(P)
```

The etherchannels on DSW1 and DSW2 are operational. Next step is to check if they are in trunk mode and if VLAN 10 is allowed or not.

```
DSW1#show interfaces po1 trunk

Port      Mode           Encapsulation  Status        Native vlan
Po1       on             802.1q         trunking      1

Port      Vlans allowed on trunk
Po1       1-4094

Port      Vlans allowed and active in management domain
Po1       1,10,20,200

Port      Vlans in spanning tree forwarding state and not pruned
Po1       1,10,20,200
```

```
DSW1#show interfaces po3 trunk

Port      Mode           Encapsulation  Status        Native vlan
Po3       on             802.1q         trunking      1

Port      Vlans allowed on trunk
Po3       1-4094

Port      Vlans allowed and active in management domain
Po3       1,10,20,200

Port      Vlans in spanning tree forwarding state and not pruned
Po3       1,10,20,200
```

Interface port-channel 1 is the one that is connected between ASW1 and DSW1. VLAN 10 is allowed on it so this should normally be enough. To make sure redundancy is intact I'm going to check the other interfaces as well.

```
DSW2#show interfaces po2 trunk

Port      Mode           Encapsulation  Status        Native vlan
Po2       on             802.1q         trunking      1
```

```
Port        Vlans allowed on trunk
Po2         1-4094

Port        Vlans allowed and active in management domain
Po2         1,10,20,200

Port        Vlans in spanning tree forwarding state and not pruned
Po2         1,10,20,200
```

```
DSW2#show interfaces po3 trunk

Port        Mode        Encapsulation   Status      Native vlan
Po3         on          802.1q          trunking    1

Port        Vlans allowed on trunk
Po3         1-4094

Port        Vlans allowed and active in management domain
Po3         1,10,20,200

Port        Vlans in spanning tree forwarding state and not pruned
Po3         10,20,200
```

We can verify that VLAN 10 is now operational on ASW1, DSW1 and DSW2. I didn't bother with the interfaces that are connected to ASW2 because VLAN 10 is not active there.

```
Client2#show ip interface brief
Interface               IP-Address      OK? Method Status  Protocol
FastEthernet0/0         unassigned      YES DHCP   up      up
```

```
Client1#show ip interface brief
Interface               IP-Address      OK? Method Status  Protocol
FastEthernet0/0         unassigned      YES DHCP   up      up
```

We fixed all layer 2 and DHCP related issues but the clients are still not getting an IP address. What else could be wrong?

Let's check if our DHCP server is receiving the DHCP messages from our clients:

```
R4#show ip dhcp server statistics
Memory usage        31953
Address pools       1
Database agents     0
```

```
Automatic bindings      2
Manual bindings         0
Expired bindings        0
Malformed messages      0
Secure arp entries      0

Message                 Received
BOOTREQUEST             0
DHCPDISCOVER            216
DHCPREQUEST             0
DHCPDECLINE             0
DHCPRELEASE             0
DHCPINFORM              0

Message                 Sent
BOOTREPLY               0
DHCPOFFER               216
DHCPACK                 0
DHCPNAK                 0
```

Great! At least R4 is receiving the DHCP discover messages from our clients. I don't see any DHCP ACK messages so something somewhere is going wrong. Let's do a debug:

```
R4#debug ip dhcp server packet
```

We'll enable the debug to see DHCP packets.

```
R4# DHCPD: DHCPDISCOVER received from client
0063.6973.636f.2d63.3230.382e.3066.6134.2e30.3030.302d.4661.302f
.30 through relay 10.2.1.2.
DHCPD: Sending DHCPOFFER to client
0063.6973.636f.2d63.3230.382e.3066.6134.2e30.3030.302d.4661.302f
.30 (10.2.1.11).
DHCPD: unicasting BOOTREPLY for client c208.0fa4.0000 to relay
10.2.1.2.
DHCPD: DHCPDISCOVER received from client
0063.6973.636f.2d63.3230.382e.3066.6134.2e30.3030.302d.4661.302f
.30 through relay 10.2.1.1.
DHCPD: Sending DHCPOFFER to client
0063.6973.636f.2d63.3230.382e.3066.6134.2e30.3030.302d.4661.302f
.30 (10.2.1.11).
R4#
DHCPD: unicasting BOOTREPLY for client c208.0fa4.0000 to relay
10.2.1.1.
```

R4 is receiving and sending DHCP messages for VLAN 10 and they are relayed to IP address 10.2.1.1 (DSW1) and 10.2.1.2 (DSW2). Is R4 able to reach these IP addresses?

```
R4#ping 10.2.1.1

Type escape sequence to abort.
Sending 5, 100-byte ICMP Echos to 10.2.1.1, timeout is 2
seconds:
.....
Success rate is 0 percent (0/5)
```

```
R4#ping 10.2.1.2

Type escape sequence to abort.
Sending 5, 100-byte ICMP Echos to 10.2.1.2, timeout is 2
seconds:
.....
Success rate is 0 percent (0/5)
```

R4 is unable to reach these IP addresses so that's why DHCP is not working now.

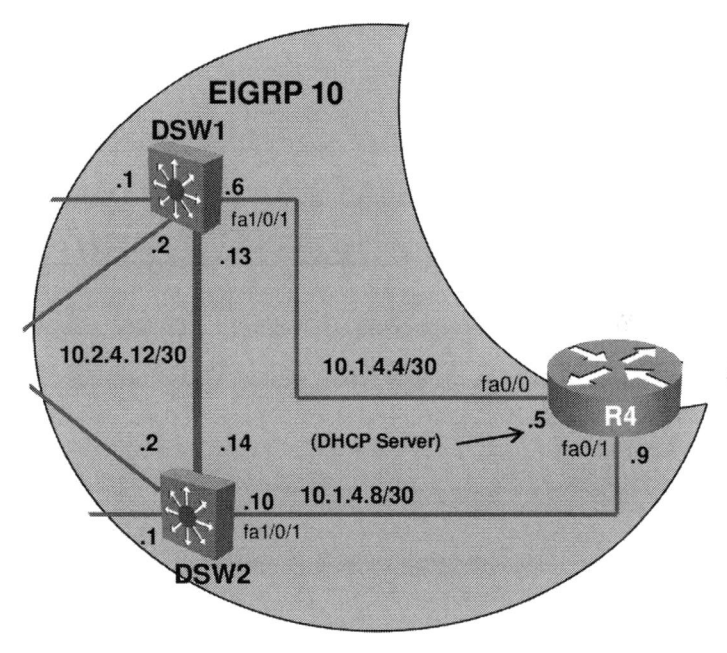

Back to the drawing board. Our topology picture shows up that DSW1, DSW2 and R4 are configured for EIGRP AS 10. R4 should learn about the 10.2.1.0 /24 prefix through EIGRP.

```
R4#show ip eigrp neighbors
IP-EIGRP neighbors for process 10
```

R4 doesn't have any EIGRP neighbors however.

```
R4#show ip protocols
```

```
Routing Protocol is "eigrp 10"
  Outgoing update filter list for all interfaces is not set
  Incoming update filter list for all interfaces is not set
  Default networks flagged in outgoing updates
  Default networks accepted from incoming updates
  EIGRP metric weight K1=1, K2=0, K3=1, K4=0, K5=0
  EIGRP maximum hopcount 100
  EIGRP maximum metric variance 1
  Redistributing: eigrp 10, ospf 1
  EIGRP NSF-aware route hold timer is 240s
  Automatic network summarization is not in effect
  Maximum path: 4
  Routing for Networks:
    10.1.4.4/30
  Passive Interface(s):
    FastEthernet1/0
  Routing Information Sources:
    Gateway         Distance      Last Update
  Distance: internal 90 external 170
```

We'll do a quick show ip protocols to see if we can find anything. There are two interesting things here:

- The passive interface for FastEthernet1/0 (that's the interface to DSW1).
- No network command for 10.1.4.8 /30 (that's the interface to DSW2).

```
R4(config)#router eigrp 10
R4(config-router)#no passive-interface fastEthernet 1/0
R4(config-router)#network 10.1.4.8 0.0.0.3
```

Let's make the appriopate changes.

```
R4#show ip eigrp neighbors
IP-EIGRP neighbors for process 10
H   Address              Interface        Hold Uptime   SRTT
RTO  Q   Seq
                                          (sec)         (ms)
Cnt Num
1   10.1.4.10            Fa2/0            11 00:00:34   12
200  0   19
0   10.1.4.6             Fa1/0            13 00:00:43   10
200  0   21
```

Seems we now have EIGRP neighbors!

```
R4#show ip dhcp server statistics
Memory usage         31953
Address pools        1
Database agents      0
Automatic bindings   2
```

```
Manual bindings           0
Expired bindings          0
Malformed messages        0
Secure arp entries        0

Message                   Received
BOOTREQUEST               0
DHCPDISCOVER              340
DHCPREQUEST               4
DHCPDECLINE               0
DHCPRELEASE               0
DHCPINFORM                0

Message                   Sent
BOOTREPLY                 0
DHCPOFFER                 340
DHCPACK                   4
DHCPNAK                   0
```

This is looking better!

```
Client1#show ip interface brief
Interface              IP-Address      OK? Method Status    Protocol
FastEthernet0/0        10.2.1.11       YES DHCP   up        up
```

```
Client2#show ip interface brief
Interface              IP-Address      OK? Method Status    Protocol
FastEthernet0/0        10.2.1.12       YES DHCP   up        up
```

Finally the clients are receiving IP addresses through DHCP! This ticket is solved.

Let's move onto the next one:

- **Ticket #2**: After fixing the issue with Client1 you receive another ticket that users from VLAN 10 are complaining that they are unable to connect to the FTP server.

DHCP is working but it seems our clients are unable to reach the FTP server. This FTP server is in another subnet so traffic has to be routed. The first thing I would check is to see if they can reach their default gateway or not.

```
Client1#show ip route
Default gateway is 10.2.1.254
```

```
Host            Gateway              Last Use     Total Uses
Interface
ICMP redirect cache is empty
```

IP address 10.2.1.254 is supposed to be the default gateway.

```
Client1#ping 10.2.1.254

Type escape sequence to abort.
Sending 5, 100-byte ICMP Echos to 10.2.1.254, timeout is 2
seconds:
.....
Success rate is 0 percent (0/5)
```

I'm unable to ping the default gateway IP address. Let's take a look at our diagram to see what device is the default gateway for VLAN 10.

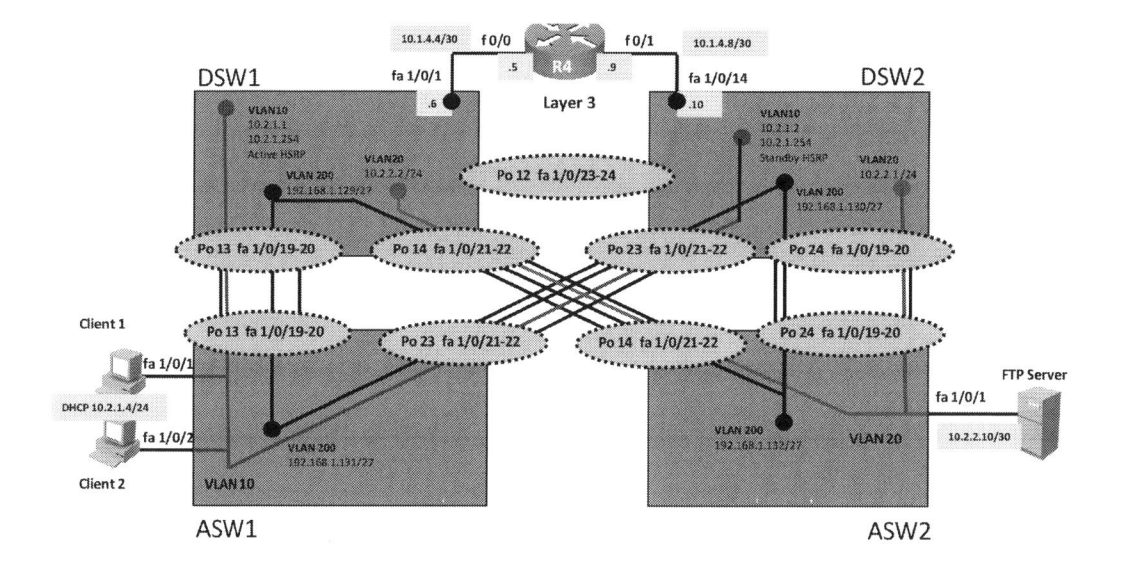

DSW1 and DSW2 are configured to use HSRP with virtual IP address 10.2.1.254. We can try if our clients can reach IP address 10.2.1.1 (DSW1) and/or 10.2.1.2 (DSW2).

```
Client1#ping 10.2.1.1

Type escape sequence to abort.
Sending 5, 100-byte ICMP Echos to 10.2.1.1, timeout is 2
seconds:
!!!!!
Success rate is 100 percent (5/5), round-trip min/avg/max =
4/210/1028 ms
```

```
Client1#ping 10.2.1.2

Type escape sequence to abort.
Sending 5, 100-byte ICMP Echos to 10.2.1.2, timeout is 2
seconds:
!!!!!
Success rate is 100 percent (5/5), round-trip min/avg/max =
4/205/1004 ms
```

Pinging the SVI interfaces for VLAN 10 on DSW1 and DSW2 is no problem. This makes me feel like checking the HSRP configuration.

```
DSW1#show standby
Vlan10 - Group 10
  State is Active
    2 state changes, last state change 02:45:04
  Virtual IP address is 10.2.1.200
  Active virtual MAC address is 0000.0c07.ac0a
    Local virtual MAC address is 0000.0c07.ac0a (v1 default)
  Hello time 3 sec, hold time 10 sec
    Next hello sent in 0.008 secs
  Preemption enabled
  Active router is local
  Standby router is 10.2.1.2, priority 120 (expires in 8.660 sec)
  Priority 200 (configured 200)
  Group name is "hsrp-Vl10-10" (default)
DSW2#show standby
Vlan10 - Group 10
  State is Standby
    4 state changes, last state change 02:45:32
  Virtual IP address is 10.2.1.254
  Active virtual MAC address is 0000.0c07.ac0a
    Local virtual MAC address is 0000.0c07.ac0a (v1 default)
  Hello time 3 sec, hold time 10 sec
    Next hello sent in 1.456 secs
  Preemption enabled
  Active router is 10.2.1.1, priority 200 (expires in 9.848 sec)
  Standby router is local
  Priority 120 (configured 120)
  Group name is "hsrp-Vl10-10" (default)
```

This is an interesting output. DSW1 has been elected as the active router but the virtual IP address is 10.2.1.200. DSW2 is configured with the correct virtual IP address.

```
DSW1(config)#interface vlan 10
DSW1(config-if)#standby 10 ip 10.2.1.254
```

This is the correct virtual IP address for VLAN 10.

```
DSW1(config)#interface vlan 10
```

```
DSW1(config-if)#shutdown
DSW1(config-if)#no shutdown
```

In my case I had to shutdown and no shutdown the SVI interface before DSW1 would use the correct virtual IP address.

```
Client1#ping 10.2.1.254

Type escape sequence to abort.
Sending 5, 100-byte ICMP Echos to 10.2.1.254, timeout is 2
seconds:
!!!!!
Success rate is 100 percent (5/5), round-trip min/avg/max =
1/5/12 ms
```

We can now reach the default gateway from within VLAN 10.

```
Client1#ping 10.2.2.10

Type escape sequence to abort.
Sending 5, 100-byte ICMP Echos to 10.2.2.10, timeout is 2
seconds:
!!!!!
Success rate is 100 percent (5/5), round-trip min/avg/max =
8/9/12 ms
```

And we can reach the FTP server...problem solved! Let's move on to ticket #3!

- **Ticket #3**: Your users are happy that they can connect to the FTP server but they are still unable to reach the webserver.

I'm very stubborn so let's see if this is true or not:

```
Client1#ping 209.65.200.241

Type escape sequence to abort.
Sending 5, 100-byte ICMP Echos to 209.65.200.241, timeout is 2
seconds:
U.U.U
Success rate is 0 percent (0/5)
```

I can send a quick ping to check connectivity. The U.U.U reveals me that this IP address my default gateway doesn't know how to reach this destination.

```
Client1#ping 209.65.200.241

Type escape sequence to abort.
Sending 5, 100-byte ICMP Echos to 209.65.200.241, timeout is 2
seconds:
.....
```

```
Success rate is 0 percent (0/5)
```

If I would have seen this then I still don't know if the destination is unreachable or that ICMP is being filtered. It would be better then to connect to TCP port 80 to test connectivity to the webserver:

```
Client1#telnet 209.65.200.241 80
Trying 209.65.200.241, 80 ...
% Destination unreachable; gateway or host down
```

That's promising...we can't connect to TCP port 80.

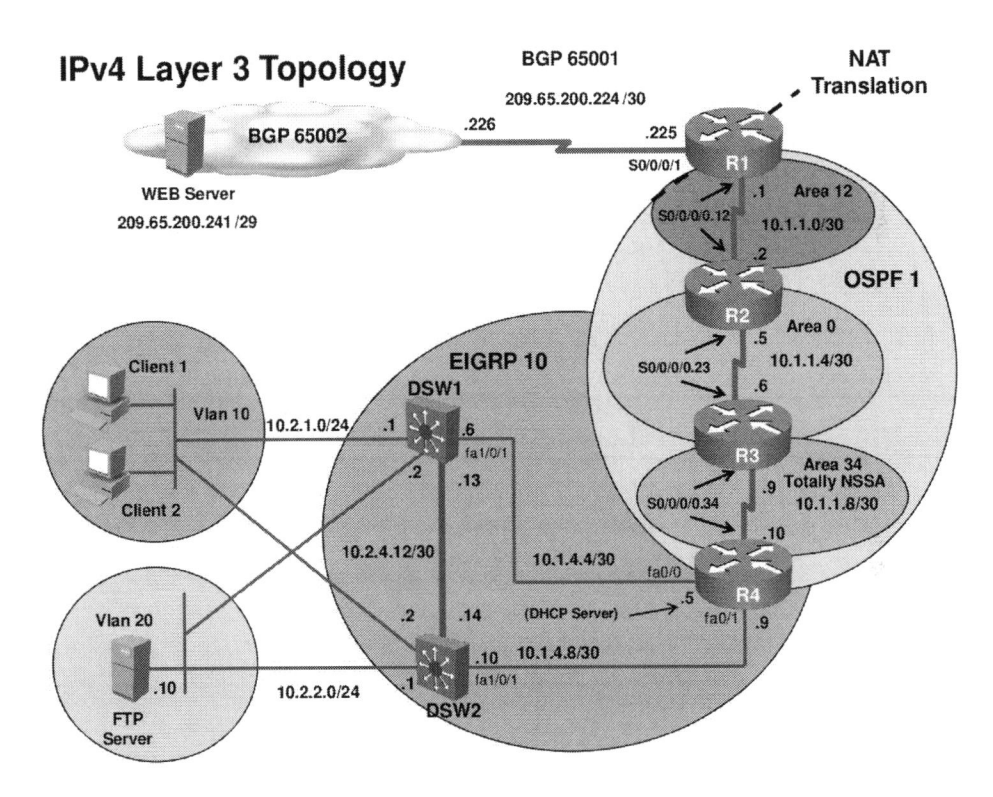

IPv4 Layer 3 Topology

Let's take a good look at the layer 3 topology of this network. There are quite some devices in between VLAN 10 and the webserver. In our previous efforts we fixed VLAN 10 and we know that the clients can reach their default gateway.

We will have to focus on the following area for now:

301

IPv4 Layer 3 Topology

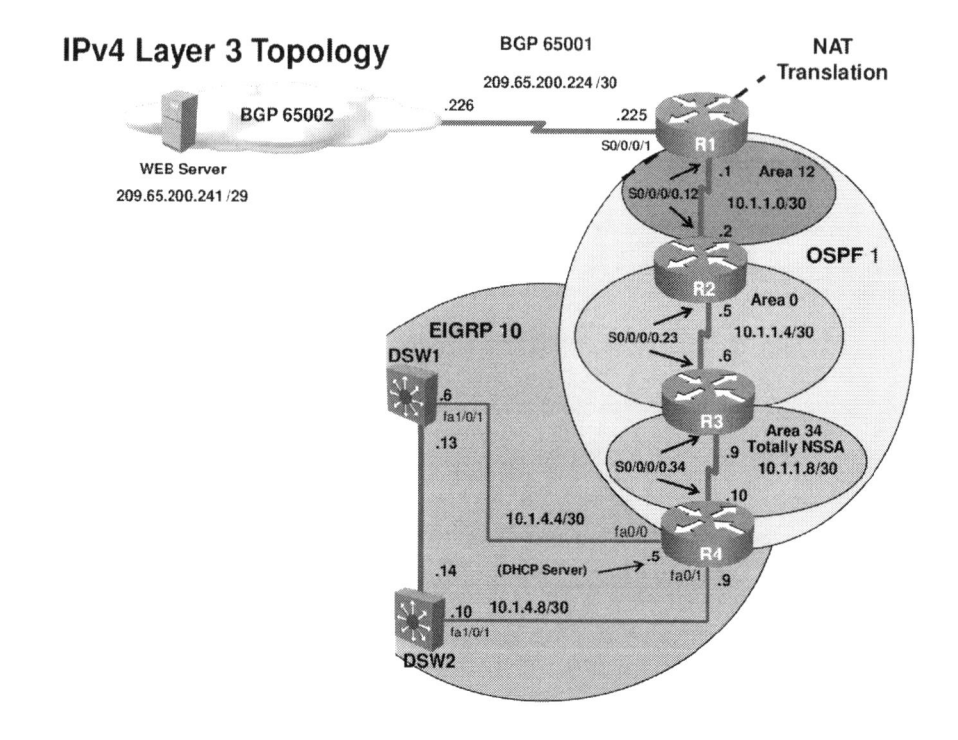

The clients can reach the default gateway in VLAN 10 so I'm not worried about layer 2 issues anymore. There is a lot of stuff in between DSW1 and DSW2:

- Multi-area OSPF on a frame-relay network.
- EIGRP between DSW1, DSW2 and R4.
- BGP between R1 and the ISP router.
- NAT on R1.
- There could be access-lists or vlan-access maps that filter traffic.

Where are we going to start? Everything is fair game when there are so many components that could cause issues.

```
Client1#ping 209.65.200.241

Type escape sequence to abort.
Sending 5, 100-byte ICMP Echos to 209.65.200.241, timeout is 2
seconds:
U.U.U
Success rate is 0 percent (0/5)
```

This message told me that the default gateway (DSW1 or DSW2) don't know how to reach this IP address. It sounds like a good idea to check these devices first.

```
DSW1#show ip route 209.65.200.241
% Network not in table
```

DSW1 is the active router for HSRP so that's where I'll start looking. We can see that it doesn't know how to reach IP address 209.65.200.241 so it's a routing issue.

```
DSW1#show ip route
Codes: C - connected, S - static, R - RIP, M - mobile, B - BGP
       D - EIGRP, EX - EIGRP external, O - OSPF, IA - OSPF inter area
       N1 - OSPF NSSA external type 1, N2 - OSPF NSSA external type 2
       E1 - OSPF external type 1, E2 - OSPF external type 2
       i - IS-IS, su - IS-IS summary, L1 - IS-IS level-1, L2 - IS-IS level-2
       ia - IS-IS inter area, * - candidate default, U - per-user static route
       o - ODR, P - periodic downloaded static route

Gateway of last resort is not set

     10.0.0.0/8 is variably subnetted, 5 subnets, 3 masks
D       10.1.4.8/30 [90/30720] via 192.168.1.130, 00:36:33, Vlan200
                   [90/30720] via 10.2.2.1, 00:36:33, Vlan20
                   [90/30720] via 10.2.1.2, 00:36:33, Vlan10
                   [90/30720] via 10.1.4.5, 00:36:33, FastEthernet0/0
C       10.2.1.0/24 is directly connected, Vlan10
C       10.2.2.0/24 is directly connected, Vlan20
D       10.0.0.0/8 is a summary, 00:36:33, Null0
C       10.1.4.4/30 is directly connected, FastEthernet0/0
     192.168.1.0/24 is variably subnetted, 2 subnets, 2 masks
D       192.168.1.0/24 is a summary, 00:36:33, Null0
C       192.168.1.128/27 is directly connected, Vlan200
```

I'm only seeing the "D" for EIGRP internal prefixes. If I want to reach networks beyond R4 then we should have "D EX" (EIGRP external prefixes) or at least a default route. R4 is the router that is configured for both OSPF and EIGRP so let's check it out.

```
R4#show ip route
Codes: C - connected, S - static, R - RIP, M - mobile, B - BGP
       D - EIGRP, EX - EIGRP external, O - OSPF, IA - OSPF inter area
       N1 - OSPF NSSA external type 1, N2 - OSPF NSSA external type 2
       E1 - OSPF external type 1, E2 - OSPF external type 2
       i - IS-IS, su - IS-IS summary, L1 - IS-IS level-1, L2 IS-IS level-2
       ia - IS-IS inter area, * - candidate default, per-user static route
       o - ODR, P - periodic downloaded static route
```

```
Gateway of last resort is not set

     10.0.0.0/8 is variably subnetted, 7 subnets, 3 masks
C       10.1.1.8/30 is directly connected, Serial0/0.34
C       10.1.4.8/30 is directly connected, FastEthernet2/0
D       10.2.1.0/24 [90/30720] via 10.1.4.10, 00:38:38,
FastEthernet2/0
                   [90/30720] via 10.1.4.6, 00:38:38,
FastEthernet1/0
D       10.2.2.0/24 [90/30720] via 10.1.4.10, 00:56:14,
FastEthernet2/0
                   [90/30720] via 10.1.4.6, 00:56:14,
FastEthernet1/0
D       10.0.0.0/8 [90/33280] via 10.1.4.10, 00:56:14,
FastEthernet2/0
C       10.1.4.4/30 is directly connected, FastEthernet1/0
O IA    10.1.1.4/30 [110/128] via 10.1.1.9, 03:27:43,
Serial0/0.34
     192.168.1.0/24 is variably subnetted, 2 subnets, 2 masks
D       192.168.1.0/24 [90/30720] via 10.1.4.6, 00:56:14,
FastEthernet1/0
D       192.168.1.128/27 [90/30720] via 10.1.4.10,
00:56:14,FastEthernet2/0
```

I see OSPF and EIGRP routes on R4. A mental note to make is that R4 also has no clue how to reach 209.65.200.241 /29 (the network where the webserver is located). Right now I have two choices:

- Am I going to fix R4 so it knows how to reach 209.65.200.241 /29.
- Or will I look at R4 so I can help DSW1 and DSW2 to learn some EIGRP external prefixes.

It doesn't really matter much since we have to deal with both issues. I will first see if I can help DSW1 and DSW2 so I don't have to think about it later.

```
R4#show run | section router eigrp
router eigrp 10
 redistribute ospf 1
 network 10.1.4.4 0.0.0.3
 network 10.1.4.8 0.0.0.3
 no auto-summary
```

R4 is configured for redistribution from OSPF into EIGRP. You can see however that no seed metrics have been configured so it will be unreachable for EIGRP. Let's fix it:

```
R4(config)#router eigrp 10
R4(config-router)#redistribute ospf 1 metric 1500 1000 255 1
1500
```

I don't care about these values since R4 is the only router doing redistribution anyway.

```
DSW1#show ip route eigrp
     10.0.0.0/8 is variably subnetted, 7 subnets, 3 masks
D EX    10.1.1.8/30 [170/1965056] via 10.1.4.5, 00:00:18,
FastEthernet0/0
D       10.1.4.8/30 [90/30720] via 192.168.1.130, 00:46:50,
Vlan200
                    [90/30720] via 10.2.2.1, 00:46:50, Vlan20
                    [90/30720] via 10.2.1.2, 00:46:50, Vlan10
                    [90/30720] via 10.1.4.5, 00:46:50,
FastEthernet0/0
D       10.0.0.0/8 is a summary, 00:46:50, Null0
D EX    10.1.1.4/30 [170/1965056] via 10.1.4.5, 00:00:18,
FastEthernet0/0
     192.168.1.0/24 is variably subnetted, 2 subnets, 2 masks
D       192.168.1.0/24 is a summary, 00:46:50, Null0
```

DSW1 has learned some EIGRP external prefixes so at least it can get to the networks beyond R4. Before we continue let's also verify if redistribution from EIGRP into OSPF has been done correctly. Otherwise IP packets might make it from DSW1 and DSW2 to beyond R4 but there might be no way back.

```
R3#show ip route ospf
     10.0.0.0/8 is variably subnetted, 3 subnets, 2 masks
O N2    10.0.0.0/8 [110/20] via 10.1.1.10, 01:06:35,
Serial0/0.34
O N2 192.168.1.0/24 [110/20] via 10.1.1.10, 01:06:44,
Serial0/0.34
```

I can take a quick look at R3 to see if it has learned any O E1 or E2 prefixes (OSPF external). It has two "O N2" entries. One for 1.0.0.0/8 and another for 192.168.1.0 /24. This means that redistribution on R4 has been configured but the keyword "subnets" has been left out.

This shouldn't be a problem in this topology but it does mean that R3 will send everything that matches 1.0.0.0 /8 and 192.168.1.0 /24 towards R4 if it doesn't have any more specific routes.

I'm done with R4 now because EIGRP and OSPF are both operational and redistribution is working. If you look closely at R3 you can see that it doesn't have any other OSPF prefixes. It should learn about 10.1.1.0 /30 in area 12 from R2 however. Let's check R3 more closely:

```
R3#show ip ospf neighbor

Neighbor ID     Pri   State           Dead Time   Address
Interface
10.1.4.9         0    FULL/    -      00:00:38    10.1.1.10
Serial0/0.34
```

Interesting... R3 doesn't have an OSPF neighbor adjacency with R2. Let's find out why! I have two options:

- Check the serial interfaces and frame-relay configuration (bottom-up).
- Jump into the OSPF configuration.

```
R3#show ip protocols
Routing Protocol is "ospf 1"
  Outgoing update filter list for all interfaces is not set
  Incoming update filter list for all interfaces is not set
  Router ID 10.1.1.9
  It is an area border and autonomous system boundary router
  Redistributing External Routes from,
  Number of areas in this router is 2. 1 normal 0 stub 1 nssa
  Maximum path: 4
  Routing for Networks:
    10.1.1.6 0.0.0.0 area 0
    10.1.1.9 0.0.0.0 area 34
  Reference bandwidth unit is 100 mbps
  Routing Information Sources:
    Gateway         Distance       Last Update
    10.1.1.9            110        03:46:26
    10.1.4.9            110        00:06:19
  Distance: (default is 110)
```

I'll jump into the OSPF configuration first so we'll assume the frame-relay interface is configured correctly...if I'm right I'll save time.

OSPF is activated on the serial0/0.23 interface that connects to R2. Something else is preventing it from becoming OSPF neighbors.

```
R3#show ip ospf interface s0/0.23
Serial0/0.23 is up, line protocol is up
  Internet Address 10.1.1.6/30, Area 0
  Process ID 1, Router ID 10.1.1.9, Network Type POINT_TO_POINT, Cost: 64
  Transmit Delay is 1 sec, State POINT_TO_POINT
  Timer intervals configured, Hello 7, Dead 28, Wait 28, Retransmit 5
```

We'll check some of the obvious things like the OSPF network type and timers. I'll do the same on R2. If I wouldn't have had access to R2 I could do a debug for OSPF to see if there's a mismatch somewhere.

```
R2#show ip protocols
Routing Protocol is "ospf 1"
  Outgoing update filter list for all interfaces is not set
  Incoming update filter list for all interfaces is not set
  Router ID 10.1.1.5
  It is an area border router
  Number of areas in this router is 2. 2 normal 0 stub 0 nssa
  Maximum path: 4
  Routing for Networks:
    10.1.1.2 0.0.0.0 area 12
    10.1.1.5 0.0.0.0 area 0
  Reference bandwidth unit is 100 mbps
  Routing Information Sources:
    Gateway           Distance         Last Update
    10.1.1.5             110           03:51:55
    209.65.200.225       110           03:51:55
  Distance: (default is 110)
```

The network command is correct.

```
R2#show ip ospf interface serial 0/0.23
Serial0/0.23 is up, line protocol is up
  Internet Address 10.1.1.5/30, Area 0
  Process ID 1, Router ID 10.1.1.5, Network Type POINT_TO_POINT,
Cost: 64
  Transmit Delay is 1 sec, State POINT_TO_POINT
  Timer intervals configured, Hello 10, Dead 40, Wait 40,
Retransmit 5
```

The OSPF network type is the same but the timers are different. This will prevent OSPF from becoming neighbors for sure.

```
R3(config)#interface s0/0.23
R3(config-subif)#ip ospf hello-interval 10
```

We'll change it to 10 seconds on R3.

```
R3#show ip ospf neighbor

Neighbor ID     Pri    State         Dead Time     Address
Interface
10.1.1.5         0     FULL/  -      00:00:39      10.1.1.5
Serial0/0.23
10.1.4.9         0     FULL/  -      00:00:34      10.1.1.10
Serial0/0.34
```

That's better! We are now OSPF neighbors.

```
R3#show ip route ospf
     209.65.200.0/30 is subnetted, 1 subnets
O IA    209.65.200.224 [110/192] via 10.1.1.5, 00:02:38,
Serial0/0.23
     10.0.0.0/8 is variably subnetted, 4 subnets, 2 masks
O IA    10.1.1.0/30 [110/128] via 10.1.1.5, 00:02:38,
Serial0/0.23
O N2    10.0.0.0/8 [110/20] via 10.1.1.10, 01:26:03,
Serial0/0.34
O N2 192.168.1.0/24 [110/20] via 10.1.1.10, 01:26:11,
Serial0/0.34
```

We'll take a quick look at the routing table of R3. You can see that is has learned how to reach 209.65.200.224 /30 through OSPF. This is the network between R1 and the ISP. It doesn't know how to reach 209.65.200.241 /29 however.

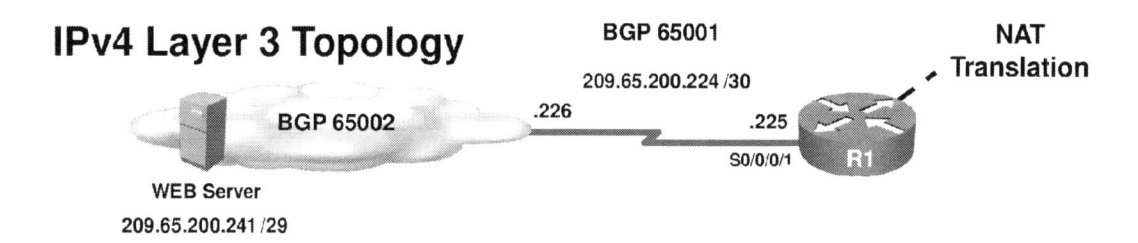

IPv4 Layer 3 Topology

BGP 65001
209.65.200.224 /30
.226   .225
BGP 65002
S0/0/0/1   R1
WEB Server
209.65.200.241 /29
NAT Translation

R1 is the router that is advertising 209.65.200.224 /29 into OSPF. Since that's being advertised I'm not concerned with the OSPF configuration at this moment. 209.65.200.241 /29 is advertised through BGP so I'm curious if this prefix is in the routing table of R1.

```
R1#show ip route 209.65.200.241
% Subnet not in table
```

R1 has no clue where it is. Is BGP working correctly?

```
R1#show ip bgp summary
BGP router identifier 209.65.200.225, local AS number 65001
BGP table version is 1, main routing table version 1

Neighbor         V    AS MsgRcvd MsgSent    TblVer  InQ OutQ
Up/Down   State/PfxRcd
209.65.200.224   4 65002       0       0         0    0    0 never
Active
```

We don't have any operational BGP neighbors. If you look closely the IP address of our BGP neighbor is incorrect. This is the network address, not the IP address of the ISP router. Let's change it:

```
R1(config)#router bgp 65001
R1(config-router)#no neighbor 209.65.200.224 remote-as 65002
R1(config-router)#neighbor 209.65.200.226 remote-as 65002
```

This is a long day...;)

```
R1#show ip bgp summary
BGP router identifier 209.65.200.225, local AS number 65001
BGP table version is 2, main routing table version 2
1 network entries using 120 bytes of memory
1 path entries using 52 bytes of memory
2/1 BGP path/bestpath attribute entries using 248 bytes of
memory
1 BGP AS-PATH entries using 24 bytes of memory
0 BGP route-map cache entries using 0 bytes of memory
0 BGP filter-list cache entries using 0 bytes of memory
Bitfield cache entries: current 1 (at peak 1) using 32 bytes of
memory
BGP using 476 total bytes of memory
BGP activity 1/0 prefixes, 1/0 paths, scan interval 60 secs

Neighbor        V    AS MsgRcvd MsgSent   TblVer  InQ OutQ
Up/Down   State/PfxRcd
209.65.200.226  4 65002       7       7        2    0    0
00:02:54          1
```

Excellent we now have a BGP neighbor and we received 1 prefix.

```
R1#show ip route 209.65.200.241
Routing entry for 209.65.200.240/29
  Known via "bgp 65001", distance 20, metric 0
  Tag 65002, type external
  Redistributing via ospf 1
  Advertised by ospf 1 subnets
  Last update from 209.65.200.226 00:03:30 ago
  Routing Descriptor Blocks:
  * 209.65.200.226, from 209.65.200.226, 00:03:30 ago
      Route metric is 0, traffic share count is 1
      AS Hops 1
      Route tag 65002
```

This is what we were looking for. R1 now has it in the routing table.

```
R2#show ip route 209.65.200.240
Routing entry for 209.65.200.240/29
  Known via "ospf 1", distance 110, metric 1
  Tag 65002, type extern 2, forward metric 64
  Last update from 10.1.1.1 on Serial0/0.12, 00:05:39 ago
  Routing Descriptor Blocks:
  * 10.1.1.1, from 209.65.200.225, 00:05:39 ago, via
Serial0/0.12
```

```
     Route metric is 1, traffic share count is 1
     Route tag 65002
```

I'll take a quick look on R2 because R1 still has to redistribute 209.65.200.240/29 from BGP into OSPF. This seems to be the case.

```
R3#show ip route 209.65.200.240
Routing entry for 209.65.200.240/29
  Known via "ospf 1", distance 110, metric 1
  Tag 65002, type extern 2, forward metric 128
  Last update from 10.1.1.5 on Serial0/0.23, 00:07:04 ago
  Routing Descriptor Blocks:
  * 10.1.1.5, from 209.65.200.225, 00:07:04 ago, via Serial0/0.23
      Route metric is 1, traffic share count is 1
      Route tag 65002
```

R3 also knows about this prefix.

```
R4#show ip route 209.65.200.240
% Subnet not in table
```

R4 doesn't know about it. Why is this happening?

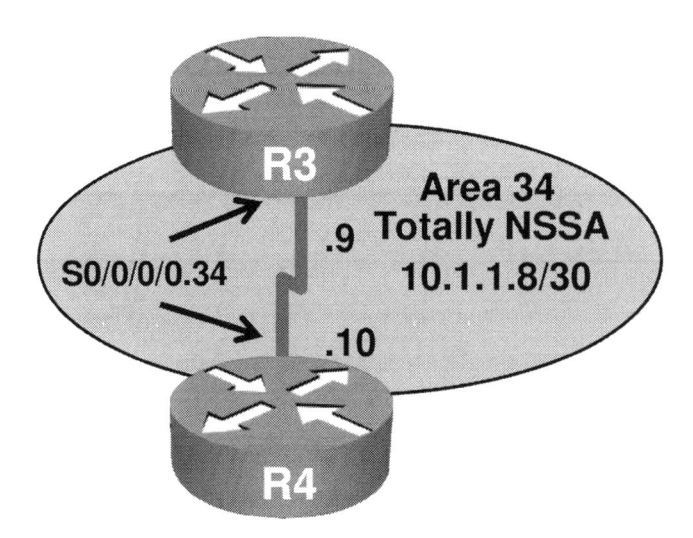

If you look at our OSPF configuration you can see that area 34 between R3 and R4 is a totally NSSA. This means it will block LSA type 5 (OSPF external) prefixes. We can either change the area type or we can generate a default route on R3 so that R4, DSW1 and DSW2 know how to reach 209.65.200.240/29.

```
R3(config)#router ospf 1
```

```
R3(config-router)#area 34 nssa no-summary default-information-
originate
```

We'll use the default route this time.

```
R4#show ip route ospf
O*IA 0.0.0.0/0 [110/65] via 10.1.1.9, 00:01:44, Serial0/0.34
```

R4 now has a default route that we can use to reach the webserver. All routers should now be able to send their IP packets towards the webserver. Let's take a leap of faith and see if we can reach the webserver from our clients.

```
Client1#telnet 209.65.200.241 80
Trying 209.65.200.241, 80 ...
% Connection timed out; remote host not responding
```

Too bad...I'm unable to reach the webserver. Let's take a look at the topology again:

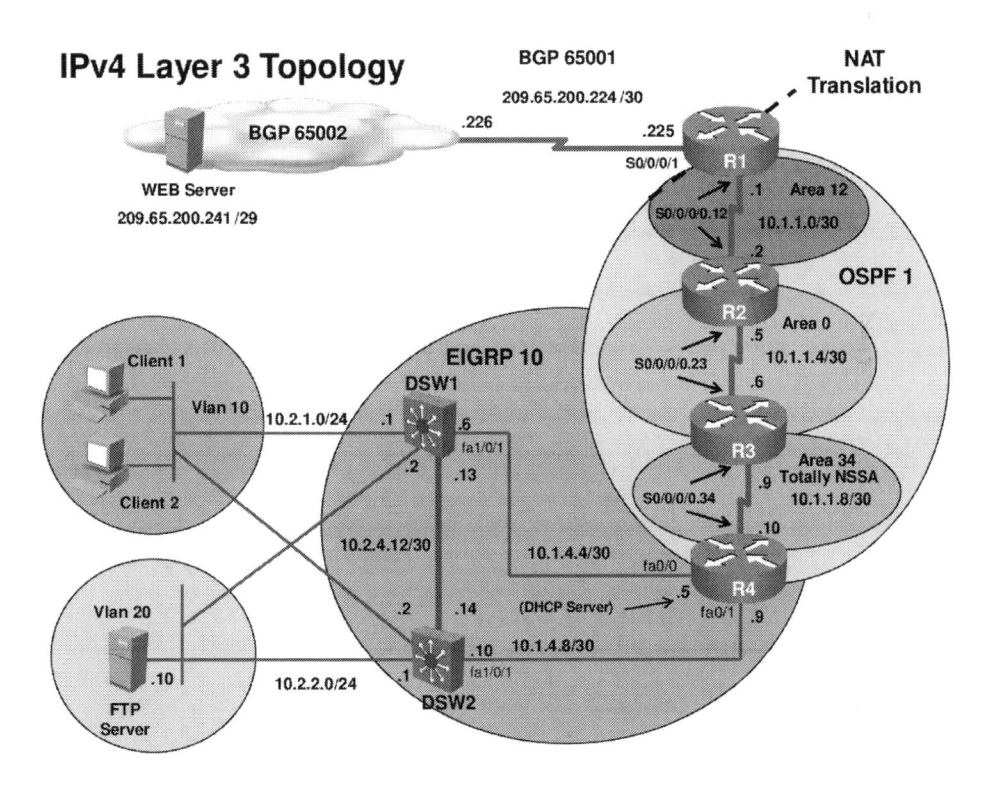

IPv4 Layer 3 Topology

We verified that routing within AS 65001 is working correctly. All routers know where to send traffic towards 209.65.200.241 /29 to. Still, my clients are unable to connect to the webserver. If you look at the topology picture there are a number of things we have to realize:

311

- Traffic might be able to make it from AS 65001 to AS 65002 but perhaps it's unable to get back.
- R1 is configured for NAT.
- AS 65001 is using subnets from 10.0.0.0 /8, this is a private range.

When IP packets leave AS 65001 they should be translated using NAT. If IP address 209.65.200.225 on R1 is used for this then the ISP shouldn't have any issues sending traffic back to AS 65001 since this is directly connected for the ISP router.
If NAT is configured to use a pool of IP addresses then the ISP router will have to know how to reach those IP addresses.

Let's verify our NAT configuration:

```
R1#show ip nat statistics
Total active translations: 0 (0 static, 0 dynamic; 0 extended)
Outside interfaces:
  Serial0/1
Inside interfaces:
  Serial0/0.12
Hits: 0  Misses: 0
CEF Translated packets: 0, CEF Punted packets: 0
Expired translations: 0
Dynamic mappings:
-- Inside Source
[Id: 1] access-list 1 pool TSHOOT refcount 0
 pool TSHOOT: netmask 255.255.255.252
        start 209.65.200.225 end 209.65.200.225
        type generic, total addresses 1, allocated 0 (0%),
misses 0
Appl doors: 0
Normal doors: 0
Queued Packets: 0
```

Our NAT configuration tells us that the inside and outside interfaces are configured correctly. Access-list 1 is used to match the inside hosts and there's a pool called TSHOOT which only uses IP address 209.65.200.225 (the IP address on the outside interface of R1).

Let's take a closer look at the access-list:

```
R1#show access-lists
Standard IP access list 1
    10 permit 0.0.0.0, wildcard bits 255.255.255.0
    20 permit 192.168.0.0, wildcard bits 0.0.255.255
```

This is a typical Monday morning problem. Someone made an error with the access-list.

```
R1(config)#ip access-list standard 1
R1(config-std-nacl)#no 10
R1(config-std-nacl)#10 permit 10.0.0.0 0.255.255.255
```

We'll change it so everything within 10.0.0.0 /8 will be translated using NAT.

```
Client1#telnet 209.65.200.241 80
Trying 209.65.200.241, 80 ... Open
```

Yes! The client can now connect….another ticket (finally) bites the dust!

- **Ticket #4**: The IPv6 team left a ticket for you that they are unable to reach 2026::12:/122 from DSW1 or DSW2.

This is the last ticket we will look at. It's about IPv6. Seems we can't reach 2026::12/122 from DSW1 or DSW2.

IPv6 Layer 3 Topology

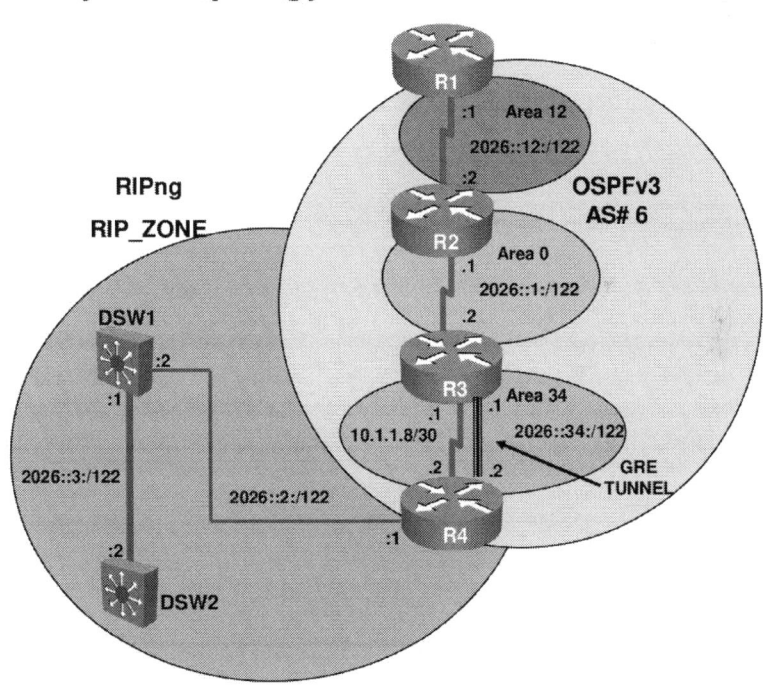

This is what the IPv6 topology looks like. Due to our previous configurations / verifications we know that the layer 2 interfaces in between these devices are operational. One mental sidenote is that R1, R2, R3 and R4 are using frame-relay links so it's possible that there are frame-relay maps for IPv4 but not for IPv6.

```
DSW1#show ipv6 route rip
IPv6 Routing Table - 6 entries
Codes: C - Connected, L - Local, S - Static, R - RIP, B - BGP
       U - Per-user Static route, M - MIPv6
       I1 - ISIS L1, I2 - ISIS L2, IA - ISIS interarea, IS -
ISIS summary
       O - OSPF intra, OI - OSPF inter, OE1 - OSPF ext 1, OE2 -
OSPF ext 2
       ON1 - OSPF NSSA ext 1, ON2 - OSPF NSSA ext 2
       D - EIGRP, EX - EIGRP external
R   2026::34:0/122 [120/2]
    via FE80::C000:FFF:FE86:10, FastEthernet0/0
```

```
DSW2#show ipv6 route rip
IPv6 Routing Table - 5 entries
Codes: C - Connected, L - Local, S - Static, R - RIP, B - BGP
       U - Per-user Static route, M - MIPv6
       I1 - ISIS L1, I2 - ISIS L2, IA - ISIS interarea, IS -
ISIS summary
       O - OSPF intra, OI - OSPF inter, OE1 - OSPF ext 1, OE2 -
OSPF ext 2
       ON1 - OSPF NSSA ext 1, ON2 - OSPF NSSA ext 2
       D - EIGRP, EX - EIGRP external
R   2026::2:0/122 [120/2]
    via FE80::C00B:13FF:FEE1:1, Vlan10
R   2026::34:0/122 [120/3]
    via FE80::C00B:13FF:FEE1:1, Vlan10
```

DSW1 and DSW1 both learned about 2026::34:0/122 so this proves that RIPNG is working and that R4 is redistributing OSPFv3 into RIPNG. Why don't we see 2026::1:/122 and 2026::12:/122?

- Maybe not all prefixes are being redistributed from OSPFv3 into RIPNG.
- Maybe there's something wrong with R3 and/or R2.

Let's check R4 to see if it has an OSPFv3 neighbor adjacency with R3:

```
R4#show ipv6 ospf neighbor
```

No neighbors...

```
R4#show ipv6 protocols
IPv6 Routing Protocol is "connected"
IPv6 Routing Protocol is "static"
IPv6 Routing Protocol is "ospf 6"
  Interfaces (Area 34):
    Tunnel34
  Redistribution:
    Redistributing protocol connected with metric 1
```

```
Redistributing protocol rip RIPNG with metric 1
```

OSPFv3 is enabled on a tunnel34 interface so that's looking good.

```
R4#show ipv6 ospf interface tunnel 34
Tunnel34 is up, line protocol is up
  Link Local Address FE80::C000:FFF:FE86:0, Interface ID 17
  Area 34, Process ID 6, Instance ID 0, Router ID 10.1.4.9
  Network Type NON_BROADCAST, Cost: 11111
  Transmit Delay is 1 sec, State DR, Priority 1
  Designated Router (ID) 10.1.4.9, local address
FE80::C000:FFF:FE86:0
  No backup designated router on this network
  Timer intervals configured, Hello 30, Dead 120, Wait 120,
Retransmit 5
```

The tunnel34 interface is up and running and the OSPF network type is non-broadcast. We can also see the timers. Let's compare this to what we see on R3.

```
R3#show ipv6 protocols
IPv6 Routing Protocol is "connected"
IPv6 Routing Protocol is "static"
IPv6 Routing Protocol is "ospf 6"
  Interfaces (Area 0):
    Serial0/0.23
  Interfaces (Area 34):
    Tunnel34
  Redistribution:
    None
```

OSPFv3 is enabled on the tunnel34 interface.

```
R3#show ipv6 ospf interface tunnel 34
Tunnel34 is up, line protocol is up
  Link Local Address FE80::C333:13FF:FEC3:0, Interface ID 15
  Area 34, Process ID 6, Instance ID 0, Router ID 10.1.1.9
  Network Type POINT_TO_POINT, Cost: 11111
  Transmit Delay is 1 sec, State POINT_TO_POINT,
  Timer intervals configured, Hello 10, Dead 40, Wait 40,
Retransmit 5
```

On this side we are using a different network type. The timers are also different but this is because of the network type.

```
R4(config)#int tunnel 34
R4(config-if)#ipv6 ospf network point-to-point
```

I'll change R4 to the point-to-point network type or we'll have to worry about a DR/BDR election.

```
R4#show ipv6 ospf neighbor

Neighbor ID     Pri   State         Dead Time    Interface ID
Interface
10.1.1.9         1    FULL/ -       00:00:33     15
Tunnel34
```

There we go, we have a neighbor.

```
DSW1#show ipv6 route rip
IPv6 Routing Table - 8 entries
Codes: C - Connected, L - Local, S - Static, R - RIP, B - BGP
       U - Per-user Static route, M - MIPv6
       I1 - ISIS L1, I2 - ISIS L2, IA - ISIS interarea, IS -
ISIS summary
       O - OSPF intra, OI - OSPF inter, OE1 - OSPF ext 1, OE2 -
OSPF ext 2
       ON1 - OSPF NSSA ext 1, ON2 - OSPF NSSA ext 2
       D - EIGRP, EX - EIGRP external
R   2026::1:0/122 [120/2]
     via FE80::C000:FFF:FE86:10, FastEthernet0/0
R   2026::12:0/122 [120/2]
     via FE80::C000:FFF:FE86:10, FastEthernet0/0
R   2026::34:0/122 [120/2]
     via FE80::C000:FFF:FE86:10, FastEthernet0/0
```

Now we see all prefixes in the routing table.

```
DSW1#ping 2026::12:1

Type escape sequence to abort.
Sending 5, 100-byte ICMP Echos to 2026::12:1, timeout is 2
seconds:
!!!!!
Success rate is 100 percent (5/5), round-trip min/avg/max =
4/12/28 ms

DSW1#ping 2026::1:1

Type escape sequence to abort.
Sending 5, 100-byte ICMP Echos to 2026::1:1, timeout is 2
seconds:
!!!!!
Success rate is 100 percent (5/5), round-trip min/avg/max =
8/8/8 ms
```

```
DSW2#ping 2026::12:1

Type escape sequence to abort.
```

```
Sending 5, 100-byte ICMP Echos to 2026::12:1, timeout is 2
seconds:
!!!!!
Success rate is 100 percent (5/5), round-trip min/avg/max =
4/12/28 ms

DSW1#ping 2026::1:1

Type escape sequence to abort.
Sending 5, 100-byte ICMP Echos to 2026::1:1, timeout is 2
seconds:
!!!!!
Success rate is 100 percent (5/5), round-trip min/avg/max =
8/8/8 ms
```

There we go! We can now reach these prefixes from DSW1 and DSW2. Problem solved!

That means we made it to the end of this chapter. I hope this was useful to you to get an insight how I would troubleshoot a "full lab". Of course there are many different approaches and the best way to learn this is by doing troubleshooting labs yourself.

12. Final Thoughts

Here we are, you worked your way through all the different chapters that showed you how you can master the CCNP TSHOOT exam. There is only one thing left for you to do and that's *labs, labs and even more labs!* The CCNP TSHOOT exam is different than the ROUTE and SWITCH exams because in this exam you will get questions (troubleshooting tickets) on a given topology that has errors. If you read the previous chapter you are now familiar with the official Cisco CCNP TSHOOT topology and the topology that I recreated in GNS3.

If you want to know what the exam looks like you can take a look at a demo that Cisco offers:

https://learningnetwork.cisco.com/docs/DOC-6738

If you want more labs just visit http://gns3vault.com where I have about everything on CCNP TSHOOT level. If you feel there is something missing drop me a message/mail/PM/twitter and I'll make sure to add a new lab.

One last word of advice: If you do a Cisco exam you always do the tutorial before you start the exam which takes 15 minutes. These 15 minutes are not taken from your exam time so this is valuable time you can spend creating your own cheat sheet or anything else you would like to dump from your brain onto paper.

I hope you enjoyed reading my book and truly learned something! If you have any questions or comments how you feel I could improve the book please let me know by sending an e-mail to info@gns3vault.com or drop a message at my website: http://gns3vault.com.

I wish you good luck practicing and mastering that CCNP TSHOOT exam!

Appendix A – How to create mindmaps

A mindmap is a diagram which consists of text, images or relationships between different items. Everything is ordered in a tree-like structure. In the middle of the mindmap you write down your subject. All the topics that have to do with your subject can be written down as a branch of your main subject. Each branch can have multiple branches where the pieces of information are leaves. Mindmaps are great because they show the relationship between different items where notes are just lists...

You can create mindmaps by drawing them yourself or use your computer. I prefer the second method because I can save / print them but also because I'm a faster at typing than writing.

You can download Xmind over here, it's free:

http://www.xmind.net/

Once you have installed it and started a new project you can add some items.

Here's an example I created for CCNP TSHOOT with some of the items you could check when troubleshooting OSPF, just to give you an impression:

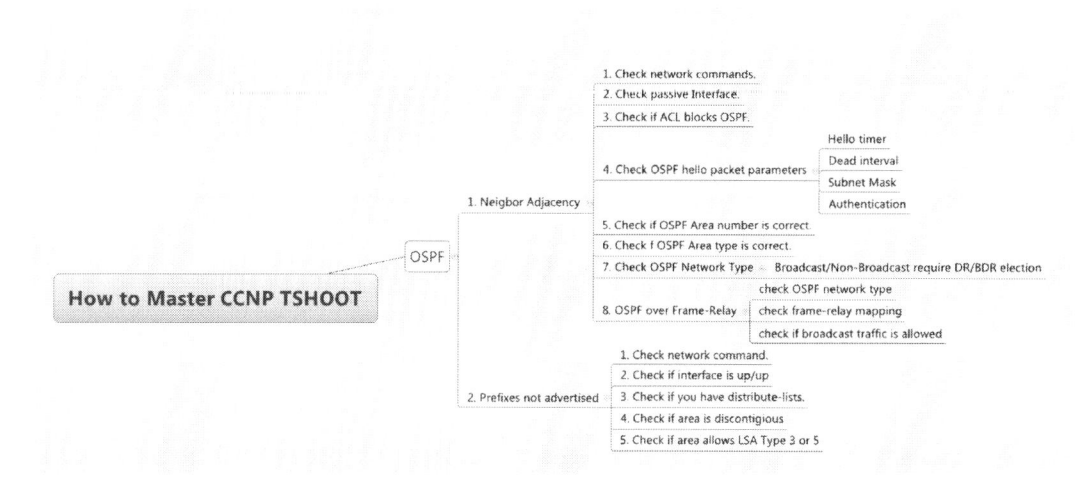

Just add all the items and build your own mind-map using your own words. Now you have a nice overview with all the stuff you need to remember but also the relationship between items. Give it a shot and see if you like it!

Printed in Great Britain
by Amazon